Nonviolence and Peace Psychology

For other titles published in this series, go to
www.springer.com/series/7298

Daniel M. Mayton II

Nonviolence and Peace Psychology

Intrapersonal, Interpersonal, Societal,
and World Peace

 Springer

Daniel M. Mayton II
Lewis-Clark State College
Lewiston
ID
USA

ISBN 978-0-387-89347-1   e-ISBN 978-0-387-89348-8
DOI 10.1007/978-0-387-89348-8
Springer Dordrecht Heidelberg London New York

Library of Congress Control Number: 2009922610

Printed on acid-free paper

Springer is part of Springer Science+Business Media (www.springer.com)

Foreword

The UNESCO constitution, written in 1945, states, "Since wars begin in the minds of men, it is in the minds of men that the defenses of peace must be constructed." This is an appeal for peace psychology. It is a call to understand the values, philosophies, and competencies needed to build and maintain intrapersonal, interpersonal, intergroup, and international peace. Peace psychology involves the information, attitudes, values, and behavioral competencies needed to resolve conflicts without violence and to build and maintain mutually beneficial, harmonious relationships. The ultimate goal of peace psychology is for individuals to be able to maintain peace among aspects of themselves (intrapersonal peace), individuals (interpersonal peace), groups (intergroup peace), and countries, societies, and cultures (international peace).

For centuries, peace was primarily discussed in the teachings of religious leaders such as Lao Tse, Jesus Christ, Buddha, the Dali Lama, and Bahá'u'lláh, who taught that people were supposed to promote peace in their lives and in the world as a whole. Compassion, empathy, and nonviolence were presented as some of the ways in which to do so. In the middle ages, the discussion of peace expanded beyond religion into education (the Czech educator Comenius believed that peace depended on universally shared knowledge) and philosophy (Immanuel Kant believed that peace was achieved through legal and judicial systems). Late in the nineteenth century, William James wrote an article opposing imperialism and the "war fever" with which it was associated. In the twentieth century, Maria Montessori advocated teaching children to be independent decision makers, who would not automatically follow authoritarian rulers urging them to war. Perhaps the most famous advocate of nonviolence in the twentieth century was Mahatma Gandhi, who used it as a means for ending oppression. The first academic peace studies program was established in 1948 at Manchester College in Indiana. Peace psychology gained momentum during the Cold War, when activists worked to prevent nuclear war in organizations such as the Committee for a Sane Nuclear Policy (SANE), which was founded in 1957. In the 1950s, Martin Luther King advocated nonviolence in the United States Civil Rights Movement as the only moral and practical method for oppressed people to gain their freedom. Modern peace psychology has its roots in the concern about the possibility of nuclear war and the use of nonviolence to end the oppression. Since the 1970s, peace programs have been initiated at every level of education. Over 300 colleges and universities now have peace studies programs and in many countries elementary and secondary schools have programs that could be described as peace education.

It is not easy to define peace. In English, "pax," is the Latin root word for peace, which means a settlement or common understanding that ends or averts hostilities. In Hebrew and Arabic the root word for peace (i.e., shalom, salaam) is shalev, which means whole or undivided. In Chinese, peace is written with two characters, one meaning harmony and the other equality or balance; thus, peace is harmony in balance. In Japanese, peace is represented by two characters meaning harmony, simplicity, and quietness. Hindu and Sanskrit have several words for peace (i.e., avirodha, shanty, chaina) which mean the absence of war, spiritual or inner peace, and mental peace or calmness. From these root words it may be concluded that peace is more than the absence of war, just as health is more than the absence of disease. Besides the absence of war or violence, peace involves mutually beneficial, cooperative, harmonious relationships among relevant parties. For peace to be achieved, violence and oppression must be ended in a way that creates a relationship characterized by cooperative efforts, positive feelings, mutual benefit, and justice.

Nonviolence, as advocated by Gandhi and King, promotes peace by seeking the high power party's friendship, understanding, and cooperation (rather than defeat and humiliation). Nonviolence is a means for awakening a sense of injustice and moral shame in the high-power parties. It defeats injustice by showing high-power parties they have more to gain by ending injustice and oppression than by maintaining them. It is aimed at creating redemption, reconciliation, and a community characterized by equal justice and mutual benefit. Advocates of nonviolence recommend it as making the means of achieving peace and the nature of the peace achieved indivisible.

For nonviolence to succeed as a method for social change, there are certain conditions that must be met. The first is the creation of a cooperative relationship among relevant parties. As long as parties compete, they will be motivated to seek to dominate other parties and ensure that no other party can dominate them. Nonviolence is most effective when it highlights the positive interdependence existing among the parties and the need for joint efforts to achieve mutual benefits. Its success depends on a basic shift from negative interdependence among goals (i.e., competition) to positive interdependence among goals (i.e., cooperation). It is only within a cooperative context that nonviolence can achieve a lasting peace. The second is the initiation of integrative (as opposed to distributive) negotiations. Integrative agreements maximize mutual benefits. Just because peace has been established does not mean that different parties will have identical interests. Ongoing integrative negotiations are necessary to keep the focus on cooperative efforts to maximize joint benefits. A third condition is the use of a procedure of decision making that creates a synthesis or integration of the different preferences of the involved parties. Decisions must be made in a way that takes everyone's perspectives and conclusions into account. Constructive controversy is an example of such a decision making procedure.

What has been lacking in the literature on nonviolence is a scholarly review of the social science theories and research underlying its effective use. Nonviolence has been examined from religious, philosophical, historical, and political perspectives. But until this book, there have been few attempts to examine the theory and research underlying the use of nonviolence. This book provides a clear and concise conceptualization of the nature of nonviolence, reviews the major theories of nonviolence, and nonviolence at the intrapersonal, interpersonal, societal, and world levels, and proposes new directions for the research on nonviolence. Dan Mayton brings together into one place some of the more thoughtful theories and discussions of nonviolence. He has written an admirable and much needed book that advances the scholarship in the field. It is thus a landmark publication and a valuable resource for all social scientists and students interested in nonviolence, peace, and constructive conflict resolution.

Minneapolis, MN   David W. Johnson
                                                    Roger T. Johnson

Preface

The twentieth century has been called the bloodiest century in human history, marked by the loss of more than 100 million lives in war. Besides its bloody legacy, a story that is less often told about the twentieth century is the success of nonviolent people power movements. The twentieth was the first century in human history in which many large-scale nonviolent movements successfully toppled oppressive regimes, often in the face of overwhelming military power. Even as we have transitioned into the twenty-first century, violent human encounters in Afghanistan, Iraq, Darfur, Congo, and other places capture our attention and eclipse the many and varied nonviolent social movements that are taking place around the world. One purpose of this book is to heighten awareness of nonviolent movements that continue to take place as the twenty-first century unfolds.

Most people are familiar with nonviolence through the lives of Mohandas K. Gandhi and Martin Luther King Jr. The nonviolent activism of these two individuals has helped shape our understanding of nonviolence as both a philosophy of life and as a political strategy. Despite the success of the nonviolent social change movements of Gandhi and King, individuals are often reluctant to participate or even consider a nonviolent action as a means of pursuing goals. Part of this reticence is based on a view that sees active nonviolence as ineffective in transforming social conditions. People often lament that "Gandhi was great but that was a long time ago and he was dealing with the British. My situation is different." Or "I can't do what they did because I am dealing with violent people." These types of comments are not only misinformed but, unfortunately, by default, they support violent approaches to problems. The second purpose of this book is to demonstrate the effectiveness of nonviolent action in a broad number of contexts and in the past two decades.

By writing this book, I not only hope to increase awareness of the prevalence of nonviolent action and its successful use in diverse settings, but equally important is to make it clear how nonviolence is based on a range of theories and sound social science principles. This book is interdisciplinary, as I discuss theories and perspectives of nonviolence drawn from the fields of anthropology, political science, psychology, religious studies, and sociology. Individuals in each of these disciplines will see major work within their own field plus they will realize interconnections to related fields.

While multidisciplinary discussions will appear throughout the book, this book will be written from the point of view of a psychologist. Ever since the beginning of modern psychology, psychologists have been concerned about the problem of war. William James, one of the founders of modern psychology, wrote an important article at the beginning of the twentieth century entitled "The Moral Equivalent of War." James (1995/1910) argued that war instilled in people some positive qualities including patriotism and discipline. What was needed, he suggested, was a suitable substitute for war that would instill these same qualities. For James, that substitute was mandatory service and hard labor for the country. In a sense, this book takes James' challenge seriously, and highlights ways in which contemporary nonviolent social movements around the world are providing a "moral equivalent of war." As I will point out, participation in these movements requires great courage, solidarity, and discipline as participants face well organized, heavily financed, and often armed resistance to change.

In addition, my psychological approach to nonviolence is distinguished from others because it emphasizes beliefs, motives, values, and other mainstream social psychological concepts in a manner that is intended to be informative to psychologists and understandable to nonpsychologists. Realizing the dynamics of human psychology are always embedded in sociohistorical and cultural contexts, I situate the analyses of nonviolence within cross-cultural contexts. Above all, I want to provide a comprehensive conceptualization of nonviolent behavior that can be used in a variety of contexts by adherents of many disciplines.

The final focus of the book is to review selected methodological issues that are important to social scientists interested in conducting research or utilizing the results on nonviolence and nonviolent action. Important measurement issues, micro and macrolevel concerns, mediating variables in nonviolent behaviors, and directions for further research will be presented to achieve this purpose.

I want to thank many people for their support, feedback and critiques during different aspects of the writing process. First, I want to thank David Johnson and Roger Johnson for writing the Forward to this book. Their comments nicely situate nonviolence into the larger field of peace psychology. Additionally, I want to thank Dan Christie, editor of the peace psychology series of Springer Publishing, for his encouragement to write this book and his insight and input throughout the process of making this book a reality. I also appreciated the comments and recommendations of anonymous reviewers of the book prospectus that have pushed my writings in directions that were beneficial to the final product. In addition, I want to thank Anna Tobias and the staff at Springer for their help in bringing this book to press.

Second, I am indebted to critical comments, guidance, and support for my research on nonviolence from many peace psychologists over the years. This group includes Linden Nelson, Dan Christie, Dick Wagner, Mike Wessells, Deborah DuNann Winter, Milt Schwebel, Marc Pilisuk, Kathleen Kostelny, Paul Kimmel, Judy Van Hoorn, Steve Fabick, Eduardo Diaz, Diane Perlman, Anne Anderson, Todd Sloan, Amal Winter, Tony Marsella, Tina Montiel, Judy Kuriansky, Klaus Boehnke, Linda Wolff, V. K. Kool, Abelardo Brenes and many, many more. The support of this peace psychology community was unbelievably helpful to me.

Third, I want to thank my colleagues at Lewis-Clark State College for granting me a sabbatical in the initial stages of writing and in supporting me throughout the writing process. I am grateful for the assistance and critiques provided by Rhett Diessner on the section of the book dealing with the Bahá'í faith. I am also appreciative of the assistance the Lewis-Clark State College library provided in locating much of the material cited in this book. I especially want to thank Becky Grinolds and Samantha Thompson-Franklin for the hours they logged for me for interlibrary loans and collection development. I also want to express thanks to the students in my Peace, Conflict and Violence class and my Advanced Research Seminar who read early drafts of sections of this manuscript and provided some good suggestions for modification and improvement of the book. I particularly want to acknowledge the excellent, constructive feedback from Becca Solom and Christina Browne. I also want to thank Linda Scott, a good friend and artist, who worked on early versions of the cover design.

Last and definitely not least, I want to thank my family for their understanding and tolerance that allowed me the time away from my usual family activities to complete the writing of this book. My wife and best friend, Andrea, started me on the direction of peace and nonviolence research years ago when she admonished me to do something of consequence with my professional life and focus on peace. During the writing, she took on an increased burden at home that was truly appreciated. My sons, Michael and Joey, and my daughters, Caitlin and ZJ, spent the last year and a half without as much interaction from their father as they should have experienced yet were patient and encouraging in my writing. Michael's intense conversations about many aspects of nonviolence and the book were helpful in organizing material in my mind. Joey read early drafts and with the help of his friend, Manar, gave excellent feedback about the section on Islam. Caitlin provided very useful input with the content related to women's issues. ZJ gave me great moral support by just putting a hand on my shoulder from time to time and saying, "How's the book coming Dad?"

As you move through the pages of this book, I ask you to keep in mind the words of Martin Luther King Jr. when he said, "Nonviolence is the answer to the crucial political and moral questions of our time; the need for man to overcome oppression and violence without resorting to oppression and violence. Mankind must evolve for all human conflict a method which rejects revenge, aggression, and retaliation (cited in Groves, 2008, p. 159)." Each of us can play some role in making that happen.

Lewiston, ID   Daniel M. Mayton II

Contents

Chapter 1
Meaning of Nonviolence and Pacifism

Nonviolence is a deceptively complex concept. It has been written about for well over two millennia and, as would be expected, it is very nuanced. If fully understood and routinely applied within human interaction, it has the potential to transform our communities and the greater society in profound and positive ways. The challenge of understanding nonviolence is the focus of this book.

When nonviolence is mentioned in conversation, one might be referring to a religious virtue or belief (e.g. Sharma, 1965), a philosophy (e.g. Bondurant, 1965; Gandhi, 1951), or a political behavior or strategy (e.g. Gandhi, 1957/19731927; King, 1963; Sharp, 1973). Major texts on nonviolence, including those by Gandhi (1957/1927), Sharp (1973), Pelton (1974), Harak (2000), Hare and Blumberg (1968), Holmes and Gan (2005), Kool (1990, 1993a, 2008), Sponsel and Gregor (1994), and Ackerman and Kruegler (1994), have approached the topic from anthropological, historical, psychological, political scientific, sociological, strategic, and pragmatic perspectives.

As is the case for many concepts, the words used in many languages to represent the concept of nonviolence are not totally reflective of the meaning. As I clarify the nature of nonviolence and before I begin to trace its recent history, I want to discuss the similarities and differences with a range of related terms and concepts by answering the following questions. What do aggression and violence mean? How does nonviolence compare to aggression and violence? How are nonviolence and pacifism similar and different from one another?

Prominence of Aggression and Violence Research in Social Sciences

The academic literature in the social sciences focuses more on violence and aggression than nonviolence and pacifism. The emphases within the social sciences can be clearly seen by searching some of the most popular databases within the different disciplines. Within the field of psychology, a search of the PsycINFO database for the key term aggression located 27,245 articles. The key term violence resulted in 31,569 hits and the use of aggression or violence yielded 54,245 separate articles.

D.M. Mayton II, *Nonviolence and Peace Psychology*,
DOI 10.1007/978-0-387-89348-8_1, © Springer Science+Business Media, LLC 2009

A similar search of PsycINFO for the key term nonviolence identified only 236 articles. Pacifism resulted in 125 hits and the combination of pacifism or nonviolence yielded 355 separate articles. This pattern reflects over 150 times more published articles on violence or aggression than articles on nonviolence or pacifism. Searches of the Social Science Index yield similar results though a little less extreme. The key terms aggression or violence located 43,666 articles compared to the terms nonviolence or pacifism which identified 800 articles. This differential is a factor of 54 to 1. Within the Communication and Mass Media Complete database the differential is a factor 50 to 1.

Sponsel and Gregor (1994) have observed that similar patterns can be found within the anthropological literature on conflict with regard to the term peace. They note that within a 366-page bibliography on the anthropology of conflict, only four pages were devoted to peace and conflict resolution. The pattern of profoundly more attention to violence and aggression exists throughout the social sciences.

Aggression

While many use the terms aggression and violence interchangeably, social psychologists prefer to use the term aggression in theory development and in conducting research. Kool (1993b) attributes this psychological preference for the term aggression to the increased focus on individual behavior, whereas violence is more often used in the context of institutional or group actions.

Aggression is typically defined by social psychologists as "any behavior whose proximate intent is harm to another person" (Fiske, 2004, p. 363) or "any form of behavior directed toward the goal of harming or injuring another living being who is motivated to avoid such treatment" (Baron & Richardson, 1994, p. 7). Berkowitz (1993) defines aggression "as any form of behavior that is intended to injure someone physically or psychologically (p. 3)." An aggressive action might be physical or verbal and the harm intended might be either physical or psychological in nature. Intent to harm or injure is the central component of aggression. An aggressive behavior may or may not result in actual harm, but to be an aggressive act, the intention to do harm must be present. A behavior that results in harm to someone may not be aggression at all if the intention to harm is not present. Fiske specifies the intent to be proximate or the most immediate intent since the determination of the primary or ultimate intent for an aggressive act can be difficult to establish due to multiple motives.

Researchers have delineated two basic forms of aggression: hostile aggression and instrumental aggression. Hostile aggression involves aggression that seeks to inflict injury or harm as the primary goal (Fiske, 2004). This type of aggression, also referred to as angry or affective aggression, is impulsive and automatic. Instrumental aggression seeks to harm, not as a primary motive, but as a means to achieve some other goal. As such, instrumental aggression tends to be more premeditated and controlled. However, Fiske describes times in which this type of aggression may be more impulsive and hostile aggression might be more controlled. For instance, a child who has another child take a toy may impulsively hit the child to get the toy back and this would be instrumental aggression. An angry child may plan to start a rumor about another child for revenge and this would be hostile aggression.

Violence

Kool (1993a) notes how most social psychological researchers rarely even use the word violence in their books. Even though violence seems to be the preferred term over aggression among other social sciences and disciplines, O'Moore (n.d.) points out how remarkable it is that violence is rarely defined, especially considering the preponderance of public concern about violence in schools and throughout society.

As for aggression, there are a variety of definitions of violence. Webster's Third New International Dictionary (1971) defines violence as the "exertion of any physical force so as to injure or abuse." Violence is the unlawful exercise of physical force in the Concise Oxford dictionary. These dictionary definitions do not reflect some of the nuances of the meaning of violence reflected in popular usage. From a psychological point of view, Pelton (1974) defines violence as an "action that is initiated with some expectation that it will physically injure another living being (p. 4)." Within this definition the intention is introduced as it was for aggression. Hastings (2005) views violence as direct physical harm to someone else that may involve verbal, psychological, or emotional violence. Bondurant (1965), a political scientist, also defines violence with intention and as she puts it as a "willful application of force in such a way that it is intentionally injurious to the person or group against whom it is applied (p. 9)." Bondurant also notes that violence may encompass threats as well as actual physical force and the injury might be either physical or psychological.

From a philosophical standpoint several definitions of violence are available. Holmes (1971) characterizes physical violence as "the intentional use of physical force to cause harm, injury or suffering or death to persons against their will (p. 109)." Holmes acknowledges the importance of a second kind of violence that is psychological in nature. Audi (1971) extends the realization of both a physical and a psychological aspect of violence in his three-part definition by adding violence directed toward property. From his perspective violence may be "the physical attack upon, or the vigorous physical abuse of, or vigorous physical struggle against, a person or animal; or the highly vigorous psychological abuse of, or the sharp, caustic attack upon a person or animal; or the highly vigorous or incendiary, or malicious and vigorous, destruction or damaging of property or potential property (pp. 61–62)." Miller (1971) provides another philosophical perspective as he views violence as an action taken by a person that "(1) involves great force, (2) in itself capable of injuring, damaging, or destroying, and (3) is done with the intent of injuring, damaging or destroying… where the damage or destruction… [is] not done with the intention of doing something of value (pp. 25–26)."

One of the more comprehensive definitions of violence was developed by the World Health Organization (Krug, Dahlberg, Mercy, Zwi, & Lozano, 2002). Krug et al. define violence as "The intentional use of physical force or power, threatened or actual, against oneself, another person, or against a group or community, that either results in or has a high likelihood of resulting in injury, death, psychological harm, maldevelopment or deprivation (p. 5)." Krug et al. are clear to acknowledge that their WHO definition of violence does have a component of intentionality just as is the case for the concept of aggression. Whereas, with aggression the intention is to do harm, with the WHO definition, the intent is to use or threaten physical force that may be a culturally determined behavior that the person does not even consider to be violent. Krug et al. also point out that the WHO definition implicitly includes both public and private acts that could be reactive to provocations or proactive or instrumental. Violent acts can be physical, sexual, psychological, or involve deprivation or neglect.

Krug et al. (2002) delineate a typology of violence that includes three general categories. Self-inflicted violence involves suicide and self-abuse. Interpersonal violence includes family and intimate partner violence along with violence directed towards individuals within one's community. Child abuse, elderly abuse, rape or sexual violence, youth violence, and violence in institutional settings like schools, government offices, and workplaces all are included within this type of violence. Collective violence is committed by large groups of individuals or states and has social, political, or economic implications. Mob violence, terrorist acts, state violence, and war are all examples of collective violence.

Christie, Wagner, and Winter (2001) developed a four-way model of peace psychology that includes two types of violence: direct violence and structural violence. Direct violence is the type of violence defined by Krug et al. (2002) in which specific actions intentionally produce harm. This violence includes episodic behaviors that result in relatively immediate injury or death and is preventable in overt ways. Structural violence harms and kills in slower and oftentimes indirect ways. This type of violence includes more impersonal and commonplace violence where the perpetrator and the exact action are difficult to observe. The death of an infant because the mother did not receive prenatal care because she did not have access to health insurance is an example of structural violence.

After looking at the general definitions of aggression and violence (especially the World Health Organization definition), it seems as though the terms are very similar indeed. Both aggression and violence can be classified into a range of types to reflect differences in the variety of actions and intentions. Violence does seem to incorporate the use of power as a definitional component whereas aggression does not, however, using the terms interchangeably does not seem to be problematic at all.

Pacifism

Pacifism is a relatively new word that only dates back to the early part of the twentieth century (Teichman, 1986). Teichman notes that the 1904 *Complete Oxford Dictionary* does not include the word. Pacifism was coined a few years later by a

Frenchman to mean "anti-war-ism". While the word is comparatively new, the underlying concepts that it reflects have been around for quite some time.

If you are a pacifist, you believe war is wrong and that it is inappropriate to engage in it (Holmes & Gan, 2005). While some use pacifism and nonviolence synonymously, Little (1995) views pacifism as a theory about the use of nonviolence. As such, pacifism can be seen as doctrines indicating the moral or religious grounds about why and when nonviolence should be used.

Teichman (1986) considers pacifism to actually be a collection of related theories as there are several types of pacifism. Little (1995) delineates absolute or strict pacifism that dictates nonviolent action as a matter of principle. Holmes and Gan (2005) note that absolute pacifists view war as wrong in all possible situations. This is different from pragmatic or situational pacifism (Little) or conditional pacifism (Holmes & Gan), which advocates nonviolent action in some situations but not all.

Yoder (1992), a Mennonite professor of theology, developed a comprehensive classification of over two-dozen different types of pacifism. Several types of pacifism presented by Yoder are discussed here to give a sense of the range of pacifistic views. Yoder's pacifism of the "honest study of cases" is also referred to as just-war pacifism. Within this approach to pacifism, each war is evaluated separately and, if a concrete situation is considered to be just, then war is considered as appropriate. If the particular situation is evaluated as unjust, then the just-war pacifist would say it is wrong to fight it. The major problem with this type of pacifism is in the subjective and inexact nature for determining whether a war is just or not. "Pacifism of absolute principle" considers *all* intentional killing of human beings as wrong. A third type of pacifism is to reject all war yet allow for violent self-defense measures to be taken. From this perspective war is wrong but if you or your loved ones are attacked, being violent in warding off the attack is permissible. As Yoder points out this interpretation of pacifism creates one exception to absolute pacifism, which is an intellectual problem, yet it does silence critics of a pacifistic stance on the very key issue of self-defense. Several subtypes of political pacifism are included in Yoder's typology. The "pacifism of programmatic political alternatives" claims that war is not the best solution to any national problem and works at the governmental level to develop programs and policies to resolve conflicts without resorting to war. The "pacifism of nonviolent social change" is a political pacifism that is based on the work of Mohandas Gandhi and Martin Luther King Jr. This approach to pacifism holds that it is in everybody's interest to live in a society built on justice and advocates techniques of nonviolent action, conscientious objection, etc. to affect a more just society. "Pacifism of absolute conscience" postulates that an individual's conscience tells each person when it is right or wrong to engage in violent activities. While absolute conscience pacifism lacks a theological or moral criteria for right and wrong, the "pacifism of categorical imperative" requires an individual to adopt nonviolent responses in situations where the world would be better off if most people also adopted this particular nonviolent approach. In addition to these types of pacifism Yoder describes pacifisms of prophetic protest, proclamation, utopian purism, redemptive personalism, and the virtuous minority with differing religious undertones.

Nonviolence

Many people who study nonviolence are quick to point out that nonviolence means more than an absence of violence (e.g. Bondurant, 1965; Pelton, 1974). Others have clarified or narrowed the concept of nonviolence by adding descriptors such as nonviolent action (e.g. Sharp, 1973), pragmatic and principled nonviolence (e.g. Holmes & Gan, 2005), and strategic nonviolent conflict (Ackerman & Kruegler, 1994).

Nonviolence as a Philosophy

Mohandas K. Gandhi viewed nonviolence as a philosophy of life (e.g. Bondurant, 1965; Fischer, 1954; Mayton, 2000, 2001; Pelton, 1974). To fully understand Gandhi's philosophy of nonviolence one needs to look closely at three basic principles that guided his life. These are *ahimsa, satyagraha*, and *tapasya*. All of these principles were deeply embedded in his religious beliefs and permeated all he did in his personal and public life.

Ahimsa is a Sanskrit word that has traditionally been translated as nonviolence in the West (Altman, 1980; Teixeira, 1987). However, in the East it is more often translated as noninjury as "himsa" means injury and the "a" prefix means non (Bondurant, 1965). In a deeper way *ahimsa* refers to love (Gandhi, 1951). Altman characterizes *ahimsa* as dynamic compassion that is expressed in a positive and an active way. King (2000) has elucidated the importance of Buddhism in understanding the true nature of *ahimsa*.

Initially, Gandhi used the term passive resistance to reflect the nonviolent approach in dealing with injustice in South Africa (Diwakar, 1948). Because of the realization that this expression did not capture the true essence of what was he was doing, Gandhi (1957/1927) sponsored a contest in 1906 to identify a better label. The word, *satyagraha*, was born from that endeavor. This term has two connotations. While *satyagraha* can be viewed as a political action, it also is an integral part of Gandhi's philosophy of nonviolence. In this context Gandhi translates it as "holding onto truth" (p. 3). Since truth was viewed as soul or spirit, Gandhi also considered *satyagraha* to be a truth-force or soul-force in which humans needed to strive for absolute truth on a continual basis throughout life.

Tapasya involves the principle of self-suffering in that one is willing to suffer for one's goals (Nakhre, 1982). *Ahimsa* and *tapasya* are the characteristics of the means to ascertain absolute truth in one's life (*satyagraha*). Since the quest to discover absolute truth can never be fully realized, one can obtain only relative truth for a particular situation at a particular time. When a conflict arises, neither side can be sure that their view of the truth is correct or not. Therefore, Gandhi believed it would be presumptuous to be anything but nonviolent (*ahimsa*) since any violence might be directed toward individuals who were closer to the absolute truth than you were. *Tapasya* involves a willingness to accept the burden of suffering on oneself rather than one's opponent in a conflict in order to break the cycle of violence with a minimal amount of total violence (Nakhre, 1982).

Groves (2000) finds four themes regarding *tapasya* in Gandhi's writing. First, *tapasya* involves a freedom from fear. This is critical as the second theme involves a willingness to die. *Tapasya* or self-suffering is also based on a religious understanding of the nature of sacrifice. In addition *tapasya* is a necessary characteristic that those engaging in a nonviolent action must have. Groves explains that for Gandhi suffering that is unearned has a redemptive or purifying nature. This view was not held by Martin Luther King Jr. and many other leaders and proponents of nonviolent action. *Tapasya* is in fact one of the most controversial components of Gandhi's philosophy of nonviolence.

Nonviolence as a Behavior

As a behavior, nonviolence has been defined as "… non injury in thought, word, and deed to all forms of life" (Sharp, 1979, p. 134). Hastings (2005) sees nonviolence as "assertive action that protects humans, the Earth and principles, often involving risk to the actionist but which forswears violence (p. xx)." Nonviolence according to Bondurant (1965) is "the exercise of power or influence to reflect change without injury to the opponent (p. 9)."

Little (1995) describes nonviolence as a pattern of attitudes and behavior with four basic characteristics. These characteristics include (1) a pedagogical intent lacking a violent component, (2) a willingness to absorb suffering rather than to reflect it directly to reduce the cause for retaliation, (3) a willingness to share the cost and assume the responsibility of achieving peace, and (4) noncooperation with evil. Little also cites Martin Luther King Jr.'s view of nonviolence as a five part definition. According to King, nonviolence is (1) spiritually aggressive but not physically aggressive, (2) designed to obtain the opponents understanding, not to humiliate them, (3) directed at the forces of evil, not the persons caught in those forces, (4) avoids both physical violence and internal spiritual violence, and (5) based on the conviction that the world is a just place.

Situating Nonviolence Among Related Concepts

Nonviolence is not the absence of aggression or violence but the absence of direct violence. There are times in which the intent of a nonviolent action is to create structural violence in order to convince one's opponent to seriously consider one's point of view in a conflict situation. For instance, when activists picket a store to stop it from discriminating against an ethnic group, the store owner may lose the business of other customers who would have shopped there but refuse to cross the picket line. Forcing the store owner to experience the pain of not being able to pay their own bills was intended to make the store understand the pain experienced by the group that was discriminated against and to subsequent end the practice of discrimination. While both violence and nonviolence involve the use of power, nonviolence is an action and not merely the absence of violent behavior.

While some writers clearly differentiate between pacifism and nonviolence, like the differences between aggression and violence, many define pacifism and nonviolence in very similar ways. Pacifism is more commonly used in relation to war whereas nonviolence is just as likely to be used in any type of conflict. Many different degrees of pacifism exist depending on the dynamics of the situation at hand. Nonviolent action is not linked within the definition to situational constraints in the same way. Pacifism is generally viewed more as a belief and not an action in the way nonviolence is conceptualized. Nonviolent action may be a result of principled or moral beliefs but it may be used even without deep moral commitment because it is often seen as the most efficacious way to resolve a conflict (Ackerman & Kreugler, 1994). Like the characteristics of violence, nonviolence utilizes personal power whereas this is absent from the notion of pacifism. However, both pacifists and nonviolent people may have an underlining moral belief system that violent behavior in certain situations is wrong.

Christie, Wagner, and Winter's (2001) four-way model of peace psychology has relevance to the understanding of nonviolence and pacifism. Peacemaking involves activities calculated to reduce the frequency and intensity of direct violence. Peacebuilding involves activities intended to reduce structural violence. Nonviolence has relevance for both of these quadrants of this model, however, the deep meaning of nonviolence implies a stronger relation to peacebuilding. This peacebuilding aspect of nonviolence will be elaborated on in the chapter on theories of nonviolence.

An Integrated View of Nonviolence

To most writers nonviolence is more than the absence of violence. Nonviolence is an action that uses power and influence to reach one's goal without direct injury or violence to the person or persons working to thwart one's goal achievement. It is clear that nonviolence is a multifaceted concept. Nonviolence appears similar to an attitude in that it may be defined with cognitive, affective, and behavioral components. Drawing from the work of Burrowes (1996), Ritter (2005), Ackerman and Kruegler (1994), and others, a person who is nonviolent may be regarded as someone who holds nonviolent attitudes with cognitive, affective, and behavioral components consistent with each other. As such, a principled nonviolent person consistently

1. believes that violent behavior and retaliations are to be avoided,
2. desires to understand the truth within a conflict,
3. accepts the burden of suffering to break the cycle of violence,
4. believes in the noncooperation with evil, and
5. engages in behaviors that confront injustice with the intent to increase social justice in a manner consistent with the above mentioned beliefs without using direct violence.

Pragmatic nonviolent persons would be different than principled nonviolent persons in that they

1. believe that nonviolent behavior is an effective method to resolve conflict,
2. do not maintain a philosophy of life consistent with principled nonviolence, and
3. engage in nonviolent behaviors that confront a conflict situation without using direct violence.

Two points must be raised to clarify the application of these definitions to particular people. First, a nonviolent person may deviate from one or more of these from time to time but is generally consistent in adhering to all of the above. No one, not even Jesus or Gandhi, were able to be perfectly reliable across all aspects all the time. Second, a nonviolent person does not use direct violence, but may in fact engage in behaviors that result in harming others in the conflict situation. For instance, during the sit-ins at the lunch counters in the segregated south, the intent of the civil rights workers was to publicize the inequities in the treatment of whites and blacks. The demonstrators did not behave aggressively and were trained to avoid any violent retaliation for any verbal or physical attacks directed towards them. However, the owners of the lunch counters did lose business on the days of the sit-ins and this loss, as well as the adverse publicity, may indeed have monetary harm and psychological harm.

Recommended Readings

Ackerman, P., & Kruegler, C. (1994). *Strategic nonviolent conflict: The dynamics of people power in the twentieth century*. Westport, CT: Praeger Publishers.
   Ackerman and Kreugler present a comprehensive interpretation of nonviolence as political strategy. The authors describe six historical episodes including the Russian Revolution of 1904–1906, the *Ruhrkampf* in 1923 Germany, the 1930–1931 Indian independence movement, Denmark's resistance to Nazi occupation, the 1944 civil strike in El Salvador, and the Polish Solidarity Movement in 1980–1981.

Bondurant, J. V. (1965). *Conquest of violence: The Gandhian philosophy of conflict* (Rev. Ed.). Berkeley, CA: University of California Press.
   This is a classic text summarizing the philosophy and the political strategy of Mohandas K. Gandhi. Bondurant's analysis is based on her travel to India to meet with Gandhi and to discuss his work first hand. Excellent discussion of the components of a satyagraha in general and of the Salt Satyagraha specifically.

Holmes, R. L. & Gan, B. L. (Eds.) (2005). *Nonviolence in theory and practice* (2nd ed.). Long Grove, IL: Waveland Press.

This is the revised edition of a book of readings that addresses the origins of pacifism and nonviolence from secular and nonsecular perspectives. Holmes and Gan carefully examine the work of Tolstoy, Gandhi, and King and the impact of women in the field of nonviolence.

Sharp, G. (1973). *The politics of nonviolent action*. Boston, MA: Porter Sargent Books.

This book by Gene Sharp is the classic treatise on nonviolence and a must read for anyone interested in nonviolence. Sharp provides a careful analysis of power and relates this discussion to nonviolent actions. He also outlines a taxonomic view of nonviolent action. His account is peppered with a myriad of detailed historical examples of nonviolence.

Smock, D. R. (Ed.) (1995). *Perspectives on pacifism: Christian, Jewish, and Muslim views on nonviolence and international conflict*. Washington, DC: United States Institute of Peace Press.

Smock summarizes highlights of the presentations and discussions at a one-day symposium on religious perspectives on pacifism under the auspices of the Unites States Institute of Peace. Religious leaders from Christian, Jewish, and Muslim persuasions provide a sense of the nuanced views of pacifism in the world today.

Yoder, J.H. (1992). *Nevertheless: Varieties of religious pacifism*. Scottsdale, PA: Herald Press.

This book summarizes over two dozen views of pacifism. Yoder's approach to study pacifism is primarily from a religious perspective and his typology or taxonomy of pacifism clearly shows the breadth to pacifistic positions from absolute pacifism through a myriad of nuanced options.

Chapter 2
Recent History of Nonviolent Responses to Conflict

Sharp (1973) noted that a considerable amount of nonviolent actions throughout history have been poorly documented, if documented at all, because of a lack of interest to do so. Wars and the outcomes of war are carefully described in our history books. Historians describe the winners and the losers in wars in great detail along with the causes and the implications of their outcomes. Nonviolent struggles are not recorded or recounted with the same regularity and vividness, as are wars and violent interchanges. Despite this propensity, hundreds of nonviolent struggles can be identified throughout recorded history (e.g., Lynd & Lynd, 1995; Sharp). Sharp in fact traces nonviolent action back to 494 B.C. when lower and middle class Romans refused to perform their usual functions until the leadership agreed to make improvement in the conditions of their lives and their status. The ancient Greek playwright, Aristophanes (1944), depicts an effective nonviolent action by Spartan women in his play, *Lysistrata*. In his play the women agree to withhold sex from their husbands to end the Peloponnesian War and to secure peace.

Some have referred to the twentieth century as the century of war (e.g., Kolko, 1995). The twentieth century has also been called the bloodiest century in human history, marked by the loss of more than 100 million lives in war. Besides its bloody legacy, a story that is less often told about the twentieth century is the success of nonviolent people power movements. Actually, during the twentieth century, dozens of major examples of nonviolent campaigns were initiated across the globe (e.g., Ackerman & Duval, 2000; Ackerman & Kruegler, 1994; Holmes & Gan, 2005; Lynd & Lynd, 1995; Sharp, 1973; Zunes, Kurtz, & Asher, 1999). In fact the twentieth was the first century in human history in which many large-scale nonviolent movements successfully toppled oppressive regimes, often in the face of overwhelming military power. However, even into the early part of the twenty-first century, violent human encounters capture our attention and eclipse the many and varied nonviolent social movements that are taking place around the world.

D.M. Mayton II, *Nonviolence and Peace Psychology*,
DOI 10.1007/978-0-387-89348-8_2, © Springer Science+Business Media, LLC 2009

Nonviolent Action in the First Half of the Twentieth Century

During the first half of the twentieth century, the nonviolent work of Mohandas K. Gandhi in South Africa and India is certainly the most famous (Mayton, 2009). Many examples of nonviolent efforts by others are noteworthy and in many cases these efforts were quite successful. Table 2.1 presents a brief, selective time line of nonviolent actions during the first half of the twentieth century. Each of these specific nonviolent campaigns will be highlighted to illustrate the breadth of purposes that can be addressed by nonviolent action and to illustrate the variety of nonviolent actions taken across the globe during this time frame.

Trade Unionists/IWW. Many nonviolent political actions during the twentieth century were initiated because individuals and groups believed their ability to make a living under reasonable conditions and to provide for themselves and their family was severely limited. The Trade Unionists and the Industrial Workers of the World in the United States mounted several nonviolent efforts starting in 1905 and continuing for several years (Lynd & Lynd, 1995). The intent of the strikes was to force the government to enforce the labor law violations of mine owners and manufacturers. For instance, miners and other workers were required to work up to 13 h a day when state laws provided for an 8-h workday.

Gandhi in South Africa. To many Mohandas K. Gandhi is a name that is practically synonymous with nonviolence. Born in India and educated in England, Gandhi's law practice and experiences in South Africa were instrumental in molding his politics and his drive to rid the world of injustice. Early in his years in South Africa, Gandhi was traveling on a train in a first class compartment that was forbidden for "colored people" at that time. When discovered, he refused to vacate his seat

Table 2.1 Brief timeline of selected nonviolent political action in the first half of the twentieth century

Time	Title/Descriptors	Place	Reference(s)
1905+	Trade Unionists/IWW	USA	Lynd and Lynd (1995)
1905–1906	Russian Empire	Russia	Sharp (1973)
1906	Transvaal Asiatic Law	South Africa	Fischer (1954)
1917	Suffragette-Hunger Strike	USA	Lynd and Lynd (1995)
1920	Kappist *coup d'etat*	Germany	Sharp (1973)
1923	Ruhrampf	Germany	Sharp (1973)
1924–1925	Vykom Temple Road	India	Bondurant (1965)
1928	Bardoli Peasants vs Bombay	India	Bondurant (1965)
1930–1931	Salt Act Reform	India	Bondurant (1965)
1940–1944	Occupation and Resistance	Denmark	Ackerman and Kruegler (1994)
1940–1941	Nazi Union of Teachers Freedom of Religion	Norway	Holmes (1990)
1943	Women's Rosenstrasse Protest	Germany	Stolzfus (1996)
1944	Civil Strike of 1944	El Salvador	Ackerman and Kruegler (1994)
1944	Ubico's dictatorship	Guatemala	Sharp (1973)

and was literally thrown off the train into the desolate cold at the next stop. This experience humiliated Gandhi and was critical in focusing his attention on the injustices experienced by nonwhites in South Africa at the dawn of the twentieth century (Fischer, 1954; Mayton, 2000).

When Gandhi decided to stay in South Africa while huddled in the cold train station, it was because he wanted to remove the injustices felt by his fellow Indian expatriates. Numerous efforts were initiated at multiple levels to achieve this difficult goal. One of the most dramatic was the nonviolent action taken to stop the registration efforts for all South Africans of Asiatic descent. The Transvaal Asiatic Law Amendment Ordinance required all Indians eight years and older to register with the government and carry papers at all times or be subject to imprisonment. The enforcement provisions of the ordinance gave the police powers of search and left the Indian population with little privacy and few civil liberties. So on September 11, 1906, Gandhi spoke to a large meeting of Indians and outlined a nonviolent response designed to end the unjust law. By refusing to register and carry the papers dictated by the ordinance many Indians were arrested and placed in jail. So many, in fact that the prison system overflowed and while the ordinance was not repealed, eventually the impact of the law was markedly lessened by the government (Fischer, 1954).

Russian Empire. Many nonviolent actions have taken place across the globe in which citizens have strived to bring about more democratic forms of government in their own country. Between 1905 and 1906, many Russians interested in changing the Tsarist government to a more representative government used nonviolent actions. Russian workers engaged in marches, general strikes, the withdrawal of funds from banks, and the nonpayment of debts to get the Tsar to act on their demands, unfortunately to no avail (Sharp, 1973; Ackerman & DuVall, 2000).

South American Response to Autocratic Rule. In 1944 dictators in both Guatemala and El Salvador were removed from office with civil resistance (Sharp, 1973). Guatemalan teachers, displeased with wages under the dictatorship of General Jorge Ubico, petitioned the government to hear their concerns and raise their wages. When these teachers were arrested and charged with conspiracy against the government, other teachers boycotted a scheduled celebration in honor of Ubico and were fired, imprisoned, or both. Within a few weeks, university students, lawyers, and other professionals joined their fellow citizens in calling for the resignation of Ubico. During a state of emergency in which there were beatings and more arrests, Ubico issued the challenge that he would resign if 300 respected citizens of his country asked him to. When 311 courageous Guatemalans signed a memorandum to just that effect, the state-directed violence towards the demonstrators intensified and during a silent procession of praying women the military attacked, wounding many and killing one. This precipitated a general strike where workers stayed home and businessmen shut their doors. While the continued strike was successful in getting Ubico to step down, democracy did not follow (Sharp).

General Martinez ruled El Salvador as a dictator from 1931 until 1944 (Ackerman & Kruegler, 1994; Ackerman & DuVall, 2000). While having popular support initially, repressive actions and the ruthlessness used in the consolidation and maintenance of power seriously eroded the support of the Martinez regime.

Martinez modified the constitution a second time so he could remain in power after 1943. This act provided the opposition throughout many sectors of society and became a focus for their accumulated frustrations. Following a violent insurrection that Ackerman and Kruegler describe as an unmitigated disaster, many people were sentenced to death for their involvement. The opposition then resolved to carry out a civil strike to bring down the Martinez regime. In April 1944 university students, doctors, lawyers, engineers, and other professionals, government workers, and members of the business community organized a national strike to bring El Salvador to a halt. From the latter part of April through the early part of May more and more people honored the strike and supported each other in the process until Martinez resigned on May 10.

Suffragette-Hunger Strike. Another early twentieth century nonviolent action in the US involved the 1917 Suffragette-Hunger Strike (Lynd & Lynd, 1995). Following imprisonment for picketing to obtain the right to vote for women, the suffragettes demanded to be treated as political prisoners and not common criminals. The response of the prison system was to place these petitioners in solitary confinement. Their hunger strike to protest this treatment was the first in the United States to be organized and sustained for a significant amount of time (Lynd & Lynd).

Vykom Temple Road. After returning to permanently live in India in 1915, Gandhi led and participated in dozens of nonviolent campaigns or *satyagrahas*. These campaigns addressed a number of issues (e.g., Bondurant, 1965; Buck, 1984), although I have only listed three here.

First is the Vykom *satyagraha* that took place from 1924 until 1925. The issue at question here was the restriction that kept members of the lowest Hindu cast, the untouchables, from walking in front of an orthodox Hindu temple of the Brahman or highest caste (Bondurant, 1965). The fact that an untouchable was forbidden from passing in front of the orthodox temple in Vykom was a particular burden since it necessitated that they must walk a considerable distance in order to return to their homes each day after work. Gandhi, some high-caste reformers, and some untouchables decided to walk in front of the temple in question and stop directly in front of it. When they did, the marchers were attacked and some were sentenced to prison. Once this happened, the original marchers not in jail were joined by others from throughout the country and, even though they were not allowed to enter the road that passed in front of the temple, a vigil was started at the entrance to the road. The 24/7-prayer vigil continued through the rainy season with considerable hardship to the reformers who prevailed after sixteen months. The Brahman leadership allowed the untouchables to use the road after this nonviolent action.

Bardoli Peasants vs Bombay. In 1928 the Bardoli *satyagraha* was initiated to deal with unfair taxes (Bondurant, 1965). The grievance was based on increased assessment of land value that increased the tax revenue owed. This new assessment was viewed as being inaccurate, unwarranted, and unjust. The objective of the nonviolent campaign was to persuade the officials in Bombay (Mumbai) to reassess the land revenue process by making an impartial inquiry. Gandhi viewed this as a very strategic effort since this unfair method of tax increases existed in many other locations in India and would set an important precedent. This campaign lasted six months and included noncooperation, technical trespass, submission to arrest, resignations of offices, and social boycott. The objective was resolved in a manner that allowed the government officials to save face and set the groundwork for cooperation between the people and the officials in the future.

Salt Act Reform. The British Salt Act made it illegal for Indians to manufacture salt and it levied an increase in the tariff that was placed on the salt that the British collected by selling it. The nonviolent campaign that Gandhi helped organize in 1930 was a multifaceted approach designed to give power to the Indian people and ultimately to repeal the Salt Act. This nonviolent campaign also had strategic value to Gandhi and his fellow Indians who believed that by characterizing the British government as unrepresentative and alien, India would move closer to complete independence (Bondurant, 1965). A multilayered-system of leadership was organized and the campaign began with Gandhi's historical march to the sea to make salt in defiance of British law. Following Gandhi's civil disobedience of making salt at the seaport of Dandi on April 5, he declared that all Indians had the right to do so. When thousands of Indians also defied the law, the British government arrested all the lawbreakers and put them in prison. As the prisons filled, the economy suffered with shops that could not open because their owners were jailed. Resignations from public office in support of the campaign also made commerce and normal business practices slow. The demonstration at the Dharsana Salt Works in May resulted in violent retaliation by government police, but the worldwide publicity of the brutality weakened the British image even more. The demonstrations, boycotts of British goods, noncooperation, and other types of civil disobedience all continued until March 1931 when Gandhi and Viceroy Irwin signed a historic agreement. By the time this yearlong campaign ended, hundreds of thousands of Indians had participated in over a thousand different nonviolent activities (Bondurant). While the Salt Acts were not totally repealed, provisions for the poor were granted to alleviate the monetary difficulties imposed by the law. The British also agreed to allow more involvement of representatives of the Indian National Congress in deliberations regarding constitutional reforms.

Post World War I Nonviolence in Germany. During the 1920s, German citizens initiated two nonviolent actions. First, in Berlin in 1920 an attempted *coup d'état* against the ruling Weimar Republic planned by Dr. Kapp with military assistance was thwarted nonviolently by a general strike and noncooperation by the bureaucracy and ordinary civil servants (Sharp, 1973). Without popular support the Kappist regime lasted only a few days. Second, in 1923 German industrialists and civil servants used noncooperation and both passive and active resistance against French and Belgian occupiers of the Ruhr (Ackerman & Kruegler, 1994; Ackerman & DuVall, 2000). While Sharp points out that this Ruhrampf action was not very successful, the French and the Belgians were not able to take the level of reparations from Germany as they had hoped.

Nonviolent Actions Against Nazi Germany. Several nonviolent actions have been documented against the Nazi government during the 1940s. Between 1940 and 1944 during the Nazi occupation of Denmark, the Danish people engaged in a broad set of strategies to maintain their national culture and sense of integrity

(Ackerman & Kruegler, 1994; Ackerman & DuVall, 2000). Initially, citizens performed their jobs in intentionally poor fashion by working slowly with as many mistakes as possible. These activities were combined with boycotts of Nazi stores and goods plus worker strikes during the latter part of the occupation. Stolzfus (1996) describes a nonviolent protest in Germany directed at the German Gestapo. A group of non-Jewish wives demonstrated for the release of their Jewish husbands who were being retained. These 6,000 courageous women and their supporters stood outside the Gestapo headquarters at Rosentrasse and they were able to have their husbands released.

Nonviolent Action in the Last Half of the Twentieth Century

The second half of the twentieth century witnessed many large-scale nonviolent actions in every inhabited continent on earth. Table 2.2 presents a brief, selective time line of nonviolent actions during this time period.

Table 2.2 Brief timeline of selected nonviolent political action in the second half of the twentieth century

Time	Title/Descriptors	Place	Reference
1953	Vorkuta labor camps	Soviet Union	Sharp (1973)
1955–1956	Montgomery bus boycott	USA	Cortright (2006)
1958	Comm. for Nonviolent Action	USA	Lynd and Lynd (1995)
1961–1965	Voter rights/Desegregation	USA	King (1963); Lynd and Lynd (1995)
1968	Reform movement	Czechoslovakia	Sharp (1973)
1966–1973	Vietnam War Protests	USA	Lynd and Lynd (1995)
1971–1972	United Farm Workers	USA	Cortright (2006)
1980–1981	Solidarity vs. Communism	Poland	Ackerman and DuVall (2000)
1981–1982	Druze of Golan Heights	Israel/Syria	Holmes (1990)
1982–1998	Active Peace & Liberation Movement	East Timor	Montiel (2006)
1984–1994	Apartheid to Democracy	South Africa	Ackerman and DuVall (2000)
1986	People Power Revolution	Philippines	Ackerman and DuVall (2000)
1986–1999	Orange Hats	Washington DC	Anderson (2000)
1988–1995	NLD Popular Revolt	Burma	Oishi (2002)
1989	Velvet Revolution	Czechoslovakia	Smithey and Kurtz (1999)
1991	Stopping Military Coup	Russia	Ackerman and DuVall (2000)
1992–1996	Dhammayietra Walks for Peace	Cambodia	Montiel (2006)

Montgomery bus boycott. Just as Gandhi was the most recognized proponent of nonviolent action in the first half of the twentieth century, Martin Luther King Jr. was clearly the most notable advocate of nonviolence during the last half. Martin Luther King Jr. was born in 1929 in Atlanta Georgia into a Baptist family. He was a very precocious child academically, skipping some grades so he could enter Morehouse College at 15. After graduation from college he went on to receive two degrees in religion including a PhD from Boston University. Following in his father's footsteps, King became a minister (Washington, 1992).

In 1954 King took his first ministry at the Dexter Avenue Baptist Church, in Montgomery, Alabama (King, 1969). While he was presiding at this church, one of King's parishioners was Rosa Parks who decided to keep her seat on a bus instead of giving it to a white man. Many in the African American community in Montgomery were ready to act against racial injustice and the actions of Parks provided a clear opportunity. Even though more senior leaders might have taken up the mantel, King was somewhat reluctantly thrust into a leadership position in the Montgomery Bus Boycott because of his energy and his speaking skills. The bus boycott requested all African Americans to refrain from riding the city buses until the law requiring them to sit in the back of the bus was overturned. There was a near unanimous compliance with the boycott among the African American community and the loss of revenue for the city of Montgomery was considerable. As the spokesperson for this 382-day boycott, King was harassed, threatened, arrested, and his home was bombed. The Montgomery African Americans persevered with the boycott for over a year. The boycott ended when the Supreme court outlawed segregation on public transportation systems (King, 1963; Sharp, 1973).

Voter rights/Desegregation. The civil rights movement in the American south during the 1950s and 1960s may be associated with Martin Luther King Jr. but there were many nonviolent events designed to improve the lives of African Americans in which King was not involved. When four students from North Carolina A & T sat down at the whites-only lunch counter in the Greensboro Woolworth's store in February 1960, were refused service, and continued to sit in their seats, the sit-in movement was launched (Ackerman & DuVall, 2000). By the end of that year over 70,000 African Americans and whites had been involved in sit-ins to end segregation in restaurants throughout the American south (Sharp, 1973). As the number of arrests neared 4,000 over this 7-month period, businesses and government from local to federal levels felt pressure to change the levels of segregation within their communities and jurisdictions.

Voter registration was another type of injustice that affected African Americans during the Civil Rights period in the United States (Lynd & Lynd, 1995). Once formed in 1960, the Student Nonviolent Coordinating Committee (SNCC) soon coordinated its activities to increase voter registration of African Americans in rural southwestern Georgia and in Mississippi. Efforts to register voters were met with violence including beatings and murder and at one point the entire staff of SNCC in a county of Mississippi were jailed. The brave workers persisted and more and more citizens were registered to vote and more and more people throughout the world became aware of the difficulties the SNCC faced in completing their task.

In an effort to end segregation on interstate buses and long distance bus services in the south, the Freedom Riders, consisting of white and black passengers, defied segregation laws by boarding buses in Washington DC and traveling together to Mississippi, Alabama, and other locations in the deep south (Ackerman & DuVall, 2000). During this series of actions, the KKK and its sympathizers engaged in ambushes, beatings, and other types of violent intimidations. These attacks were so severe that President Kennedy ordered the National Guard to protect the Freedom Riders (Aspey, 2005).

In addition to the bus boycott to deal with segregation Martin Luther King Jr. tried to reduce levels of segregation in other ways. In April 1963 King was arrested in Birmingham during a demonstration in support of the desegregation of restaurants. It was during this tumultuous time that he was urged by many to stop his actions because they were resulting in such violent responses by the segregationists. When television coverage of the white mobs beating the nonviolent Freedom Riders was broadcast throughout the country, a moral outrage spread along with a deeper understanding of the oppression experienced by African Americans. In the cramped quarters of a crowded cell King wrote his eloquent response to his critics that is known as the "Letter from Birmingham Jail" (Holmes & Gan, 2005). In this letter King responded to his critics who abhorred the turmoil and violence created by the demonstrations that King led. He reminding his fellow clergymen and other critics that the suffering among members of the African American community from many injustices was already tragic and should be deplored also. King outlined a guide for nonviolent social action including the four steps of (1) collecting the facts, (2) engaging in negotiation and dialogue with one's adversary, (3) purifying oneself and preparing for sacrifice, and (4) taking direct action (Cortright, 2006). Furthermore, King pointed to the tension the demonstrations would create as necessary since those in charge of the segregated south were not apt to relinquish their power unless they were pushed out of their comfort zone. In other words additional time for the white southern leadership to act had little chance of success in ending racial discrimination.

United Farm Workers. Cortright (2006) has described Cesar Chavez as the Gandhi of the fields. Chavez and the United Farm Workers pursued efforts to alleviate the oppression of workers in the United States (Holmes, 1990). Specifically, the concern was that workers were being paid very low wages (less than a dollar an hour) and also faced a range of dehumanizing working conditions. A series of boycotts for lettuce and grapes were organized starting in 1965 and these continued into the 1970s. When other unions like the longshoreman refused to move boycotted grapes, the impact on effected growers was immediately felt. The boycotts expanded to the national levels as consumers across the country listened to the United Farm Workers of America (UFWA) activists who were taking their case to the press. The boycotts and strikes were effective and by mid 1970, major grape growers signed labor contracts with the UFWA. When another labor dispute with lettuce growers emerged in the same year, the same methodology of boycotts and strikes was used.

Many other labor disputes in the United States used nonviolent actions to overcome differences with management and to improve working conditions. In 1968 sanitation workers in the city of Memphis Tennessee went on strike for a living wage, fair treatment, and safety issues. Martin Luther King Jr. joined the sanitation workers in a march through downtown that uncharacteristically erupted into violent acts by some protesters. While the leadership of the strike worked to refocus their nonviolent efforts, King gave his memorable "I have been to the Mountaintop" speech on April 3 and was assassinated the following day. Despite the rioting throughout Memphis sparked by King's murder, meetings continued between the strikers and Memphis city officials. An agreement was reached within two weeks that increased wages and committed the city to end racial discrimination on the job.

Anti-Nuclear Weapons/ Vietnam War Protests. Formed in 1957 with only a dozen members, the Committee for Nonviolent Action (CNVA) promoted a bold action to try to slow the development of nuclear weapons (Lynd & Lynd, 1995). With Albert Bigelow, a former naval commander, at the helm the 30-foot boat, Golden Rule, sailed into the nuclear testing area in the Pacific Ocean. The press coverage of the voyage and subsequent arrest and imprisonment of the crew served to make the cause of the CNVA known to the world.

Zinn (2002) has analyzed the immorality and historical folly of US actions in Vietnam that led to many nonviolent protests in the United States and around the world. King (2002/1967) spoke out against the Vietnam War on moral and pragmatic grounds in 1967. Protests and nonviolent actions designed to stop the war in Vietnam were initiated starting in the mid 1960s in the United States (Chatfield, 1999). The activities employed were diverse and included picketing, vigils, teach-ins, street theatre, and the display of buttons and bumper stickers. Dozens of antiwar groups were formed with civilian and veteran members alike. Chatfield asserts that while the antiwar Vietnam War movement did not directly bring about the withdrawal of US troops, it was a contributing factor in ending the US involvement in the war.

Nonviolent Actions of Warsaw Pact Countries. In the nearly five decades following the end of World War II the countries under the sphere of influence of the Soviet Union used nonviolent actions to varying degrees of success to increase their autonomy. The Czechoslovakian reform movement of 1968 (Sharp, 1973), the Polish Solidarity Movement of 1980-1981 (Ackerman & DuVall, 2000), the Velvet Revolution in Czechoslovakia in 1989 (Ackerman & Kruegler; Van Inwegen, 2006), and thwarting the military coup in Russia in 1991 (Ackerman & Kruegler) are all particularly relevant here.

The Czechoslovakian reform movement of 1968 was an ill-fated attempt to wrest freedoms from the communist regime via a populist movement (Sharp, 1973). Realizing the futility of violent revolt after watching the Hungarian attempts in 1956, the Czechs and Slovaks used nonviolent resistance to support their leaders' efforts to break from the Soviet-backed Warsaw Pact and the repression it maintained. When the Soviet leaders ordered a half a million Warsaw Treaty Organization troops to orchestrate a *coup d'état* to replace the reform leadership with a pro-Moscow government, many in Czechoslovakia refused to follow the orders of the invaders. Radio stations did not air pro-Soviet messages, clandestine radio stations called for short general strikes and slow work downs plus it successfully discouraged collaboration with the invaders. Sharp indicates that while the Soviet-backed military invasion was totally successful, the organized civil resistance of the Czech and Slovak people made the political victory more dubious. The Czechoslovakian reform leadership maintained some political power and was part of the new government for nearly a year after the invasion.

Ackerman and DuVall (2000) have outlined the key aspects of the demands and actions of the workers at the Polish shipyards in Gdansk in 1980–1981 that led to a nonviolent restructuring of Polish government and society. As Ackerman and DuVall point out, the approach taken by the workers and their supporters and the effectiveness of these actions in 1980 were a function of a series of earlier failed actions by Polish workers to achieve similar demands. Among other things workers wanted a pay raise, longer maternity leave, and the right to form their own independent, self-governing trade union. The latter demand was strategic in that even though it was an economic demand for more freedom in the work place, granting this demand would necessitate a major change in the power and structure of the communist government.

Many of the leaders and participants in what has become to be known as the Polish Solidarity Movement in the early 1980s had been believers in their country's communist party when they were younger (Ackerman & DuVall, 2000). Failure of the government to deliver on its promise of a prosperous economy became painfully obvious when the costs of food rose and the wages dropped. Exacerbated by the knowledge that it was going to be hard to feed one's family, workers engaged in a series of strikes that yielded only minimal gains on minor demands. In 1970, workers engaged in a strike to protest another hike in the price of food which resulted in a violent backlash by the government. Ackerman and DuVall point out that others in Polish society took note and realized that the way to increase the freedoms experienced by Polish citizens via government change was going to be through the actions of the workers. Groundwork to support the cause of the workers was laid during the next decade and when economic issues flared up in the late 1970s many elements of Polish society consciously decided to support the workers in their struggle against the government. Thus, the solidarity movement emerged into a very strong force by 1980. When the decision was made by the workers to strike and occupy the shipyard to prevent normal business in August 1980 and action was taken, the resources at the disposal of the nonviolent strategic action were multifaceted and effective in obtaining most of the workers' demands. The right of the Gdansk workers to form a free trade union ultimately changed the entire country although the first half of the decade was tumultuous within the government as the communist leaders were divided and many attempted to cling to their old ways and power. The rapid spread of independent unions into many segments of Polish society resulted in widespread government crackdowns and imprisonment of many union leaders including Solidarity activists like Lech Walesea. Because of the breadth of the support within the country, the movement continued with new leadership and in 1989, the communist dictatorship in Poland was over (Ackerman & DuVall).

Efforts to gain freedom via nonviolent social movements also occurred in the 1980s in other European countries under the sphere of Soviet influence. Smithey & Kurtz (1999) report that Hungary was transforming itself nonviolently at the same time as Poland was. They also note that East German citizens used the opportunities provided by neighboring Hungary when it removed border fences in May 1989 to put pressure on their government for changes. Demonstrations and a mass exodus of East Germans led to the resignation of the communist leader, Erich Honnecker, on October 18. In about a year the Berlin Wall came down and East and West Germany were unified. The Velvet Revolution in Czechoslovakia gained momentum in 1989 as well. Popular demonstrations by student groups in November 1989 were joined by many other dissident groups and in combination with general strikes led to the fall of the communist government and the installation of Vaclav Havel as the new president by the end of December.

Stopping Russian Military Coup. Mikhail Gorbachev and his *perestroika* dramatically changed the lives of his Soviet comrades as he worked to implement new economic mechanisms. The dissolution of the Soviet Union created much upheaval for the new Russian citizen and many hardliners were not pleased with the direction their country was taking. In August 1991 a military coup was attempted to end the moral danger to the Motherland (Ackerman & DuVall, 2000). Many in the country were not surprised by the military revolt and Gorbachev's arrest, however, Boris Yeltsin, the former mayor of Moscow and the elected president of the Russian Federation responded in a dramatic way to thwart the coup. Yeltsin made a concerted plea to the Russian people and the military personnel to the commitment they had for Mother Russia. He climbed on top of a tank defending the Russian White House government building and read a powerful statement to remind the soldiers that their allegiance was to the people and to not spill the blood of those you have taken an oath to protect. His actions and words convinced many to build barricades around the White House and to convince the military to lay down their arms. He asked others not to cooperate with the members of the coup. Many aspects of Russian society including the media refused to comply with the demands of the leaders of the coup. The situation at the White House was broadcast so others could see the bravery of Yeltsin and others in the face of the massed military strength. As military leaders sent to arrest government leaders changed their allegiance from the junta to Yeltsin and positioned their armor to protect the White House the dynamics of the military takeover changed quickly. The attack on the government was cancelled and many in the KGB and the military voiced their support for Yeltsin (Ackerman & DuVall).

Asia has been in the forefront of nonviolent actions over the last half of the twentieth century as well. Montiel (2006) describes many of the recent nonviolent movements in Southeast Asia including the People Power Revolution in the Philippines, the Buddhist Walk for Peace in Cambodia, and the peace and liberation movement in East Timor. Another nonviolent movement was the NDL Popular Revolt and the work of Aung San Suu Kyi in Burma (Hunt, 2002; Oishi, 2002).

People Power Revolution. The People Power Movement in the Philippines was a response to the actions of the corrupt regime of President Ferdinand Marcos. When the exiled opposition leader Benigno Aquino was shot on the tarmac immediately as he returned to his country in 1983, the public became outraged and a martyr was created (Ackerman & DuVall, 2000). Demonstrations ensued but their impact was marred by violent episodes. Over the next few years Marcos realized that his support from the United States was eroding so he agreed to a snap election three months off. The campaign of Corazon Aquino, widow of the assassinated Benigno, was well organized and its message brought out many supporters across the country to her rallies. Aquino's campaign seemed to be the antithesis of that of the incumbent Marcos. However, the election process was severely flawed with the intimidation of voters, widespread reports of vote buying, and vote counting irregularities (Ackerman & DuVall). Despite considerable evidence that the outcome would be different, Marcos claimed electoral victory.

Zunes (1999b) makes the case that the success of the nonviolent campaign that followed was the result of many years of planning and preparation following unsuccessful and sometimes violent efforts to overthrow Marcos. The immediate and organized demonstrations were possible because Aquino's supporters anticipated that Marcos would engage in some type of fraud to steal the election. As the disciplined nonviolent demonstrations were large in number (some estimated to be over a million) and well conceived, they began to win over many in the military and many international observers and leaders to the cause of a strong democracy for the Philippines. Marcos was pushed into making concessions to make the elections fair. This ultimately opened the door for Corazon Aquino to become president of the Philippines.

Active Peace & Liberation Movement. The active peace and liberation movement in East Timor was also designed to bring democratic rule to the people. East Timor was invaded and occupied by Indonesia in 1975. An armed struggle to obtain independence began almost immediately. Nonviolent efforts for self-rule were initiated starting in 1982 and were continued sporadically until Indonesian President Suharto resigned under pressure in 1998. Despite the violent retaliation of the occupiers to the nonviolent activists, the East Timorese voted in favor of their independence in 1999. Montiel (2006) analyzed the nonviolent prodemocracy movement in East Timor and posits that it was not as effective as other similar movements because of the lack of international support for the efforts of the nonviolent activists.

Dhammayietra Walks for Peace. Cambodians have instituted *Dhammayietras* or Buddhists Walks for Peace on multiple occasions starting in 1992 (Montiel, 2006). The first *Dhammayietra* was a month long and was orchestrated to unite Cambodian refugees on the Thai border with the local Cambodian population. Subsequent *Dhammayietra* addressed the need for democratic polls, the civil war, land mines, and deforestation.

NLD Popular Revolt. Nonviolent action also found a significant place in the political arena for Burma, another Southeast Asian country. Burma does not have a long history of nonviolent movements, but that changed in the late 1980s (Beer, 1999; Oishi, 2002). Under a repressive military government that totally controlled the economy a growing unrest was intensified by high inflation, corruption, and a lowered standard of living (Hunt, 2002). In the summer of 1988 a student-led prodemocracy movement resulted in massive street protests. A heavy-handed military crackdown on the demonstrations resulted in the deaths of hundreds of nonviolent protesters. Following the massacre, many intellectuals, retired military, and other concerned people including Aung San Suu Kyi, the daughter of General Aung San the World War II military hero of Burma, became involved in the prodemocracy movement (Oishi). When the government responded to political demands for a democracy with civilians calling for elections, the opposition was ready. Suu Kyi as the National League for Democracy (NLD) candidate advocated nonviolent actions in her campaign to become the leader of Burma in spite of being threatened and harassed sometimes at gunpoint. While the election did occur with a landslide victory for Suu Kyi and the NLD, the military junta refused to honor the results and most leaders of the NLD including Suu Kyi were imprisoned or put under house arrest. As these imprisonments have continued over the subsequent years, a unique alliance of armed resistance and nonviolent action has worked together to bring about a civilian-led democracy in the country. Beers has analyzed this type of alliance and points out the dangers and pitfalls that it brings. However, even if movement is relatively slow, a greater international understanding of the struggle resulted in the 1991 Nobel Peace Prize being awarded to Aung San Suu Kyi that in turn increased international awareness even more. The release of many NLD leaders in 1995 has been a good positive outcome even if restrictions for the NLD leadership still persist.

Apartheid to Democracy. Africa has had its share of nonviolent actions designed to change governments to a less repressive and more democratic form. The military-dominated government of Mali was replaced by a democracy due to a nonviolent insurrection although efforts in Sudan and Niger were not as successful (Zunes, 1999a). Like many other struggles to remove a repressive regime, the struggle in South Africa to end apartheid had violent and nonviolent aspects. Racism as an organizing principle of the governing white Europeans in South African society was present since their arrival in the seventeenth century and was made explicit policy in the 1920s (Ackerman & DuVall, 2000). In the late 1940s apartheid became a formal policy with a range of very restrictive laws that banned the indigenous peoples of the region and those classified as Coloured (other dark skinned people often of Asian descent) from politics and high wage jobs and also kept them separate from the white minority (Ackerman & DuVall). This institutionalized racism kept the African and Coloured majority from experiencing numerous freedoms. The resistance to racism and apartheid policies spanned many decades even before the Actions of Gandhi in the first part of the twentieth century. Organizations, like the African National Congress (ANC) and the United Democratic Front (UDF), were formed to work to eliminate apartheid. The fact that violent episodes were relatively common over the years weakened the impact of the nonviolent actions and probably delayed the changes that fundamentally restructured the government South Africa into a representative democracy (Zunes, 1999c).

One of the key figures in the South African struggle was Nelson Mandela, one of the leaders of the ANC. While Mandela was an advocate for violent action against the oppression of the white minority rule and was imprisoned in 1962 for his violent attacks, he came to see the wisdom of nonviolent means. During his stay at the Robben Island prison, Mandela and other ANC leaders had time to discuss political action among themselves and with newly arrested younger activists. The realization that color was not the issue but the goal was to work together to obtain true democracy was communicated and this helped build a coherent group of people ready to accomplish what the ANC had set out to do years before. Therefore, it is not surprising that Mandela came to symbolize a more democratic South Africa and, upon winning his release from prison, he was a critical focal point of the non-violent actions taken by many of his fellow countrymen (Presbey, 2006).

Outside of the Robben Island prison, many people were moving the cause of a truly democratic South Africa. The emerging mass democratic movement included informal alliances among the ANC, UDF, and several other organizations making a coalition of 700 + organizations (Zunes, 1999c). While some within this movement still supported an armed resistance, many refocused their energy on nonviolent actions to bring down apartheid. Because the domination by the white minority depended on nonwhite labor, strikes were planned and executed very skillfully and effectively. The heavy handed response of the South African police to nonviolent actions resulted in many whites in the country and many in the international community to see the inhumanity of the apartheid policies and laws. The antiapartheid forces combined strikes with boycotts. For instance, when workers went on strike in the beef industry, people throughout the country supported the strike by boycotting beef products. When potato workers were on strike, there was a widespread boycott on potatoes. Community boycotts became national boycotts and were joined by the international community to apply consider-able pressure on the apartheid government (Zunes).

The work of antiapartheid leadership like, Popo Molefe, Mkhuseli Jack, and Archbishop Desmond Tutu and international boycotts of South African goods took their toll. By the late 1980s many in the South African government realized a shift from apartheid policies and law was eminent. Secret meetings were held between government officials and Nelson Mandela (Ackerman & DuVall, 2000). Mandela was clear in his goal that majority rule was necessary but also asserted that whites could expect to find a place in democratic South Africa. The commitment to "non-racialism" created a climate that made for more rapid changes than might have otherwise occurred. Changes happened quickly following Mandela's release from prison in 1990. In four years a fully franchised citizenry elected Nelson Mandela as President of South Africa. After decades, apartheid laws were gone.

Nonviolent Actions in the Middle East. The Middle East as the birthplace of west-ern civilization has experienced considerable violence and war. The view that Arabs, Jews, and Christians have been in conflict with each other in the Middle East for mil-lennia is true. Within hours after the establishment of the modern state of Israel, war again became a reality for the region. From the time of Christ to the Crusades to the 1967 Arab-Israeli War to the Israeli-Lebanese War during the summer of 2006, mili-taries and militias have wrought considerable violence on each other. However preva-lent war and violence has been to this region, this does not mean that there have not been times of peace and that nonviolent actions have not been used to obtain some type of resolution to the many conflicts. Zunes (1999a) indicates that Egyptian inde-pendence in 1919 was preceded by several months of civil disobedience.

Awad (1990) comments on the Palestinian strike in 1936 as a modern beginning point for nonviolent action. Many people from a variety of backgrounds living within the expanded borders of Israel have engaged in nonviolent action over the last half of the twentieth century to achieve a variety of goals. McCarthy and Sharp (1997) observe that on numerous occasions citizens have engaged in nonviolent action to increase their voice in political life and to express their resistance to war and militarization of the country. Zunes (1999a) indicates that in the latter case over 50 Israeli peace groups either were created or reemerged during the 1980s alone.

The outcome of the 1967 war between Israel and several Arab nations was an impetus for considerable nonviolent as well as armed action between Palestinians living within the new Israeli borders and the Israeli military and settlers. At the end of the 1967 war, Israel occupied the West Bank and the Gaza Strip areas that were both previously Palestinian territory. They also occupied the Golan Heights that was previously Syrian territory.

As people in the Golan Heights began to adjust to life under Israeli rule, one element of the population took steps to maintain their ethnic and religious autonomy (Kennedy, 1990). The Druze of the Golan Heights are an offshoot of Shi'ite Islam that synthesizes Islam with aspects of Christianity, Hellenism, and other sources to form a belief system that views Mohammed as an important prophet but only one of several incarnations of Allah on earth (Kennedy). This has resulted in the group's persecution by both Sunni and Shi'ite Moslems over the centuries. While a tight-knit community and generally secretive about their religious beliefs, Kennedy characterizes the Druze as both politically flexible and pragmatic. In 1982 the Druze used nonviolent techniques to stand up to the Israeli administration over the offer to obtain Israeli citizenship following the annexation of the Golan Heights by Israel in 1981. Druze laborers refused to become Israeli citizens and refused to work in Israeli industry and this seriously hurt the economy. Efforts to isolate Druze villages by the Israeli Defense Forces (IDF) were thwarted by the Druze. As a village ran out of food, Druze from other villages would walk in very large numbers to deliver supplies and would overwhelm the IDF by their sheer numbers to accomplish their goal. Curfews were ignored to harvest crops, village collectives emerged, and a variety of activities were instituted to convince the IDF to leave the Druze villages. The Druze even engaged in a reverse strike where they organized to complete work instead of a typical strike where groups organize to refuse to complete work. In this instance the Druze built a sewer system that the Israeli's refused to build as a public works project (Zunes, 1999a). The Israeli's escalated their efforts to get the Druze to accept Israeli citizenship by imposing a 43-day siege with as many as 15,000 members of the IDF. During the siege, IDF were ordered to go door to door, forcibly enter each Druze home, confiscate identification papers from the time of Syrian rule, and leave Israeli identification papers in their place. When villagers littered their town squares with Israeli identity cards, the Israeli effort to force the Golani Druze to become Israeli citizens was suspended (Kennedy).

The Palestinian *Intifada* is another action taken against the Israeli occupiers. *Intifada* commonly referred to as "uprising" literally means "to shake up" or "to shake off" (Dajani, 1999). The first *Intifada* began in 1987 and occurred in the West Bank and the Gaza Strip until 1992 (McCarthy & Sharp, 1997). While the *Intifada* did have some well-publicized episodes of violence, it explicitly endorsed nonviolent means because of the realization that armed action was not successful (Zunes, 1999a). Peaceful demonstrations, strikes, tax refusal, the development of alternative institutions, and other nonviolent actions were used by the Palestinians to obtain greater self-determination. Dajani posits that while this *Intifada* did change both

Palestinian and Israeli societies, the types of changes were mixed in terms of the effect they have on Palestinian independence and future peace in the region.

Orange Hats. An example of nonviolent action designed to make communities safer was the neighborhood "Orange Hats" in Washington DC (Anderson, 2000). During the late 1980s, one neighborhood was forced to confront an influx of drug dealers and an increase in violent crime. Anderson described the purpose of the Metro Orange Hat Coalition was to take back the streets, neighborhoods, and community. In particular the Metro Orange Hat Coalition wanted to remove the drug dealers, prostitutes, and gangs members and the turf wars, drive-by shootings, public drinking, and rowdy and threatening behavior that made it unsafe for children and adults to enjoy their own neighborhood. Legal means were tried but were ineffective as dealers had warnings of police raids and witnesses of crimes were intimidated and evidence was not readily available for prosecutors. So people within DC communities decided to act on their own.

Small neighborhood groups kept a low profile as they worked anonymously to make their neighborhoods safe so people did not feel the need to stay shut up in their homes. Anderson (2000) describes many activities of these groups but I will describe the actions of James Foreman, one group leader, to reduce drug traffic in his neighborhood. Foreman wanted to rid his neighborhood of drug dealers and wanted to avoid any violent confrontations between his neighbors and the drug dealers at the same time. To do this he established contacts with the police and developed a communication system so the neighborhood group could stay in touch with each other and still contact the police quickly. Since this was before cell phones, his group was equipped with powerful walkie-talkies and all had access to a "home base" with quick access to the police in an emergency. Anonymity was aided by code name "handles" and a rule not to use last names during communication.

Foreman identified a location that served as an open-air drug market to focus his efforts. This place was a grassy area between two streets that formed a triangular-park of sorts. This is where he planned for a community picnic to be held. He organized extensive planning meetings to be sure the community members would be comfortable at the picnic and it would serve their purpose. Community members were to wear orange hats and move around the drug market area introducing themselves by handle or first names to everyone present. Many present would be there for the picnic while others would be there to sell or buy drugs. This community building activity was designed to make things very personal. On the day of the picnic community people descended on the grassy triangle with their charcoal grills ready to feast on chicken, corn on the cob, beans, chips, and more. The drug dealers were invited to the picnic and the interactions were friendly. Even some police who were invited stopped for the festivities. Drug deals were not possible as prospective customers were quite befuddled to see the block party at the location they expected to make their drug purchase. Many cars slowed down only to drive rapidly away. The Orange Hats stayed all day and came back several days running to the grassy triangle. Each time they wrote down license plate numbers of cars driving by and brought the drug sales to a stand still until the location no longer was a viable one for the dealers (Anderson, 2000).

The knowledge of success of efforts like this spread through other DC neighborhoods and other locations instituted similar efforts. It seemed to take about three days of community presence to shut down an open-air drug market (Anderson, 2000). Once a neighborhood had mobilized to remove drug dealers, other issues that could make their communities safer were addressed.

Nonviolent Action in the Twenty-First Century

With the attacks on September 11, 2001 and the US invasion of Iraq so dominantly in the news many would suggest that the violence of the twentieth century is continuing at a deplorable pace. However, even in the first few years of the twenty-first century, nonviolent actions have emerged to deal with injustices. Table 2.3 presents a brief time line of nonviolent actions that have already been used during the twenty-first century.

People Power Revolution II. The Philippines experienced a second large scale People Power nonviolent social movement in 2001. Macapagal & Nario-Galace (2003) describe the circumstances and social psychological processes in this People Power II movement that successfully ended the presidency of a formerly popular leader who was viewed as corrupt and to have used government resources for his own personal benefit. President Joseph Estrada, a popular movie actor, was elected in 1998 and within two short years his administration was embroiled in controversy. Bribery, kickbacks, and a betrayal of the public trust were all concerns that led to the filing of impeachment by the Congress in 2000. Apprehension about the fairness of Estrada's impeachment trial grew until People Power II was instituted to force the president's resignation. As Macapagal and Nario-Glace point out, the history of people power in the Philippines that ended the Marcos regime meant that People Power II happened in a rapid and highly organized manner. When President Estrada used his influence to suppress incriminating evidence from his trial, the organizations and committees concerned about the welfare of democracy in the Philippines initiated their action within minutes. Cell phones and text messages were used to tell anti-Estrada Filipinos to go to Epifanio Delos Santos Avenue to demonstrate peacefully. Thousands converged on that street in Manila over a 4-day period. As influential Filipinos, including cabinet members and the military leadership, joined the movement, the pressure on Estrada to resign became too much and he resigned (Macapagal & Nario-Glace). So within the period of fifteen years, the people of the Philippines had twice taken back the democratic principles that their corrupt leaders had taken away from them.

Orange Revolution. Just as nonviolent revolutions had enabled many members of former Soviet-bloc countries in Eastern Europe (e.g., Poland) to obtain more

Table 2.3 Brief timeline of selected nonviolent political action in the first part of the twenty-first century

Time	Title/descriptors	Place	Reference(s)
2001	People Power Revolution II	Philippines	Macapagal and Nario-Galace (2003)
2004	Orange Revolution	Ukraine	Karatnycky (2005)
2005	Courage to Refuse	Israel	Derfner (2006)

democratic forms of government, the same process was happening within many former Soviet Republics (e.g., Ukraine) to achieve independence from Russia. Under communism, elections did in fact occur although the outcome was always a forgone conclusion. With a true democracy there was a need for fair elections and a fully franchised citizenry. The 2004 election in Ukraine resulted in a hotly contested outcome and an Orange Revolution was initiated to rectify the problem (Karatnycky, 2005). Viktor Yuschenko, the opposition candidate and former chairman of the national bank, was vying to unseat Prime Minister Viktor Yanukovich. Despite an array of dirty political tricks, including a very serious dioxin poisoning that kept Yuschenko from campaigning for almost a month, it seemed like he would still win decisively. However, the official results gave the election to Yanukovich and given strong evidence of election fraud, this sparked the Orange Revolution.

On the day after the troubled election, cars, trucks, and other vehicles in the capital city of Kiev were honking their horns in a distinctive way to show their support of Yuschenko. Orange banners were everywhere and demonstrators that converged onto Kiev's Independence Square were wearing orange. Hundreds of thousands of Ukrainians demonstrated for days and this show of support for fair elections could not be stopped or ignored. When the parliament voted to declare election results invalid and the Supreme Court upheld this declaration, another election was needed. Under the careful watch of over 12,000 election observers and monitors from Europe, Asia, and North America, Yuschenko was handily elected (Karatnycky, 2005).

Courage to Refuse. Following the breakdown of the active peace efforts of the 1990s between Israeli and Palestinian interests, a second *Intifada* began in 2000 after Israeli Prime Minister Ariel Sharon visited the Temple Mount a holy Muslim site. Sharon's visit did not show the necessary respect and his actions outraged many Muslims. The second *Intifada*, like the first, was a mix of nonviolent and violent actions. However, the second *Intifada* did not seem to have the same level of commitment to nonviolence as the first *Intifada*.

Another active area for nonviolent action has been carried out by members of Israel's reserve military forces for years and it continues to this day. Although military service is compulsory in Israel, many veteran military personnel are refusing to serve in combat roles in the Occupied Territories. Derfner (2006) describes the phenomenon where elite warriors and battlefield veterans selectively draw the line where they are not willing to fight. Believing that the Israeli occupation is unjust and that the actions taken against the Palestinians living in the Gaza Strip or West Bank is unjust, these veterans and reservists make their feelings known to their commanders and willingly serve the prison terms as a statement to their government. These draft resisters are not draft dodgers in the sense that they are willing to serve their country in what they believe are truly defensive or protective missions; instead, they refuse to serve because they do not believe that military actions as collective punishment against the Palestinian civilians is making Israelis safer. As Derfner points out, this draft resistance has been going on since the 1982-1985 Lebanon War and also during the first and second *Intifada*. This group has also tried to make their concerns known more widely by signing a Pilot's Letter (27 Air Force signees) in 2003 refusing to fly "targeted assassination runs." The organizations, Yesh Gvul (There is a Limit) and *Courage to Refuse*, encourage military personnel to refuse to serve. *Courage to Refuse* obtained over 600 signatures of soldiers and officers who pledged to refuse to serve in the West Bank and Gaza Strip based on the immorality of the IDF occupation and the suffering of the Palestinian civilians living there. Derfner indicates that while the effect of the draft resisters was mixed depending on the particular war in question and multiple factors within Israeli society influence war policy decisions, it is "widely believed that the refusal of the pilots and Sayeret Matkal members had a telling effect on prime minister Ariel Sharon, and played a part in leading him to decide on disengagement from Gaza."

While not all these nonviolent actions led to short-term and long-term success, most have. Even if many individuals might be more familiar with the wars and armed conflicts of the twentieth century, the dozens of nonviolent actions noted attest to the prevalence and success of this concept as a political strategy in multiple locations (e.g., Europe, Asia, Africa, the Americas), multiple contexts (e.g., occupied countries, democracies, communist countries, dictatorships), and across time. Nonviolent political action has involved the active engagement with dehumanizing human conditions with the practical goal of transforming such conditions to more humane social situations.

Recommended Readings

Ackerman, P., & Duvall, J. (2000). *A force more powerful: A century of nonviolent conflict.* New York: Palgrave.

Ackerman, an authority on nonviolent strategy, and DuVall, a veteran writer, tell how popular movements have used nonviolent weapons to overthrow dictators, obstruct military invaders, and secure human rights in country after country over the past century. The book depicts how nonviolent sanctions—such as noncooperation, strikes, boycotts, and civil disobedience—can separate brutal regimes from their means of control. It also includes inside stories of how ordinary people take extraordinary action to end oppression, and historical photographs of nonviolent leaders and events from the last century.

Ackerman, P., & Kruegler, C. (1994). *Strategic nonviolent conflict: The dynamics of people power in the twentieth century.* Westport, CT: Praeger Publishers.

Ackerman and Kruegler present a comprehensive interpretation of nonviolence as political strategy. The authors describe six historical episodes including the Russian Revolution of 1904–1906, the *Ruhrkampf* in 1923 Germany, the 1930–1931 Indian independence movement, Denmark's resistance to Nazi occupation, the 1944 civil strike in El Salvador, and the Polish Solidarity Movement in 1980–1981.

Bondurant, J. V. (1965). *Conquest of violence: The Gandhian philosophy of conflict* (Rev. ed.). Berkeley, CA: University of California Press.

This is a classic text summarizing the philosophy and the political strategy of Mohandas K. Gandhi. Bondurant's analysis is based on her travel to India to meet with Gandhi and to discuss his work first hand. Excellent discussion of the components of a satyagraha in general and of the Salt Satyagraha specifically.

Cortright, D. (2006). *Gandhi and beyond: Nonviolence for the age of terrorism.* Boulder, CO: Paradigm Books.

Cortright provides a detailed analysis of the people involved in many nonviolent actions. His analyses focus extensively on Gandhi, Martin Luther King Jr., Cesar Chavez, Dorothy Day, and Barbara Deming. The discussion does not describe the specific actions of each person in detail but looks to help the reader understand the personality of each person and the implications of their actions for the twenty-first century. The final chapters provide specific and practical guidance as to how nonviolence might best be applied in the age of terrorism.

Holmes, R. L., & Gan, B. L. (Eds.) (2005). *Nonviolence in theory and practice* (2nd ed.). Long Grove, IL: Waveland Press.

Holmes and Gan carefully examine the work of Tolstoy, Gandhi, and King and the impact of women in the field of nonviolence. This book also describes a wide range of nonviolent actions that have been used in the Middle East, Africa, Asia, Europe, as well as, North America.

Hunt, S. C. (2002). *The future of peace: On the front lines with the world's great peacemakers.* San Francisco: Harper Collins.

Hunt traveled the world to meet and interview many people who have been at the forefront of making the world a more peaceful place through nonviolent actions. He writes about three Nobel Laureates: Dalai Lama, Aung San Suu Kyi, and Oscar Arias. He also writes about Thich Quang Do from Vietnam, Maha Ghosananda from Cambodia, and Jane Goodall.

Sharp, G. (1973). *The politics of nonviolent action.* Boston, MA: Porter Sargent Books.

This book by Gene Sharp is the classic treatise on nonviolence and a must read for anyone interested in nonviolence. Sharp provides a careful analysis of power and relates this discussion to nonviolent actions. He also outlines a taxonomic view of nonviolent action. His account is peppered with a myriad of detailed historical examples of nonviolence.

Zinn, H. (Ed.) (2002). *The power of nonviolence: Writings of advocates of peace.* Boston, MA: Beacon Press.

Zinn, a famous nonviolent activist in his own right, has compiled a volume of short entries from many writers about nonviolence and many leaders in nonviolent movements from Buddha to Thoreau to Gandhi to King and many in between. Lesser-known contributors to the nonviolent literature include William Penn, Ralph Waldo Emerson, A. J. Muste, and Arunhati Roy. Zinn organizes the writings according to time periods with pretwentieth century entries, early twentieth century to the cold war, the cold war and Vietnam, and post Vietnam eras.

Zunes, S., Kurtz, L. R., & Asher, S. B. (Eds.) (1999). *Nonviolent social movements: A geographical perspective.* Malden, MA: Blackwell Publishers.

This book summarizes a large number of nonviolent social movements that took place during the twentieth century with a geographical organization. Following an summative introductory chapter by Kenneth Boulding, the editors discuss nonviolent movements that have taken place in the Middle East, Europe, Asia, Africa, Latin America, and North America.

Recommended Films and Videos

A Force More Powerful – Documentary Television Series

This is an award winning and critically acclaimed 3-h film series that was shown on PBS. It parallels the examples cited in the Ackerman and Duvall (2000) book of the same name. Historical footage is accompanied by great narration to make eight separate nonviolent examples come to life. Information for ordering may be found at http://www.aforcemorepowerful.org/films/afmp/index.php

Gandhi – Feature Film

This 1982 biographical film directed by Richard Attenborough won the Academy Award for best picture. Attenborough took great pains to make this an accurate depiction on Gandhi and his life by finding old photographs and using them to recreate the settings in his films. Highly recommended.

Chapter 3
Theories of Nonviolence

The role of sound theory is vital in psychology and within all fields in the social sciences. A good theory puts forth conjectures about causal relationships and causal inferences in coherent, parsimonious, and general terms that are falsifiable (Fiske, 2004). An important function of theory is to derive hypotheses that direct research and advancing knowledge within a field. Therefore, if our understanding of nonviolence and nonviolent action is to move forward, theories of nonviolence are crucial.

McCarthy and Kruegler (1993) make a strong case for good theory building and productive research to advance our understanding of nonviolent action. They stress that the study of nonviolent action needs theories that suggest productive research questions. These important research questions should focus the attention of researchers to the significant variables within the context of a nonviolent action or conflict in which nonviolent responses are being considered. McCarthy and Kruegler believe "that research will be most fruitful when focused on nonviolent action as purposive behavior in conflicts and on the problems and possibilities that nonviolent action raises for actors in conflicts (p. 2)." They also encourage researchers to use data sources not previously utilized. In addition, they underscore that the use of good theories will permit researchers of nonviolence to abandon unproductive avenues of research.

Within this chapter, I will discuss theories of nonviolence and nonviolent action from the perspective of several disciplines within the social sciences. Placing each theory of nonviolence into a particular discipline is somewhat arbitrary as several of them are multidisciplinary, so the classification is primarily being done based on the discipline of the authors. Beginning with the philosophical approaches, I will move through sociological, anthropological, and psychological perspectives, and then I will discuss the approaches of political scientists. Finally, I will discuss two theories that are multidisciplinary in nature. In presenting each theory my concern is to first summarize the theory in a manner consistent with the intent of the theorist. A discussion of the relevance of each theory for the field of nonviolence and nonviolent action and the merits of the theories for research will be presented in later chapters as appropriate.

D.M. Mayton II, *Nonviolence and Peace Psychology*,
DOI 10.1007/978-0-387-89348-8_3, © Springer Science+Business Media, LLC 2009

Philosophical Views of Nonviolence

Many philosophers have written about nonviolence but few have attempted to define a theory of nonviolence. Gandhi's lifestyle and actions have been interpreted as a philosophy of nonviolence but he did not specifically delineate a theory of nonviolence (Fischer, 1954). Gandhi's philosophy of nonviolence was discussed in Chap. 1.

Holmes' Theory of Nonviolence

Holmes (1971) presents a theory of nonviolence from a philosophical perspective. His theory is based on the assumption that nonviolence involves a significant degree of power and is a forceful concept. He broadly defines nonviolence as either a tactic, a way of life, or a philosophy. To set up his discussion of nonviolence further, Holmes distinguishes two types of violence. He refers to physical violence or violence$_1$ as actions committed with the intent to do physical harm and to psychological violence or violence$_2$ as actions intended to do psychological harm. Likewise, he defines two types of nonviolence as nonviolence$_1$ and nonviolence$_2$ where the former is a rejection of physical violence or violence$_1$ and the latter is a rejection of psychological violence or violence$_2$. Holmes notes that one may advocate nonviolence$_1$ without advocating nonviolence$_2$ but one cannot practice nonviolence$_2$ generally speaking without practicing nonviolence$_1$.

Nonviolence$_1$ and nonviolence$_2$ are more specifically differentiated by Holmes (1971) based on moral issues and the form of action taken. In this vein Holmes develops a model whereby nonviolence$_1$ and nonviolence$_2$ might be manifest via three actions. These are nonresistance (willingly suffering evil without action of any sort), passive resistance (noncooperation), and militant nonviolence (nonviolent direct action). The subsequent two-dimensional model is presented in Fig. 3.1.

Holmes (1971) outlines four ethical rules or principles that are relevant for the understanding of nonviolence$_1$ and nonviolence$_2$. These are:

1. One ought not to kill.
2. One ought not to wage war.
3. One ought not to use violence$_1$.
4. One ought not to use violence$_2$ (p. 116).

Holmes uses these rules to establish differences between pacifists (who believe in rules one or two or both) and those who believe in nonviolence from an ethical stance. This group, which he refers to as *nonviolentists*, believe in rule three or rule four or both. From this, Holmes indicates a *nonviolentist* would be a pacifist, but a pacifist need not be a *nonviolentist*. The critical aspect of Holmes' thesis is the difference between an absolutist and conditional interpretation of pacifist or *nonviolentist* views. While absolutist pacifists and absolutist nonviolentists have clear responses to issues like being a conscientious objector, their positions are quite vulnerable to counterexamples. For instance if one is an absolute pacifist, the position

	Nonviolence$_1$	Nonviolence$_2$
Nonresistance		
Passive resistance		
Militant resistance		

Fig. 3.1 Holmes' model of nonviolence. Reprinted from Holmes (1971) by permission of the author

that one ought not kill in all circumstances is difficult to support when one is confronted with someone who is attacking a child or loved one. On the other hand the conditional pacifist may determine certain wars, like the war in Iraq to be wrong but other wars, like World War II, to be appropriate and moral. This creates potential difficulties in establishing conscientious objector status even if it can be supported with a valid argument when the type of war in question is consistently applied. In a similar vein one might freely declare that defending one's child using violence is acceptable yet engaging in a preemptive war with another country is not. Holmes concludes that only conditional pacifism and conditional nonviolence$_1$ and conditional nonviolence$_2$ are defensible.

Holmes (1971) makes the case that violence is not justifiable based on the belief that it is the only effective means of preventing the spread of evil in the world. To make his argument work he looks specifically at the use of violence and nonviolence as tactics and considers the relative effectiveness of each in achieving the same type of ends. Holmes places the moral burden to justify the use of violence on those who advocate it and the moral burden to justify nonviolence on nonviolentists. His analysis focuses on World War II and Hitler's Nazi Germany to challenge the assumptions of supporters of violent means. While he places doubt on the assumptions of advocates of violence, Holmes is not able to provide evidence for the clear efficacy of nonviolent means. He concludes by pointing out the need for a more concerted effort to test the practicality of alternatives to violence. He says we cannot know if nonviolence is truly more effective than violence until we spend a comparable amount of money on nonviolent alternatives as we currently do on war and other violent methods.

Anthropological Views of Nonviolence

Like many of the social sciences, anthropologists have been studying and writing about conflict and aggression for a considerable amount of time but peace and nonviolence has not been discussed nearly as much (Sponsel & Gregor, 1994). Sponsel (1994) argues that anthropology has much to give to the study of peace and nonviolence and at the same time peace studies can positively impact anthropology. Most of the research and writing within the field of anthropology that is relevant to nonviolence has been in the analysis of tribal and other societies that are primarily peaceful and nonviolent (e.g., Bonta, 1996, 1997; Goldschmidt, 1994; Gregor, 1994). While informative, this body of research is primarily descriptive and does not present anthropological theories of nonviolence. However, the work of Flemish anthropologist, Patfoort (1987, 2002), does outline a conceptual framework of nonviolence from an anthropological perspective.

Patfoort's Conceptual Framework of Nonviolence

Patfoort (1987) has worked in a wide variety of contexts as a faculty member, a mediator, and a trainer for groups and organizations to resolve conflict and to achieve reconciliation. She conceives nonviolence as based on two principles. The first principle of no violence needs to be balanced with the second principle of personal power. The principle of no violence refers to the need to refrain from violence against others, but according to Patfoort, nonviolence is much more than that. Personal power speaks to the notion that nonviolence is not passive but is a position of strength and power. As such, Patfoort believes her second principle involves no violence against oneself. In this way nonviolence includes "power with no violence (p. 12)." A balance between the two principles is the dynamic within Patfoort's conceptualization. To communicate this balance she refers to *isononviolence* to highlight the dual nature and the fluidity of the two principles of nonviolence. She reminds us that in working for the balance one can approach being nonviolent and can become more nonviolent but one can never achieve perfect nonviolence.

In striving for a balance between no violence and personal power Patfoort (1987) notes how critical it is for one to consider multiple sides of a conflict situation. Considering one's own point of view is easy but to be nonviolent one must consider the side of one's opponent as well. Nonviolent thinking requires one to consider the varying viewpoints in a conflict in a calm and peaceful manner. Realizing that someone else may interpret things differently than you is also important. Patfoort points out that actions you consider nonviolent, like yelling for instance, might be considered violent by someone else, or vice versa. Being nonviolent therefore requires that everyone understand how others interpret their actions in their lives. Patfoort views power as being efficacious. To wield our personal power one needs to become aware of our capabilities, learn to develop them, and realize how best to use our talents and skills. Balance requires that one know how to live with individual differences and to communicate during a conflict to acknowledge one's understanding of different perspectives in a manner that is not defensive. According to Patfoort, the less we allow violence directed towards us to occur, the more it is possible for us to behave nonviolently towards others. In this way we can break the cycle of violence.

Additional skills that Patfoort (1987) believes one needs to be nonviolent include patience, creativity, quick self-mastery, the ability to focus our anger in a positive way, and the ability to develop and follow strategies of cooperation and solidarity. When these skills are combined with good communication skills, success at achieving nonviolence is more likely.

Patfoort (2002) has developed a conception of the process involved in violent and nonviolent action. When an individual's self preservation instinct is triggered, the individual is energized to act. These actions might be either aggressive or nonviolent in an assertive way. A violent action is based on an underlying assumption that there are major players (powerful) and minor players (those oppressed by the powerful) in a conflict and works toward retributive justice. Patfoort names this violent process the Major–minor model or the M–m model. Thus, the root of violence is based on a hierarchical power relationship. While many may view the aggressive response to threat as inherently human, Parfoort believes that the desire to move out of the minor or threatened position is what is self-preserving or instinctual. The characteristics of our actions need not be violent to accomplish that. A nonviolent action is based on an equivalency model (E-model) that is not hierarchical but strives for restorative justice in resolving the conflict. Patfoort has developed extensive training programs based on her conceptualization of nonviolence. She has applied it at many levels from the individual to the national in a variety of contexts addressing issues within the family, the workplace, in prisons, and many cases of ethnic conflict (i.e. Kosovo, Rwanda, East Congo).

Sociological Views of Nonviolence

The first academic book on nonviolence, *Nonviolent Coercion*, was published in 1923 by a sociologist, Clarence Case (Hare, 1968a). While Case did analyze historical examples of nonviolence in terms of socializing influences, he did not develop a theory of nonviolence. Lakey (1968), a sociologist and a participant and observer of nonviolent direct action, has outlined three mechanisms that make nonviolent actions successful. Coercion, conversion, and persuasion are the three methods Lakey documents through examples dating back to the early Roman empire. Oppenheimer (cited in Hare) outlines seven tenets of nonviolent ideology that are heavily influences by the writings and teachings of Gandhi. These tenets are as follows:

1. Action based on "truth-force" or love.
2. A need to communicate with an opponent to bring a change of heart.
3. Never attempting to overcome evil with evil, only with good.

4. Enduring unmerited suffering.
5. The search for truth in which it is not for a man to judge man irrevocably by killing him or using physical violence.
6. Respect for the individual.
7. Religious feeling, because the resister needs this kind of security when his life is at stake (p. 12).

Steihm (1968) differentiates two types of nonviolent social movements based on the underlying values. She labels the first school of thought as conscientious and the second as pragmatic. The conscientious approach to nonviolence assumes a basic social harmony in humans and attempts to convert one's opponent to one's position and not to coerce them. The pragmatic approach assumes conflict is healthy, normal, and desirable. The pragmatic approach is an economic alternative to violence to resolve a conflict. Unless those engaged in a nonviolent movement are following the same approach, confusion and counterproductive activities can prevail and the success of a nonviolent social movement will be reduced. While Lidz (1968) views the conscientious form as a useful appeal for raising money to support a movement, he believes ultimately that conscientious nonviolence is the first stage of a movement and the pragmatic approach is the final stage. This runs counter to the theorizing of Ritter (2005).

Ritter's Two-Dimensional Theory of Nonviolence

Ritter (2005) recently developed a two-dimensional theory of nonviolence based on the philosophy and writings of Gandhi. Ritter's theory analyzes the nature of the means and the ends of the parties within a conflict into a 2 × 2 model in which both might be either violent or nonviolent in nature. This theory defines violent and nonviolent means consistently with the typical ways these two concepts have been discussed in the literature of peace. Violent means involve actions intended to do physical and psychological harm to one's opponent. Nonviolent means eschew violent actions and use tactics that are not physically or psychologically violent. Ritter also differentiates violent ends and nonviolent ends. If a goal is to be considered violent it implies that the intent is to improve one's own situation following the resolution of a conflict at the expense of one's opponent. If one is seeking a nonviolent ends, one needs to both approach the conflict with intense goodwill towards one's opponent and maintain the desire to convert the opponent so all parties are able to live peacefully when the conflict is resolved.

Before looking at the theory itself, the underlying assumptions are important to consider. Ritter (2005) outlines his assumptions as follows:

1. Conflicts are inherent in the human experience.
2. Conflicts provide humans with opportunities for positive change.
3. Humans are neither good nor evil.

4. Religious conviction is not a requirement for nonviolence.
5. Gandhi reached the highest understanding of nonviolence.
6. Principled nonviolence is possible on a grand scale (pp. 6–9).

These assumptions communicate Ritter's realistic perspectives and his biases. Most agree that conflicts are inevitable and many agree that human nature is neither inherently good nor evil, however, the other assumptions are not so widely accepted. Ritter is adamant that a strong religious belief is not a necessary condition for nonviolence even though he notes that the best example of nonviolence expressed in the writings, beliefs, and actions of any human being was in Gandhi who was very religious. Ritter acknowledges that Gandhi's actions were not purely non-violent, but Gandhi's teachings were and this is what drives the two-dimensional theory.

Ritter's (2005) two-dimensional theory of nonviolence allows us to classify an effort to resolve a conflict into the four basic types of (1) violent means and violent ends, (2) violent means and nonviolent ends, (3) nonviolent means and violent ends, and (4) nonviolent means and nonviolent ends. Ritter calls struggles that use violent means and violent ends destructive action or principled violence. Examples of destructive violence include the Holocaust and more recent efforts toward ethnic cleansing. Conflicts that use violent means with the goal of nonviolent ends are referred to as suppressive action or strategic violence. Ritter looks at World War I or the "war to end all wars" as a classic example of this type of conflict. Once this type of conflict is concluded, there will be a lasting peace. Most conventional wars have this expectation at some level as well.

The combination of nonviolent means and violent ends seems intuitively prob-lematic until the definition of violent means employed by Ritter (2005) is recalled. This type of struggle is labeled coercive action or strategic nonviolence and prac-tices nonviolence as a tactic fueled by an intent to win and oftentimes hatred toward one's adversary. Nonviolent means are practiced in this type of struggle to compel the opponent to change in the desired way with little empathy or love. While Ritter acknowledges that coercive action can interrupt the cycle of violence because of the means used, the end result without compassion for one's opponent will make the interruption short lived as the hatred between groups festers and leads to worsening relationships and interactions. Ritter cites examples of strategic nonviolence as the Indian independence movement and the American civil rights movement. Some leaders in both did have nonviolent ends in mind but the majority did not and this made the aftermath of significant gains more conflicted than they might have been.

Principled nonviolence or conversion is a conflict behavior in which nonviolent means are combined with nonviolent ends. Ritter views this as the truly effective nonviolent response and one that is apt to break the cycle of violence. Because principled nonviolence is fueled by love and not hatred, it is more likely to break the cycle of violence than any of the other three responses to conflict. The goal here is to achieve positive outcomes for all and since it includes mutual understanding and tolerance, a lasting peace is more probable.

For Ritter (2005) a conflict does not exist on a continuum from violent to nonviolent but for understanding requires that we look at both the means and the desired ends to fully classify it. He realizes that the four types do not easily apply to conflicts either since any conflict includes many different combinations of violent and nonviolent actions and goals. Figure 3.2 depicts a more fluid view of Ritter's theory on a two-dimensional plane. The bottom left quadrant of Fig. 3.2 reflects destructive action and the upper left quadrant reflects suppressive action. Strategic nonviolence occupies the lower right quadrant and principled nonviolence is in the upper right quadrant. This upper right quadrant of conversion denotes the optimal placement for a conflict to be successful in breaking the cycle of violence in Ritter's theory of nonviolence.

It is through conversion or principled nonviolence that Ritter (2005) believes nonviolent campaigns will be most successful. He firmly believes in the centrality of a nonviolent mentality to be critical for the ultimate long-term success of nonviolent efforts to resolve conflict. This is exemplified when Ritter says "it is unrealistic to expect nonviolence to be a successful tool if it is simply a tool. Nonviolence is one of those strange phenomena that are most effective when the obsession with efficiency is abandoned. Nonviolence must therefore be practiced for the sake of practice, and not because one hopes to accomplish certain objectives (p. 4)." Ritter notes the very few examples of conversion have been documented in large-scale nonviolent campaigns. However, he also points out that they do exist for smaller scale efforts.

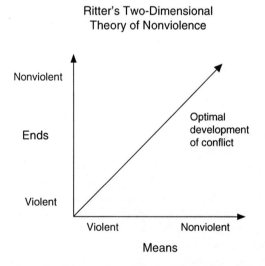

Fig. 3.2 Ritter's two-dimensional theory of nonviolence. Reprinted from Ritter (2005) by permission of the author

Psychological Views of Nonviolence

William James, the father of American psychology, has been referred to as the first peace psychologist (Deutsch, 1995). James (1995/1910) encouraged psychologists to wage a war against war by providing an alternative to the aspects of war that so fascinate humans and have drawn them into war so often over millennia. According to James, war serves a moral function in that it provides a type of discipline to societies waging war and it provides heroes for generations to come. While noting the cruelty of the killing, rape, and plunder, he finds a society at war to have a positive cohesiveness as well. Given what James calls the pugnacity that has been bred into modern man, he encourages psychologists and other professionals to develop imaginative alternatives to deal with the fear-regime of modern civilization. He asks for a moral equivalent to war that substitutes for war yet contains the thrilling and heroic opportunities of war.

Even though James (1995/1910) over emphasizes the inherited aspects of the need to fight and wage war, he is correct to draw attention to the emotional aspect of war that is so appealing. Hedges (2002) recognizes this truth when he refers to war as a force that gives us "purpose, meaning, [and] a reason for living (p. 3)." Deutsch (1995) comments on the mixed feelings James had toward war that acknowledged the impact of the US Civil War on his generation. Finding war appealing in certain aspects and abhorrent in others, James encourages us to use our imaginations to challenge the political–military–industrial complex in ways to reduce the chance for war while allowing for other avenues to achieve the heroic ends that society craves (Deutsch). Doing so would provide a nonviolent option or set of options to replace war.

In this section five social psychological views or theories of nonviolence will be summarized. The perspectives of Blumberg (1968) and Hare (1968b) will be presented first, followed by the theories of Kool (1990, 1993b) and Teixeira (1999), and then the model of Brenes (1999) will be reviewed.

Blumberg's Utility Model of Nonviolent Mass Demonstrations

Blumberg (1968) outlines a three-step conceptual model for nonviolent mass demonstrations. The first step in the process is evolution whereby a number of activities are tried by the demonstrators until the most efficacious are determined and chosen to be used in the future of the movement. This is where specific types of activities are ruled out or decided upon based on analysis of previous demonstrations that are similar and the practical considerations of the demonstration being planned. The second step involves what Blumberg calls contagion where the chosen form of protest spreads from one member of the demonstration through others. People are added to the mass demonstration and people become clear as to the aims of the activities and the way to conduct themselves during the demonstrations. The third step is reinforcement where the rewards for actually carrying out the activities at a specific site within the demonstration are concretely rewarded.

Hare's Social-Psychological Perspective on Nonviolent Action

Hare (1968b) has presented a social-psychological explanation of the dynamics of nonviolent action by synthesizing the theories of Homans (1961), Leary (1957), and Bales (1968). Hare uses the exchange theory of Homans that is drawn from behavioral psychology and economics. This exchange theory views human activity as an exchange of actions and rewards between people. If the cost of engaging in the activity on behalf of someone else is commensurate with the reward then the person will be pleased. If costs exceed rewards, then the person is likely to be angry.

Leary (1957) and Bales (1968) have developed models of human interaction that categorize an individual's actions in order to predict the response of others. Leary explained personality using a two-dimensional model with the vertical dimension being dominance-submission and the horizontal dimension is hostility-love that Hare refers to as upwards–downwards and negative–positive, respectively. Bales added a third dimension of goal-oriented (conforming)-deviant that is orthogonal to the first two dimensions. This third dimension also reflects a forward thinking versus a backward thinking orientation.

Hare (1968b) uses these theories to describe the behavior of nonviolent activists in three separate and diverse case studies. He indicates that the conduct of individuals engaging in nonviolent direct actions can be classified into three quadrants in the three-dimensional space. In all three types of nonviolent activists Hare describes their behavior as submissive or downwards which tends to elicit dominant behavior from others. Nonviolent activists also would be classified along the backward thinking dimension in which actions are deviant in the sense that they do not conform to the goals of the status quo or those in power. On the third dimension the nonviolent actor might be positive, negative, or neutral depending on his or her ability to express love toward the opponent. The submissive-backward-positive action would be consistent with the teachings of Gandhi and King. In all cases the behavior or intent of the actor may be miscommunicated to others and it is the interpretation of others that will determine their reactions.

Hare (1968b) predicts from his model that the submissive-backward-positive role will precipitate a dominant-positive response. This response by the opponents in a nonviolent struggle would lead to sought-after change. If the nonviolent actor is submissive-backward-negative or is perceived to be, then Hare predicts the response of the opponent will be dominant-negative. In this situation the opponent will become angry, as the costs of their own action may be perceived to be greater than any likely reward. Therefore, a violent reaction to the nonviolent activists is probable when this type of nonviolent actor behavior is perceived.

Kool's Theory of Nonviolence

Kool (1993b) has outlined many important issues that ought to be considered when developing a theory of nonviolence. Acknowledging the early psychological work on peace of James (1995/1910), Tolman (1942), Osgood (1962), and May (1972), Kool situates nonviolence within current psychological theory and concepts while incorporating the work of Sharp (1979) as well.

First, Kool (1993b) differentiates acts of nonviolence from nonviolent acts. Acts of nonviolence are categorical in nature and substitute for violence. The use of these acts attempt to communicate that alternatives to violence are possible and can be used to avoid injury to one's opponent. Acts of nonviolence have a particular purpose: to resolve conflict in areas where aggression or violence might be a legitimate response. An act of nonviolence might be a consumer boycott, a march, or a demonstration. Nonviolent acts are different in that these behaviors do not use violence and are normative patterns of behavior. Kool uses caring for animals or nurturing children as examples of a nonviolent act. He notes that nonviolent acts are less salient because of the normative expectations that we should engage in them in our everyday activities. Kool notes that James (1995/1910) alluded to the need to make these nonviolent acts, which we take for granted as part of our culture, more salient and highlighted within our communities if the moral equivalent of war is ever to be obtained. Since these are the behaviors we associate with the actions of individuals in the helping professions, Kool believes the helping professions should work to make nonviolent acts more salient to demonstrate the futility of violence in society. He feels that the psychology of nonviolence should acknowledge the survival value of aggression. However, the long-term value of engaging in nonviolent acts should be emphasized and the situational cues that make it a more likely behavior should be studied.

A second concept discussed by Kool (1993b) in analyzing the psychology of nonviolence is moral development. Drawing upon the work of Piaget, Kohlberg, Gilligan, Erikson, and Rest, Kool makes a case that nonviolence has a moral dimension that includes both a justice perspective and a caring perspective. A person high on justice and low on caring is concerned about following rules like equity and equality. A person high on caring and low on justice exhibits supreme compassion. If someone is low on both justice and caring perspectives then what works in a particular instance is good. A person high on both justice and caring perspectives looks for and acts upon alternatives that are fair and compassionate ones.

The third component integrated into Kool's (1993b) treatment of nonviolence is power or the capacity to influence the behavior of others. Kool draws on the views on power developed by Sharp (1973), Boulding (1977, 1989), Hagberg (1984), and May (1972). While people use many different types of power, the power that Kool views as most relevant to nonviolence is integrative power. Integrative power derives from the trust and good will given to those who are in positions of power by their followers. Kool believes that when nonviolent individuals attempt to achieve social harmony via moral behavior they obtain power that affects the conscience of the perpetrators of violence.

Kool (1993b) outlines a three-dimensional model of nonviolence in which the dimensions are defined as (1) aggression (high vs. low), (2) moral concerns (high vs. low), and (3) power (others vs. self). This model is represented in Fig. 3.3. He believes that a robust theory of nonviolence should study the cognitive components of the relation of aggression to the concepts of morality and power.

Within the model presented in Fig. 3.3, nonviolent individuals would be in the bottom right quadrant of the cube and would represent low levels of aggression along with high moral concerns and other-oriented power (Kool, 1993b). To Kool the high moral concern is a Gestalt-like concept that includes being highly principled, caring, concerned about social justice, and also committed to utilitarian issues. While the placement of moral thought within Kool's model has face validity, several researchers have not observed a relationship between nonviolence and moral reasoning (e.g., Keniston, 1990; Kool & Keyes, 1990; Mayton, Diessner, & Granby, 1993). Kool (2008) describes nonviolent individuals as those who utilize integrative power in their relationships and conflicts.

Teixeira's Theory of Nonviolence

Teixeira (1999) has synthesized a holistic theory of nonviolence that has a strongly humanistic orientation. For Teixeira nonviolence consists of actions void of any harmful intent and requires the means and ends of an action to be congruent. Nonviolence is a phenomenon with a global character, as it has existed for a considerable time throughout the world. It is neither a recent experience nor an ethno-specific one as it has a rich historical and evolutionary perspective. Teixeira makes the case that nonviolence is

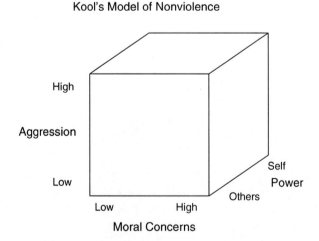

Kool's Model of Nonviolence

Fig. 3.3 Kool's model of nonviolence. Reprinted from Kool (1993b) by permission of the Rowman & Littlefield Publishing Group

preferable to violence and has been practiced for centuries by many indigenous peoples through diverse Western cultures.

Teixeira (1999) describes a very pragmatic, holistic theory of nonviolence with the overarching goal to achieve "a pluralistic society, multiethnic, multicultural, and multifaith (p. 558)." This is accomplished via a process of individual and societal transformation. At the intrapersonal level nonviolent action should produce and enhance high self-esteem that includes believing in oneself as significant, valuable, and powerful. At the interpersonal level self-respect is extended to a respect for others. This respect for others embraces our views of both friends and foes. Teixeira goes on to elaborate that nonviolence addresses "fundamental ways of perceiving and thinking about oneself and the world" and "assumes an interconnectedness that is transpersonal or spiritual (p. 558)." It is the transpersonal or spiritual aspect that enables the nonviolent practitioner like Gandhi or King to be willing and able to suffer instead of harming one's opponent in a conflict.

At the socio-critical level of nonviolence the goal is the fostering of pluralistic society (Teixeira, 1999). The social change process via nonviolence should emphasize an inclusive approach for the marginalized members of society. Teixeira explains that when the needs of the marginalized or neglected groups in a society are addressed, these outcast groups can oftentimes be mobilized into self-aware nonviolent groups to assist in bringing about a more complete social change for society as a whole. When a marginalized group is actively pursuing nonviolent methods, a society is pushed to reflect on its beliefs and values that govern its treatment of all groups and this can have a transformative effect at the societal level. An awareness of our ecological interdependence on this planet is also important for nonviolence to minimize social and environmental disruptions.

The practical strand of Teixeira's (1999) general theory of nonviolence is reflected in the process and goal of achieving a more humane world. This theory acknowledges the inevitability of the human emotion of anger to exist during times of conflict that are also inevitable in human interaction. Nonviolence does not deny anger but hopes to channel the energy created by the experience of the emotion into respectful, preventative, and active change tactics. In fact this theory of nonviolence looks at anger as a positive motivator for change if it is focused in a socially responsible fashion.

The holistic nonviolence theory of Teixeira (1999) is portrayed in a circular model that is presented in Fig. 3.4. In this model the central core value is interconnectedness with the individual aspects, the relationships, and the social systems relevant to nonviolence in the sequential circles moving from the center. One obvious aspect of Teixeira's model is the centrality of interconnectedness at multiple levels of analysis as one moves from the inner to the outer circles of the model.

Teixeira's model (1999) has a preventative aspect as it moves from theory to the practice of nonviolence. The outer ring reflects the social systems that encourage either violence or nonviolence among its members. Child rearing practices, educational systems, reward structures within a society, and conflict resolution strategies that are the encouraged norms impact an individual's relationships at the intrapersonal, interpersonal, and transpersonal levels. As such, Teixeira notes that if we are

Teixeira's Model of Nonviolence

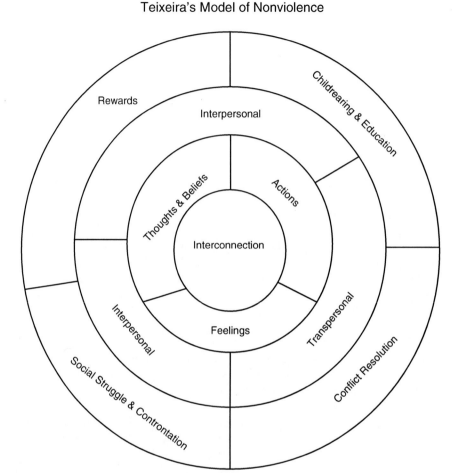

Fig. 3.4 Teixeir's model of nonviolence. Reprinted from Teixeira (1999) by permission of Elsevier Press

to obtain a nonviolent future we must direct the oppression that society creates so that we might move toward "unmasking prejudice, dismantling discrimination, and replacing them with a celebration of human diversity (p. 662)."

An additional aspect involved in the practice of Teixeira's (1999) model is being confrontational in the sense that one must actively engage in social conflicts. Initially, dialogue with one's opponent is required, and if not successful in dealing with a conflict, persuasion and negotiation need to be initiated. If these methods fail to resolve a conflict, noncooperation, civil disobedience, and the development of alternative social structures should be pursued to effect change. Thus, confrontation within this nonviolent context requires a progressive escalation until resolution is achieved.

Brenes' Model of Peaceful Selfhood

Brenes (1999) has synthesized a model of peaceful selfhood that implicitly involves a psychological theory of nonviolence. Brenes developed his model within the context of the United Nations University of Peace program entitled "Culture of Peace and Democracy in Central America" between 1994 and 1999. Brenes' model of peaceful selfhood is presented in Fig. 3.5.

The peaceful selfhood model attempts to answer the question "What kind of person is needed to promote a culture of peace (p. 5)?" Within the model peace is the hub of concentric circles that radiate from the center in three separate themes. These are peace with the body, health for all, and the natural balance of things. As one moves from the center of the model to the peripheral rings at each level there

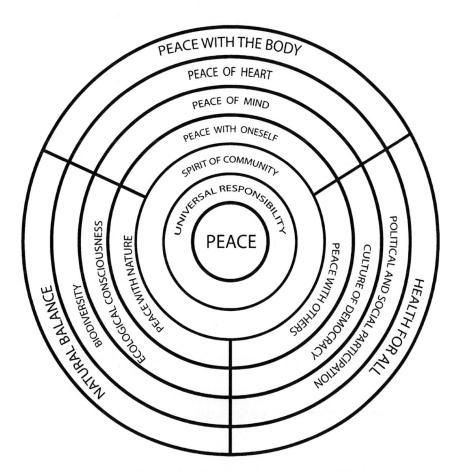

Fig. 3.5 Brenes' model of peaceful selfhood. Adapted from Brenes (2004) by permission of SUNY Press

are relevant values and a broadening context in which each value is applied. These fundamental values and traits for Brenes' normative model of peaceful selfhood are drawn from his work with the United Nations cultures of peace projects.

The model of peaceful selfhood posits three levels for the expression of peace with oneself that are peace in the body, peace in the heart, and peace in the mind. These three dimensions presuppose three necessary shifts in consciousness to allow for nonviolent or peaceful selfhood. These are: (1) equanimity (capacity to treat all human beings with an equal sense of benevolence), (2) equality of self and others (shift from an egotistical orientation to a more collective one), and (3) commitment to altruistic life practices.

Peace with others is a second spoke of the model of peaceful selfhood. Social justice from a democratic perspective is the theme that is elucidated through values of responsibility, solidarity and participation in the promotion of the common good. The expectation is that all within a society that is a culture of peace will have their health and economic security assured.

The third spoke of the Brenes' model deals with peace with nature and a natural balance within a culture of peace. The values of conservation, identity with the cosmos, and respect for all life leads to an ecological consciousness and a strong ethic for sustainability.

For Brenes (2004) nonviolence is an integral part of the conflict resolution process in which the persuasion of one's adversary about the justice of one's own cause is the responsible approach. This then falls primarily within the second spoke of the model under peace with others, democratic participation, and the promotion of the common good. Nonviolence also can be seen in the first spoke of the model or peace with oneself. Love and compassion play a central role in this section of the model along with self realization, inner harmony, and enlightened self-interest.

Political Views of Nonviolence

To this point the discussion has focused on principled views or moral aspects of nonviolent action. However, nonviolent action need not be considered synonymous with principled action but can be viewed as an efficacious political behavior (Ackerman & Kruegler, 1994). The political views of nonviolence espoused by Gandhi (1951, 1957/1927; Bondurant, 1965), Sharp (1973, 1979, 1990, 1992, 1999), and Ackerman and Kruegler will be summarized in this section.

Gandhi's Political Theory of Nonviolence

Mohandas K. Gandhi wrote, spoke, and acted out his theories of nonviolence from a philosophical, as well as, a pragmatic political way. Gandhi's (1951, 1957/1927) philosophy of nonviolence was grounded in his belief that humans are innately nonviolent. As Bondurant (1965) points out, Gandhi did not explicitly develop a political theory but was more of a political actionist. However, his political actions can be construed into a political view of nonviolence that was both practical and constantly evolving. The importance of Gandhi's actions to "political theory... [and] the practical field of politics, is inestimable" (Bondurant, p. 189). His overarching goal in life was to achieve *sarvodaya* or the welfare and good of all (Bose, 1987). Gandhi strongly believed that the means to achieve any ends needed to be congruent with one's ultimate goal.

Central to Gandhi's political views of nonviolence is his second meaning for the term *satyagraha*. As was discussed earlier, one meaning of *satyagraha* means "holding onto the truth." From the second perspective *satyagraha* comprises a nonviolent action to bring about social justice or *sarvodaya*. Gandhi (1957/1927) referred to those who participated in a *satyagraha* as *satyagrahi*. Throughout his life, Gandhi continued to develop different strategies or types of *satyagraha* that he referred to as his "experiments with truth." The objectives of each *satyagraha* varied from the rights of the downtrodden including women and the untouchables, to unfair taxation, to Indian self-determination, and ultimately to India's independence from Great Britain.

Through a generally inductive process, the principles of *satyagraha* were refined by Gandhi over a fifty year period in South Africa and India. Bondurant (1965) summarizes the fundamental rules for the political action of *satyagraha* as follows:

1. Self-reliance at all times
2. Initiative in the hands of the *satyagrahis*
3. Propagation of the objectives, strategy, and tactics of the campaign
4. Reduction of demands to a minimum consistent with truth
5. Progressive advancement of the movement through steps and stages determined to be appropriate within the given situation
6. Examination of the weaknesses within the satyagraha group
7. Persistent search for avenues of cooperation with the adversary on honorable terms
8. Refusal to surrender essentials in negotiation
9. Insistence upon full agreement on fundamentals before accepting a settlement (pp. 38–39)

Using these fundamental rules, the *satyagraha* campaign typically follows these nine steps:

1. Negotiation and arbitration
2. Preparation of the group for direct action
3. Agitation
4. Issuing of an ultimatum
5. Economic boycott and forms of strike
6. Noncooperation
7. Civil disobedience
8. Usurping of the functions of government
9. Parallel government (Bondurant, 1965, pp. 40-41)

As a pragmatic individual, Gandhi followed no-ism (Fischer, 1954) nor adhered to any political ideology (Bondurant, 1965). The nonviolent action, which he referred to as *satyagraha*, was a political means to achieve his goals that was consistent with his philosophy of nonviolence.

Sharp's Political Theory of Nonviolence

Sharp (1959, 1973, 1979, 1992, 1999, 2003) has been a major analyst and proponent of nonviolent political action for well over three decades. Sharp defines nonviolent action as "A technique of action in conflicts in which participants conduct the struggle by doing – or refusing to do – certain acts without using physical violence (p. 567)." As Sharp notes, the concept of nonviolent political action is first an *action* and not inaction. It is an active response in a conflict situation and not inaction, apathy, cowardice, or general inertia.

Sharp (1959) developed a typology of nonviolence early in his career. The six types of nonviolence he identified were (1) nonresistance, (2) active reconciliation, (3) moral resistance, (4) selective nonviolence, (5) *satyagraha*, and (6) nonviolent revolution. Later, Sharp (1967) added passive resistance, peaceful resistance and nonviolent direct action to his typological analysis of nonviolence.

According to Sharp (1973), nonviolent political action is based on the postulate that when people do not do what they are told to do or do what is forbidden to them, they reduce the power held by their adversaries and increase their own power. Thus, an understanding of the power differentials and the means to wield power is central to the practice of nonviolent action. In fact Sharp (1990) places power at the apex of nonviolent action when he indicates, "The practice, dynamics, and consequences of nonviolent struggle are all directly dependent upon the wielding of power and its effects on the power of the opponent group (p. 1)."

Sharp (1973) outlines two views on the nature of political power. One perspective considers the people as dependent upon the good will of the government or those above them in the hierarchical system. The other perspective considers the government or entire hierarchical system as dependent on the good will and support of the people. A ruler or one high within the hierarchy in question may have a traditional social basis for their political power vested in their authority, human and material resources, skills and knowledge and other intangibles. However, nonviolent action is based on the second view of power and it can make these traditional trappings of power fragile and ineffective. The key is that these characteristics of power are successful only when the people are obedient and cooperate with those attempting to wield them. This dependency also extends to the knowledge, skills, labor, and other abilities that make the government, economy, and other institutions function smoothly and effectively.

Nonviolent responses or nonviolent struggle to different conflict situations may involve many types of conduct or methods. Sharp (1999) places the number of specific nonviolent methods utilized throughout history at around 200. Sharp classifies all these nonviolent political actions into three general types of political responses (1) nonviolent protest and persuasion, (2) nonviolent noncooperation, and (3) nonviolent intervention. Nonviolent protest and persuasion includes techniques like picketing, holding vigils, wearing or displaying symbols, conducting mock trials or funerals, humorous skits, and conducting marches or parades. Nonviolent noncooperation includes actions such as political or economic boycotts, strikes or slowdowns, refusal of awards or honors, and temporarily withdrawing or withholding cooperation in social, economic, or political relationships with ones opponent in the conflict situation. Nonviolent intervention involves actions that actively disrupt the workings of the system such as sit-ins, teach-ins, hunger strikes, overloading administrative systems or facilities, and the development of parallel government or systems.

The three types of nonviolent political action outlined by Sharp form an increasing continuum of strength in the amount of power that is wielded by those engaging in the nonviolent action, as well as, the simultaneous loss of power by the oppressive systems and governments involved in the conflict. Nonviolent protest and persuasion wields the smallest amount of power. Nonviolent noncooperation is a more powerful type of nonviolent action and the third and most powerful class of nonviolent political action is nonviolent intervention.

Ackerman and Kruegler's Political Theory of Nonviolence

Ackerman and Kruegler (1994) have built a dynamic political perspective of strategic nonviolent conflict that combines the theoretical literature on nonviolent action with the literature of military strategy. They carefully explain how many but not all of the social and political struggles of the twentieth century, including those in South Africa, Thailand, the Philippines, and Russia, were positively shaped and influenced by nonviolent actions. They further contend that the mobilization of civilians to use nonviolent direct action in these great struggles was the most effective and efficient option available.

Ackerman and Kruegler's (1994) approach is pragmatic and does not concern itself with principled nonviolence or pacifism at all. Their view is that nonviolent actions are reasonable and effective whether or not those engaging in the nonviolent action are principled, moral, and good. In fact they assert that in most cases of nonviolent struggle, choices are made based on the motivation to defeat an opponent using the most effective and least costly way and not by a principled commitment to avoid violence. Based on the assumption that conflict is adversarial, Ackerman and Kruegler believe one should select options that have the best probability of success in achieving one's goals whether your actions are military or nonviolent. They note that over many centuries, the military has studied conflict situations to determine optimal strategies and the use of a military framework to understand nonviolent strategies can prove to be efficacious. Ackerman and Kruegler's thesis is that "the quality of strategic choices made by nonviolent protagonists matters to the outcome of nonviolent struggle (p. 2)."

Instead of using the term nonviolent actions, Ackerman and Kruegler (1994) prefer the term "nonviolent sanctions" which they define as "methods capable of bringing pressure to bear against even the most ruthless opponents by mobilizing social, economic, and political power, without recourse to killing or otherwise causing direct physical injury to the opponents or their agents (p. 4)." Again, from their perspective nonviolent sanctions may or may not be accompanied with a belief in principled nonviolence. Ackerman and Kruegler define a strategy as "the process by which one analyzes a given conflict and determines how to gain objectives at minimum expense and risk (p. 6)." While recognizing that nearly all conflicts involve violent methods at some level even if violence is only a perceived threat, they view a strategic nonviolent campaign as an organized collection of strategic nonviolent sanctions designed to achieve known goals. It also has an identifiable beginning, middle, and ending. How to choose which strategic nonviolent sanctions to use in a campaign should be based on a careful analysis of the nature of the conflict, resources available to participants,

Ackerman and Kruegler (1994) use these assumptions and definitions to outline three categories of principles: principles of development, engagement, and conception. In addition, there are twelve principles of strategic nonviolent conflict within the three categories. There is overlap in these categories and following them is not a purely sequential process.

Principles of development are designed to answer the question "What can be done to create the most advantageous environment for strategic nonviolent conflict?" (Ackerman & Kruegler, 1994, p. 23). The principles in this category are meant to be considered before the implementation of a nonviolent sanction and should be an ongoing consideration during the implementation phase of a campaign as well. The five principles of development are:

1. Formulate functional objectives
2. Develop organizational strength
3. Secure access to critical material resources
4. Cultivate external assistance
5. Expand the repertoire of sanctions (p. 23)

Ackerman and Kruegler emphatically note that it is imperative to have an ultimate goal that constitutes success for the campaign. The goal needs to be specific and concrete and achievable in a reasonable amount of time. A good goal should preserve the vital interests of the nonviolent campaigners, resonate with and attract support from societies affected by the conflict. In addition to an overarching goal intermediate goals are also important to help assess the progress in a campaign.

With sound goals in hand groups pursuing a nonviolent strategic campaign need to become organized and capable of completing the nonviolent sanctions necessary for success. Leadership capable of quick and appropriate response to shifting conditions in a conflict must be established and methods to deal with a replacement for leadership vacuums created when existing leaders are arrested, killed, or otherwise removed from their positions in the campaign. Ackerman and Kruegler (1994) suggest that in addition to leadership, which is analogous to the high command in a military, two additional tiers in the nonviolent campaign must be fully organized. The second tier after the leadership is equivalent to the officer corps in the military and the third tier is analogous to the foot soldiers. The second tier or operational corps have a communication function from the leadership to those carrying out the nonviolent sanctions, an intelligence function to inform the leadership of the status of sanctions,

Principles of engagement are designed to answer the question "Once the conflict is joined, how should we interact with the opponents so that nonviolent sanctions will have maximum effect?" (Ackerman & Kruegler, 1994, p. 23). The four principles of engagement are:

1. Attack the opponents' strategy for consolidating control.
2. Mute the impact of the opponents' violent weapons.
3. Alienate opponents from expected bases of support.
4. Maintain nonviolent discipline (p. 23).

These principles of engagement encourage the fine-tuning of strategic nonviolent sanctions to deal with the inevitable friction during the evolving conflict within a campaign. Ackerman and Kruegler contend that the wide use of nonviolent sanctions in the early phases of a campaign can reduce the opponent's ability to consolidate and maintain control. When the opponent's ability to coerce or threaten is compromised, their ability to dominate and control is limited. A nonviolent campaign must work to mute or lessen the impact of an opponents' violent weapons. This is accomplished through a range of nonviolent sanctions including demolition and carefully focused sabotage that take the sting out of many of an opponents' violent actions. Efforts to alienate opponents from their anticipated bases of support, when they use violence, are an effective approach in any nonviolent campaign. By doing this, an opponent's violent actions may be turned in a way that harms the opponent's strategy via a type of political jujitsu. Maintaining nonviolent discipline by adopting clear codes of conduct and methods for keeping people in line during a nonviolent campaign is an important principle of engagement. Ackerman and Kruegler recognize that the level of disciple needed in a nonviolent campaign is similar to that needed of soldiers in a military campaign. Even though being part of a nonviolent campaign can be dangerous and sometimes deadly, the material and psychological rewards to the resisters can be powerful. The critical aspect of maintaining the necessary discipline is that nonviolent resisters account for their own and their immediate cohort's actions.

Principles of conception ask the question "How should we think about what we have already done to the opponents and what are we trying to do to them as the conflict continues (Ackerman & Kruegler, 1994, p. 23)?" The three principles of conception are:

1. Assess events and options in light of levels of strategic decision-making.
2. Adjust offensive and defensive operations according to the relative vulnerabilities of the protagonists.
3. Sustain continuity between sanctions, mechanisms, and objectives (p. 23).

It is here at the levels of policy, operational planning, strategy, tactics, and logistics that strategic decision-making becomes critical and each must be constantly kept in mind to be sure that important tasks are not overlooked. From a policy perspective nonviolent resisters need to ask whether the campaign is worth pursuing and how will we know if we have succeeded or failed. Once the policy to engage in the campaign is established, operational planning is needed to specifically outline the concrete steps to achieve the desired goals before any actions are taken. Once the policy and plan are articulated, Ackerman and Kruegler note that the strategy or how the group will deploy its resources within the campaign is much easier. Tactics or the methods and logic of individual encounters with one's opponents are subordinate to strategy and are developed with an understanding of the specifics on the ground. Logistics involves the marshalling of resources and the communications needed to support the implementation of strategy and tactics.

Ackerman and Kruegler (1994) point out that any nonviolent campaign involves both offensive and defensive operations that require adjustment based on the shifting situations during a conflict. Sanctions are defensive operations if they protect the nonviolent resister's ability to stay in the conflict to eventually prevail. As such defensive operations are not an admission of defeat. Offensive operations are designed to reduce an opponents' power. Ackerman and Kruegler note that a competent strategist might not be concerned about a strict dichotomy as there is considerable overlap between defensive and offensive operations but would look at operations along a defense–offense continuum. Nonviolent sanctions should be a mix of offense and defense and will need to be adjusted throughout a campaign to maximize their effectiveness.

Sustaining continuity between sanctions, mechanisms, and objectives is the final principle of conception proposed by Ackerman and Kruegler (1994). Here the important aspect is the correspondence between the mechanisms of change and the objectives and specific sanctions employed. The desired change might involve totally changing one's opponents' mind regarding the nature of the conflict, having one's opponent simply decide that a settlement is preferable, coercing one's opponent to realize that continuing in the conflict is not possible, or disintegrating the political cohesion of one's opponent to the point at which they do not exist as an opponent any longer. Strategists need to select specific sanctions to best match the type of change that the nonviolent campaign is seeking. Recognizing when unanticipated opportunities arise and to implement and modify the best sanctions to employ at the time to reach the desired objectives is vital to realize success.

Ackerman and Kruegler (1994) have begun to use these principles to analyze the effectiveness of nonviolent sanctions that have been used in a variety of contexts. Their preliminary analysis is encouraging to help understand why some nonviolent sanctions were successful and others not. As more nonviolent actions are investigated with this model, the refinement and elaboration of these principles may prove to be useful as a blueprint for effective nonviolent action.

Multidisciplinary Views of Nonviolence

Several nonviolent theories are more general in nature and certainly draw heavily on several disciplines and do not rely primarily on a single discipline. The theories of nonviolence discussed in this section also have a systems perspective in their design to either change society or to keep society from changing in undesirable ways.

The two theories discussed are considered to be two different conceptions of "nonviolent defense" (Burrowes, 1996). Civilian-based defense is a defense system that replaces or supplements military defense and utilizes nonviolent resistance by civilians along with economic and diplomatic sanctions to deter and defend against unwanted military aggression. Civilian-based defense is concerned with the defense of the government and territory of a country and is intended to be adopted by governments as policy. The second type of nonviolent defense is what Burrowes refers to as social defense. Social defense also uses nonviolent protests, noncooperation, and intervention in response to military aggression. However, it is more principled in its use of nonviolence than the more pragmatic civilian-based defense. Social defense also emphasizes more structural changes and is more focused on defending the values and social fabric of society and not the government per se. As such, social defense is more of a grass roots or community-based cooperative effort.

Sharp's Civilian-Based Defense

Civilian-based defense has been championed by Sharp (1970, 1985) as an approach to nonviolence that may be employed by civilians in lieu of military defense but for similar purposes. Based on the belief that most countries need alternatives to military deterrence and military defense policies, civilian-based defense was developed as a national defense strategy to be used against foreign invaders and those within a country that attempt to change society's institutions without popular support and through illegitimate means. Sharp indicates the aim of civilian-based defense is "to deny attackers their objectives, to become politically unrulable by would be tyrants, and to subvert the attackers' troops and functionaries to unreliability and even mutiny (p. 9)." Sharp believes this type of nonviolent noncooperation would potentially serve as a kind of deterrent for rational would-be aggressors.

Sharp (1985) makes several specific points about civilian-based defense. First, there is a genuine need for an effective national defense and given that past attempts to peace have met with limited utility at best an alternative to military defense is needed. Second, Sharp draws attention to the significant and growing information about nonviolent techniques that may be political, social, psychological, and economic that have been effective against many different regimes including many tyrannical and violent ones. While nonviolent struggle has been used for national defense purposes during the twentieth century, Sharp rightfully notes that these efforts generally lacked systematic planning, research, and training. However, if a refined and viable technique of nonviolent struggle could be developed and if civilian populations were trained to carry out the policy, civilian-based defense could seriously lessen the need for military defense and the expenses associated with military preparedness. Thus a phased program might be instituted to build up the civilian-based defense components while building down the military defense components. This would break what Sharp refers to as the technological weaponry spiral and help restore self-defense capabilities to countries that are ill prepared economically to support an extensive military. Sharp reports that several European countries are studying civilian-based defense possibilities.

Burrowes' Strategic Theory of Nonviolent Defense

Burrowes (1996) has synthesized a theory of social defense that draws upon the strategic theory of von Clausewitz, the literature of human needs, the nonviolent approach of Gandhi, and recent research on conflict theory. Nonviolent defense to Burrowes is similar to civilian-based defense in that it may potentially be used to defeat military invasions and occupations and to thwart or deter internal coups without the use of military force.

Burrowes (1996) rejects the assumption "that a society is an integrated social system or that it strives to become this (p. 43)." Central to his assumption about the dominant social cosmology in a society is the belief in the importance of shared values and the role of coercion to maintain the power structure. He believes conflict to be structurally generated as a result of the inherent contradictions in modern society and among nation-states. He believes security is a cooperative concept. Security within a society is obtained when a condition of certainty exists "regarding the ongoing viability of the ecological, political, economic, social, and psychological circumstances necessary for all individuals and identity groups, as well as the Earth and all its species, to satisfy their needs, to live in harmony, and to survive indefinitely (p. 149)."

Like Clausewitz, Burrowes (1996) accepts the premise that a good strategy should be an extension of society and policy. Burrowes' theory of nonviolent defense also follows the principle of the superiority of a defense over offense and the view that the capacity for resistance is a function of power and will. He also adapts into his theory the notion of center of gravity or the assumption that the social order has stability as described by Causewitz. For Burrowes the center of gravity is the social order within a society that is fluid and can shift to serve a self-defensive role. He believes a good strategic theory has three functions. These are:

1. To explain the nature and causes of conflict in the international system and to identify the causes of conflict in any particular situation.
2. To identify the appropriate strategic aims for dealing with a particular conflict and to guide the formulation of a strategy to achieve those aims, and
3. To provide tactical guidance within the context of this strategy (p. 125).

Burrowes considers international conflict to result when the satisfaction of human needs is prevented in a national context.

The human-needs perspective is viewed as a workable alternative to political realism by Burrowes (1996). While the realist would look to the maximization of power as the driving force, Burrowes argues that the satisfaction of human needs is critical in determining human nature and in understanding human motivation. Central to his human-needs theory is "that the frustration or denial of human needs… leads to conflictual behaviors; if needs generally are not satisfied, then deep-rooted problems and protracted conflicts arise (p. 126)." Burrowes considers human needs as both innate and universal. Although he does not provide a definitive list of human needs, he does include needs for security, meaning, self-esteem, and latency as minimal needs plus he recognizes the importance of many other including needs for freedom, distributive justice, participation, and identity in his writings. His human-needs theory also assumes that the human drive to control our environment in order to satisfy our needs is cross-cultural and the ultimate determinant of behavior. For Burrowes human nature is neither a priori good nor evil. Individuals will be good if society provides ample opportunity for them to meet their needs. Individuals will be evil if society frustrates their needs.

Burrowes (1996) builds on the work of Gandhi and identifies four major approaches to nonviolence. The model that he describes places principled and pragmatic nonviolence at the ends of one axis. Reformist and revolutionary nonviolence are at the ends of the second axis. This two-dimensional model or matrix of nonviolence as he calls it is presented in Fig. 3.6. The four approaches to nonviolence are reflected in each of the four quadrants of the matrix.

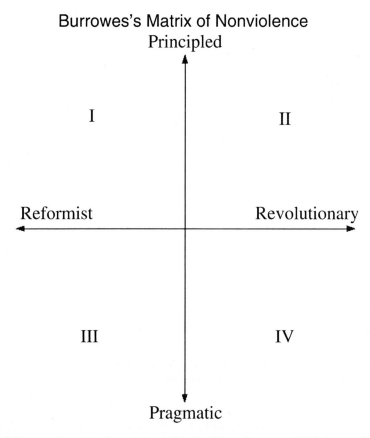

Fig. 3.6 Burrowes' matrix of nonviolence. Reprinted from Burrowes (1996) by permission of SUNY Press

The principled-pragmatic dimension indicates the characteristics of the commitment to nonviolence that activists have as they engage in nonviolent actions (Burrowes, 1996). The principled person views nonviolence as ethically the best thing to do and does not separate the means and the ends in working to resolve the conflict at hand. The pragmatic activist views nonviolent action as the most effective method to resolve the conflict and is not so concerned about any inconsistencies between means and ends. Whereas principled nonviolent activists probably view nonviolence as a way of life, the pragmatic nonviolent person does not. The principled nonviolent activist views the means and ends as inextricable (Spense & McLeod, 2002). Principled nonviolent activists approach the conflict as a shared problem with their opponent and are willing to accept suffering at the hands of their opponent, this is not the case for pragmatic activists who view the conflict as based on incompatible interests with their opponent and are more inclined to inflict suffering on their opponent than to accept it themselves (Burrowes).

The reformist-revolutionary dimension reflects the ultimate goal and the timeframe utilized by activists to achieve their goal (Burrowes, 1996). Reformist nonviolent activists conceptualize the problem as a policy issue and use shorter-term campaigns to change the policies within existing social structures. Revolutionary activists work for a fundamental structural change in society as their goal. Practitioners of revolutionary nonviolence engage in more long-term campaigns because they realize that the structural problem is deeply rooted and necessitates a longer commitment for success to be realized. Spense and McLeod (2002) note that the revolutionary nonviolent activists work to undermine the sources of their opponent's power. Pragmatic-reformist nonviolence (quadrant III in Fig. 3.6) might be illustrated by environmentalists who use nonviolent actions to officially obtain endangered species status for a particular animal. The People Power Movement in the Philippines represents this quadrant as well. Burrowes classifies the Palestinian Intifada as an example of the pragmatic-revolutionary nonviolence (quadrant IV in Fig. 3.6). The Solidarity Movement in Poland and the South African Campaign against Apartheid are other examples within quadrant IV. The nonviolent actions by Martin Luther King Jr. are examples of principled-reformist nonviolence (quadrant I in Fig. 3.6). The Montgomery Bus Boycott for instance was based on principled nonviolence but was not designed to fundamentally change the structures within American society. Instead, the goal was to have the principles within the US Constitution enforced (Burrowes). According to Burrowes, the principled-revolutionary nonviolence (quadrant II in Fig. 3.6) is exemplified by Gandhi's approach. Gandhi led the Salt Satyagraha and other *satyagraha* movements based on principled beliefs regarding nonviolence in order to remove the British occupiers and to obtain self-rule for India. This is an obvious structural change within Indian society. Burrowes comments that Gandhi also rejected capitalism and pursued this structural change as well.

While Burrowes (1996) analyzes a number of conflict theories, he is clearly drawn to the views of Gandhi regarding conflict. Both view conflict as positive and desirable plus they distinguish the conflict from the parties involved in it. With this view of conflict as natural and inevitable conflict resolution should proceed by seeking and developing a better understanding of truth (*satyagraha*) via nonviolent action. Burrowes, like Gandhi, sees this process as "goal-revealing" and at the same time useful in converting one's opponent into a friend. In addition to Gandhi's ideas Burrowes combines conceptions of conflict with the views of Johan Galtung and John Burton as a basis for his theory of nonviolent defense. For Burrowes conflict will be resolved when the human needs of those in conflict are satisfied. Additionally, when one or more parties in the conflict refuse to engage in problem solving, he posits the most effective means of compelling participation is nonviolent action.

Burrowes (1996) outlines a strategic framework for his theory of nonviolent defense to provide guidance for planning strategies for implementation. This framework is presented as a strategy wheel in Fig. 3.7.

The hub of the wheel demonstrates the importance of political and strategic assessment at the onset. The political purpose derived from strategic theory and the political demands of the particular context must be determined to better understand and develop strong strategic aims and intermediate goals within the nonviolent

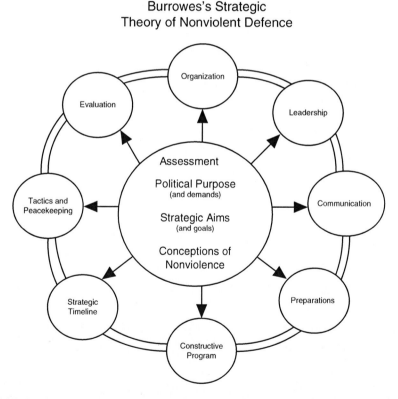

Burrowes's Strategic Theory of Nonviolent Defence

Organization

Evaluation

Leadership

Assessment

Political Purpose
(and demands)

Tactics and
Peacekeeping

Communication

Strategic Aims
(and goals)

Conceptions of
Nonviolence

Strategic
Timeline

Preparations

Constructive
Program

Fig. 3.7 Burrowes' strategic theory of nonviolent defense. Reprinted from Burrowes (1996) by permission of SUNY Press

campaign. Burrowes also highlights as central the importance of agreement on the conception of nonviolence to be used in the campaign. The eight concepts on the outer rim of the strategic wheel identify the specifics to attend to as the nonviolent campaign proceeds in order to maximize success.

Locating Nonviolence Within Peace Psychology

Christie, Wagner, and Winter (2001) define peace psychology as a discipline that "seeks to develop theories and practices aimed at the prevention and mitigation of direct and structural violence. Framed positively, peace psychology promotes the nonviolent management of conflict and the pursuit of social justice, what we refer to as peacemaking and peacebuilding, respectively (p. 7)." As indicated in Chap. 1, the scope of peace psychology can be represented with a four-way model that includes direct violence, structural violence, peacemaking, and peacebuilding (Christie et al.). Peacemaking addresses the problem of direct violence and is designed to make direct violence less frequent and less intense (Wagner, 2001). Peacebuilding is a process designed to prevent or reduce structural violence (Christie, 2001). Whereas both take a positive approach to peace and emphasize nonviolence, peacemaking is more reactive to the more dramatic and episodic nature of direct violence and peace-building is more proactive as it promotes social justice. Peacemaking activities are generally not a threat to the status quo but peacebuilding often is a threat to those in power and the system that gives them their power.

Nonviolence has been described as being either pragmatic or principled (e.g., Burrowes, 1996; Ritter, 2005; Steihm, 1968). Both types of nonviolence might be practiced in peacemaking and peacebuilding. However, peacemaking is consistent with the reformist nonviolence and peacebuilding with revolutionary nonviolence discussed by Burrowes. Spense and McLeod (2002) make a case that the combination of principled and revolutionary nonviolence (Burrowes quadrant II in Fig. 3.6) is most relevant for peacebuilding since "a reformist conception of nonviolence would not adequately address the structural causes of conflict, while a pragmatic conception could easily overlook the values, attitudes, and behaviors that sustain life (p. 63)." Peacebuilding empowers those who have little control over their lives and addresses inequalities and injustices within healthcare, education, and other structures in a society (Christie, 2001). Thus, peacebuilding fits the principled-revolutionary nonviolence very well.

Recommended Readings

Ackerman, P., & Kruegler, C. (1994). *Strategic nonviolent conflict: The dynamics of people power in the twentieth century*. Westport, CT: Praeger Publishers.
   Ackerman and Kreugler present a comprehensive interpretation of nonviolence as political strategy. The authors develop a concrete theory of nonviolent strategic action and investigate how the principles derived from their theory apply to six historical episodes.

Bondurant, J. V. (1965). *Conquest of violence: The Gandhian philosophy of conflict* (Rev. ed.). Berkeley, CA: University of California Press.

This is a classic text summarizing the philosophy and the political strategy of Mohandas K. Gandhi. Bondurant's analysis may be the best explication of Gandhi's work into a "theory of nonviolence" available to date.

Burrowes, R. J. (1996). *The strategy of nonviolent defense: A Gandhian approach*. Albany, NY: State University of New York Press.

This book presents a strong case for Burrowes' comprehensive theory of nonviolent defense. Burrowes gives a nice summary of strategy theories, need theories, and conflict theories and then elaborates how these are applied to develop his theory of nonviolent defense.

Hare, A. P., & Blumberg, H. H. (1968). *Nonviolent direct action: American cases-social psychological analysis*. Washington CD: Corpus Books.

This book has pulled together a large number of previously published articles on nonviolence in sociological and psychological journals and has added some new selections. While this book was published nearly four decades ago, it does a good job analyzing the civil rights movement in the United States as it was happening.

Holmes, R. L., & Gan, B. L. (Eds.). (2005). *Nonviolence in theory and practice* (2nd ed.). Long Grove, IL: Waveland Press.

This is the revised edition of a book of readings that addresses the origins of pacifism and nonviolence from secular and nonsecular perspectives. Holmes and Gan carefully examine the work of Tolstoy, Gandhi, and King and the impact of women in the field of nonviolence. This book also describes a wide range of nonviolent actions that have been used in the Middle East, Africa, Asia, Europe, as well as, North America.

Kool, K. K. (Ed.). (1990). *Perspectives on nonviolence*. New York: Springer-Verlag.

This book is a compilation of papers presented at a symposium on nonviolence at the University of Wisconsin, Eau Claire in 1988. The papers address the psychological, sociological, philosophical, social work, political, and historical perspectives of nonviolence. Kool develops his early ideas about nonviolent personality.

Kool, V. K. (Ed.). (1993a). *Nonviolence: Social and psychological issues*. New York: University Press of America, Inc.

This book is a compilation of papers that were presented at a symposium convened by Kool at SUNY, Utica in 1992. The papers span a wide range of issues related to nonviolence with a strong psychological emphasis. Kool describes his theory of nonviolence in this volume.

McCarthy, R. M., & Kruegler, C. (1993). *Toward research and theory building in the study of nonviolent action*. (Monograph Series Number 7) Cambridge, MA: The Albert Einstein Institute.

This monograph outlines the importance of developing theories of nonviolence and the need for more careful research in the field of nonviolence. While the authors do not recommend a specific research agenda that should be completed, they do provide guidance as to how a sound knowledge base might be generated by testing theory and by addressing a range of variables relevant to nonviolent action.

Pelton, L. H. (1974). *The psychology of nonviolence*. New York: Pergamon Press.

Pelton's book is one of the first to relate mainstream concepts in psychology to nonviolence, nonviolent protest, noncooperation, and reconciliation. He specifically explains how the cognitive dynamics of nonviolence including values, cognitive consistency, and cognitive structure are relevant to nonviolent action. He also relates nonviolence to the roles of power and information.

Sharp, G. (1985). *National security through civilian-based defense*. Omaha, NE: Association for Transarmament Studies.

Originally published in 1970, this volume summarizes the concept of civilian-based defense by one of its primary supporters. Gene Sharp provides a strong rationale for the use of this security strategy during the cold was, however, the implications of this practice in today's world can be extrapolated.

Chapter 4
Intrapersonal Perspectives of Nonviolence

> *The question of real, lasting world peace concerns human beings, so basic human feelings are also at its roots. Through inner peace, genuine world peace can be achieved. In this the importance of individual responsibility is quite clear; an atmosphere of peace must be created within ourselves, then gradually expanded to include our families, our communities, and ultimately the whole planet.*
>
> Dalai Lama, cited in Kraft, 1992a, p. 2

The Dalai Lama also acknowledges the importance of intrapersonal perspectives for nonviolence when he states, "Although attempting to bring about world peace through the internal transformation of individuals is difficult, it is the only way (Hahn, 1991, p. vii)."

This chapter focuses on inner peace and the intrapersonal aspects of nonviolence. Intrapersonal nonviolence is discussed from both individualist and collectivist perspectives. This distinction between individualist cultures and collectivist cultures is based on the work of many cross-cultural social scientists including Hofstede (1980, 2001), Smith and Bond (1993), and Triandis (1995). Hofstede (2001) defines individualism societal norms as loose ties between individuals where "Everyone is expected to look after him/herself and her/his family only (p. 225)." He goes on to define collectivism social norms as existing in "a society in which people from birth onwards are integrated into strong, cohesive in-groups, which throughout people's lifetime continue to protect them in exchange for unquestioning loyalty (p. 225)." The United States, Canada, Australia, and many Western European countries contain strong individualism social norms while many countries in East Asia, South America, and Africa have strong collectivism social norms.

The individualist focus with its strong Western influence will carefully look at the theory and research on the independent self and related concepts. The psychological notions of anger, anxiety, needs, happiness, contentment, and positive psychology will also be part of the individualistic discussion. The personality correlates of nonviolent behavior and the personality characteristics of a peaceful or nonviolent person will be discussed as well. The collectivist focus with its strong Eastern influence will draw on the notion of an interdependent self and Buddhist traditions through the writings of Buddhist peace activists Thich Nhat Hahn, the Dalai Lama,

D.M. Mayton II, *Nonviolence and Peace Psychology*,
DOI 10.1007/978-0-387-89348-8_4, © Springer Science+Business Media, LLC 2009

and Joanna Macy. The Jain and Hindu perspectives of inner peace will also be included among the collectivist discussion of intrapersonal nonviolence.

Intrapersonal Nonviolence from an Individualistic Perspective

The self is a powerful, multifaceted concept in psychology. Dozens of "self terms" abound in the social psychological literature. The list includes self-concept, self-esteem, self-efficacy, self-schemas, self-presentation, self-monitoring, self-handicapping and goes on and on.

The Independent Self and Nonviolence

In looking at the relation of the self to intrapersonal nonviolence, several concepts are particularly relevant: self-concept, self-esteem, and self-efficacy. Self-concept is our cognitive representation of ourselves or how and what we think about ourselves (Fiske, 2004). Self-concept includes all our knowledge of our personal qualities (Smith & Mackie, 2000). Self-esteem is our affective evaluation of our selves. Our self-esteem reflects how we feel about ourselves and may include both positive and negative evaluations. Self-efficacy is an aspect of human agency and a major component of action. Bandura (1997) defines it as "beliefs in one's capabilities to organize and execute the courses of action required to produce given attainments (p. 3)." Bandura's research has shown that self-efficacy is a powerful predictor of well being and a wide variety of human accomplishments

Culture plays a large role in how the self is defined and structured (Smith & Bond, 1993). Individualism and collectivism social norms impact the nature of the self. European and North American cultures emphasize the autonomous person and are individualistic while many African, Asian, South American cultures emphasize groups and generally exhibit more collectivist patterns (Fiske, 2004). People in individualistic cultures look out for themselves and define their identity by personal choice and achievement whereas people in collectivist cultures expect the groups to which they belong to look out for them and define their identity by the nature of the collective groups to which they are loyal members (Moghaddam, 1998). The notion of an independent self is more relevant to people in individualistic cultures and the idea of an interdependent self is more relevant for collectivist cultures (Smith & Mackie, 2000).

The independent self is a view of the self that emphasizes the uniqueness of individuals and the separateness of the individual from others in their culture. The values of freedom and self-determination are important aspects of the independent self (Smith & Bond, 1993). The independent self is autonomous and not universal (Fiske, 2004). In addition men are expected to exhibit characteristics of an independent self-concept more so than women (Baron, Byrne, & Branscombe, 2007).

How the self is viewed may have a considerable impact on intrapersonal nonviolence. If people maintain an independent self-concept, they want to be unique and will view others as different from themselves. Independent self-conceptions can make a person overestimate personal contributions to a team effort, take credit for successes, and blame others when failures happen (Kassin, Fein, & Markus, 2008). Because those with an independent self-concept experience themselves as less similar to others, they may experience less empathy toward others and may express less forgiveness toward others. Those with an independent self-concept may also have a tendency to be more impulsive (Baumeister & Bushman, 2008).

Personality Characteristics of a "Peaceful Person"

Nelson (2005) built on the work of Ziller, Moriarty, and Phillips (1999) and challenged peace psychologists to make the concept of a "peaceful person" a focus of their research. Nelson outlined five domains to describe peaceful states, attitudes, and behaviors. These include (1) peace within self, (2) peace with other individuals, (3) peace with groups and nations, (4) peace with humanity, and (5) peace with nature. Nelson made a case for an empirically based model of a peaceful person based on selected variables within these domains. The underlying variables based on empirical research that Nelson suggested for the "peace within self" dimension of his model included agreeableness, anger control, empathic concern and empathic perspective taking, positive orientation to democratic principles and values, and the values of universalism and benevolence. Other variables that Nelson suggested should be tentatively included among the underlying variables even though the research basis for them is not as strong are forgiveness and optimism. Other variables in Nelson's model including the variables of cooperativeness, forgiveness, tolerance, social dominance orientation, perspective-taking, and the social values of freedom and equality will be discussed in the chapters dealing with "peace with other individuals" and "peace with groups and nations."

Mayton et al. (2007) conducted an empirical study to investigate the relationship between several of the variables in Nelson's model of the peaceful person plus several additional constructs as well. For their study a peaceful person was defined as someone who scored above the median value on four of the five subscales of the Teenage Nonviolent Test (TNT, see Chap. 9 for a full discussion of this instrument.). A nonpeaceful person was defined as someone scoring below the median on four of five TNT subscales. The results of the Mayton et al. study will be discussed as each variable in Nelson's (2005) model is presented below.

Agreeableness

Agreeableness is a personality trait that finds its roots in Adler's concept of social interest (Graziano & Eisenberg, 1997). As one of the big five personality traits, agreeableness has been defined as "a trait characterized by being trusting and helpful, as opposed to suspicious and uncooperative (Ewan, 1998, p. 285)." The facets of the agreeableness factor include trust, straightforwardness, altruism, compliance, modesty, and tender-mindedness (Engler, 2003).

Agreeableness is relevant to Nelson's peaceful person on more than one level. Its relevance to peace within the self will be discussed here and its relevance to peace with other individuals and peace with groups and nations will be discussed in relation to conflict resolution in the next two chapters. Regarding intrapersonal peace, the agreeableness facets of trust, modesty, and tender-mindedness are consistent with the nonviolent philosophy of Gandhi.

Heuchert (2003) investigated the relationship between agreeableness measured with the NEO-Personality Inventory-R and beliefs on the Peace Test with an undergraduate population. He found college students who were more supportive of peace had significantly higher levels of agreeableness than students who were more likely to support war. Heuchert also concludes that students with high agreeableness are "more likely to resist moral disengagement and resist violent impulses and tendencies toward war (p. 10)." Holding attitudes that support peace is not synonymous with being nonviolent but as a personality trait it is consistent with intrapersonal peace.

Anger Control

Anger is an emotion that has been well studied. Plutchik (1962) states that with the possible exception of fear, anger is probably the emotion discussed most in the literature. Anger often is considered a basic emotion that fuels aggressive acts (Myers, 2001). Like other pure or primary emotions, anger has an adaptive value as others can recognize the need to stop what they are doing or remove themselves from the situation when they see someone is angry (Feshbach & Weiner, 1982; Plutchik).

Because anger makes people fiercer and better able to defend themselves with aggressive actions, anger management is an important aspect of nonviolence and inner peace. How a person interprets a situation determines if anger is experienced or not. A peaceful person may be more likely to take the perspective of others and therefore would be less likely to experience anger in the first place (Feshbach & Weiner, 1982). If an angry person is able to think before acting and consider a range of nonviolent responses to a challenging situation, violent acts may be avoided. Anger management would help a peaceful person maintain consistency between their beliefs and behaviors.

Mayton et al. (2007) used a combination of *The Anger Profile* (Psychology Today, 2006) & *The Anger Quiz* (Boston University, 2006) to assess levels of anger management among peaceful persons. They found peaceful persons were significantly less likely to be expressing anger than their nonpeaceful peers. Mayton et al. (2008) replicated this finding with the Novaco Anger Inventory – Short Form (Novaco, 1975). While peaceful people in their study did experience anger, they seemed to have the ability and propensity to reason through potential conflicts and were less likely to impulsively react on anger.

Empathy

Empathy is a process of social understanding and is defined as "the ability to discriminate and label feelings in others, to assume the perspective and role of another person, and to experience and respond with feeling (Feshbach & Weiner, 1982, p. 514)." Davis (1994) conceptualizes empathy using a multidimensional approach such that it includes a set of related constructs pertaining to the reaction of an observer to the experiences of someone else. These reactions have both cognitive and affective components, focus on process and outcome, and depend upon the disposition of the observer and the situation in which the observations are made. Goleman (2006) notes that empathy has three distinct varieties including "*knowing* anther person's feelings; *feeling* what that person feels; and *responding compassionately* to another's distress (p. 58)." Research has shown that empathy is an important factor in mediating prosocial behavior like altruism (Phares, 1984) and cooperativeness (Feshbach & Weiner). In addition empathy has also been associated with lower levels of aggressiveness in children (Feshbach & Weiner). Based on analyses of interviews and studies of the Holocaust and other genocides, Staub (1993) characterizes the incapacity for empathy as a critical and nearly a sufficient condition for an individual in the "right" situation to be a perpetrator of torture and mass killing.

Peace psychologists have addressed the issue of empathy from several perspectives (e.g., Schwebel, 2006; Staub, 1992; White, 1991). White (1984, 1986) used the term realistic empathy to describe the orientation needed to understand and deal with one's enemy in a nonviolent fashion. "Realistic" is added to empathy to differentiate it from sympathy, compassion, and approval. Realistic empathy, or understanding how a situation looks to someone else, enables one to recognize the fear in our enemies such as the Soviet Union in the 1980s. He also highlighted this same principle with Saddam Hussein in the 1990s (White, 1991). White's ten steps to realistic empathy are

1. Defining empathy clearly.
2. Immersing oneself in the available and relevant evidence.
3. Using the self-discrepancy methods, such as criticism sources, that a trained historian would use.
4. Listening to the best-informed observers, including (but with much skepticism) the person himself.
5. Asking, in many contexts, the simple question, "How would I feel, and what would I do, in his situation?"
6. Asking, in other contexts, the chess players' question, "What would he do next?"
7. Taking into account the other's expectable misperceptions.
8. Taking into account also one's own expectable misperceptions.
9. But not leaning over backwards in an effort to be fair and objective.
10. Taking the other's cultural background into account (1991, pp. 393–398).

White applies this approach to realistic empathy in developing a response to Saddam Hussein's invasion of Kuwait. From White's perspective realistic empathy can lay the groundwork for the successful negotiation of conflict and the avoidance of violent responses within volatile situations.

Nelson (2003) studied the relationship between perspective taking and empathic concern with peaceful tendencies. Empathic concern was significantly correlated with nonviolent attitudes regarding national policies. Christie (2003) found that empathic concern contributed to socially responsible beliefs and the pursuit of social justice. Mayton et al. (2007) found peaceful persons to possess significantly higher emotional empathy than nonpeaceful persons. Nelson (2007) found a positive correlation between self-reported peaceful feelings and nonviolence as measured by items from the Nonviolence Test (Kool & Sen, 1984) for males but not females.

Need for Cognition

Cacioppo and Petty (1982) describe people with a high need for cognition as tending to engage in and enjoy thinking. Those who do not have a high need for cognition may avoid thinking when possible and do not enjoy it when the situation requires it.

Waller (1993) found college students with low need for cognition to harbor more racial prejudices than those with high need for cognition. Watt and Blanchard (1994) found a similar population with low need for cognition to be more likely to experience boredom and the negative emotions that are associated with it.

Mayton et al. (2007) assessed need for cognition in peaceful persons using the 18-item short form of the Need for Cognition Scale (Cacioppo, Petty, & Kao, 1984). As predicted, peaceful persons expressed a higher need for cognition than others in their study. Peaceful persons are less likely to be cognitive misers and be persuaded by weak arguments. They are more likely to engage in effortful thinking and be persuaded by strong arguments.

Spirituality

Mattis (2004) defines spirituality as "beliefs and practices that are grounded in the conviction that there is a transcendent (nonphysical) dimension of life. These beliefs are persuasive, pervasive, and stable (p. 609)." Spirituality is a concept that the founders of positive psychology have identified and included in their list of strengths or virtues (Peterson & Seligman, 2004). People who possess the character strength of spirituality believe that there is a higher power holding them accountable for their actions. Such people tend to have lower levels of conflict in all areas of their lives (Mattis). Current research into the development of the character strength of spirituality shows that social network factors have essential roles in spiritual development (Mattis).

Mayton et al. (2007) used the 16-item Daily Spiritual Experience Scale (Underwood & Teresi, 2002) to assess the levels of spirituality of peaceful persons as compared to nonpeaceful persons. Their results found a person's perception of the divine in one's daily life to be a strong characteristic of peaceful persons.

Materialism

Materialism is the importance people ascribe to their possessions and the process of their acquisition (Richins & Dawson, 1992). People who are materialistic pursue happiness through the acquisition of material goods. Richins and Dawson view materialism as having the three dimensions of acquisition centrality, acquisition as the pursuit of happiness, and possession defined success.

Materialism is negatively correlated with nonviolence tendencies and is not indicative of peaceful persons. Mayton et al. (2007) used the 18-item materialism scale developed by Richins and Dawson (1992) and found that peaceful persons had significantly lower materialism scores.

Optimism

Optimism is a personality characteristic that predisposes people to expect positive outcomes. Seligman (1991) made the case that optimism could be learned and when it is adopted can lead to positive mental health. A person who is optimistic reports fewer illnesses and health problems, plus when setbacks do occur, they adjust better than their pessimistic peers (Brehm, Kassin, & Fein, 2005).

Optimism and hope are two personality characteristics that have been hypothesized to be important characteristics for peaceful persons (Nelson, 2005). While many nonviolent activists like Gandhi and Martin Luther King Jr. seemed to have optimism about human nature, no empirical research can be found that specifically relates optimism to nonviolence.

Forgiveness

Forgiveness involves "giving up the desire to punish those who have hurt us, and seeking instead to act in kind, helpful ways toward them (Baron, Byrne, & Branscombe, 2007, p. 327)." Forgiveness is a prosocial behavior that involves giving up revenge as a response when someone has harmed you. A striking example of forgiveness occurred in Nickel Mines, Pennsylvania after a disturbed man walked into a rural school and shot several schoolgirls execution style in October 2006. As the Amish community grieved for its small slain residents, they forgave the killer and reached out to comfort his family during their time of suffering. This Amish community also ceased to feel angry toward the person who murdered their children which is another important component of forgiveness (Baumeister & Bushman, 2008).

People who more readily forgive others tend to be more agreeable and to possess higher levels of emotional stability (Baron, Byrne, & Branscombe, 2007). Forgiveness seems to have many clear benefits to both the wrong doer and the forgiver. When forgiven, the person who did something wrong has personal guilt feelings reduced and may feel less defensive. The person who forgives the wrong doer tends to feel better both physically and mentally than those who continue to bear a grudge

(Baumeister & Bushman, 2008). The process of forgiving can reduce levels of stress hormones and lower blood pressure (Goleman, 2006).

Forgiveness has often been described as an important human value (Rokeach, 1973, 1979). All of the empirical research that has been conducted to assess the relationship between forgiveness and nonviolence or the nature of a peaceful person has approached assessment from the value perspective and this research will be described later in this chapter.

Happiness

Happiness may be referred to as a primary emotion (Plutchik, 1962), a terminal value of being contented (Rocheach, 1973), satisfaction with life (Myers, 2001), feeling good at a particular time (Baumeister & Bushman, 2008), or experiencing subjective well-being (Kassin, Fein, & Markus, 2008). Happy persons do tend to be optimistic, agreeable, and in individualistic cultures have a higher self-esteem (Myers). While happy moods may make positive information salient and enable us to remember this information better, empirical research assessing the relation between happiness and nonviolence has not been identified.

Positive Psychology

The notion of a profile that encompasses the qualities of the typical peaceful person fits nicely into the framework of the fairly new field of positive psychology (Peterson, 2006; Peterson & Seligman, 2004). Peterson describes positive psychology as the scientific study of the aspects of human existence that make life worth living throughout the life span. At the heart of positive psychology lie 24 character strengths, or virtues, that represent the potential for good in every person. Several traits including spirituality, happiness, and forgiveness have already been discussed. Others, such as prudence, self-regulation, mercy, perspective, open-mindedness (tolerance), and kindness closely resemble those traits identified as being present in the peaceful person. The application of this approach to future research on the profile of a peaceful person seems warranted and likely to be quite fruitful.

Values of a "Peaceful Person"

Rokeach and Values

Human values have been discussed by numerous social scientists including important work by Kluckholn (1951), Allport, Vernon, and Lindzey (1960), Kluckholn and Stodtbeck (1961), Scott (1965), Williams (1968), and Smith (1968). The understanding of human values based on this early work in the field has been important. However, the seminal work of Rokeach (1968, 1973) moved values theory and research enormously. Rokeach's innovative contributions significantly increased the attention of social scientists to values and values research through the last decades of the twentieth century (Mayton, Ball-Rokeach, & Loges, 1994).

Rokeach's (1973) approach to values was based on five assumptions. He assumed:

1. the total number of values that a person possesses is relatively small;
2. all men everywhere possess the same values to different degrees;
3. values are organized into value systems;
4. the antecedents of human values can be traced to culture, society and its institutions, and personality;
5. the consequences of human values will be manifested in virtually all phenomena that social scientists might consider worth investigating and understanding (p. 3).

Rokeach defined values as enduring prescriptive or proscriptive beliefs that a specific mode of conduct or end-state of existence is preferred to another mode of conduct or end-state. Values transcend attitudes toward specific objects and situations and serve as standards that guide our behavior. The modes of conduct he referred to as instrumental values and the end states of existence as terminal values. Instrumental values might be either moral values (values with an interpersonal focus and when not followed arouse feelings of guilt) or competence values (values related to self-actualization that make us feel inadequate when not followed). Terminal values might be either personal (self-centered) or social (society-centered).

While not without its critics, for many years the standard for measuring human values was the Rokeach Value Survey (RVS, Rokeach, 1973). The RVS requires respondents to separately rank 18 terminal values (a comfortable life, an exciting life, a sense of accomplishment, a world at peace, a world of beauty, equality, family security, freedom, happiness (switched to health in later work), inner harmony, mature love, national security, pleasure, salvation, self-respect, social recognition, true friendship, and wisdom) and 18 instrumental values (ambitious, broad-minded, capable, cheerful, clean, courageous, forgiving, happiness (switched to loyalty in later research), helpful, honest, imaginative, independent, intellectual, logical, loving, obedient, polite, responsible, and self-controlled) according to their importance as a guiding principle in their lives. The highest terminal value is assigned a 1, the second highest value a number 2, and this process continues until the lowest value is assigned the number 18. The same process is followed for the instrumental values. While the forced choice nature of this assessment process has undesirable psychometric characteristics, Rokeach contends this is the dynamic the real world demands of our values within our personal value systems. Many people who have completed the RVS complain that they are forced to rank a particular value low because other values are more important even though the value in question is in fact quite important to them. People are forced to make choices between possibilities that are highly prized. A trip to Europe or a new car, go fishing or go to the football game, buy a new dress or a new pair of shoes, attend one child's activity or the other child's activity when they occur at the same time are but a few of the difficult choices life forces us to make and the RVS simply reflects these dilemmas we all must face.

One's value system is the organization of our values along a continuum of personal priorities or relative importance. Many value researchers agree that people do not necessarily differ in the values they hold but in the priority they place on the values. When value systems are measured by the ranking of two lists of 18 terminal and 18 instrumental values, the number of different priority patterns possible is tremendously large. The number of permutations in ranking just the 18 terminal values alone is $6.40237371 \times 10^{15}$ or over six thousand trillion! The notion that Rokeach's method of assessing value systems is limiting is far from the truth.

Belief system theory was developed to both understand and explain stability and change within value systems (Ball-Rokeach, Rokeach, & Grube, 1984). According to belief system theory, values are the hub or central components of an individual's personality. Values surround the self to maintain one's self-esteem whenever necessary and to enhance one's self-esteem whenever possible. Ball-Rokeach, Rokeach, and Grube assume that people "will believe and behave in ways that are consistent with a need to maintain and enhance their self-esteem. (p. 20)." They posit that either explicitly or implicitly people want to see their view of themselves as consistent with their view of themselves as competent and moral. Values are the criteria people use to select and justify their actions and to interpret and evaluate their world (Schwartz, 1992; Schwartz & Bilsky, 1987, 1990).

Some of the values that Nelson (2005) implicated as relevant to understanding a peaceful person are reflected in Rokeach's conceptualization of values and the RVS. These instrumental values are forgiveness, tolerance, and self-control. Being forgiving or willing to pardon others is an instrumental value described previously as a personal characteristic relevant to nonviolent responses to conflict situations. Tolerance is reflected in another instrumental value of broadminded or open-mindedness. Being self-controlled or self-disciplined is the third value that ought to be mentioned even if Nelson did not list it. The actions of the satyagrahi under Gandhi and the civil rights demonstrators in the 1960s in the American South required a considerable amount of discipline and self-control. In fact many have argued that nonviolent activists need to have the same level of discipline and training as a well-trained soldier.

Research on values with the RVS has looked at the salience of the nuclear threat (Mayton, 1989a), attitudes toward Cold War policy (Mayton, 1987a, 1987b, 1989b, 1992a; Mayton & Sangster, 1992), militarism (Mayton, Peters, & Owens, 1999), and nuclear activist behavior and attitudes during the Cold War (Mayton & Furnhan, 1991, 1994). Mayton (1989a) investigated the salience of the nuclear threat using an incomplete sentences method among college students along with their value priorities. He surveyed junior and senior high adolescents but found no differences between those concerned about nuclear war and the priorities they placed on the values of broadminded, forgiving, or self-controlled. Mayton (1987a) surveyed senior high age adolescents and found respondents who placed a higher priority on being broadminded held attitudes skeptical of the success of civil defense measures during nuclear war. Respondents who placed high priorities on broadmindedness and forgiveness also thought we should not escalate a military action in order to win a conflict. Adolescents who more strongly valued being broadminded reported lower levels of nuclear denial. Adolescents who placed higher priorities on being self-controlled were more supportive of escalating a conflict militarily to win. Mayton (1989b) found no significant relationships among the values of being broadminded, forgiving, or self-controlled and attitudes toward the Soviet Union as an evil empire. Mayton and Furnhan reported the results of a cross-national study involving samples of college students and adult samples from England, Japan New Zealand and the United States. Being broadminded or tolerant was positively correlated with antinuclear activist behaviors in four of the five countries. The value of self-control was positively correlated with antinuclear activist behavior in three of five countries surveyed whereas being forgiving was only significant for the adult sample from the United States.

These RVS results reflect the relationships between values and variables that are tangentially related to nonviolence at best. While the results are mixed, the picture is somewhat encouraging and more research looking at the importance for these values as characteristics of a peaceful person seems warranted.

Schwartz and Values

Schwartz and his colleagues have developed a comprehensive theory of human values that builds from the work by Rokeach and extends it by utilizing multivariate analysis techniques (Schwartz, 1990, 1992, 1994a, 1994b; Schwartz & Bilsky, 1987, 1990). Schwartz defines a value as "a (1) belief, (2) pertaining to desirable end states or modes of conduct, that (3) transcends specific situations, (4) guides selection or evaluation of behavior, people, and events, and (5) is ordered by importance relative to other values to form a system of value priorities (1994a, p. 20)." According to Schwartz and Bilsky, the structure of human values consists of a typology with ten motivational value types. The names and definition of each value type are as follows:

1. Power: Social status and prestige, control or dominance over people and resources.
2. Achievement: Personal success through demonstrating competence according to social standards.
3. Hedonism: Pleasure and gratification for oneself.
4. Stimulation: Excitement, novelty, and challenge in life.
5. Self-direction: Independent thought and action – choosing, creating, and exploring.
6. Universalism: Understanding, appreciation, tolerance, and protection for the welfare of *all* people and for nature.
7. Benevolence: Preservation and enhancement of the welfare of people with whom one is in frequent personal contact.
8. Tradition: Respect, commitment, and acceptance of the customs and ideas that traditional culture or religion provide.
9. Conformity: Restraint of actions, inclinations, and impulses likely to upset or harm others and violate social expectations or norms.
10. Security: Safety, harmony, and stability of society, of relationships, and of self. (Schwartz, 1994a, p. 22)

Schwartz (1990, 1992, 1994a) and Schwartz et al. (2001) have engaged in a rigorous program of cross-cultural research to determine the exhaustive nature of his theory of values using his 56-item Schwartz Values Survey (SVS) and his 40-item Portrait Values Questionnaire (PVQ, Schwartz, 2003). Translated into dozens of languages and administered in well over five-dozen countries, Schwartz has strong data to support the claim that the ten value types are cross-culturally valid. While these ten value types may not be exhaustive as a spiritual value type is missing and some cultures may possess values not reflected in the SVS or PVS such as Confucian value type in China (Smith & Bond, 1993), the structure of values theorized by Schwartz is extremely robust.

The ten motivational value types of the Schwartz model can be depicted within a circular structure. Value types adjacent to each other share similar motivational emphases and value types across the circular model are in opposition to each other.

The characteristics of a peaceful person seem to directly involve the three value types of universalism, benevolence, and conformity. Universalism consists of the nine self-transcendent values. Being broad-minded or tolerant of different ideas and beliefs is one of several values that make this value type particularly germane. Other pertinent values and their descriptive phrases on the SVS are inner harmony (at peace with myself), a world at peace (free of war and conflict), social justice (correcting injustice, care for the weak), wisdom (a mature understanding of life), and equality (equal opportunity for all). These values are consistent with the notion of a positive peace and the philosophy of nonviolence espoused by Gandhi. When these values are combined with protecting the environment, a world of beauty, and unity with nature, the importance of universalism to being a peaceful person is clear. The other self-transcendent value type is benevolence and this value type includes being forgiving or willing to pardon others plus the value of helping. Adjacent to benevolence is the value type conformity that includes the value of self-discipline or self-restraint and resistance to temptation. Benevolence and conformity emphasize normative behavior in the promotion of close relationships.

Mayton and Furnham (1994) aggregated their cross-national value data from the RVS to reflect nine of the ten Schwartz value types. Universalism values were significantly correlated with self-reported antinuclear activism behavior for three of four college-age samples and both adult samples. Benevolence was not correlated with antiwar activism over any samples and the two samples that conformity significantly correlated with it were in the opposite direction from the predictions.

Mayton, Diessner, and Granby (1996) assessed the values of college students who demonstrated nonviolent tendencies and those who did not. They measured values using the SVS and nonviolent predispositions using the Nonviolence Test (NVT, Kool & Sen, 1984). Nonviolent college students held significantly higher benevolence values, universalism values, and conformity values. Persons with more violent inclinations held significantly higher power values and hedonism values than those with nonviolent predispositions. Mayton (1992b) found significant positive correlations between the benevolence, conformity, and universalism values and nonviolent dispositions. A replication of value and nonviolent relationships showed the same significant positive correlations between nonviolent dispositions and benevolence, universalism, and conformity value types (Mayton, 1994).

Hossner et al. (2004) conducted values research with high school students ages sixteen to eighteen years old. They used the Portrait Values Questionnaire (PVQ) to assess the Schwartz value types and the Teenage Nonviolence Test (TNT, Mayton et al., 1998) to assess nonviolence. The TNT provides five subscale scores underlying the concept of nonviolence. These subscales are physical nonviolence, psychological nonviolence, helping, *satyagraha* (search for wisdom), and *tapasya* (self-suffering). Physical nonviolence scores were positively correlated with benevolence, universalism, and conformity values types and negatively correlated with power and hedonism values at statistically significant levels. The same significant relationships were identified for the psychological nonviolence subscale and these value types. Tapasya scores were significantly correlated with the values types of benevolence, universalism, and conformity in a positive direction as well. The same relationships were significant for the satyagraha, or search for wisdom subscale, and the helping/empathy subscale of the TNT. While the hedonism value type was not correlated with the TNT helping/empathy subscale, there were significant negative correlations between hedonistic values and the other TNT subscales. Hossner et al. conclude that the results for adolescents mirror the results with college students. The value types of benevolence, universalism, and conformity are associated with nonviolent predispositions and those with nonviolent predispositions put lower priorities on power and hedonism values.

Mayton et al. (2007) investigated the value hierarchies of peaceful persons. They defined a peaceful person for their study as someone who scored above the median value on four of the five subscales of the TNT and compare them to nonpeaceful persons who scored below the median value on four of the five subscales. Benevolence values, the desire to be positive toward others to whom one is close, were the strongest value type for peaceful persons and significantly differentiated peaceful from nonpeaceful persons. Benevolence values were significantly correlated with all TNT subscales. While universalism values and conformity values were significantly correlated with the helping/empathy and *satyagraha* subscales, these values did not differentiate peaceful from nonpeaceful persons nor did they correlate with the physical or psychological nonviolence subscales. Mayton et al. did determine that power values and hedonism values were significantly lower priorities for peaceful persons when compared to their nonpeaceful peers.

Tentative Profile of a Nonviolent or Peaceful Person

A case has been made that certain individual values based on the methods of Rokeach (1973, 1979) and certain value types based on the approach of Schwartz (1992, 1994a) are related to nonviolence and to the notion of a peaceful person (Nelson, 2005). Some empirical data based on samples of adolescents and college students supports most of these value assertions. Some research studies are consistent with the view that being forgiving, tolerant (broadminded), and self-controlled (self-disciplined) may be part of a nonviolent predisposition or are characteristics of a peaceful person. Other studies were cited that consistently indicate the value hierarchy of those with nonviolent predispositions and peaceful persons place high priorities on benevolence values and low priorities on power and hedonism values. While not quite as consistent, the studies reviewed generally point to the values of a nonviolent or peaceful person as also reflecting universalism and conforming values.

Peaceful persons were found to be very different from nonpeaceful persons in many ways over a wide variety of other personality or social psychological constructs. Peaceful persons were significantly more spiritual, and had higher emotional empathy and had a higher need for cognition. Peaceful persons were less materialistic and less angry as well. There have been no studies to ascertain whether optimism, happiness, or other character strengths or virtues described within positive psychology are also an integral part of the disposition of a peaceful person.

With the data we have at the present time we are able to describe many aspects of a peaceful person. Peaceful persons tend to work hard to preserve and enhance the welfare of others close to them plus they understand, appreciate, tolerate, and protect the welfare of all people and nature. Their ability to recognize the feelings of others and to act in kind and helpful ways without the need to be vengeful enables them to realize these values. They are able to restrain their actions, inclinations, and impulses that might upset or harm others or violate social expectations and norms. Anger management is a strength of peaceful persons. Peaceful persons tend to believe in a higher power, metaphysical reality or God and enjoy thinking about the complexities of life. Peaceful persons are not very interested in materialistic possessions, social status and prestige, and control or dominance of other people or resources. Pleasure or sensual gratification is a lower priority for peaceful persons as well.

Intrapersonal Nonviolence from a Collectivistic Perspective

The Interdependent Self and Nonviolence

The interdependent self is closely aligned with the characteristics of the groups to which one belongs and this dependence creates fuzzier boundaries between the self and those groups. The preservation of harmony within groups is a major focal point for the interdependent self (Smith & Bond, 1993). The interdependent self is enmeshed in the many different roles and groups that one is involved (Fiske, 2004). Women from most cultures are more likely to exhibit an interdependent self-concept than men from the same culture (Baron, Byrne, & Branscombe, 2007).

A person with an interdependent self-concept readily sees similarities with others and therefore may be more inclined to be empathic and forgiving. Seeing one's own role as less important in relation to other members of the group may result in fewer self-serving biases and allow those with interdependent self-concepts to interpret their own actions more accurately. The interdependent self-concept should enable a person to focus on the situation at hand more fully and clearly and therefore result in a better understanding of others and their point of view. The need for personal vengeance might be lessened while the push to save face for one's collectivities would be increased.

Nonviolence from Eastern Religious Perspectives

Many religions have placed nonviolent behavior as a significant part of their beliefs. Buddhism (Gomez, 1992; Hahn, 1993; Niwano, 1977; Sharp, 1992), Christianity (Aspey, 1990; Fried, 1999, Kimelman, 2005), Hinduism (Fried; Hunter, 1990), Islam (Abu-Nimer, 2003; Flinders & Easwaran, 2005; Siddiqui, 2005), Jainism (Sharma, 1965), and Judaism (Kimelman, 2005) all speak to nonviolence as an appropriate behavior for religious followers, to varying degrees. The Christian, Jewish, and Muslim views of nonviolence will be discussed more fully in Chap. 7. The Hindu, Buddhist, and Jain views will be presented here. A brief description of the historical context and some of the major tenets and practices of each religious perspective will precede the discussion of the intrapersonal aspects of nonviolence encompassed in each religion.

Hinduism

Hinduism is the world's third largest religion and has its roots on the subcontinent of India. Hinduism is the oldest of the major religions of the world and is practiced in India, Nepal, Pakistan, Bangladesh, Sri Lanka, Indonesia, Malaysia and many smaller countries by about one billion followers (Monroe, 1995). "Hinduism is that complex of culture, religious practice, myth, belief that are felt to be a continuation of the Vedic tradition (Buitenen cited in McCasland, Cairns, & Yu, 1969, p. 391)." However, instead of being a religion of sacrifice as was the case for the Vedic religion, Hinduism emphasizes meditation and devotional worship.

Hindu Beliefs and Rituals

The ultimate mission for a Hindu is to prepare one's soul to become an integral part of the absolute soul after death. This process may take many millennia of reincarnations depending on the good deeds accumulated over the many lifetimes. The positive deeds one is able to accrue over all lifetimes result in good *karma* (Monroe, 1995). Important Hindu texts like the *Bhagavad-Gita* and the *Upanishads* prescribe guidance as to the methods of meditation, prayer, and devotion to the gods in both home and temple to develop good *karma*. The many gods worshiped by Hindus include Brahman, Trimurti, Brahma, Vishnu, Shiva, Devi, Saravati, Ganesha, Karttikkeya, Indra, and many more (McCasland, Cairns, & Yu, 1969).

Ceremonies or rituals are performed to celebrate the life cycle for Hindus. These life cycle rituals, usually only for boys, start at birth and include several for small children. Some rituals also honor marriage and others focus on the time of death and cremation. The number of rituals varies according to an individual's caste. Daily rites include the ritual of worship and the celebration of religious holidays throughout the year. No weekly holy day exists during the Hindu week but there is an expectation that some days of fasting will occur each month. There are also expectations for Hindus to engage in pilgrimages to sacred places and holy cities (McCasland, Cairns, & Yu, 1969).

There are four paths to *moksha* or liberation in Hinduism. These include the path of knowledge, the path of love, the path of yoga or the union of the soul with God, and the path of works. A person may use any of these paths to be liberated from karma and be united with the absolute reality and this is typically done based on personality predispositions. Intellectuals and thinkers choose the path of knowledge while the emotional person would favor the path of love. The more scientific method for obtaining *moksha* is the path of yoga that involves moral restraint and observances, control of the body, and concentration of the mind. Mohandas Gandhi was a wonderful example of an individual who followed the path of works. This path allows one to perform the regular tasks of the world in a very active life as long as these actions are performed egolessly and the work is devoted to absolute reality and not for personal reward (McCasland, Cairns, & Yu, 1969).

Hindu Views of Nonviolence

Ahimsa, or nonviolence, is deeply embedded in Hinduism (Hunter, 1990). The term is listed in early Hindu texts as one of five ethical virtues (Bondurant, 1965). Where violence maintains one's position in the cycle of reincarnation, nonviolence moves the Hindu closer to spiritual enlightenment and is therefore more desirable (Fried, 1999). Despite this belief, the Hindu nation of India is not less violent than other nations in terms of violent disturbances and intolerance (e.g., Fischer, 1954).

Shastri and Shastri (1998) observe that from a Hindu perspective, *ahimsa* is a concept with philosophical, religious, and ethical connotations. As a "positive doctrine of love, friendship and equality among all living beings in the universe (p. 68)," *ahimsa* is an antidote to violence in the world. It embraces both the pursuit of the good of humanity and devotion to the good of all living beings and the environment.

Hunter (1990) highlights the interpretations both Thoreau and Gandhi had of the *Bhagavad-Gita* that are relevant to nonviolent behavior. Both men recognized the *Gita* encourages people to act in harmony with their real selves. Gandhi did not view the *Gita* as supporting the use of violence but as "pre-eminently a description of the duel that goes on in our hearts. The divine author has used a historical incident for inculcating the lesson of doing one's duty even at the peril of one's life. It inculcates performance of duty irrespective of the consequences, for, we mortals, limited by our physical frames, are incapable of controlling actions save our own" (cited in Hunter, p. 17). As an allegory where the battlefield is the soul, Gandhi viewed the real struggle as that between a person's higher impulses and evil.

Ego-attachment and possessiveness lead to selfishness and jealousy and results in violence. From the Hindu perspective the major task is to move human beings toward truth through unselfish, open-minded and nonviolent thoughts and behavior (Hunter).

Shastri and Shastri (1998) cite four Vedas to support the Hindu position on non-violence. They note the Hindu reference to the concept of the golden rule predated rabbinic and Christian writings by hundreds of years. Shastri and Shastri point out the critical role the experience of separateness from others plays in causing hatred and violence. Hindu texts encourage followers to avoid a sense of duality and "see one's own self in everything and everything in one's own self (p. 71)." It is through the realization of unity with others and God that peace can prevail (Shastri & Shastri). The unity with others is consistent with the interdependent view of the self. Gandhi (1999) captures this principle well when he says God "has saved me often against myself and left me not a vestige of independence.... No one can see God face to face who has aught of an 'I' in him.... God triumphs in us, never we (p. 87)."

The term *shanti* is used for peace in the Hindu tradition (Shastri & Shastri, 1998). *Shanti* may refer to spiritual peace or to peace in society and nature. Shastri and Shastri regard the ultimate goal of Hindus to be the attainment of spiritual peace and this goal is achieved by giving up one's plurality and separateness and identifying with all beings in the universe. Societal peace might be achieved if everyone attained spiritual peace, but since this is not the case, Hindu texts encouraged the passage of laws that invoked punishments to bring about peace within a society.

Buddhism

Buddhism is the fifth largest religion in the world today and is based on the teachings of Siddhartha Gautama, an Indian prince from the fifth century BCE (Monroe, 1995). He became known as the Buddha or the enlightened one (Lester, 1987). Despite its Indian legacy, the main traditions of Buddhism practiced around the world are Theravâda Buddhism, East Asian Buddhism, Tibetan Buddhism, and Zen Buddhism and are found primarily in China, Japan, Tibet and many Southeast Asian countries.

Buddhist Beliefs

The Buddhist path to nirvana or enlightenment begins with faith as expressed through confidence in the three jewels of the Buddha, Dharma, and Sangha (Lester, 1987). It is important to take refuge in the Buddha as a symbol of one who conquered suffering and pain. The Dharma involves the path that Buddha spoke of as the four noble truths of enlightenment (Monroe, 1995). The first truth, or *dukkha*, notes that human existence includes suffering and pleasure as essential ingredients.

The second truth, or *tanha*, explains that human desire is what causes pain and suffering. The third truth, or *nirodha*, explains that the escape from the destruction of all desires and ego drives is a way to escape from pain and suffering. The fourth truth, known as Buddha's way, describes the eighth paths to nirvana. Monroe describes the eightfold path to nirvana as being analogous to the Judeo-Christian Ten Commandments. These eight paths are as follows:

1. Right knowledge, that is, accept the four noble truths.
2. Right aspiration or thought.
3. Right speech, avoidance of obscenity and words that demean others. Avoid gossip and lies.
4. Right behavior, no stealing, sexual immorality, drunkenness, or murder.
5. Right effort, the necessary willpower to do right actions.
6. Right livelihood. The command to do honest work faithfully, never cheating, stealing, or loafing on the job. Refrain from prostitution, selling drugs, alcohol, meat, armaments, or engaging in slavery.
7. Right mindfulness, a statement that what we are and will become is determined by our thoughts.
8. Right concentration, or the practice of correct meditations and yogas. (Monroe, p. 114)

The Sangha is the community of monks who follow the Buddhist way. The Buddhist monks provide positive resources that involve prayer, ritual, and offerings (Lester). The Sangha is also a type of planned social movement as the monastic community serves as a "nonviolent army of peace (Kraft, 1992a, p. 4)."

Just as in other religions, there are several main types of Buddhism that follow the same general beliefs with some variation in emphasis. Theravada Buddhism follows the preeminent virtues of self-restraint and generosity. Mahayana Buddhism emphasizes wisdom and compassion (Kraft, 1992b).

Buddhist Views and Nonviolence

While recognizing that Buddhists throughout history have not been involved in military crusades, Sharp (1992) points out that "political conditions in predominately Buddhist countries are not exemplary or notably nonviolent (p. 111)." Queen (1998) comments on the adaptation of Buddhist teachings and monastic discipline to train armies to defend and to conquer. Swearer (1992) also comments on the condoning, promotion, and participation in violence by Buddhist followers. According to the Tibetan Buddhist tradition, a person may be "compelled to kill someone if that is the only way he can save the life of many people, though killing violates a fundamental monastic and ethical precept. Yet even if he has to take life in order to save life, he does not do so aggressively. He acts with regret and love toward the person he must kill (Thurman, 1992, p. 78)." Sharp goes on to note that considerable suffering in the form of domestic crises, coup d'état, mass slaughter of civilians, and dictatorships have occurred in predominately Buddhist countries or previously

Buddhist countries. However, there is generally support for the promotion of both nonviolent domestic and foreign policies with the view that this doctrine of nonviolence leads to greater social harmony. Buddhist teachings provide numerous examples of how enlightened and compassionate kings and leaders can rule their domains nonviolently and how Buddhism can contribute to a more peaceful and nonviolent world (Swearer).

Niwano (1977) characterizes Buddhism as a religion of peace. Queen (1998) observes that while Buddhism is extolled for its teachings of peace and nonviolence, it is the perspectives and techniques developed by Buddhists for achieving peace that is really exemplary. Within the Buddhist tradition, the way to relieve human suffering and pain is found in cardinal moral precept of *ahimsa* or refraining from harming living beings. Hahn (1987), a Vietnamese Buddhist monk, describes many guidelines for Buddhist behavior including the one against killing. This particular precept indicates that people should use nonviolent means and, whenever possible work "to protect life and prevent war (p. 19)." The fourth path to virtue states that one should engage in right behavior and not to murder. The Buddhist ideal of *ahimsa* includes abstaining from harming others, as well as, removing the causes of harm to others (Kraft, 1992b). Queen also points to the "practices of lovingkindness, compassion, sympathetic joy, and equanimity (*brachmaviharas*); the doctrines of selfishness (*anatta*); interdependence (*paticcasamuppada*), and nondualism (*sunyatta*) (p. 25)" as important to the realization of peaceful and nonviolent methods.

In order to practice nonviolence, Buddhists work to counter the three roots of evil: hatred, greed, and delusion. Hatred is countered by lovingkindness, compassion, and goodwill toward others. Greed is countered by generosity and delusion by wisdom. Meditation about lovingkindness and mindfulness is the approach to develop inner peace and a propensity toward nonviolence (Queen, 1998).

Fleischman (2002) adds fear to the emotions that move people to violent actions. He explains that nonviolence is a necessary aspect of self-development for a beginning student of Buddhism. Eventually, nonviolence embodies the essence of a quality life as it liberates the mind and heart from hate, fear, and self-delusion. Fleischman summarizes this aspect of Buddhist thought by saying "Ultimately, nonviolence is a recognition of the simple facts that the quality of our life is the same as the quality of our moment-to-moment thoughts and feelings, and that enmity, hatred, and violence never improve our state of mind (p. 10)." However, Fleischman clearly points out that while the Buddha's teaching encouraged nonviolence, these teachings did not demand absolute pacifism. Buddha did not council kings to refrain from raising armies in defense of their kingdoms, nor did he judge them adversely for their militaristic behaviors. Despite concern for the welfare of all animals, the Buddha did not demand strict vegetarianism even on the part of monks.

As Kraft (1992b) notes, the question of whether Buddhists might engage in violence as self-defense, the defense of loved ones and innocent people, or the defense of their country has resulted in different interpretations. Responses have varied from the view that one should refrain from hate and thought about killing any living creature to support for the mobilization of armies to battle invaders.

Hahn (1987, 1991, 1993, 2005) is a Vietnamese Zen Buddhist monk who worked to relieve the suffering of his Vietnamese people during the US-Vietnamese War during the 1960s and 1970s. He has been a human rights activist and was nominated for the Nobel Peace Prize by Martin Luther King Jr. in 1967. He has worked with American military veterans who served in Vietnam, with law enforcement officers, with many in public service, as well as victims of conflict and activists to ease the stress and negative emotions each might be experiencing through Buddhist principles.

Buddhism includes a notion of the peaceful mind and universal harmony that incorporates the principle of nonviolence. Within the Buddhist doctrine of nonviolence, the mind comes first and peace in the world follows (Gomez, 1992). Hahn (1993) stresses that in order to practice nonviolence or "ahimsa," it must happen within ourselves first. He views the essence of nonviolence to be love that leads one to act in a selfless manner. As a process and not a dogma, nonviolence develops from an awareness of human suffering and is nurtured by love. If people are able to use their love and act selflessly, Hahn believes they will find effective tactics and techniques for their nonviolent struggle. When it comes to changing a society, the Buddhist orientation focuses on inner work and inner change as a necessary precursor to social change.

Hahn (1987) does not make the distinction between one's inner world of the mind and the outer world. He views them as the same reality. Because of this, it is important for one to strive to be in touch with the here and now or have what he refers to as the spirit of *tiep hien*. He coined the term interbeing to reflect this notion. Interbeing also emphasizes the "inter"-relationships and "inter"-dependencies between so many aspects of our reality (Hahn, 1991).

Interbeing is realized by following the fourteen guidelines for engaged Buddhism that are based on the eight paths to nirvana described above (Hahn, 1987). Meditation and mindfulness activities are used to move one toward interbeing (Hahn, 2005). If we want to bring nonviolence to the world, Hahn (1987) asserts we need to become aware of our inner world including our perceptions, our positive and negative emotions, plus our thoughts to experience our "true mind." In addition we need to experience the outer world including the physical world and the joys and sufferings of human kind. In other words we need to stop and smell the roses and listen sincerely to the people around us. This allows us to realize understanding and compassion and develop an inner calmness and serenity. Only after we attain this inner calmness and peacefulness can we share it with others and make the world a more nonviolent place.

Mindfulness and interbeing can be thwarted by emotions that dominate our attention. There is no place for anger, hatred, and blame within this process of interbeing and nonviolent action. Anger results in the condemnation of others and this makes healing and the reduction of suffering more difficult to accomplish (Hahn, 1993). Hatred takes us out of the here and now and away from mindful living and can lead to despair (Macy, 1983). Hahn uses the metaphor of growing lettuce to show the futility of blame. "When you plant lettuce, if it does not grow well, you do not blame the lettuce. You look into the reasons it is not doing well.

It may need fertilizer, or more water, or less sun. You never blame the lettuce. Yet if we have a problem with our friends or our family, we blame the other person. But if we know how to take care of them, they will grow well, like lettuce (Hahn, 1991, p. 78)." Even positive emotions like hope can thwart the process of interbeing and mindfulness. When we cling to hope during times of hardship, Hahn reminds us we are focusing on the future and not staying in the present to discover the joys that are already present around us.

While Hahn (1993) believes that true harmony and inner peace are necessary precursors to nonviolent action, an "engaged Buddhist" does address nonviolent actions that go beyond the mind. He addresses nonviolent action of speech and the body as well as nonviolent inaction. Sometimes what we do not say and do not do can make the situation better whether it is due to our positive presence that calms those around us or by refraining to say something that is hurtful and causes someone to suffer. Just like action, some inaction can cause great suffering as well.

Like many Buddhist scholars, Hahn (1993) acknowledges the difficulties in being totally nonviolent in one's actions and totally violent as well. Strict vegetarians who boil their vegetables certainly kill microorganism. Soldiers who conduct their military operations to avoid killing innocent civilians are behaving nonviolently.

Meditation and mindfulness activities have been used to move people toward interbeing (Macy, 1983, 2000; Hahn, 2005). Macy (1983) initially employed Buddhist principles along with psychological systems theory to address the despair and powerlessness that was fostered during the tense times of the Cold War. Her methods of empowerment training were designed to assist people in dealing with the repression of fears of pain, appearing stupid, unpatriotic, and too emotional, guilt, provoking panic, sowing disaster, and religious doubt. The activities were based on the five principles of "(1) feelings of pain for our world are natural and healthy, (2) pain is morbid only if denied, (3) information alone is not enough, (4) unblocking repressed feelings releases energy, clears the mind, and (5) unblocking our pain for the world reconnects us with the larger web of life (Macy, 1983, pp. 22–23)." Macy outlines dozens of activities that she used in many workshops with some appropriate for elementary age children, teenagers, and adults. Initially, these workshops encourage participants to acknowledge and experience their pain and to discuss it so they and others might realize that it is a common experience. The next stage of the despair work encourages participants to develop a deep understanding of the destruction and suffering in the world in order to work through personal repression of the feelings of anger, guilt, and grief. This middle stage of the workshop turns to an awareness of the interconnectedness of participants with others. The final stage of Macy's workshops provide methods for participants to recognize the power they possess to become social change agents. This empowerment phase encourages participants to develop a vision of what is possible and to develop skills to work toward that vision. More recently, Macy (2000) has described activities designed and used specifically with social activists. Hahn also presents many activities based on fundamental Buddhist precepts to assist workers within the helping professions to deal with the stress inherent in their jobs and to enable them to remain productive.

The Buddhist tradition continues to be very germane to the world today (Sivaraksa, 1992). It is a very tolerant religion that encourages inner peace and the settling of conflict in nonviolent ways. The Dalai Lama describes how changing our thought processes and interpretations of the world can reduce personal suffering and lead to inner tranquility and peace (Mehrotra, 2005).

Jainism

Jainism is a religion originating in India that developed out of Hinduism. While much smaller than the other two religions with Indian roots, Jainas have had a profound impact on culture and other religions to this day. There are fewer than 10 million followers of Jainism world-wide (McCasland, Cairns, & Yu, 1969). The name of this religion, Jain, is derived from the word jina that means conqueror as the religion is designed to conquer human suffering (Chapple, 1992).

Jaina Beliefs

Vardhamana Mahavira, who lived from 599–527 BCE, was the major ascetic prophet for Jainism (Monroe, 1995). While there is no documentation that he ever met the Buddha, they were contemporaries. The sacred texts of the Jainas were passed down from one generation to the next orally for centuries but at the dawning of the common era the clear essence of these religious teachings appears to have been lost or at least corrupted to some degree (McCasland, Cairns, & Yu, 1969).

Like Hindus and Buddhists, Jains believe life is trapped within the birth and rebirth cycle (Monroe, 1995). The path to salvation for Jains, as for Hindus and Buddhists, is to escape this cycle. Monroe describes the five codes of conduct prescribed within Jaina teachings as "(1) destroy no life, (2) do not lie, (3) practice charity, (4) practice chastity, and (5) possess nothing and want nothing (p. 128)." For Jainas the soul ultimately needs to escape from the material world of the body and *karma* represents the material world. Conduct consistent with the five principles outlined above would result in good deeds that would create very little negative karma and hasten the release of the soul (Monroe).

Acharya Tulsi modernized the code of conduct in 1949 to promote nonviolence and peace throughout India. His guidelines were as follows:

1. I will not willfully kill any innocent creature.
2. I will not attack anybody.
3. I will not take part in violent agitations or in any destructive activities.
4. I will believe in human dignity.
5. I will practice religious toleration.
6. I will observe rectitude in business and general behavior.
7. I will set limits to the practice of acquisition.
8. I will not resort to unethical practices in elections.

9. I will not encourage socially evil customs.
10. I will lead a life free from addictions.
11. I will always be alert to the problem of keeping the environment pollution-free. (Chapple, 1998, p. 21)

Jaina Views of Nonviolence

Within Jainism, *ahimsa* or "non-violence is the highest virtue" (Sharma, 1965, p. 12). Nonviolence, which is synonymous with compassion, includes mental, verbal, and physical nonviolence. Restraining one's mind (mental or intrapersonal nonviolence), controlling one's tongue (verbal or interpersonal nonviolence), being careful as one travels, removing living creatures from one's path, and eating in daylight to avoid accidentally eating insects with one's food (Chapple, 1992). Jainas view physical nonviolence as inappropriate toward humans, animals, insects, and even some plants (Chapple, 1998). For the ascetic Jaina there is no difference between avoidable and unavoidable violence. All violence and injury is the same and is not acceptable if one is to rise above worldly practices to achieve spiritual liberation. Jainism does allow for the nonascetic to adopt principles that are less severe yet incorporate the essence of nonviolence.

The identity of a Jain holds nonviolence or *ahimsa* as the central component. The nonviolent ethic requires considerable personal discipline as it is practiced. The advanced monks or ascetic Jains have considerable restrictions on their behaviors to maintain nonviolence. Food intake is limited, travel has serious limitations, sexual behavior is renounced, as are personal possessions. In refraining from possessions some Jains renounce all clothing. In addition there are prohibitions for ascetics to dig, bathe, light or extinguish fires, or even fan themselves. Jain laypersons are permitted to follow less rigorous guidelines for behavior. Violence that is unintentional, related to one's occupation, or is used in self-defense is permitted. All Jains are vegetarians and may eat milk products (Chapple, 1992).

Summations of Intrapersonal Nonviolence

Intrapersonal nonviolence was described from both individualist and collectivist perspectives of the self. From the individualist perspective, intrapersonal nonviolence was addressed using a variety of personality constructs, individual values, and value types. The concept of a peaceful person was used to pull these characteristics together. From the collectivist perspective of intrapersonal nonviolence, the Eastern religions of Hinduism, Buddhism, and Jainism were analyzed to understand nonviolence.

Many personality traits and values described as aspects of a peaceful person can be seen as consistent with the beliefs and teachings of the Eastern religions. The self-transcendence values (benevolence and universalism) of peaceful persons are consistent with the Hindu, Buddhist, and Jain views that unity with others is important, as is the need to behave unselfishly and with an open-mind. The practice of charity and relieving of human suffering is a part of these self-transcendent values and eastern thought. The Eastern religious beliefs that ego-attachment is problematic and that people need to move beyond personal pleasure are consistent with the low priority peaceful persons place on hedonistic values.

Recommended Readings

Kraft, K. (Ed.) (1992a). *Inner peace, world peace: Essays on Buddhism and nonviolence.* Albany, NY: State University of New York Press.
  Kraft has edited a first-rate volume of eight essays on Buddhism and peace. The articles address the nature of Buddhist thought, relationships between Buddhism and society, inner peace, and Buddhism's relevance to our world today. Besides discussing Buddhism from different orientations, comparisons and interrelationships between Buddhism and both Jainism and Christianity are also analyzed.
Hahn, T. N. (1987). *Interbeing: Fourteen guidelines for engaged Buddhism.* Berkeley CA: Parallax Press.
  This book by the Zen Buddhist monk explains the meaning of interbeing and carefully presents the fourteen guidelines for engaged Buddhism in an easily comprehensible way. Nhat Hahn relates these fourteen precepts in a manner that is very relevant for the twenty-first century.
Hahn, T. N. (2005). *Keeping the peace: Mindfulness and public service.* Berkeley CA: Parallax Press.
  This book by Nhat Hahn is directed toward developing mindfulness among people working in people-oriented jobs that are stressful and frustrating. It is very different than his previous books that are often compendia of short essays or lectures as here he provides examples of activities or "workplace practices" to cultivate the inner peace of civil servants.
Peterson, C., & Seligman, M. E. P..(Eds.). (2004). *Character strengths and virtues: A handbook and classification.* Washington DC: American Psychological Association.
  This handbook brings many ideas that have previously been within the domains of moral philosophy, politics, and other social science disciplines together in a coherent and organized way for any scholar interested in positive psychology. The authors describe their work as analogous to the Diagnostic and Statistical Manual of Mental Disorders except that their work is more like a "Manual of the Sanities." The strengths of wisdom and knowledge, courage, humanity, justice, temperance, and transcendence are presented.
Rokeach, M. (1973). *The nature of human values.* New York: Free Press.
  This is the classic text of value theory developed by Milton Rokeach. The delineation of his theory and measurement techniques are clearly explained with references and summaries of many empirical studies throughout. Other references highly recommended are Ball-Rokeach, Rokeach, and Grube (1984) and Rokeach and Ball-Rokeach (1989). The later reports the most recent US national sample data available.
Schwartz, S. H. (1992). Universals in the content and structure of values: Theoretical advances and empirical tests in 20 countries. *Advances in Experimental Social Psychology, 20,* 1–65.
  While many articles might be recommended to understand the value theory developed by Shalom Schwartz, this article does an excellent job of providing the reader with the historical development of the theory, the measurement and analysis procedures used to empirically support his theory, and cross-cultural data to show the robustness of his approach. Other articles that are also recommended are Schwartz (1994a) and Schwartz (2003).

Smith-Christopher, D. L. (Ed.). (1998a). *Subverting hatred: The challenge of nonviolence in religious traditions*. Cambridge, MA: Boston Research Center for the 21st Century.

This little volume includes eight articles that present the place of nonviolent within eight different religions including Jainism, Confucianism and Daoism, Buddhism, Hinduism, Judaism, Christianity, Islam, and the spirituality of the Cheyenne a Native American culture. The eight essays, written by religious scholars quite knowledgeable in the religious tradition being addressed, when taken in combination, allow for clear comparisons and contrasts to be made.

Chapter 5
Interpersonal Perspectives of Nonviolence

Nonviolence is a weapon fabricated of love. It is a sword that heals. Our nonviolent direct action program has as its objective not the creation of tensions, but the surfacing of tensions already present. We set out to precipitate a crisis situation that must open the door to negotiation. I am not afraid of the words 'crisis' and 'tension.' I deeply oppose violence, but constructive crisis and tension are necessary for growth. Innate in all life, and all growth, is tension. Only in death is there an absence of tension.
Martin Luther King Jr., cited in Scholl, 2002, p. 43

The more I think about peace, I think peace starts and ends in connection. When we connect, we learn about 'the other.' It is not tolerance but understanding, acceptance. In the connection, everything starts to happen.
Isabella Allende, cited in Groves, 2008, p. 76

This chapter addresses aspects of nonviolence that are relevant to interpersonal relationships. While violence within interpersonal relationships has been predominant in research, nonviolence is an important albeit neglected aspect to consider. The role of cooperation (Deutsch, 2000; Johnson & Johnson, 2003), negotiation (Fisher & Shapiro, 2005; Fisher, Ury, & Patton, 1991), and other nonviolent conflict resolution strategies are examined as they pertain to intimate relationships, friendships, and small group interactions. Mediation (Leviton & Greenstone, 1997), conflict resolution (Bunker & Rubin, 1995; Deutsch & Coleman, 2000; Jones, 2004; Sanson & Bretherton, 2001), violence prevention (Gottfredson & Gottfredson, 2002), nonviolence education (1999a, 1999b), and peace education programs (Forcey & Harris, 1999; Harris, 1988, 2002a; Harris & Morrison, 2003; Nelson & Christie, 1995; Reardon, 1988a) designed for participants across the life span are reviewed with recommendations concerning usage by peace researchers and peace practitioners.

Nature of Conflict

Rubin, Pruitt, and Kim (1994) define conflict as the "perceived divergence of interest, or a belief that parties' current aspirations cannot be achieved simultaneously (p. 5)." Deutsch (1973) defines a conflict between two or more parties as perceptual differences

D.M. Mayton II, *Nonviolence and Peace Psychology*,
DOI 10.1007/978-0-387-89348-8_5, © Springer Science+Business Media, LLC 2009

regarding interests, goals, and aspirations that exist with the belief that these differences cannot be resolved. Kriesberg (2007) defines social conflicts as existing "when two or more persons or groups manifest the belief that they have incompatible objectives (p. 2)." Whether these differences are real, or just perceived to be so, is immaterial for a conflict to exist (Rubin & Levinger, 1995). The existence of a conflict necessarily implies some level of interdependence (Deutsch, 2000).

Deutsch (1973) describes a typology of conflicts based on the objective state of differences and the perceptions of the state of the differences held by the parties in the conflict. This typology identifies six types of conflicts that are not mutually exclusive. Veridical conflict exists when there is a true conflict and the parties in the conflict perceive it as so. Contingent conflict exists when there is an objective conflict between the two parties, both parties perceive it to be a conflict, and it is dependent on both parties failure to recognize that it might easily be resolved using available resources. This type of conflict requires the two parties to get beyond their misperceptions of the conflict by broadening their perspectives and being flexible. Displaced conflict exists when there is an objective conflict and the two parties perceive a conflict between them, however, there is a misperception about the issues in the conflict. Deutsch describes this conflict being one where the parties are arguing about the wrong issues. A misattributed conflict exists when the objective conflict is not dealt with by the true parties to it and instead is taken up by the wrong parties. Deutsch views the "divide and conquer" strategy as an example of misattributed conflict. Deutsch demonstrates this type of conflict with the example of job shortages in which a conflict between two racial factions within labor might be incited by industry to take the focus off the need for labor and management to cooperatively work together. Latent conflict exists when an objective conflict between two parties is not perceived as being a conflict at all. Deutsch uses the conflict between men and women in a patriarchal society that is accepted as legitimate as an example of latent conflict. Women who view their domination by men as appropriate see no conflict. However, once awareness of subjugation occurs via a consciousness-raising experience, this latent conflict will morph into a perceived and conscious conflict. The final conflict in Deutsch's typology, false conflict, has no objective reality but is misperceived to be a conflict.

Fellman (1998) analyzes the underlying assumptions about conflict that people hold. He differentiates the adversarial inclination from a mutualistic viewpoint. Some parties assume a win–lose outcome will occur and other parties assume the possibility of a win–win outcome exists.

Conflict exists within a cultural context of norms, practices, and institutions (Fry & Bjorkqvist, 1997). As a cultural phenomenon, the ways in which conflicts are perceived and responded to depend upon societal assumptions, attitudes, and beliefs about conflicts and this may be transparent to members of the society as they experience it (Fry & Fry, 1997).

Galtung and Tschudi (2001) describe conflict as ubiquitous and if it is not so, it certainly seems to be a regular occurrence in human interactions. While conflict may have negative consequences, Sanson and Bretherton (2001) note that the outcome of a conflict may be positive, so conflicts should be viewed as "value-neutral."

A conflict between two lovers may result in a quarrel or violent exchange or it might result in a dialogue that leads to a deeper understanding of each other's needs and desires. Likewise, conflicts between friends, business partners, and between small groups may be seen to have negative or positive consequences depending on the processes used to resolve the conflict. Deutsch (1973) makes the distinction between a destructive conflict, in which participants are displeased with their outcome, and a constructive conflict, in which the participants are satisfied with the outcome. Given this distinction, Deutsch rightfully frames the basic concern as preventing conflicts from being destructive and facilitating constructive conflict solutions. However, as Deutsch (1994) points out, conflicts clearly tend to involved mixed motives, so the parties in most conflicts have competitive and cooperative interests and therefore these conflicts potentially can be either destructive or constructive.

Both personality characteristics and personal behaviors or skills might assist anyone in securing a positive outcome to conflict. Individuals who are agreeable, forgiving, tolerant, and cooperative are more inclined to resolve conflicts in nonviolent ways, as are people in tune to the needs of others. Individuals skilled in methods of negotiation, mediation, and other conflict resolution strategies are more likely to resolve conflicts nonviolently as well.

Personality and Behavioral Tendencies of Peaceful Persons and Conflict Resolution

In the previous chapter, the notion of a peaceful person was discussed in terms of intrapersonal nonviolence. Many of the characteristics of a peaceful person including agreeableness, forgiveness, cooperativeness, and trust are also relevant to interpersonal nonviolence and are discussed next.

Agreeableness

As stated in the previous chapter, agreeableness is one of the big five personality traits that comprises "trust, straightforwardness, altruism, compliance, modesty, and tender-mindedness (Mathews, Deary, & Whiteman, 2003, p. 24)." While agreeableness has been viewed as perhaps least well understood of the big five personality traits (Jensen-Campbell & Graziano, 2001), Mathews et al. report its relationship to many positive aspects of interpersonal relationships. They summarize research that showed individuals with high agreeableness are less involved in aggressive behavior and are in fewer conflicts with others than individuals with low levels of agreeableness. Mathews et al. also report the results of research on marital couples. Individuals with low levels of agreeability are more likely to anger and to be upset in their marital relationship. They also point to research that shows high agreeableness is associated with higher levels of distress and a lowering of self-esteem following interpersonal disputes.

Jensen-Campbell and Graziano studied the link between agreeableness and interpersonal conflicts with middle school children. Compromise was deemed a more appropriate response to conflict for students with high agreeability and less so for those with low agreeability. More agreeable adolescents approved of constructive conflict tactics and disapproved of destructive conflict tactics than their peers who had low agreeableness scores. When asked to consider the appropriateness of hypothetical use of force and endorsement of threats, Jensen-Campbell and Graziano found their adolescent participants to behave consistently with their expectations with judgments inversely related to agreeableness. Graziano and Tobin (2002) investigated the conflict tactics chosen as most appropriate by undergraduate students in dealing with a series of conflict vignettes. They reported that negotiation was preferred most and power assertions tactics the least by highly agreeable respondents and selection levels for both tactics were significantly different than their low agreeableness cohorts. Jensen-Campbell, Gleason, Adams, and Malcolm (2003) conducted two studies with fifth and sixth grade elementary students to see if personality variables including agreeableness predicted conflict resolution and coping choices. Children with higher agreeableness scores endorsed constructive conflict resolution strategies, submission, disengagement, and third-party intervention at significantly higher levels than their peers with lower agreeableness scores. Children with lower agreeableness scores endorsed destructive conflict resolution strategies, manipulation, guilt, and physical force at significantly higher levels than their peers with higher agreeableness scores. In a second study Jensen-Campbell et al. found children high in agreeableness to show constructive conflict behaviors in conflicts whether or not their partners in the experiment demonstrated agreeableness or not. Antonioni (1999) investigated the conflict management style preferences of university students and business managers in terms of the big five personality factors. As in the previous studies, high agreeableness was associated with constructive conflict resolution strategies. For both groups of participants, Antonioni reports agreeableness is positively related with an integrating style of conflict management and negatively related to a dominating style.

Forgiveness

Forgiveness is the act of pardoning someone for a mistake or misconduct of some kind. While forgiveness may be about minor transgressions, like closing a door on someone's face, it may also be about life and death issues caused by severe forms of violence. For instance, in Northern Ireland in the late 1980s a father with his 20-year-old daughter was in a crowd devastated by an IRA bomb. The last words of his dying daughter as they laid holding hands in the rubble were "Daddy, I love you so much." From his hospital bed [the father] said, "I have lost my daughter, but I bear no grudge. Bitter talk is not going to bring [my daughter] back to life.

I shall pray, tonight and every night, that God will forgive them (Worthington, 2001, p. 161)." This is an example of supreme forgiveness.

The complexity of forgiveness can be seen in its cultural, religious, and political underpinnings (Anderson, 2007). Forgiveness occurs when a "motivated decision by victims of an offense to let go of their legitimate anger and resentment toward the offender and to evaluate him or her more favorably (Eaton & Struthers, 2006, p. 196)." Forgiveness replaces extreme anger and fear with positive emotions (Worthington, 2001). The process changes what would otherwise be a vengeful, negative response to a situation positive response (Maio, Thomas, Fincham, & Carnelley, 2008). Maio et al. characterize the forgiver as consciously engaging in positive thoughts, feelings, and behaviors toward the transgressor in a conflict while pushing any negative responses out of mind. In the Hindu scripture, the Bhagavad-Gita, Gita declares, "If you want to see the brave, look at those who can forgive. If you want to see the heroic, look at those who can love in return for hatred (Scholl, 2002, p. 23)."

Kalayjian (1999) speaks to the potential of forgiveness as an important step in dealing with the genocide of the Ottoman Turks against the Armenians in the late nineteenth and early twentieth centuries. Following up on a suggestion made to her by Viktor Frankel, a Holocaust survivor, Kalayjian has advocated for Armenians to make a very difficult first step to forgive the Turks who committed the atrocities toward her people. She is quick to point out that forgiveness, as the first step toward healing and ending the psychic genocide that Armenians around the world are still facing, is not forgetting or subverting the truth about what happened. Kalayjian views forgiveness as a process to free a person of the anger, resentment, and hatred and as one does this the structural violence of the lingering injustice in one's psyche can be removed and this can enable the person to achieve their potential in ways prevented before. One of her poems captures this idea when she says "With love and forgiveness, we will help one another to break the cycle of violence, and to prevent future genocides, by reasserting our humanness (p. 119)."

Forgiveness has strong roots in religion and is very commonly linked to religion (Anderson, 2007). Petersen (2001) notes the centrality of the wisdom of forgiveness in Judaic and Christian traditions and discusses how the Islamic emphasis on mercy and the Buddhist emphasis on compassion tap into the same dynamics of forgiveness. While recognizing forgiveness has often been subsumed as being in the domain of religion, Peterson identifies how it is also important to see its relevance to everyday life and to public policy issues.

Maio et al. (2008) add the purpose of relationship in which forgiveness is embedded as an important contextual variable. The roles of the persons in the relationship and the psychological needs of all in the relationship must be included in the contextual analysis as well. Because the purpose of relationships is different, Maio et al. expect forgiveness to be designed to serve different needs in different types of relationships. When two lovers quarrel, forgiveness may serve different needs than when a mother forgives her daughter. Maio et al. developed measures of forgiveness in family dyads and embarked on a 1-year longitudinal study to monitor the effects of levels of forgiveness within families. While they identified asymmetries between the levels of forgiveness of different family members, forgiveness was associated with better quality relationships and the experience of a more positive family environment. Forgiveness also was associated with lower numbers of repeat offences.

Eaton and Struthers (2006) document the ways in which forgiveness reduces aggression and promotes prosocial behavior within interpersonal interactions including romantic partners, school friends, and coworkers. While forgiveness reduces subsequent aggression, they investigated the role repentance or an apology by the transgressor can have on smoothing the way for forgiveness by the victim. Their path analysis model across three types of relationships was supported by their study involving college students for the use of repentance and forgiveness and followed the same pattern for relationships with romantic partners, school friends, and coworkers. Eaton and Struthers report a significant negative correlation between forgiveness and subsequent psychological aggression across all relationship types studied.

While forgiveness by members of the victim group of genocide may seem unimaginable, Staub and Pearlman (2001) write that even though it is difficult it is not only possible but also necessary and desirable. Using examples of collective violence in Rwanda, South Africa, and Bosnia, Staub and Pearlman discuss how the forgiving benefits those harmed by improving their psychological well-being, reducing their anger and its burden, and reducing their desire for revenge. Forgiveness makes the process of reconciliation more likely too. The security and feelings of safety of the surviving victims is also enhanced following forgiveness and reconciliation.

Cooperativeness

Cooperativeness can be seen as a positive attitude that predisposes an individual to accept the influence of others, to believe in the mutual benefits of the relationship, and to believe that you are supportive of the other and they are supportive to you (Deutsch, 2000). Deutsch characterizes cooperative relationships as having friendly and helpful orientations to interpersonal interaction, effective communication patterns with a desire to coordinate efforts with the other and avoid obstructive efforts, a willingness to enhance the other person's power, and a tendency to see problems as mutual and to be approached in a collaborative way. Keashly and Warters (2000) also describe cooperative attitudes as trusting, friendly, and helpful and elaborate that cooperative people are sensitive to similarities with others plus they minimize perceived differences in beliefs and values as they communicate openly yet respectfully.

"We who seek justice will have to do justice to others (Gandhi, cited in ME WE, 2007, p. 30)." This quote reflects Deutsch's *crude law of social relations* which says, "The characteristic processes and effects elicited by a given type of social relationship also tend to elicit that type of social relationship (Deutsch, 2000, p. 29)." Goleman (2006) describes an incident early in the recent US invasion of Iraq that nicely demonstrates Deutsch's *crude law of social relations*. While US soldiers were looking for a town's chief cleric to discuss the distribution of relief supplies, they found themselves surrounded by a hostile mob of residents concerned about the intentions of the soldiers toward their leader and the town in general. The US commanding officer told his troops to kneel on one knee and smile. After US forces assumed this nonhostile demeanor, many in the crowd reciprocated and responded in kind, smiling at the soldiers, and engaging in positive gestures. This defused a volatile situation without injury to anyone involved.

Based on Deutsch's *crude law of social relations*, one would expect that cooperativeness would bring out cooperativeness in others and that is in fact what research has demonstrated (e.g., Deutsch, 1973; Worchel, 1986). Johnson (1974) reviewed the effects of cooperative communication within the context of game behavior (e.g., Prisoner's Dilemma) and found that many cooperative behaviors influenced the other person to behave cooperatively. Johnson and Johnson (1995c) note that within a cooperative context more positive interpersonal relationships are fostered. Johnson and Johnson (1995b) see this as a result of cooperators having a more long-term focus for finding mutually beneficial solutions to conflicts so as to maintain good relationships with others because they tended to trust and like others. They also found cooperators to be more accurate in their perceptions of the needs and positions of others and are more sincere in recognizing the legitimacy of everyone's interests. Cooperators were also better communicators in that they engaged in more accurate and complete communications more often than non-cooperators. A competitive context tended to result in avoidance of communication and more destructive outcomes whereas a cooperative context tended to foster constructive outcomes with more positive long-term relationships between the people involved. While a single cooperative encounter may not significantly reduce hostility and conflict, multiple cooperative interactions eventually do result in a reduction in hostilities (Worchel).

Trust

While trust is a construct that has already been described as a component of agreeableness and cooperativeness, it is a variable important enough to discuss here in its own right. Trust may be viewed as synonymous with a social relationship and is highly dependent on context and the interconnectedness of people (Cromwell & Vogele, 2008). A person who exhibits trust has confidence in others and a belief that they will act fairly and in good faith. Webb and Worchel (1986) assert that there is no commonly accepted definition of trust as the meanings for it depends on orientation and interests of the theorists and researchers who study it. Lewicki and Bunker (1995) followed the lead of Worchel (1979) and reviewed different conceptions of trust from the perspective of personality theory, sociological or anthropological theory, and social psychology. As a personality trait, trust may be viewed as a generalized expectancy that another person is reliable in what is said and done (Rotter, 1971). Lewicki and Bunker found several theorists who considered trust to be a "faith in humanity" and this was manifested in a positive view of human nature. Others who approached trust from a personality perspective viewed it as an important developmental task or milestone (Erikson, 1963). From a social psychological perspective Worchel portrays trust as a result of interpersonal and group interaction patterns that have either fostered or reduced the expectation that others will act in a predictable way in future transactions. Lewicki and Wiethoff (2000) have synthesized these perspectives into three critical elements of trust that include the individual's disposition, situational parameters, and the history of their relationship.

There are many different types of trust described in the psychological literature. Jones, Couch, and Scott (1997) differentiate generalized trust from relational trust. They report higher levels of both types of trust are associated with better communication and greater satisfaction in relationships. Lewicki and Bunker (1995) describe calculus-based trust, knowledge-based trust, and identification-based trust based on different levels of understanding and control within a relationship. Calculus-based trust in an interpersonal interaction is determined by the perceived benefits and costs of remaining in the relationship, cheating in the relationship, and breaking the relationship. Knowledge-based trust is grounded in beliefs about the predictability of the other in a relationship and not the potential rewards or punishments that can result from the relationship. Identification-based trust involves the internalization of the desires and intentions of the other person in the relationship and leads to mutual understanding. While Lewicki and Wiethoff (2000) indicate that calculus-based trust usually develops first, the development of identification-based trust enhances the relationship. They also report that trust in a relationship makes conflict resolution easier and more effective.

Cromwell and Vogele (2008) describe the recursive aspects of trust and nonviolent action at the interpersonal level. They note that trust may lead to social benefits that include cooperation and deeper relationships that can lead to more nonviolent interpersonal interactions. Just as trust can create a context that encourages nonviolent responses to conflict, Cromwell and Vogele illustrate how nonviolent action reinforces several necessary components of trust building. Nonviolent action removes the threat of inflicting physical harm within the interpersonal interaction and this results in a removal of physical fear from the conflict. When physical safety is present, trust is promoted.

Nonviolent Communication Approaches

Rosenberg (2003) has developed a very promising approach to encourage nonviolent behavior in interpersonal relationships. He calls his strategy nonviolent communication (NVC) or compassionate communication. Rosenberg admits his approach consists of actions and strategies that have been available for a long time and little is new. However, if followed, NVC will encourage people to reconnect with their compassionate nature and be less likely to behave in a violent or exploitative way. NVC is based on the premise that if people reframe how they perceive others and how they express themselves, then they can change their habitual and automatic responses to life's conflicts and demands and recapture their humanness.

The four components of NVC model are (1) observing the concrete actions of others, (2) identifying our feelings in a particular situation, (3) understanding our underlying needs that create the feelings we have, and (4) requesting concrete actions to enrich our lives (Rosenberg, 2003). If individuals can honestly express themselves through these four components of NVC and receive empathetically through these four components, then they should be more able to (a) connect more deeply with others and themselves in a way that their natural compassion will flourish and (b) develop stronger relationships predicated on mutual respect, compassion, and cooperation.

Rosenberg (2003) notes that too often people do not really observe what is happening around them in an objective way. Observations are too often clouded with judgments and evaluations to the point in which people do not truly see what others around us actually are doing. For instance, we may see someone watching television and we tell ourselves that this is a lazy person. This is not a true observation but a moralistic judgment that can work to block our compassion toward that person and make conflict and violence more likely in our interpersonal interactions. Rosenberg describes how value judgments and social comparisons can aid us in denying personal responsibility for our actions and refusing to believe we have the ability to make different choices. Observing without evaluating is therefore a critical component in NVC and a skill that needs to be developed.

The second component of NVC is being able to identify and express our feelings. Rosenberg (2003) makes the excellent point that schooling and cultural learning teaches people to avoid their feelings. Because so much of personal experiences within school and other social institutions either call for people to repress or to ignore their own feelings and emotions, it is not easy to even identify our emotions let alone expressing our feelings to another person. Rosenberg provides clear suggestions on how to start to identify feelings from opinions and thoughts that are deceivingly cloaked in language of emotions. Saying "I feel..." does not necessarily reflect an emotion as it may reflect a thought or opinion. For instance, if one says, "I feel my spouse did the right thing," an opinion is being expressed. Before people can identify and express their feelings, they need to develop a vocabulary for emotions and distinguish feelings from thoughts.

Once feelings have been identified and expressed, people who apply NVC work to understand the needs they have that created their feelings. Rosenberg (2003) outlines the language of autonomy, celebration, integrity, interdependence, play, and physical nurture needs to guide people using NVC to an improved understanding of how needs are behind our emotions. He advocates expressing these needs, even if it may be painful, since this is an important step in valuing our own needs. Ultimately, taking responsibility for one's emotions and acknowledging one's needs is empowering.

After a person is able to objectively observe what is happening, to identify and express feelings, to understand the needs reflected in these feelings, then it is important to be able to use positive action language to request of others what would enrich one's life (Rosenberg, 2003). NVC involves making requests about what is wanted in concrete language as opposed to specifying what is not wanted. If requests are preceded by an expression of feelings and needs then they are less likely to be perceived as demands and more likely to be granted. While this leaves the person vulnerable, the human weaknesses expressed in this way allows for stronger empathy within the relationship and reduces the chance of a hostile interchange. Avoiding requests that are demands and defining our objective for the request increases the chances that the other person will really hear you and make your life better for it.

Empathy, or the ability to empty one's mind and totally listen to others, is a critical ingredient of NVC. Rosenberg (2003) describes how receiving empathically what others are communicating requires listening for what others are observing, feeling, needing, and requesting of you, regardless of what is being said. This necessitates focusing on the other person and attending to the same components you used in communicating honestly about yourself. Rosenberg recognizes how this is difficult at times and will call for you to ask for information from the other person, reflecting back what you are hearing to validate your understanding, and paraphrasing the other's message to communicate your compassion and commitment to understand their position.

Rosenberg's (2003) method of NVC synthesizes many psychological concepts into a process of communication designed to connect compassionately with others. In so doing NVC leads to nonviolent interactions designed to enrich the lives of the people in the relationship. Empathically listening to others and honestly expressing our own observations, feelings, needs, and requests may take time but Rosenberg provides anecdotal evidence of NVC's effectiveness in prisons, marital relationships, parenting relationships, international relationships in Croatia, Israel, Nigeria, Palestine, and Rwanda to name a few, and in many types of helping relationships.

Only limited, data based research on the impact could be found. Steckel (1994) applied an earlier version of NVC in a 7-h workshop with adults to determine the effect on empathy and self-compassion. Using a small matched pairs design, the experimental group exhibited significantly higher levels of empathy and self-compassion than the control group. Blake (2002) investigated the effect of NVC training via a 2-day workshop within communication classes at a university and a community college. Her quasiexperimental research showed NVC did not seem to impact empathy. Verbal aggression was lowered more than the control group for university students but not for the community college students. Cox and Dannahy (2005) studied the effectiveness of NVC within online course communications at a university in the United Kingdom. Their qualitative analysis determined that by focusing on feelings and needs in e-mentoring relationships, more trusting and open relationships were fostered. While considerable anecdotal support for NVC exists, more data based research is needed to validate the use of NVC.

Nonviolent Methods of Dealing with Conflict: Specific Conflict Resolution Approaches

Sanson and Bretherton (2001) view conflict resolution as a broad concept referring to a range of methods of resolving conflict or disagreements. Conflict resolution utilizes knowledge of psychological processes to "maximize the positive potential inherent in a conflict and to prevent its destructive consequences (p. 193)." The four basic principles of conflict resolution include cooperation, integrative solutions, understanding the interests of all parties, and nonviolent process and outcomes.

Picard (2002) places the different methods of nonviolent conflict resolution on a continuum. This conflict resolution continuum is presented in Fig. 5.1. Negotiation is on the extreme left and represents a method in which the parties arrive at a solution without outside assistance. As one moves to the right on the continuum from negotiation, to mediation, to conciliation, to arbitration, and finally to adjudication at the extreme right, a third-party has increasing involvement in resolving the conflict and acquires more and more power in determining the nature of the solution.

Negotiation

Negotiation is derived from a Latin verb *negociare* meaning "to conduct business" (Rubin, 1994). Negotiation is a back and forth communication process designed to get what you want from others (Fisher et al., 1991). It also has been referred to as "a discussion between two or more parties aimed at resolving incompatible goals (Pruitt & Carnevale, 1993, p. xv)." Negotiation is a joint-decision-making process in which the parties involved in the conflict work together to develop an outcome (Keashly & Warters, 2000).

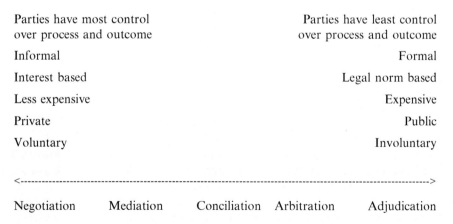

Parties have most control over process and outcome	Parties have least control over process and outcome
Informal	Formal
Interest based	Legal norm based
Less expensive	Expensive
Private	Public
Voluntary	Involuntary

<-->

Negotiation   Mediation   Conciliation   Arbitration   Adjudication

Fig. 5.1 Conflict resolution continuum (reprinted from Picard, 2002, p. 8)

Integrative Negotiation (vs. Distributive Negotiation)

Johnson and Johnson (2003) outline two basic of approaches to negotiation. Distributive negotiation is used when the intent is to seek an agreement whereby your gain is maximized at the expense of the other side. Rubin (1994) has referred to this approach to conflict management as the concession-convergence model. The integrative approach involves a negotiation where an agreement that benefits both sides is sought. This is similar to what has been described as the mutual gains model (Rubin). While Johnson and Johnson point out that the strategies of distributive negotiation are well studied and understood, they delineate the need for much more attention and research on integrative negotiation. They call for a clearer conceptualization of integrative negotiation based on the theoretical underpinnings of social interdependence theory, for specifically developed procedures to guide practitioners, and for validation research to answer the many questions that research has not addressed to date.

Integrative negotiation is theoretically grounded in social interdependence theory (Johnson, 2003; Johnson & Johnson, 1995c, 2003). Social interdependence is the state where the satisfaction of one's goals is linked to the action of another. If the achievement of one's goal is solely under one's own control then social interdependence would not exist. Interdependence might be either positive or negative. Positive interdependence occurs when one side in a negotiation believes it is only possible to reach their goal if the other party reaches theirs as well. Negative interdependence occurs when one side believes their goals can only be attained if the other side is thwarted from reaching theirs (Deutsch, 1973).

The basis of social interdependence theory is an extension of Deutsch's *crude law of social relations* that was described earlier in this chapter. Based on this crude law, if one behaves in a cooperative way toward another, this crude law of social relations predicts that the other person would behave in a cooperative manner too. Competitive behavior would beget competitive responses and so on. The basic premise of social interdependence theory speaks to the manner in which individuals interact and this interaction depends upon the way the interdependence is structured and the outcome of the situation is determined by the interaction pattern (Johnson & Johnson, 2003). Therefore, positive interdependence leads to promotive interaction that is relevant, open, and honest communication based on trust and accurate perceptions of the interests and concerns of all involved. This promotive interaction leads to a cooperative situation that might foster mutual assistance and cooperative responses by the other person(s). On the other hand negative interdependence leads to oppositional interaction that might include obstruction of the other's goal.

Integrative negotiations are cooperative interactions in which the parties in the conflict seek mutually beneficial agreements (Johnson & Johnson, 2003). The six step process for integrative negotiation presented by Johnson and Johnson are as follows (1) define the conflict as a solvable problem and not a test of dominance and accurately describe what is wanted by the negotiators, (2) state the underlying feelings about the problem at hand, (3) describe the reasons behind each negotiators wants and feelings, (4) take the perspective of the other person in the conflict,

(5) engage in creative reasoning to identify several potential solutions (at least three) that result in high levels of mutual gain, and (6) agree on a particular option for adoption.

In a meta-analysis involving 16 studies conducted in several countries with students from kindergarten through ninth grade, Johnson and Johnson (2003) found support for social interdependence theory being an appropriate framework for integrative negotiations. Just as cooperative behavior leads to cooperative behavior in others, integrative negotiation establishes a cooperative context that promotes the same type of outcomes as cooperative behavior has promoted in other research. Johnson and Johnson found students who were trained in integrative negotiation procedures for 9–15 h using the *Teaching Students to be Peacemakers* program (Johnson & Johnson, 1995a) "recalled the steps of integrative negotiations, retained their understanding over considerable time, actually used integrative negotiation procedures to resolve conflicts, retained their ability to use the procedure over time, reached more integrative agreements, transferred their use of integrative negotiation procedures to nonclassroom and non-school settings, developed more positive attitudes toward conflict, and increased academic learning when the training was integrated into academic units (p. 61)." These summary findings are quite broad and impressive.

Principled Negotiation

Fisher et al. (1991) developed the effective process of principled negotiation and their classic text, *Getting to Yes*, explains how best to negotiate using this method of negotiation. In order for a negotiation to be considered successful it should be efficient and produce a wise agreement in a manner that does not damage the relationship between all parties involved and might even improve the relationship. The agreement in a successful negotiation must meet the legitimate needs of all sides to the level possible while resolving the interests in conflict fairly. When conflicting interests do arise, principled negotiation makes decisions based on fair standards and the merits of the situation. A typical assumption many have when they enter into a negotiation is that if I am more skilled in the methods of negotiation, I will be able to get an agreement that helps me at the expense of the other side. The beauty of principled negotiation is that this type of brinkmanship is not considered advantageous at all. In fact, "Unlike almost all other strategies, if the other side learns this one, it does not become more difficult to use; it becomes easier. If they read this book, all the better (Fisher et al., p. xix)."

Fisher et al. (1991) delineate the steps of principled negotiation as (1) separating the people from the problem, (2) focusing on the interests, not positions, (3) inventing options for mutual gain, and (4) insisting on using objective criteria. It is an approach that has been well tested in a wide variety of negotiations from marital breakups to individual contract disputes between an employee and employer to national disputes involving potential military involvement.

In order to separate the problem from the people we are negotiating with, Fisher et al. (1991) caution us to remember negotiators are people first and that we need to attend to relationship interests so they are not intertwined with the problem at hand. A good principled negotiator should separate the relationship from the content and goals of the negotiation and deal directly with people problems. This necessitates attention to perceptual, emotional, and communication concerns at individual, language, and cultural levels. Principled negotiation requires negotiators to do their homework to understand cultural styles of communication including eye contact, physical distance, wait time in responding, plus formality, and hierarchical expectations. It is also advisable to know the personal history of the individuals with whom you are negotiating. However, individual negotiators do not always behave consistent with group norms or their previous tendencies so it is critical to avoid succumbing to self-fulfilling prophecies. Putting in an initial effort during negotiation to build a working relationship with the other person is well worth the time. Once this is accomplished, it becomes possible to face the problem and not the people you are negotiating with.

The next step in principled negotiation is to focus on the interests you and the other side have and not positions you both may be taking (Fisher et al., 1991). The goal is not to reconcile positions but identify interests and reconcile them since interests define the problem. A principled negotiator must ask why do I hold this position and why do they hold theirs. The answers to these questions will help identify our interests and their interests within the negotiation. If one also asks the question oneself "Why not?" about the position of the other party, one might also get some insight into interests of the other side. Understanding the multiple interests of all parties in a negotiation entails considerable reflection and analysis. People have many values, many needs, and many relevant constituencies when confronted with a conflict that needs a negotiation to resolve. The goal of looking at interests is to find shared and compatible interests or complementary interests. Ideally, interests should be made specific and concrete yet the negotiator should remain flexible.

The complexity and importance of looking at interests, instead of positions, can be seen with the issue of gun control. Gun control advocates want to restrict gun ownership while their opponents want gun ownership to be unrestricted. The interests of gun control advocates might include the desire to reduce homicides and suicides, to remove guns from dangerous people, and to reduce the chance of victimization along with the general concern that guns are dangerous and that too many guns already are in circulation and we do not need anymore. Gun ownership advocates feel they need guns for entertainment, sport, and self-defense or protection. This is a freedom issue and they believe criminals will get guns anyway and gun control is a "scapegoat" for other issues. The interests of the two sides offer a glimpse at the common needs for security, well-being, and control over one's life and while this is still a contentious issue, it is possible to see commonalities on the two sides.

Next Fisher et al. (1991) want the principled negotiator to invent options for mutual gain. This brainstorming process needs to be done prior to and separately from the decision process to avoid premature judgment. Fisher et al. caution the negotiator against searching for the single answer or option and assuming there is a fixed pie. Once brainstorming has occurred attempts should be made to broaden the available options by looking for mutual gain, inventing agreements of varying strengths, and shuttling between specific and general conceptualizations of the problem.

Instead of relying on the will or demands of the parties in the negotiation to determine the outcome, Fisher et al. (1991) encourage principled negotiators to insist on using objective criteria. Developing fair and objective criteria to use in evaluating the options at hand is critical to successful negotiations that produce wise agreements amicably and efficiently. Fair standards are independent of each side's will and are legitimate and practical. Fisher et al. provide numerous examples for a wide range of problems under negotiation. These include precedent, scientific judgment, professional standards, efficiency, costs, what a court would decide, moral standards, equal treatment, tradition, reciprocity, taking turns, and drawing lots just to name a few. The important point is that negotiating with objective criteria can reduce the pressure one experiences in making the final decision. They point out that the principled negotiator ultimately should never yield to pressure, only to the principle established by the objective criteria.

Since negotiations can break down, Fisher et al. (1991) provide useful strategies when you do run into problems. The key is to be aware of your best alternative available to you if negotiations collapse. This best alternative to a negotiated agreement is your BATNA and is what you are left with when no solution to the conflict is agreed upon. Within principled negotiation knowing your BATNA can help you to make the most of your assets and understand how much power you have in the negotiation process. A strong BATNA translates into more power and allow you to negotiate a solution to the conflict based on the merits or the objective standards. Without a BANTA you can be too committed to making an agreement and this can make you vulnerable to poor decision-making. Your BATNA is the standard to judge the proposed agreements that are minimally acceptable. Of course it is a good idea to know your opponent's BATNA to estimate the power they have as well. If all parties in a negotiation have strong BATNAs, the possibilities for a good agreement to be reached are seriously reduced. Fisher et al. encourage principled negotiators to formulate a trip wire which is a less than perfect agreement that is still better than your BATNA. Before you accept any agreement worse than the trip-wire, they recommend that you take a break and reexamine your situation.

A critical action to consider is the disclosure of your BATNA to the other side of the negotiation. Fisher et al. (1991) offer several scenarios where disclosure might be helpful and others where it would not be. If your BATNA is extremely attractive or you have an attractive BATNA and they think you do not, a discussion of your BATNA might be to your advantage. If you believe the other side is overestimating their BATNA, you might benefit from lowering their expectations. If your BATNA is not very strong or if you believe your opponent thinks it is more attractive than it really is, then sharing your BATNA may put you at a disadvantage.

Fisher et al. (1991) also provide positive recommendations to be used when negotiations become stalled for a wide-range of reasons from stubbornness to dirty tricks and deception on the part of those you are negotiating with. They encourage the use of negotiation jujitsu, a metaphor to the martial art by the same name. A principled negotiator should not push back but use the energy of your opponent to your advantage. When your adversary holds fast to their position, you should not attack it but look behind their position to discover their interests. In this way your refusal to react can break the vicious cycle of obstinacy. You can rephrase any attack on you as an attack on the problem instead. This, coupled with encouragement for your opponent to provide criticism and advise to your recasting of their attack, changes the dynamics of the discussion and the line of thinking they are using. During these types of interactions, it is important to ask questions and pause to give the other side a chance to think and get their points across. The uncomfortable nature of silence can impel the other side to think through an issue. Fisher et al. note that while statements generate resistance, questions generate answers. By assuming every position the other side takes is a real attempt to address the fundamental concerns of each side and by examining their negative judgments to better understand their interests, a principled negotiator can oftentimes apply this negotiation jujitsu in a timely fashion.

Emotions and Negotiation

Fisher and Shapiro (2005) have focused attention on the best way to use emotions to one's advantage in the negotiation process. While some methods of negotiation encourage people to avoid them, ignore them, or to deal directly with them, they point out the impossibility or futility of these approaches. Instead, Fisher and Shapiro encourage negotiators to focus on a small set of core concerns that are manageable and enable one to deal indirectly yet quite effectively with emotions during even intense negotiations. Their core concerns include appreciation, affiliation, autonomy, status, and role needs. If any of these needs are ignored or not met, emotions can easily scuttle a successful negotiation. However, if these concerns are adequately addressed and met, emotions that can sabotage the process are not stirred up and if they are, are more likely to dissipate before detrimental effects are manifest.

Fisher and Shapiro (2005) encourage negotiators to follow the guidelines of principled negotiation along with careful attention to the five core concerns during any negotiation. By doing so a host of negative emotions are avoided and a considerable number of positive emotions are fostered and this improves the chances of successful outcomes. When negotiators show appreciation of their counterparts, the other negotiators are likely to believe that their thoughts, feelings and actions are legitimate and not devalued. When negotiators are treated as colleagues as opposed to adversaries, they will experience a sense of affiliation and this will cultivate positive emotions that lead to more of a desire to work together. When negotiators believe their freedom to decide is recognized by the opposite side, their autonomy will more likely lead them to respect the autonomy of their counterparts and this can promote more creative solutions. When negotiators believe they are accorded the status they deserve, they will be more trusting, calm, and less defensive. When negotiators perceive their role as fulfilling and important, they are more liable to believe they can make a real difference and this can have a positive effect on the negotiation as well. By taking the initiative to address the core concerns of appreciation, affiliation, autonomy, status, and role, negative emotions are reduced without having to monitor and focus on them plus positive emotions are cultivated.

Mediation

Mediation has a Latin derivation meaning middle and refers to assisted negotiation with someone who is not a party to the conflict being in the middle of the communication (Picard, 2002). Mediation is another type of joint decision-making in which a third-party facilitator works with the parties to develop a solution to the conflict (Keashly & Warters, 2000). The neutral third party is the mediator who facilitates a step-by-step process to explore each party's agreements and disagreements with relevant information and potential options available to resolve the conflict through consensus (Leviton & Greenstone, 1997). Wall, Stark, and Standifer (2001) comment that mediation is a conflict resolution process that is quite old and is practiced countries worldwide.

Wall et al. (2001) delineate a useful mediation paradigm. The following description of mediation is based on their paradigm. The first step in mediation is for the disputing parties to agree to allow a third party to get involved in their conflict. Next the person who will be the mediator must agree to perform this role. The likelihood that mediation will occur is influenced by the norms held by the disputants, the laws relevant to the conflict, and the expected benefits of the mediation. Once the parties are committed to a process of mediation and a mediator has been identified, the mediation proper involves a range of techniques that may include information gathering, pressing, education or advising, empowerment, monitoring interactions or critiquing positions of the disputants, trying to sell one side's case to the other, and integrating issues in the conflict. Wall et al.'s paradigm includes three types of outcomes drawn from the mediation literature. Disputant outcomes might be agreement, satisfaction, improved relationships, and procedural or restorative justice. Outcomes relevant to the mediator include reputation and enhanced social skills. Additional outcomes affect individuals not directly involved in the mediation process.

Picard (2002) considers communication, both verbal and nonverbal, to be the key element in the resolution of interpersonal or small group conflict. Whereas, negotiation is based on the discussion of the arguments and interests of the parties in a conflict, mediation involves an outside party, the mediator, who uses communication skills to get the parties on a conflict to move away from position-based to principled-based bargaining. The success of the mediation depends on the mediator's skill to enable the conflicted parties to understand the factual and emotional issues that are relevant to the dispute at hand.

While no consensus exits as to the optimal role of a mediator, the mediator usually does not have any authority to impose an outcome of any kind (Wall et al.,

2001). Picard (2002) identifies four sets of contrasting roles that have been hypothesized and studied to determine their effectiveness. She describes the bargaining style and the therapeutic style studied by Silbey and Merry as two positive roles mediators might assume. The bargaining style assumes a structured approach on the part of mediators who work to narrow issues and focus on the bottom-line to reach a settlement. The therapeutic style focuses more on communication and the expression of feelings and attitudes in a safe environment designed to develop understanding between the disputants. Similarly, Picard relates the work of Bush and Folger in which the bargaining style is described more as a problem-solving or directive orientation taken by the mediator. This problem-solving approach conceptualizes the conflict for the disputants. In contrast to this more common problem-solving approach, Folger and Bush (1996) identify a transformative approach of mediation in which the mediator works to create an environment that empowers the parties in the conflict to be creative and recognize their abilities to see how to capitalize on the larger implications of the conflict in a relational way. In transformative approaches the mediator focuses on the process to change the mind sets of the parties to create more opportunities for mutual understanding, better communication patterns, and a positive resolution to the conflict. This approach "can strengthen people's capacity to analyze situations and make effective decisions for themselves and can strengthen people's capacity to see and consider the perspectives of others (Folger & Bush, p. 264)."

Another way to conceptualize mediator styles is to distinguish between a settlement frame vs. a communication frame, as expressed by Kolb and Associates (cited in Picard, 2002). The settlement frame is similar to the bargaining style and the problem-solving approach described above, however, in this approach the mediator is focused more on the potential deal at hand and takes an even larger directive role that includes suggesting the makeup of the best deals, opinion sharing, and persuasive attempts to make the deals happen. On the other side of the Kolb and Associates mediator style dichotomy is the communication frame which has the purpose of developing an understanding between the disputants in a comparable way to the therapeutic style.

Riskin (cited in Picard, 2002) delineates the evaluative and facilitative schemes to classify mediation. The evaluative approach is much like the settlement frame whereas the facilitative approach is analogous to the communication frame. Because the visions of the resolution process held by mediators differ, so does the role that they take within the process. In addition to vision, the role taken "is influenced by [the mediator's] past experience, training, and ideology as well as the context in which mediation takes place (Picard, p. 30)."

Mediation is currently being applied in a wide variety of contexts. It is used widely within the legal system especially in marital disputes (i.e., McKnight, 1995) and victim-offender disputes (Umbreit, 1995), within parent–child disputes (Umbreit), within the school system (Johnson & Johnson, 1995b, 2001; Powell, Muir-McClain, & Halasyamani, 1995; Umbreit), within community disputes, civil matters, and a variety of business matters (Nagel Lechman, 1997).

Conciliation

Picard (2002) describes one type of conciliation as very similar to mediation except for the fact that the third party serves as a "go-between" between two or more parties that never meet directly. Keashly and Warters (2000) also note that conciliation involves the third-party as a communication link that shuttles information between disputants who are not communicating well with each other. Another type of conciliation involves persuading the parties in the conflict to come together to discuss the relevant issues in a dispute. The third-party conciliator orchestrates the process of getting the parties into a discussion but these discussions generally occur without third-party involvement. Conciliation only involves the inclusion of a third-party in the initial stages of conflict resolution and is most often employed in international contexts (Nagel Lechman, 1997). US Secretary of State Kissinger's shuttle diplomacy in the Middle East during the Nixon administration is such an example. In this instance Kissinger traveled back and forth between Middle East leaders after the 1973 Arab-Israeli War to explain the position of the Arabs to the Israelis and the Israelis to the Arabs in order to facilitate peace between the parties.

The process of conciliation was also a major component in Graduated and Reciprocated Initiatives in Tension reduction (GRIT) developed by Osgood (1962). This alternative to military or violent action is a step-by-step process to reduce tension by making small conciliatory gestures that are hopefully matched in kind by the other side. This step-by-step process was employed successfully at the international level by Kennedy and Khrushchev in the 1960s and has been shown to induce the other side of interpersonal conflicts to cooperate more as well (Lindskold, 1986).

Arbitration

Arbitration is a decision making process that has been used for hundreds of years (Nagel Lechman, 1997). "In arbitration, the parties agree to submit their dispute to a neutral third party whom they have selected to make a decision regarding the outcome of the dispute" (Picard, 2002, p. 8). The third-party in arbitration might be a single individual or a panel of individuals who carefully listen to the presentations of each side in the conflict before rendering the decision. The decision of the third-party arbitrator might be binding and the disputants agree to follow the decision made for them or it may be nonbinding.

In private arbitration the disputants choose and pay the arbitrator. A private arbitration does not necessarily take place in a legal setting and the records of the process may or may not be made public. The determination of whether a private arbitration is either binding or nonbinding should be made before the parties in a dispute submit their cases to the arbitrator. Court-annexed arbitration is required by law or mandated by legal statute and does take place in a courthouse. The parties in the dispute do not choose the arbitrator and the decision rendered is binding.

Court-annexed arbitration may take place in local, state, or federal judicial systems (Nagel Lechman, 1997).

While arbitration provides more flexibility than adjudication in Picard's (2002) continuum of conflict resolution, Nagel Lechman (1997) describes arbitration as having strong similarities with adjudications and litigation. Legal counsel may be employed in arbitration and the arbitrator decides on the outcome after hearing the case, as does the judge in adjudications. Arbitration is commonly used in conflicts involving labor relations.

Adjudication

Picard (2002) describes adjudication as "a formal process conducted by a judge or jury in a court of law (p. 8). The basis for the decisions rendered in adjudications involve points of law rather than moral concerns or other criteria applied in arbitrations. The parties in the dispute have the least control over the process and outcome if adjudication is used and this method of conflict resolution is more public. Included within adjudication processes are private judges who make binding decisions and final-offer arbitration (Nagel Lechman, 1997).

Nonviolent Methods of Dealing with Conflict: Preventative Approaches

When a conflict exists, its resolution can consume all parties directly or indirectly involved. While Deutsch (1973) suggests that conflict may yield constructive or destructive outcomes, the possibility of a destructive outcome is a real risk. Therefore, the relative regularity of conflict in our lives encourages us to consider ways to prevent future conflicts whenever possible. Educators, psychologists, and public health professionals have all developed programs to encourage people to use nonviolent reactions to conflict at the individual, interpersonal, community, and societal levels. This section will address the preventative approaches referred to as conflict resolution education (CRE), violence prevention programs, social and emotional learning (SEL), nonviolence education, and peace education programs.

Jones (2004) summarizes the similarities between CRE, violence prevention programs, SEL programs, and peace education. She also highlights the ways CRE is different from the interventions listed above. Violence prevention programs include safety and security goals as does CRE, however, they put more focus on decreasing risk factors for violence and are more concerned about more serious violent acts in the schools like the shootings and killings at Columbine High School in 1999. CRE is concerned more about life skills that lead to nonviolent methods of dealing with conflict whereas violence prevention focuses on reducing risks that lead to substance abuse, unsafe sexual behavior, self-injurious behavior, and violence directed toward peers. The distinction between CRE and SEL programs have disappeared over the years when it comes to the specific set of emotional, cognitive, and behavioral competencies the two programs address. However, CRE goals for a safe and constructive learning environment and for a larger constructive conflict community go beyond SEL program goals.

While these categories are commonly used and useful to highlight the range of preventative approaches available to those concerned about peace and nonviolence, as can be seen, some preventative programs are truly hybrid in nature as they incorporate aspects of two or more approaches. While I will be generally following the classification process of Jones (2004) as described above in organizing the following discussion of preventative approaches, at times the distinctions become muddled because other researchers cited below do not follow the same approach in their identification of preventative programs.

Conflict Resolution Education

Jones (2004) has detailed the field and goals of CRE and reviewed relevant research on this and related educational programs. CRE "models and teaches, in culturally meaningful ways, a variety of processes, practices and skills that help address individual, interpersonal, and institutional conflicts, and create safe and welcoming communities" (Association for Conflict Resolution, cited in Jones, pp. 233–234).

Jones (2004) has synthesized four broad goals for CRE from her review of the literature. The first goal of CRE is to create a safe learning environment by decreasing the incidents of violence, decreasing intergroup conflicts (especially those based racial or ethnic problems), and decreasing suspensions, absenteeism, and dropout rates related to unsafe schools. The second goal is to create a constructive learning environment by improving the classroom and school climate, increasing respect and caring in our schools, improving classroom management abilities of teachers so they spend less time on disciplinary issues, and increasing student-centered discipline with the schools. The third goal is to enhance student's social and emotional development by increasing perspective taking and constructive conflict behaviors, improving problem-solving abilities, emotional awareness, and emotional management, while reducing aggressive orientations and hostile attributions. The fourth goal is to create a constructive conflict community by increasing parental and community involvement in school functions and activities, increasing associations between school and community CRE efforts, and reducing community tensions and incidents of violence.

In working to achieve these goals CRE encompasses many types of educational programming including education on conflict resolution skills, dialogue skills, restorative justice, prejudice and bias, bullying, and negotiation training, plus those described as SEL and peer mediation. While many would view SEL and peer mediation as separate types of interventions, Jones (2004) described them as important components of CRE. Therefore, they will be discussed here as relevant elements of CRE.

Social and Emotional Learning

SEL programs "provide systematic classroom instruction that enhances children's capabilities to recognize and manage their emotions, appreciate the perspective of others, establish prosocial goals and solve problems, and use a variety of interpersonal skills to effectively and ethically handle developmentally relevant tasks (Payton et al., 2000, p. 179)." SEL programs are often viewed as primary prevention to reduce high-risk behaviors (Elias & Weissberg, 2000). If successful, these programs teach skills needed to be ethical and responsible (Devaney, O'Brien, Tavegia, & Resnik, 2005).

The Collaborative to Advance Social and Emotional Learning (CASEL) was established in 1994 and developed a framework of important competencies for SEL programs (Payton et al., 2000). SEL programs generally address the third goal of CRE as they work to develop and enhance a person's social and emotional competencies (Jones, 2004).

Payton et al. (2000) highlight the more specific competency areas of SEL as (1) awareness of self and others, (2) positive attitudes and values, (3) responsible decision making, and (4) social interaction skills. The awareness of self and others competencies expressly focus on the awareness and management of emotions by developing the capacity to perceive, label, and regulate one's own feelings and to accurately take the perspective of others. In addition this competency addresses the importance of developing a strong sense of self that reflects one's strengths and weaknesses while building an optimistic and efficacious orientation. The positive attitudes and values component of SEL is designed to develop personal and social responsibility by building intentions to tolerate individual and group differences and to behave in a safe, honest, and appropriate way while contributing to one's community and protecting the environment. The responsible decision making competencies involve the abilities to identify problems, to analyze relevant social norms, to set positive and realistic goals, and to develop, implement, and evaluate solutions to problems. The social interaction competencies encompass active listening, verbal and nonverbal communication skills, strategies for dealing with peer and social pressures, cooperation, negotiation, and support seeking skills.

Jones (2004) has comprehensively reviewed the research on the effectiveness of SEL programs from the preschool level through high school. Based on her analysis of this research, she describes SEL to be effective in improving "interpersonal skills, quality of peer and adult relationships, and academic achievement, as well as reductions in problem behaviors such as school misbehavior and truancy, violence and aggression (p. 240)." These results are especially strong for younger age children. Devaney et al. (2005) add positive health behaviors, ethical development, citizenship, and motivation to achieve to the list of significant outcomes of SEL programs. Considerable research evidence also exists to say that SEL can increase school achievement and success (Zins, Weissberg, Wang, & Walberg, 2004). Ross, Powell, and Elias (2002) also make the case that SEL programs increase the likelihood that students will avoid high-risk activities and engage in behaviors that foster good health. Based on an extensive body of research, Payton et al. (2000) point to the increased effectiveness of SEL when it is implemented in an integrated curriculum over two or more years. Greenberg et al. (2003) also report that "short-term preventative interventions produce short-lived results" and "multiyear, multicomponent programs are more likely to foster enduring benefits (p. 470)." These benefits include a reduction of violence and aggression as well as other high-risk behaviors like drug use, truancy, and unsafe sexual behaviors plus increased self-awareness and confidence, improved interpersonal skills, higher quality peer and adult relationships, better academic goal-setting behavior, increased organizational skills, and higher levels of academic performance. Greenberg et al. stipulate that the effectiveness of SEL programs is enhanced if they are implemented before pressures to perform risky and antisocial behaviors are intense during adolescence. Combining social and emotional skill building across at least five SEL competencies with school-wide and community-wide components are highly advantageous.

Peer Mediation in the Schools

Peer mediation is the oldest type of CRE intervention and is used more often than any other type of CRE intervention (Jones, 2004). Peer mediation programs attempt "to teach students how to deal with anger constructively, how to communicate feelings and concerns without using violence and abusive language, how to think critically about alternative solutions, and how to agree to solutions in which all parties win (Kort, cited in Morse & Andrea, 1994, p. 76)." Most peer mediation programs are designed to have the mediators assist in resolving student–student disputes although some programs include student-teacher disputes and student–other adult disputes (Hall, 1999). Peer mediation programs have been delivered using at least three basic models. Jones outlines the three types of peer mediation delivery as the cadre approach, the curriculum or classroom-linked approach, and the mentoring approach. When the cadre model is followed, students are trained in mediation techniques and then they are expected to mediate disputes between students in a special location removed from the rest of the school population. This approach has been implemented at all educational levels. When the curriculum model is followed, the full class receives training in negotiation and mediation methods. Class members then become mediators on a rotating basis conducting mediations in class at the request of their peers or teacher. This approach is more commonly used at the elementary school level. When the mentoring model is followed, students who have been trained and have experience in mediation are required to train younger students. This approach is more commonly used within secondary schools.

An increasing amount of research has looked at the effects of peer mediation in its many forms (Flecknoe, 2005; Johnson & Johnson, 2001; Jones, 2004; Powell et al., 1995). Jones reports the results of a meta-analysis published in 2003 by Burrell, Zirbel, and Allen in which overwhelming support for peer mediation was identified. Student's knowledge and skills regarding conflicts significantly increased when peer mediation was implemented and negative behavior in the schools decreased as school climate improved.

Some who have reviewed this research refer to mixed outcomes (Flecknoe, 2005; Hall, 1999), find inadequate implementation problems, and report differing effects based on the model of peer mediation used (Jones, 2004). Flecknoe points to mixed outcomes as a function of the methodological difficulties in segregating children into treatment and control groups within a school since students mix with each other in so many ways throughout the school day and before and after school too. Powell et al. (1995) found considerable variance in the way some peer mediation programs are implemented. They saw implementation problems in several peer mediation programs as a function of the inadequate teacher and student training. However, even with these limitations, some strong research designs have been employed and a body of sound research is growing. Many who have looked at this research evidence regarding peer mediation see strong empirical support for it (Johnson & Johnson, 2001; Jones).

Peer mediation does have significant effects on the cadre trained in mediation techniques in both elementary and middle schools (Jones, 2004). Johnson, Johnson, Dudley, and Magnuson (1995) analyzed the effects of conflict resolution training including peer mediation in elementary students in the second through fifth grade. Students who were taught peer mediation learned the process, were able to use peer mediation in their day-to-day school life, and were able to do so throughout the entire school year. Johnson, Johnson, Dudley, Ward, and Magnuson (1995) report that the strategies for conflict resolution learned in peer mediation generalize and are used at home as often as they are in school. Johnson and Johnson (2001) looked at the effects peer mediation for third and fourth grade mediators within a K-4 elementary school. Prior to the implementation all reported conflicts were resolved with physical force and after the training the students in conflict primarily agreed to avoid each other in the future or apologized and forgave each other. Jones found several studies that supported these findings regarding increased knowledge and abilities of peer mediators plus peer mediators have fewer disciplinary referrals than their peers who did not have the training. She also reports of studies that replicated these results with special need students and at-risk students. Jones also reviewed several studies that reported elementary peer mediators have consistently increased their perspective taking abilities.

Elementary students throughout an entire school are sometimes trained in peer mediation within the curriculum or classroom-linked peer mediation model. Johnson and Johnson (2001) reported the results of a meta-analysis of their Teaching Students to be Peacemakers Program (TSPP) for both the elementary school and middle school levels. The findings indicate that students learned the mediation techniques over a year-long timeframe, and as for the cadre approaches, they were able to apply what they learned both in the schools and in their lives at home and outside of school. Some but not all studies showed TSPP to increase academic performance while decreasing suspensions and classroom management problems. Jones (2004) reports the effectiveness of the Responding in Peaceful and Positive Ways (RIPP) program at the middle school level. Like for the TSPP, RIPP participants had fewer suspensions and disciplinary problems. RIPP students also demonstrated less physical aggression and more peer support for nonviolent behaviors than a control group.

Research evaluating and supporting the mentoring model for peer mediation is available only for the elementary level (Jones, 2004). The Winning Against Violent Environments (WAVE) program cited by Jones provides positive validation for the mentoring model as it was implemented in the urban environment of the Cleveland Municipal School District. Jones summarizes the program evaluation of WAVE as positive for both mediators and nonmediators alike. Both groups understand conflict better, believe the school climate is better, and have more informed attitudes about conflict. WAVE schools had lower suspension rates and school academic achievement scores rose more than the non-WAVE schools in the district.

Jones (2004) describes the preliminary outcome of a comparative research project conducted in three cities by herself and her colleagues. This 2-year research project utilized a 3×3 field experiment design to assess the impact of peer mediation model (cadre, curriculum linked/whole school, control) at three school levels (elementary, middle, and high school). Jones and her colleagues found that "peer mediation programs provide significant benefit in developing constructive social and conflict behavior in children of all education levels. It is clear that exposure to peer mediation, whether cadre or whole school, has a significant lasting impact on students' conflict attitudes and behaviors (p. 250)." The positive outcome measures that were identified in this comprehensive study include decreases in aggressiveness, increases in prosocial values, perspective taking, and the tendency to help others with conflicts. These findings were long lasting and especially true for those trained in peer mediation. While peer mediation programs did produce more positive school climates, this was only the case for the elementary school level and not for middle or high school levels.

Violence Prevention Programs

Violence prevention programs have the goal of creating safe school climates through the reduction in violence, crime, drug usage, and the peer pressures that push students toward these antisocial behaviors (Harris, 1999a). Congress provided a strong impetus for school-based violence prevention when it passed national education goals that included one that stated "every school in the United states will be free of drugs, violence, and unauthorized presence of firearms and will offer a disciplined environment conducive to learning (Greene, 2005, p. 236)." Greene has identified school violence prevention programs that include a wide array of program components. These include security apparatuses and policies such as surveillance cameras and metal detectors at the entrances to school buildings and property, discipline policies and rules such as graduated sanctions for violent acts and incentives for positive behavior, peer-led programs such as peer counseling or peer mediation, threat assessment and crisis response teams, psychosocial and psychoeducational programs such as year-long curricular interventions, plus social climate strategies such as bullying prevention targeting an entire school or school district. Unfortunately, Greene found little evaluation research to support the effectiveness of security measures, peer-led programs, threat assessment, and crisis response approaches. While some specific psychosocial and psychoeducational programs have research support for the reduction of school violence when implemented, Greene pushes for more multi-level program evaluation of fully integrated school-based violence prevention strategies that analyze organization barriers for success.

Gottfredson and Gottfredson (2002) reviewed over 3,000 school-based prevention activities in a national probability sample. While many of the prevention activities reviewed were not violence prevention in nature, an important segment of their sample did include them. Gottfredson and Gottfredson's results suggest that prevention practices are generally not being implemented well and these practices would benefit from better integration into regular school functions and better organizational support for training and supervision of personnel directly implementing the programs. Johnson and Johnson (1996) view violence prevention programs as incomplete unless they include conflict resolution training.

While many violence prevention programs have been school-based, others focus on the community to prevent violence in a broader context. Sabol, Coulton, and Korbin (2004) make the case that community-based violence prevention programs typically involve community mobilization to reduce youth violence, child maltreatment, and domestic violence. They use a systems approach to develop a model that looks to increase the collective efficacy of a community to reduce violence. Social ties, local organizational ties, and ties with state and federal agencies all can build multilevel bonds that increase the shared resources within a community to reduce violence.

Community-based violence prevention programs often follow a public health model like the one outlined by the Center of Disease Control and Prevention (CDC, 2007). With the US Surgeon General's declaration that violent behavior is a public health priority in 1979 the CDC has developed a focus on building a case for violence prevention by conducting research and synthesizing the scientific results to implement its Division of Violence Prevention (DVP). The mission of the DVP is to stop violence in the United States using a four-step public health approach that includes (1) defining the problem, (2) identifying the risk and protective factors, (3) developing and testing prevention strategies, and (4) assuring widespread adoption. The types of violence that are monitored by the CDC consist of child maltreatment, intimate partner violence, sexual violence, suicide, and youth violence (e.g., bullying, dating abuse, school violence and deaths, and nonfatal injuries due to violence).

Nonviolence Education

Nonviolence education programs are specifically designed to teach people to behave in a nonviolent way. These programs draw on the lives and work of nonviolent activists and great peacemakers like Mohandas Gandhi, Martin Luther King Jr., Jesus Christ, the Buddha, and other religious leaders to serve as models for participants behavior. Nonviolence education does deal with different forms of violence, enemy images, and the role of the media in perpetuating violence, however, the overarching orientation of this approach is to develop positive images of peace and a deep understanding of the power of truth and nonviolence (Harris, 1999a).

Harris (1999a) describes an example of a K-12 nonviolence education program as the *Voices of Love and Freedom* curriculum. This curriculum like other nonviolence prevention programs is designed to counter the culture of violence on so many levels in our societies by providing students with images of positive peace. These images include resolving conflicts with win–win solutions, developing positive social skills and values, living on a sustainable planet, and having human needs met. Harris (1999b) reports nonviolence education to have had positive effects on students. Parents reported their children had fewer emotional outbursts, stayed out of fights, and followed rules of fairness more often after attending a summer nonviolence education institute.

Peace Education Programs

Harris (1988), Harris and Morrison (2003), Hicks (1988), Raviv, Oppenheimer, and Bar-Tal (1999) Reardon (1988a), and Bjerstedt (1997) provide comprehensive overviews of the general field of peace education. However, the roots of the field may be traced back to before the common era.

Brief History of Peace Education

The notion that education might potentially play a role in making the world more peaceful and less warlike dates back several millennia. Renna (1980) points to the Golden Age of Greece to see the early linkage between education and war. He interprets Plato as having proposed "civil peace was a moral effect of proper education (p. 61)." He cites some of the ideas of Aristotle as being consistent with peace education and notes the views of the Stoics plus Cicero and other Roman thinkers to support the principle that education might lead to peace as well. Renna traces this intermittent line of thinking consistent with development of peace education through the humanist tradition during the Renaissance when the belief that education is a useful method of preparing for positive citizenship consistent with peace.

Comenius, a seventeenth century Czech educator, is credited with being one of the first European peace educators because he believed that universally shared knowledge would move society towards peace (Harris, 2002b). In response to the 30 years war Comenius held out hope that the public education of all social classes might precipitate the needed social reform required to avert war (Renna, 1980). Immanuel Kant, the eighteenth century German philosopher, also provided some of the underpinnings of peace education when he wrote that war was a result of human action and not a natural or divinely determined occurrence (Vriens, 1999). Harris describes the thesis of Kant's book, *Perpetual Peace*, as the claim that people might move closer to a peaceful world by creating the legal and judicial systems to resolve conflict. While Kant and other philosophers of his time laid the philosophical foundation for the peace education that emerged in the twentieth century, they did not advocate specific actions themselves (Renna).

While the state of the world during the nineteenth century worked against advances toward peace education, the twentieth century is characterized by a significant growth in peace education (e.g. Fink, 1980; Renna, 1980). Many individuals during the twentieth century both advocated an educational intervention to bring about a more peaceful world and developed specific interventions consistent with their writings. World War I was an impetus for the development of peace education as many reacted to the atrocities of the carnage. Eminent educational philosopher and psychologist, John Dewey, was moved to a position of pacifism following World War I and encouraged the public school system to be organized and structured following democratic principles (Renna). Harris (1999a, 2002b) points to the writings and work of the Italian educator, Maria Montessori, as a person who tried to convince people to use peace education as a method of averting the tragedy created by the fascists in Europe. By structuring the educational environment in the classroom so students did not follow an authoritarian leader, Montessori believed she would graduate students who, as citizens, would not blindly follow an authoritarian leader within government and would be discerning citizens.

Defining Peace Education

There are many ways to define and conceptualize peace education. Generally speaking, peace education is "educating people to learn to live in a cooperative world, to learn to manage the inevitable conflicts that occur in a constructive rather than destructive way (Coleman & Deutsch, 2001, p. 224)." Vriens (1999) views peace education as an educational process in which an ideal view of peace in the future is balanced against an understanding of the child's current life situation. Harris (2002a) considers peace education as an educational intervention with an international or global orientation designed to create a "more tolerant and less bloody world order based on mutual respect, nonviolence, justice, and environmental sustainability (p. 28)." In addition to developing an awareness of the negative results of using violence to deal with problems, peace education instructs students about peace behaviors and strategies and their effectiveness in reducing violence in the world (Harris, 2004). To Harris (2002b) peace educators want more than just to advocate an end to violence. They want to foster an understanding of and a deep belief in the merits of a positive peace (the absence of violence combined with the presence of social justice and equality). Johnson and Johnson (2006) see the institutionalization of peace education in schools to be critical in fostering and maintaining a consensual peace.

Peace education may take the form of a specific curriculum with formal lessons like any other school subject or it may be infused into existing courses in a relatively seamless fashion. Regardless of the approach, peace education must consider the developmental levels and cognitive skills of the students it is designed to reach (Hakvoort, 2002). Formal curricular approaches have been developed for kindergarten through college. Descriptions of these formal curricula may be found in articles by Bickmore (1999), Cardella and Van Slyck (1999), Jones (2004), and

Nelson, Van Slyck, and Cardella (1999a). Reardon (1988b) provides specific examples of teacher-designed peace education activities and lessons that are appropriate for grades K-3, 4–6, 7–9, and 10–12.

Johnson and Johnson (2006) outline five characteristics that are essential if peace education is to have a maximal impact in fostering a consensual positive peace. In order to institutionalize peace we must (1) establish compulsory public education, (2) establish a mutual and positive interdependence between a peaceful society and the process of teaching students cooperation and skills needed to act peacefully in a cooperative way, (3) teach students to practice peaceful political discourse on real world issues, (4) teach skills in integrative negotiations and mediation, and (5) teach civil values at a deep level. Johnson and Johnson view peace education as content and process based. Using cooperative pedagogy enhances the positive interdependence and achievement of content goals in peace education. They advocate the use of controversy within an academic setting to build skills needed to make difficult decisions. The approach they promote here is based on their theory of constructive controversy (Avery, Johnson, Johnson, & Mitchell, 1999; Johnson & Johnson, 1979) that is based on decades of research to support it.

The infusion of peace education goals may be accomplished within nearly any subject matter at any educational level. For instance Bickmore discusses the infusion of conflict resolution skills by Adalbjarnadóttir in Icelandic elementary schools. In this application, students were engaged in discussion via open-ended questions in which teachers modeled positive strategies to deal with problems. Wagner and Bonzaft (1987) and Nelson and Christie (1995) highlight numerous ways to infuse peace education topics into the psychology curriculum at the college level. Examples are provided for usage in introduction to psychology, developmental psychology, learning theory, social psychology, personality, motivation, cognition, and the biological basis of behavior. Their approach could easily be followed to identify ways to infuse peace concepts into courses of any of the social sciences.

Peace education in schools may be an implicit part of the school day that is outside of the formal curriculum. Bickmore (1999) has highlighted several aspects of the implicit curricula of student activities, school governance, discipline practices, and any other informal interactions in school that teach students about peace, violence, and how best to resolve violence. She puts forward a strong argument that even without a formal peace education curriculum, peace education is part of the school and a formal curriculum may even be very counterproductive in developing effective skills to reduce violence and a positive view of peace.

Conceptualizing Peace Education

Peace educators conceptualize their discipline using markedly different foci and place peace education in strikingly different locations among the structural hierarchy of related concepts. Whereas Jones (2004) views CRE as a related but distinct intervention to peace education, Harris (2002b) views CRE as one of five types of peace education. For Harris peace education subsumes not only conflict resolution programs but also global peace education, violence prevention programs, developmental education, and nonviolence education as well. For Jones peace education is more focused on international issues than CRE and is more akin to Harris' global peace education.

Bar-Tal (2002) considers peace education to be elusive and condition dependent whereby it varies in terms of ideology and the context that exists within different countries. While all peace education is designed to make the world a better place, Bar-Tal places peace education within the political–societal–economic priorities for a given society. Thus the objectives, content, emphasis, and specific curricula for peace education may be expected to vary depending on the cultural and national milieu. Regardless of the context, peace education should be open-minded, relevant, and experiential according to Bar-Tal.

Many have realized that the goals and general nature of peace education has varied depending on the time of its implementation. Vriens (1999) notes that the peace education programs shifted as concerns of peace researchers changed to best reflect the perceptions of world events and future concerns. The content of peace education after World War I was very different from the content of peace education after World War II because there were radically different causes for the conflicts and dynamic differences in the number and strength of the nations who were players on the world stage. As the Cold War developed, intensified, and ended over the next four decades peace education shifted from concerns about nuclear fear, stopping the nuclear arms race, and the devastation of a nuclear war and nuclear winter, to more of an increased concern about reducing structural violence, increasing social justice at home and abroad, and achieving positive peace in the world.

Harris (1999a, 2002b, 2004) notes that the nature of peace education varies across different societies and cultures depending on the types of violence needing to be reduced. Because the causes of violence are numerous and the types of violence are also large, the goals of peace education must vary in complex ways to address the complexities of the violence of specific concern. Peace education designed to reduce violence between students is and should be different from peace education designed to reduce structural violence within a community. Peace education designed to reduce prejudice and increase tolerance among ethnic groups likewise is and should be different from education programs intended to increase awareness of environmental concerns and the need for sustainable development. Thus some peace education follows the peacekeeping orientation, some the peacemaking orientation, and some the peacebuilding orientation.

Peace education referred to as having a peacekeeping orientation by Harris (2002b) is similar to the negative peacemaking approach described by Bickmore (1999). This type of peace education might have a local (classroom, school, or community) or global focus. If locally oriented, this approach would stress developing and enforcing school rules to assure safety and control in the prevention of violence. Bickmore describes some of these programs to teach students to be polite and disciplined and while this is important for the smooth functioning of the school at some level, she notes that students may avoid conflicts since they have not learned how to be active in handling them. Bickmore adds that the control aspects of this approach may have the negative effect of reinforcing mistrust among students when it is forced upon them. This is especially the case when schools use metal detectors and weapons searches, security guards and police on school grounds, zero tolerance policies, suspensions and expulsions, and other severe punishments to intimidate students to refrain from violence (Harris, 2004). If peace education with a peacekeeping focus is globally oriented, it might stress national security systems, international organizations and law, as well as the importance of diplomatic relations (Harris, 2002b). Perkins (2002) warns of the paradox that due to the power structure needed for the implementation of peacekeeping mechanisms, war may actually be encouraged, albeit in a different form, by peacekeeping actions that are threatening. This paradox may be a real problem for peace education of this type.

Peace educators using a peacemaking orientation address ways to avoid and resolve violence. Harris (2002b) indicates this method might involve implementing a peer mediation program to teach students to resolve conflicts in a constructive manner, empathy training, or other conflict resolution strategies to deal with interpersonal violence. Harris (2004) relates the effectiveness of this approach to the effectiveness of sex education programs. Just like adolescents may understand at a cognitive level how to employ safe sex practices yet may not use them when their passions are fully aroused, students who are trained via a peacemaking approach may not be able to apply learned principles in the heat of a dispute.

By assuming problems of violence are grounded in society and not within youth the goal of the peacebuilding approach to peace education is empowerment and personal transformation by building upon the peaceful predispositions within students (Harris, 2004). This approach is designed to create a deep desire for positive peace (Harris, 2002b). Harris stresses the need for a democratically run classroom for this concept to be fully practiced and understood by students. Bickmore (1999) characterizes this democratic classroom experience as a positive liberty approach that is critical for the development of strong citizens. This is facilitated when the teacher is authoritative but not authoritarian.

Regional Context for Peace Education

Salomon (2002) makes a convincing case that peace education appropriate for one part of the world or one regional context may not be appropriate for another region at all. He argues "that neither scholarly nor practical progress can take place in the absence of clear conceptions of what peace education is and what goals it is to serve (p. 3)."

Salomon (2002) outlines three categories of peace education in which each have different assumptions, different challenges, different goals, and different methods for treating their subgroups of participants. One category of peace education would be more likely delivered in regions of relative tranquility. A second category would be delivered in regions where interethnic tensions are strong. The other category of peace education would be delivered in regions where there are intractable conflicts such as Israel, Northern Ireland, and Bosnia/Herzegovina. Each type of peace education will be discussed in this order.

Peace education in regions of relative tranquility may be viewed as education "about peace" since there are no immediate and recognizable enemy or outgroup (Salomon, 2002). Without the need to work toward reconciliation with a past and present known adversary Salomon characterizes the purpose of this type of peace education is to attain a nonviolent disposition along with a set of conflict resolution skills. He would place violence prevention programs, peer mediation programs, and conflict resolution programs based in the schools that were previously discussed into this category.

Peace education in regions where interethnic tensions are strong have different goals and generally addresses human rights issues to alleviate the tension between groups (Salomon, 2002). While this type of peace education is common in Third World countries where majority–minority tensions based on ethnic or tribal tension have a lengthy history, Salomon points out that this approach has been employed in developed countries where interethnic conquest, humiliation, and hostilities have occurred. He cited the situations in Belgium, Germany, and the United States as examples.

Peace education in intractable regions works to change the mindsets of participants by developing an understanding, respect, and tolerance of one's adversaries (Salomon, 2002). As Cairns and Hewstone (2002) found in their work in Northern Ireland, this means more than having contact with one's adversary. Oftentimes this requires addressing the "us versus them" mentality by reducing the impact of the destructive ethnic, tribal, or religious narratives. Salomon notes the importance of understanding one's own narratives, as well as, the narratives of one's adversary to break the hold that collective memories of past-atrocities have on the current perceptions of victimhood. The learning of narratives through the interaction with family and other social institutions needs to be directly countered by peace education so the parties involved can experience the present context of the conflict with new insights.

Salomon (2002) regards peace education in intractable conflict regions as the superordinate category of peace education that subsumes the goals, principles, and activities of the other two types. In other words, peace education in intractable conflicts needs to include unique components that go beyond what peace education addresses in other contexts. Specifically, peace education in intractable conflict faces three additional challenges whereby "(a) it faces a conflict that is between collectives, not between individuals; (b) it faces a conflict that is deeply rooted in collective narratives that entail a long and painful shared memory of the past; and (c) it faces a conflict that entails grave inequalities (Salomon, p. 7)." When a conflict is between collectives and not individuals, the preventative strategies appropriate to resolve conflicts between individuals are no longer relevant. When someone has a deep-seated hostility with an unjust government led by outgroup members, the person really has no quarrel with specific neighbors who are only members of the outgroup that is in power. Salomon illustrates this with the account of a Basque youth who does not view his Spanish peer living in the neighborhood as his enemy but does view the domination of the Basques by the Spanish government as terribly wrong. These feeling in intractable conflicts are fueled by collective stories or narratives that are passed down, sometimes for many, many generations, through socialization processes that include parents and family, school curricula and text-books, political figures, and the media. Each side of an intractable conflict owns a collective narrative that is distinctly different from the other side in critical ways. Markedly different interpretations of well-documented historical events keep opposite sides of conflict from establishing common ground. This situation is further exacerbated by the reality that there are, oftentimes, severe inequalities between the sides of the conflict. Whether these inequalities are a result of the power differential of minority–majority relations, socioeconomic status, indigenous populations and their newcomer/conquerors, Salomon believes the two sides need to be approached differently to best meet their needs that are challenged by the intractable conflict.

Salomon (2002, 2006) and Salomon and Nevo (2002) acknowledge when the differential between the two sides of an intractable conflict is really large, the asymmetry may create large hurdles to overcome and such difficulties if too great might in fact preclude the use of peace education as a viable option in resolving the issues. When excessive emotions, fear, animosity, and even belligerence are thrown into the mix, peaceful resolutions seem more and more difficult (Salomon, 2004).

Salomon (2002) has developed goals for peace education for intractable conflicts based on the principles just discussed. The overarching goal is to change the perceptions of the collective narratives held by the other side. Many times the parties in an intractable conflict know the others' collective narrative but that is not enough. Perceptions need to change considerably before peace education in this context can be successful. Salomon delineates four interconnected subgoals to accomplish the needed perceptual change. First, the collective narrative of the others must be legitimized and accepted. As Salomon stresses, acceptance does not mean liking, but implies giving the others narrative a sense of validity. Second, a critical examination of ones' own contribution to the intractable conflict must be completed. Salomon supports a process that moves individuals whose groups have inflicted pain to learn to accept some collective guilt even if the pain was inflicted on the others in previous generations. Third, empathy for the suffering of the others in the conflict needs to be fostered. Being able to empathize and appreciate the suffering that has been endured by the opposing group in the conflict is an important emotional goal. Fourth, each side must learn to engage the other with nonviolent means. By developing a nonviolent disposition toward the other side, Salomon sees this as a conscious decision to refrain from using violence to solve problems with the other and to seek agreement and solutions to problems that are conciliatory with the other.

Academic Controversies in Peace Education

There are times when conflict can be positive or constructive for the people involved in it (Deutsch, 1973). David W. and Roger T. Johnson and their colleagues have developed strategies for peace education that uses intellectual controversies within classrooms to stimulate students to develop the skills needed to resolve conflicts and to develop a motivation to deal directly with conflicts that arise in their lives.

Johnson, Johnson, and Tjosvold, (2000) describe constructive controversy as an experience where "one person's ideas, information, conclusions, theories, and opinions are incompatible with those of another, and the two seek to reach an agreement (p. 66)." To facilitate constructive controversy a cooperative goal structure needs to be established among students who have conflict management skills already.

The fruit of a constructive controversy or academic controversy, as it is also called, begins to develop when the students work to understand their positions more fully, prepare their arguments, present their arguments, and try to reach an agreement (Avery et al., 1999). Avery et al. indicate that these academic controversies might involve just about any topic or subject. Once a conflict is presented to students, they suggest that a teacher might guide student through the following steps. These are "(1) researching and preparing a position, (2) presenting and advocating their position, (3) engaging in an open discussion in which they refute the opposing position and rebut attacks on their own position, (4) reversing perspectives, and (5) synthesizing and integrating the best evidence and reasoning into a joint position (p. 264–265)."

Constructive controversy or academic controversy is an effective strategy in peace education at multiple grade levels in North America and overseas (Avery et al., 1999; Johnson & Johnson, 1995b; Johnson et al., 2000). In addition to a greater mastery and retention of the information surrounding the selected controversy this strategy builds more positive attitudes toward conflict and "implicitly teaches students how to maintain peace (Avery et al., p. 269)."

Evaluating Peace Education

Harris (2004) directly addresses the need for strong evaluation research on the impact of peace education. In documenting the push for peace education evaluation Harris notes the pressures that come from educational researchers, peace researchers, policy makers, public school teachers and administrators, and the general public that is providing financial support. Because of the complexities of the types of peace education programs and their varied goals, the need for multiple methodologies to assess the effectiveness of peace education is paramount. The ultimate question to be answered in evaluating peace education is "After learning about peace, do people become more peaceful or do they work for peace and hence does the intensity of violence in a given conflict reduce? (Harris, p. 18)"

Nevo and Brem (2002) provide a model to categorize peace education programs as a vehicle to summarize the results of evaluation research. Based on Guttman's facet theory, they provide a six-facet taxonomy to classify peace education research. Facet A addresses the purpose of the research which may entail efforts to either enhance certain variables like tolerance, conflict resolution skills, empathy and others or to reduce certain variables like prejudice, delinquency, violence, etc. Facet B is the age of the participants and this includes elementary school age, junior high, senior high, and college age students. Facet C addresses the didactic approach used within the peace education curriculum. These included lectures by teachers and students, watching videos, movies, and listening to tapes, writing essays, and mixed group sessions with the "other" in an ongoing conflict that may include structured meetings or open discussions. Facet D is the duration of the program that might vary from a few hours to a few years. Facet E addresses the type of research design employed in the evaluation research while Facet F addresses the type of outcome measure utilized.

A careful and thorough review of all journal articles, books and book chapters, reports, and convention papers between 1981 and 2000 enabled Nevo and Brem (2002) to find 79 peace education evaluation studies. While the small number of studies and insufficient information in the studies kept them from employing their taxonomy, they were able to look at the statistical significance of the outcomes in these peace education evaluations. Nearly two-thirds of the analyses (51 of 79) were statistically significant and for a little less that a quarter of the programs (18 of 79) some, but not all, outcome variables were significant. The remaining 12.7% of the evaluations in their analysis showed no effectiveness at all. Nevo and Brem conclude by saying that, even though they have some methodological reservations, the results are encouraging as it does appear that peace education programs do have positive effects.

Nelson, Van Slyck, and Cardella (1999a, 1999b) report the results of curricular reviews of five peace education programs designed for use in secondary schools. Each was analyzed by peace educators or peace psychologists to determine the program's grade-level appropriateness and the relative importance of concepts and goals included in the curriculum as compared to priorities set by peace psychologists. The *Making Choices About Conflict, Security, and Peacemaking: A High School Conflict Resolution Curriculum* by Lieber (1998) is a 399-page teachers manual that describes 81 different activities and was determined to be appropriate for grades 9–12 and to have a "considerable impact" on students' knowledge about interpersonal conflict, critical thinking, and conflict resolution competencies. The *Workbook for the Course in Peaceful Conflict Resolution "Alternatives to Violence"* by Looney (1995) is a 372-page workbook that provides case studies and analysis guidelines and was determined to be most appropriate for 11th and 12th graders. Reviewers viewed this curriculum as having the potential for a considerable effect on knowledge about interpersonal conflict, international conflict, and peacebuilding. It is also expected to have a strong impact on attitudes toward peace and justice. Both peace education curricula were adequate in their treatment of psychological content and issues and addressed active listening, empathy, problem solving, and integrative negotiations at reasonable levels, too. Nelson et al. (1999b) also describe over a half dozen more peace education programs that they did not have reviewed by their panel of experts but look promising to them.

Cardella and Van Slyck (1999) followed the same procedures of Nelson et al. (1999a) and asked a group of peace educators and peace psychologists to review a half dozen peace education curricula designed for usage in middle schools or junior highs. They provide both the critical reviews and constructive discussions of how existing programs might be improved by users. *Conflict Resolution in the Middle School* (Kriedler, 1997) and *Creating the Peaceable School* (Bodine, Crawford, &

Schrumpf, 1994) were both reviewed as comprehensive programs with the first taking a strong positive focus and the latter having a human needs orientation. Despite the generally good evaluations of these two programs neither these nor the others seemed fully adequate as stand-alone curricula and Van Slyck and Stern (1999) suggest that peace educators utilize more than one curriculum at a time so the strengths of one might offset the weaknesses of another.

A considerable obstacle that peace education must tackle is the reality that many events in the world and the actions of many prominent leaders run counter to the principles that are taught in peace curricula. Harris (2004) highlights the frustrations this makes for peace educators who stress human rights only to see the world community turn their back on genocides and other human rights violations or who speak about the dangers of war as nations continue to engage in civil wars or start wars with other nations. On this point Harris cogently states "Peace education does not pretend radically to change the pupils' attitudes in the course of a few lessons. It considers itself one of the factors on a long-term process of transforming ways of thinking. And it will only produce any real effect if an international solidarity is advocated by politicians or at any rate by important and influential groups in society (p. 27)." The key to the success of these preventative efforts to make the world a peaceful place is the long-term commitment.

Salomon (2006) laments the lack of research on the effectiveness of peace education in intractable conflicts. While the hurdles to be overcome in evaluating this type of peace education are huge, Salomon strikes a chord when he says the needs are great too. Whether the observed changes precipitated through peace education are deep or peripheral attitudes and beliefs, he thinks the hard task for peace education in intractable conflicts can be meaningful.

Concluding Comments on Interpersonal Nonviolence

Several personality characteristics and behavioral tendencies are related to interpersonal nonviolence. People who are agreeable, trusting, forgiving, and cooperative have predispositions to be nonviolent in interpersonal relationships. While only a limited body of research exists to support NVC, this approach to interpersonal relations based on listening empathically and communicating feelings, needs, and requests honestly seems very promising.

Conflict resolution approaches are many and range from negotiation to mediation to conciliation to arbitration to adjudication. The approaches fall along a continuum from the less formal and less expensive to the most formal and most expensive. Integrative negotiations and principled negotiations have extensive support in the literature. So does mediation.

Numerous preventative approaches were presented to assure nonviolence is maintained within interpersonal relationships. Not only is there considerable overlap between CRE, SEL, peer mediation, violence prevention programs, nonviolence education, and peace education, but many researchers, theorists, and practitioners conceptualize each differently. While this makes clear distinctions between these preventative methods problematic, the research available does show that these approaches do have research support regardless of how they are categorized. Many components of CRE and peace education do have empirical support. Successful interventions appropriate for kindergarten through college students are available for educators.

Recommended Readings

Deutsch, M., & Coleman, P. T. (Eds.) (2000). *The handbook of conflict resolution: Theory and practice*. San Francisco, CA: Jossey-Bass Publishers.

Deutsch and Coleman have compiled the best handbook of the theory and practice of conflict resolution to date. This book has a strong research focus yet is balanced nicely by issues relevant to practitioners using many methods of conflict resolution across a wide range of conflict types. Regardless of your current understanding of the field of conflict resolution, there is much to be gained from the 27 chapters in this handbook. Topics covered include cooperation-competition, negotiation, mediation, social justice, trust, culture, biases, and many more areas relevant to conflict resolution.

Fisher, R., & Ury, W. with Patton, B. (1991). *Getting to yes: Negotiating agreement without giving in. (2nd Ed.)* New York: Penguin Books.

This is the classic book on negotiation that presents a clear method of negotiation that has been shown to be successful in a wide variety of conflicts. This national bestseller is an easy read and is full of concrete examples to help the reader fully understand the processes of principled negotiation. This is a must read by anyone wishing to understand and become a skilled negotiator.

Jones, T. S. (2004). Conflict resolution education: The field, the findings, and the future. *Conflict Resolution Quarterly*, 22 (1–2), 233&267.

Jones presents an excellent overview of the field of conflict resolution education and outlines the major components addressed by this approach. After delineating the relationship between conflict resolution education and related fields, Jones thoroughly reviews the research and meta-analyses on conflict resolution education, peer mediation, social and emotional learning, bullying prevention and other related methods over the past few decades.

Picard, C. A. (2002). *Mediating interpersonal and small group conflict*. Ottawa, ON: The Golden Dog Press.

Picard outlines a useful conflict resolution continuum that helps understand the relationships between many types of conflict resolution methods used in reducing interpersonal and small group conflicts. A theory of mediation is developed and considerable attention is given to elucidating the practice of mediation. This book outlines and explains many of the skills and strategies used in mediation and conflict management.

Pruitt, D. G., & Carnevale, P. J. (1993). *Negotiation in social conflict*. Pacific Grove, CA: Brooks/ Cole Publishing Company.

Pruitt and Carnevale provide a strong overview of the dynamics of the process of negotiation. This research-based book carefully analyzes negotiation from a psychological perspective. The social norms, group processes, relationships among negotiating parties, and cognitive process are addressed in their discussion of negotiation and mediation in a variety of settings.

Rosenberg, M. B. (2003). *Nonviolent communication; A language of life*. Encinitas, CA: Puddle Dancer Press

Rosenberg describes a process of nonviolent communication that he teaches in workshops around the world. This excellent book effectively uses many examples to make this approach come alive and to make it easily accessible to the reader. Nonviolent communication can be helpful in improving many types of relationships by building mutual respect, compassion, and cooperation.

Salomon, G., & Nevo, B. (Eds.) (2002). *Peace education: The concept, principles, and practices around the world*. Mahwah, NJ: Lawrence Erlbaum Associates, Publishers.

This edited volume includes entries by major researchers and practitioners within the field of peace education. In addition to fully addressing the components, principles, and theory of peace education this book includes articles on the practice of peace education in a wide variety of countries and types of conflicts. Examples included span Israel, Northern Ireland, Rwanda, Croatia, Cyprus, Belgium, and South Africa.

Recommended Websites

Association for Conflict Resolution (ACR), http://www.acrnet.org/

The ACR is a professional organization that encourages the use of conflict resolutions skills in many contexts. Its membership is international and it includes mediators, arbitrators, educators, and other professionals engaged in conflict resolutions activities. The organization has conflict resolution internships in Washington, DC available to graduate students and advanced undergraduate students. Internships receive a "modest stipend." There are also volunteer activities possible through ACR. The ACR online bookstore has many reports, books and videos on conflict resolution for sale.

Center for the Prevention of School Violence (CPSV), http://www.ncdjjdp.org/cpsv/, http://www.ncdjjdp.org/cpsv/toolkit/index.html

The CPSV Web site provides a wealth of information on School Violence Prevention. Clicking on the toolkit option brings up a seven phase plan schools can use to help them in implementing a programs designed to find alternatives to suspending or expelling children who have committed acts in school considered to be violent, as well as various other infractions. The idea behind this program is that suspending or expelling children who commit minor acts of violence from school may not be the best discipline to undertake, and also that schools are in the best position to educate children about school violence.

Center for the Study and Prevention of Violence (CSPV), http://www.colorado.edu/cspv/safeschools/programs/overview.html

The CSPV has evaluated the efficacy of various violence prevention programs. Their top tier, Blueprints Model Programs, have passed their difficult tests for program effectiveness. The lower tier, Blueprint Promising Programs, have met some of the criteria for the model programs. Clicking on the Model Programs link brings the reader to a list of links for programs designed to reduce violence as well as substance abuse. Some of the violence prevention programs included in this tier Life Skill Training (LST), Promoting Alternative Thinking Strategies (PATHS), Functional Family Therapy (FFT), and Multisystemic Therapy (MST). Likewise, clicking on the Promising Programs Link brings up a list of links to programs that have shown promise the search for effective violence prevention programs.

Collaborative for Academic, Social, and Emotional Learning (CASEL), http://www.casel.org/home.php

The mission of CASEL is to establish social and emotional learning (SEL) as an integral part of public education. The Web site of this nonprofit organization allows you to access their newsletters, reports, articles, and publications about SEL and recent research, powerpoint presentations and general FAQs about SEL. Anyone interested in learning more about SEL and applying SEL into a classroom would find this organization and this Web site very valuable.

Conflict Resolution Education Connection. Retrieved September 13, 2007 from http://www.creducation.org/cre/home.

Conflict Resolution Education Connection (CRE) addresses conflict resolution for the following areas: researchers, policymakers, administrators, and global connections. This organization is mainly concerned with reaching global expectations for conflict resolution techniques. CRE addresses bullying, current research, peer mediation, cultural aspects and international successes.

Conflict Resolution Network. Retrieved September 13, 2007 from http://crnhq.org/index.html.
This Web site provides numerous resources dealing with conflict resolution. CRN encourages the use of their materials through their free training downloads. These consist of games, skills summaries, manuals, etc. In addition, this Web site includes resources that deal with ideas of conflict resolution and inspirations of conflict resolution. I felt this Web site was useful because it is less focused on the educational purposes of conflict resolution. Rather this Web site portrays conflict resolution from a government or society based perspective.

Educators for Social Responsibility. Retrieved September 13, 2007 from http://www.esrnational.org.
This Web site provides information for all K-12 educators. It is a great site to obtain knowledge on providing the skills to produce a learning environment that fosters peace. This Web site offers an online store and also an online teacher center where one can purchase classroom materials relevant to peer mediation, conflict resolution, and other aspects of peace education.

Harvard Negotiation Project, Retrieved November 12, 2007 from http://www.pon.harvard.edu/hnp.
Since1979, the Harvard Negotiation Project's (HNP) has worked to improve the theory, teaching, and practice of negotiation and dispute resolution. The intention is to assist people in their ability to deal more constructively with interpersonal up to international conflicts. This website provides links to research and theory papers, summary guides for researchers, educators, and practitioners in the field negotiation, radio and television interviews with HNP staff, as well as, overviews and updates on conflicts around the world.

National Youth Violence Prevention Center, http://www.safeyouth.org
The Safe Youth Web site offers a cornucopia of information related to youth violence in general, as well as more specific topics such as bullying and other violence in schools. Clicking on the school violence topic link takes the reader to a page filled with articles about anything from elements of successful school based violence prevention plans to advice on how a teacher should handle a violent student and how parents can help to reduce school violence. While in the school violence topic, the reader can click on the Federal Activities Addressing Violence in School subtopic and be taken to a page filled with links to studies and research evaluating a variety of school based violence intervention programs.

Peaceful Solution Character Education, Inc. Retrieved September 13, 2007 from http://www.peacefulsolution.org/index.html.
The Peaceful Solution Character Education Incorporated (PSCEI) is a nonprofit organization that reaches out to educational facilities including public and private schools, home schooling, and the parenting process plus prison systems. The PSCEI type of approach is different because it provides an opportunity to take peace education in all facets of life. The programs PSCEI offer are currently being used in foreign countries such as Canada, Israel, Mexico to name a few. Lastly, this Web site offers many links to workshops, trainings, and conferences available in your area.

Southern Poverty Law Center, http://www.splcenter.org/index.jsp
The Southern Poverty Law Center has grown from a small law office supporting civil rights to a multifaceted organization that addresses human rights and building tolerance throughout society. Founded by Morris Dees and Joel Leven, two lawyers committed to racial equality, in Montgomery AL, this organization has pursued law suits to break up and limit the reach of hate groups like the Aryan Nations, KKK, etc., monitors hate crimes around the country and publishes them in their *Intelligence Report* (http://www.splcenter.org/intel/intelreport/intrep.jsp), and has embarked on a K-12 educational program *Teaching Tolerance* (http://www.tolerance.org/teach/index.jsp). Their Hate Groups Map (http://www.splcenter.org/intel/map/hate.jsp) is very informative as well.

Violence Prevention at the Centers for Disease Control (CDC), http://www.cdc.gov/ncipc/dvp/dvp.htm
The Centers for Disease Control and Prevention has a specific center dealing with violence prevention in the United States. The Violence Prevention Division of CDC is committed to

stopping violence before it happens. Violence prevention is specifically directed at child mal-treatment, intimate partner violence, sexual violence, school shooting, suicide, and youth violence.

Virginia Best Practices in School-Based Violence Prevention, http://www.pubinfo.vcu.edu/VaBP/, http://www.pubinfo.vcu.edu/VaBP/best_practice_listsGo.asp?eid=4, Retrieved November 12, 2007.

This Web site offers a variety of school-based violence prevention programs. The programs are scored as either effective, model, promising, or noteworthy and brief information about the programs is provided. Hundreds of school-based violence prevention programs are reviewed in this manner.

Chapter 6
Cultural and Societal Perspectives of Nonviolence

We pray that peoples of all faiths, all races, all nations,
may have their great human needs satisfied; that those now
denied opportunity shall come to enjoy it to the full; that all
who yearn for freedom may experience its spiritual blessings;
that those who have freedom will understand, also, its heavy
responsibilities; that all who are insensitive to the needs of
others will learn charity; that the scourges of poverty, disease
and ignorance will be made to disappear from the earth, and
that, in the goodness of time, all peoples will come to live
together in a peace guaranteed by the binding force of mutual
respect and love
Dwight D. Eisenhower, cited in Ambrose, 2003, p. 124

This chapter focuses on nonviolence at the cultural or societal levels. Specifically, this chapter is organized around the concept of "cultures of peace." Numerous cultures have been identified and studied that have historically embraced nonviolence. I will initially discuss these peaceful cultures along with the features that have helped these societies to primarily utilize nonviolent behavior over violent alternatives. Next, the UN resolutions on cultures of peace and the eight key values (respect all life, reject violence, share with others, listen to understand, preserve the planet, rediscover solidarity, work for women's equality, participate in democracy) are presented and analyzed. Representative psychological and sociological research to support the development of components of cultures of peace is reviewed as well. The role of gender issues in the understanding of nonviolence at the societal level will be intertwined throughout the discussion of cultural issues of peace. A concise bibliography of readings for each component within the framework of a culture of peace is included.

Peaceful Societies

Many anthropologists and social scientists have studied peaceful cultures and peaceful societies (Bonta, 1993, 1997; Montagu, 1978; Sponsel & Gregor, 1994). While there is not a consensus on the criteria for a culture or society to be classified

D.M. Mayton II, *Nonviolence and Peace Psychology*,
DOI 10.1007/978-0-387-89348-8_6, © Springer Science + Business Media, LLC 2009

as peaceful or nonviolent, Bonta (1996) does provide a workable set of guidelines for classification. For a society to be viewed as peaceful, low-conflict, or nonviolent (words used interchangeably in this context), it should be "characterized by [1] a relatively high degree of interpersonal harmony; [2] little if any physical violence among adults, between children and adults, and between the sexes; [3] workable strategies for resolving conflicts and averting violence; [4] a commitment to avoid violence (such as warfare) with other peoples; and [5] strategies for raising children to adopt and continue these nonviolent ways (Bonta, 1996, p. 405)."

Bonta (1993) indicates that 47 peaceful cultures have been identified around the world. These include the Amish, Hutterites, Inuit, Mennonites, and Zapotec of North America, the Piaroa of South America, the Fipa, G/wi, !Kung, and Nubians of Africa, the Buid, Lepchas, Nayaka, and Semai of Asia, and the Ifaluk and Tahitians of the Pacific Islands to name a few (Bonta, 1996, 1997). Even though these peaceful societies are able to solve their conflicts nonviolently, they should not be viewed as utopias as many contain practices and customs that people from other cultures would not want to endure. For instance the harshness of being completely shunned within an Amish community by everyone including neighbors, friends, and family, even one's children and spouse, would be extremely difficult to bear. However, all of the societies use nonviolent conflict resolution strategies based on a world-view that totally rejects violence and fully embraces nonviolence as a societal norm (Bonta, 1996).

Bonta (1996) analyzed 24 peaceful peoples to determine if their methods of conflict resolution are different than the approaches employed by people living in more violent societies. In his analysis Bonta tried to assume the perspective of the members of the nonviolent cultures and not interpret the conflict resolution methods with a Western world-view that considers conflict and violence as inevitable. He defined conflict resolution in this context as "the settlement or avoidance of disputes between individuals or groups of people through solutions that refrain from violence and that attempt to reunify and re-harmonize the people involved in the internal conflicts, or that attempts to preserve amicable relations with external societies (p. 406)." Bonta found that nonviolent societies did not believe that conflict was a normal or inevitable part of their everyday experience nor was direct negotiation a common practice. The commonly held belief that within these peaceful societies violent conflict is inevitable was dispelled by the realization that about one half of these societies had no recorded violence. He concluded that most nonviolent societies preferred indirect methods of communication and therefore individuals shied away from the direct confrontation involved in the negotiation process. He ascertained many peaceful peoples do seem to practice separation and self-restraint in moving away from possible conflicts. In addition Bonta determined that, oftentimes, peaceful cultures encouraged others to intervene between parties in a conflict and to encourage involvement in meetings to impersonally discuss the issues involved in a grievance. The structure of these meetings is not confrontational but generally allows all parties to present their case or position without a focus on blame or in some cases even mentioning names. Bonta was able to find very little evidence of punishment within peaceful societies. This absence of punishment was tempered by the existence of the use of social rejection or ostracism within several nonviolent cultures. The threat of ostracism was prominent and a powerful reality among the Amish and Ladakhi peoples among others.

One common assertion about peaceful societies is that they must be either very isolated or surrounded by nonaggressive neighboring states. While this is sometimes the case, Bonta (1996) points out that it is not the rule. When peaceful societies are confronted by aggressive neighboring states, they use the same nonviolent ways to deal with these conflicts as they do with internal conflicts. Raising an army, killing, or other forms of violence are not part of their responses. Thus, their very negative view of conflict is consistently applied with their culture and in their interaction with other cultures.

Bonta (1997) carefully analyzed information available on peaceful societies to determine their orientations toward competition. Of the 25 nonviolent societies for which relevant information was available, all but two associated competition with aggression and violence and had methods designed to discourage competition. Even though most peaceful societies shun competition, Bonta points out that the existence of the two peaceful societies that allow competition while maintaining their nonviolent ways means competition is not a sufficient cause for a society to approve of violence. Likewise, cooperation without competition is not a necessary condition for a nonviolent society to exist.

Understanding the processes that nonviolent societies use to provide continuity from generation to generation may be enlightening. Bonta (1997) has identified common child rearing practices in many of these societies. One widespread parenting technique is to change the status of 2–3 year olds from receiving constant attention from parents and having their needs quickly met to one in which the children have basic needs met but are no longer as special nor the center of attention that they were as infants. As Bonta points out, this shift communicates to the children that they are just one member of the community and they are not better than any one else. Thus, they learn they are dependent upon the good will and support of others in the community and are not able to control events the way they did as infants. Parents teach their children to be sensitive to other people's needs and to avoid assertive, aggressive, or disruptive behavior. By doing this Bonta notes that rebelliousness and independence from the group are minimized early, as children learn to be obedient and exercise self-control. Fry (1994) provides data for the rejection of physical punishment for disciplining children in a peaceful Zapotec village in Mexico and cites research that is consistent in six other peaceful societies. Fry notes the preference for more positive and more nonphysical responses for child transgressions in nonviolent societies. By explaining the consequences of misdeeds and communicating the importance of respect, cooperation, humility, and nonviolence to children who misbehave, Fry believes parents model the peaceful behaviors that are important for harmony in their community.

Peaceful societies that favor cooperation and oppose competition generally also favor humility and modesty and are against the recognition of individual achievement. Bonta (1997) describes how this lowers motivation and as a result minimizes situations that generate anger and foster violence. The opposition to the recognition of individual successes also reduces hierarchical thinking and status related problems. Even among Zapotec villagers who do behave competitively in their business dealings, the virtual lack of Machismo keeps the villagers from allowing conflicts to erupt in fights.

One interesting socialization process found in many peaceful societies involves building ambiguous feelings in children regarding social relationships (Bonta, 1997). Briggs (1994) speaks of the socialization process used by Inuits in Canada's Northwest Territories whereby parents question their children in eerie ways to encourage them to experience appropriate emotional reactions to different situations. For instance, Briggs recounts how a woman asks a young girl why she did not kill her baby brother whom she was carrying. This question communicates many important messages to the girl according to Briggs' analysis. The girl learns that the woman realizes that (1) the girl may want to kill her brother, (2) thoughts of killing are all right to talk about out loud, and (3) the woman trusted the girl not to kill her brother. Briggs sees the important realization for the little girl is to see that she likes taking care of her baby brother and does not really want to kill him. Bonta views these parent–child interactions as very fear arousing, but within the context of a culture that clearly expects a child to behave nonviolently, the ambiguities created by the uncertainties and fears raised puts children on guard to their emotions and to not offend others.

Among most nonviolent societies, even competitive games are not encouraged or practiced (Bonta, 1997). The games played within these societies generally involve cooperation and/or physical activities that are engaged in for pure enjoyment. Bonta found that when competitive games were brought into a nonviolent and cooperative society, the competitive components would be dropped.

Within peaceful or nonviolent societies, cooperation is clearly the dominant orientation (Bonta, 1997). While these societies generally, but not always, avoid competition and the recognition of individual achievements, the reasons for their nonviolent behaviors are most likely to be found in their worldviews and deep and primary commitment to nonviolence (Bonta, 1996, 1997). Because of the variability in the structure of the dozens of peaceful societies, it is difficult to extrapolate clear implications for less peaceful societies. However, Bonta (1996) concludes, "If the examples of the peaceful peoples have any validity, nonviolence has to be accepted as one of the highest ideals, one of the most strongly accepted beliefs, of today's societies.... The answer is for us to build, in our societies, world-views of peacefulness that are as strong as those of the peaceful peoples (p. 416)."

Nonviolent Activities and Norms in Less Peaceful Cultures

The need to understand other cultures and to learn from them is important (Kimmel, 2001). The insights from the realization that our norms are not sacrosanct and that other approaches are possible are of great consequence to personal growth and a positively evolving culture. Observations of peaceful cultures are therefore useful. Observations of some aspects of less peaceful cultures can also be illuminating in our understanding of peacefulness and nonviolence even if our discernment is more limited than observations of peaceful cultures.

Houar (1984) discusses the practice of nonkilling warfare among some North American Indian tribal groups. Among some Plains Indians, like the Sioux, a form of warfare with adversarial tribes was nonviolent and called "counting coup" from the French for touching the enemy. The goal of this type of battle was to accomplish daring feats and not to kill members of other tribes. "To touch an enemy, to enter battle unarmed and take an opponents weapon or horse was the highest feat of bravery one could accomplish (Houar, p. 50)."

Smith-Christopher (1998b) summarizes a range of nonviolent and peaceful indigenous traditions among Native American Indians. For instance members of the Hopi nation from the Southwestern section of the United States believe so strongly in nonviolence that many became conscientious objectors during times of war and mandatory conscription through a draft. In an interview with Lawrence Hart, a Cheyenne Indian chief, Smith-Christopher uncovers the commitment to peace of the Cheyenne people that is manifest in specific ceremonies. The Cheyenne bring many "peace chiefs" into a council in which specific rules are in place to encourage verbal nonviolence and to avoid arguments. The prohibition against revenge and violent reprisals was particularly strong. Hart indicates the peace chiefs "were not to engage in any quarrels within the tribe regardless of whether their families or children were involved. They were not to engage themselves in any force or violence, even if their son was killed right in front of their tee-pee (Smith-Christopher, p. 870)." The ceremony, which included the peace pipe, took clear precedence over their consciousness. While nonviolence is not a majority view among the Cheyenne, the interview reveals that there is a strong minority view represented among the peace chiefs that negotiation, mediation, and other nonviolent conflict resolution methods be used. Efforts are made for peace chiefs to teach about the nonviolent role models of the Cheyenne and nonviolent traditions that date back hundreds of years through story telling.

Cultures of Peace

Societies exist because of the activities and social institutions that sustain and shape them (Boulding, 2000b). Whether one believes that humans are inherently aggressive or inherently peaceable, most societies use a range of social institutions to support the use of violence and war by their citizens. Schools, churches, the military, and a range of government agencies encourage people to support war and believe in its successes by inculcating values, attitudes, and behaviors consistent with a culture of war. Boulding (2000a) furthers her argument for social learning to be marshaled to foster peace by citing the positions of Mead (1940) and Adams (1991). Mead contended that war was a human invention and not a biological imperative. Adams reported the outcome of a diverse group of scientists who developed the *Seville Statement on Violence* that concluded human beings are not genetically programmed to engage in war. Therefore, societies that are violent and prone to war have learned to behave that way.

The development of the concept of a culture of peace was a clear reaction to the realization that most people in the world reside in societies that can be characterized as cultures of violence and war. The phrase "culture of peace" has emerged as a powerful umbrella concept for a worldwide movement involving diverse organizations working for peace (Adams, 2000, 2003). Boulding (2000b) describes a culture of peace as a culture that includes "patterns of belief, values, behavior, and accompanying institutional arrangements that promote mutual caring and well-being as well as equality that includes appreciation of difference, stewardship, and equitable sharing of the earth's resources among its members and with all living things (p. 1)." For Boulding a peace culture promotes diversity and a peaceableness that is action oriented and is dynamic in shaping society to sustain the well being of its people. She believes achieving cultures of peace depends on our ability to imagine what this type of society would be like. Without an image of what a culture of peace looks like, Boulding deems the paradigm shift from a culture of war to a culture of peace to be a more difficult process. She derives optimism for the development of an image for cultures of peace from her late husband Kenneth's quote "What exists is possible (cited in Boulding, 1996, p. 40)." Since examples of small peaceful cultures throughout the world already exist as discussed earlier in this chapter, these can be useful seeds for imagining cultures of peace on a larger scale.

Even though most societies are a blend of warrior cultures and peaceable cultures, the balance of these two subcultures often times is heavily weighted in favor of violence and war (Boulding, 2000b). Driven by a need to reduce the dominate "culture of war" that exists throughout the world, the United Nations (UN) and the United Nations Educational, Scientific, and Cultural Organization (UNESCO) have worked to develop and promote the ideas behind cultures of peace through conferences, programs, and declarations (*Cultures of peace,* 1997). The UN defines a culture of peace as "a set of values, attitudes, modes of behaviors that reject violence and endeavor to prevent conflicts by addressing their root causes with a view to solving problems through dialogue and negotiation among individuals, groups and nations (de Rivera, 2004b, p. 126)." The year 2000 was declared the International Year for the Culture of Peace and the decade from 2001 to 2010 was declared the Decade for a Culture of Peace and Nonviolence for Children of the World (Adams, 2000). These declarations were designed to encourage wide spread international support for developing cultures of peace. Frederico Mayor (1995), Director General of UNESCO, compared the tasks needed to create cultures of peace to orchestrating a large symphony. He said, "Every person has a part to play, within the family, the workplace, the community, the nation, multinational entities, and the international community. The role of civil society is at least as important as that of the nation-state and that of the nongovernmental organization as vital as that of intergovernmental organizations (p. 3)."

The *Manifesto*2000, adapted from the writings of several Nobel Peace Laureates, outlined the general principles of this global movement for a culture of peace. Individuals were asked to sign the following:

"Recognizing my share of responsibility for the future of humanity, especially for today's children and those of future generations, I pledge – in my daily life, in my family, my work, my community, my country and my region – to:

1. *Respect the life* and dignity of each human being without discrimination and prejudice
2. *Practice active nonviolence*, rejecting violence in all its forms: physical, sexual, psychological, economical, and social, in particular towards the most deprived and vulnerable such as children and adolescents
3. *Share my time and material resources* in a spirit of generosity to put an end to exclusion, injustice, and political and economic oppression
4. *Defend freedom of expression and cultural diversity*, giving preference always to dialogue and listening without engaging in fanaticism, defamation, and the rejection of others
5. *Promote consumer behavior that is responsible* and development practices that respect all forms of life and preserve the balance of nature on the planet
6. *Contribute to the development of my community*, with the full participation of women and respect for democratic principles, in order to create together new forms of solidarity." (Boulding, 2000a)

While the time for signing the Manifesto 2000 may be passing, you can still sign it electronically at http://www3.unesco.org/iycp/uk/uk_sum_cp.htm. (Note: You will need to click on the *Manifesto 2000* button in the column on the left and then click on the Manifesto and Sign It buttons on the top of subsequent pages to read and then electronically sign the Manifesto.) Thousands and thousands of people from all continents did sign onto this pledge and have worked to encourage the development of a culture of peace in their own sphere of influence.

Immediately prior to and during the International Year for the Culture of Peace and the Decade for a Culture of Peace and Nonviolence for Children of the World, many countries have developed and implemented initiatives to build a culture of peace within their borders. Adams (2000) has observed that the global movement for a culture of peace has served to link together many existing social movements and to subsequently strengthen them. Organizations focused on increasing the rights of women, environmental organizations, agencies designed to reduce hunger, health initiatives, and many other humanitarian groups now were linked as a transformative force in building cultures of peace. Many governmental organizations, nongovernmental organizations, grass roots organizations, and other groups now realized that they were working toward this same superordinate goal to have every human being living a life of peace and nonviolence (Boulding, 2000a; de Rivera, 2004c).

Wessells, Schwebel, and Anderson (2001) outline seven core elements of cultures of peace as:

1. *Social justice.* Institutionalized equity in the distribution and access to material, social, and political resources; truth telling, reparations, and penalties for infractions; full participation and power sharing by different groups; gender justice and full participation by women
2. *Human rights.* Rule of law and adherence to human rights standards
3. *Nonviolence.* Institutionalized arrangements for nonviolent conflict resolution and reconciliation; values and attitudes of civility; norms and processes that promote human security, cooperation, interdependence, and harmonious relationships at all levels

4. *Inclusiveness*. Respect for difference; participation by different groups; meeting identity needs; cultural sensitivity
5. *Civil society*. Strength and diversity of civic groups in sectors such as health, business, religion, and education; community action, support, and hope through these venues; full citizen participation in government
6. *Peace education*. Formal and informal, experiential education for peace at all levels; socialization of values, attitudes, and behaviors conducive to peace and social justice
7. *Sustainability*. Preservation of global resources; meeting the needs of the current generation without compromising the ability to meet the needs of future generations (pp. 351–352)

de Rivera (2004a, 2004b, 2004c) has focused on methods of determining the success of efforts to build cultures of peace. Developing a culture of peace, like a type of peacebuilding, is a process not a static goal (Boulding, 2000a). Success may be as fleeting as achieving self-actualization on a personal level. However, the task of assessing cultures of peace that de Rivera and his colleagues have begun to address is very important.

Assessing Cultures of Peace

de Rivera (2004a) organized a conference to address cultures of peace at Clark University in 2001 in which participants from several countries attended. One goal of conference organizers and participants was to establish benchmarks to assess societal characteristics that were consistent with cultures of peace, cultures of dominance or war, and the dynamic balance between the two. Group consensus was to define and treat peacefulness and a culture of peace as separate entities. Peacefulness was viewed more as a state of affairs while a peaceful culture was determined to involve social institutions, norms, and other cultural variables that served an adaptive role within a society.

de Rivera's (2004c) review of the research on assessing the peacefulness of countries found previous assessment attempts that were made in over six-dozen countries. Quality of life indicators, economic indicators, plus measures of political peace, military-diplomatic peace, and socioeconomic peace were employed. For his new study of the peacefulness of nations, de Rivera adapted objective indicators from a team of Korean peace researchers and developed some of his own to be sure that each of the eight different bases or components for a culture of peace would be assessed. His characteristics are similar yet differ in some ways from the core components outlined by Wessells et al. (2001) and presented above. The eight bases for a culture of peace used by de Rivera are from UN documentation and are as follows:

1. *Education* (and especially, education for peaceful resolution of conflict)
2. *Sustainable development* (viewed as involving the eradication of poverty, reduction of inequalities, and environmental sustainability)

3. *Human rights*
4. *Gender equality*
5. *Democratic participation*
6. *Understanding, tolerance, and solidarity* (among peoples, vulnerable groups, and migrants within the nation and among nations)
7. *Participatory communication and the free flow of information*
8. *International peace and security* (including disarmament and various positive initiatives) (de Rivera, p. 531).

Data were collected for the same 74 countries by the *Committee for the Culture of Peace* and analyzed to identify the factors underlying these indicators. de Rivera's analysis identified four factors: liberal development (freedom of the press, human rights, democracy, gender equality, adult literacy, GDP), violent inequality (high homicide rate and economic inequality), violent means (international military use and expenditure, number incarcerated), and nurturance (higher education expenditures, women in government, aiding refugees).

Further writing by de Rivera (2004b) outlines a template for assessing cultures of peace that reflects the deeper issues behind the values within the UN initiatives. Based on an extension of the discussions at the Clark University conference, he presents a method of assessment that adds new elements to the substance of the UN initiatives in order to add more coherence. The sociopolitical model he describes for cultures of peace includes three clusters: societal norms promoting a civil society, transforming sociopolitical structures to promote political stability, and governmental market policies that promote a just environment. Each subarea in the three clusters has an objective measure and, while de Rivera notes that the template for national assessments with these measures needs elaboration and is a work in progress, the process of analyzing and comparing nations with the template is clear and promising. Fernández-Dols, Hurtado-de-Mendoza, and Jiménez-de-Lucas (2004) concur with de Rivera in warning that the concepts within a culture of peace are primarily Western and this is a real limitation that needs addressing.

Later work by de Rivera and Páez (2007) points to the inclusion of the emotional climate of a country as an important variable in understanding and assessing cultures of peace. Emotional climate involves a collective emotional field that involves the emotions people experience when they think and act in a public space (de Rivera, Kurrien, & Olsen, 2007). Security, insecurity, confidence, depression, trust, fear, love, and anger are all aspects of collective sentiments that may be objectively measured to reflect emotional climate.

Basabe and Valencia (2007) applied a model to assess the extent that a culture was a culture of peace that included sociostructural dimensions, cultural values, and emotional climate. Their objective measures of social correlates included four variables: liberal development, violent inequality, state use of violent means, and nurturance. Liberal democracy involves the extent of democracy in the government, freedom of the press, human rights, adult literacy, life expectancy, GNP, and gender equality. Violent inequality for Basabe and Valencia is assessed using a UN measure called the GINI index (i.e., inequality of wealth distribution), homicide rates, and human rights violations. State use of violent means is reflected in military expenditures as a percentage of GDP and the use of the military in foreign policy crises. Nurturance involves the percentage of GNP dedicated to education, the acceptance of refugees, and the percentage of women in elected national governmental offices. Values were assessed consistent with the methodology of Hofstede (2001), Schwartz (1994b), and Inglehart (1991) with country as the unit of analysis. Data reported by Basabe and Valencia confirmed a complex picture of a culture of peace. While individualistic and egalitarian values were positively associated with two components of cultures of peace (liberal democracy and nurturance) and emotional climate, these values were not related to violent inequity or state use of violent means. These latter two components were related to the value of harmony. Therefore, Basabe and Valencia conclude, "if we wish to foster a complete culture of peace we cannot only encourage autonomy and the valuing of nonhierarchical power structures. We must also encourage harmony and a concern for economic equality and human security for all nations, and we must devise measures of emotional climate that reflects these concerns (p. 417)."

Major Components of Cultures of Peace: Implications for Theory and Research

The remainder of this chapter elucidates the major components and values within cultures of peace with implications for theory and research that. The topics follow the outline provided by Wessells et al. (2001) with a minor expansion. Some issues are relevant to more than one component and, for the sake of brevity, I elaborate only in one place and simply mention the relevance briefly in other places.

Social Justice

Social justice involves moral values, societal rules, and considerations of fairness (Opotow, 1990). It has its underpinnings in the field of ethics with values, principles, duties, and obligations for members of a society (Drevdahl, Kneipp, Canales, & Dorcy, 2001). In comparing different definitions of social justice Poe (2007) finds the most common approach incorporates the notion of distributive justice with a sharing of resources, material goods, influence, and power. Wessells et al. (2001) also describe social justice as occurring when social institutions provide for an equitable distribution and/or access to material, social, and political resources with full participation and power sharing by different groups, plus they add truth telling and reparations for infractions.

Christie (1997) has encouraged peace psychologists to incorporate human needs theory into their research and activism as a productive alternative to power politics. This is a very relevant place to do so. From a human needs perspective conflicts are managed via the pursuit of social justice by satisfying human needs. Direct violence will result in the activation of fear and the need for security. Both direct and structural violence can activate the need for identity, well-being, and self-determination. Christie points out the ways that structural violence effects need satisfaction asymmetrically within a society. Resources, material goods, influence, and power may exist within a society yet certain segments of that society experience economic hardship and are disenfranchised from the workings of their society. Christie sees the satisfaction of the human needs of security and identity as a vehicle to both prevent direct violence and war and to assist in the resolution of conflict before direct violence occurs. Political and economic inequalities can affect self-determination and well being needs among certain members of society. Focusing on quality of life factors as indicators of levels of social justice and structural violence, Christie challenges peace researchers to work to remove societal factors that keep infant mortality rates high and life expectancies and literacy rates low for particular groups. As these quality of life factors improve, critical human needs are satisfied and a more socially just society emerges.

Wessells et al. (2001) include truth telling, reparations, and penalties for infractions as important components of social justice. The trauma caused by ethnopolitical conflict has been documented in Angola (Wessells & Monteiro, 2001), Bosnia (Agger, 2001), South Africa (de la Rey, 2001), Rwanda (Staub, 2004), and many other places throughout the world. If social justice is to exist after a conflict has been resolved or ended then some form of reconciliation in the form of truth telling commissions or reparations may be needed. Staub describes how giving and hearing testimonies in postconflict Rwanda can be positive for healing and reconciliation yet there is a concern in such a process that the parties involved might be retraumatized and renewed hostilities might occur. Divided societies like South Africa during the time of apartheid make reconciliation complex and de la Rey's discussion of South Africa's Truth and Reconciliation Commission (TRC) is enlightening. She summarizes the objectives of the TRC to be truth, forgiveness, healing, and reconciliation. Her analysis of the ultimate goal of the TRC reveals a web of levels and connections in the reconciliation process that include building relationships, agreeing on the truth within the past, acknowledging the other, apologizing, forgiving, and obtaining reparations and justice. Ultimately, to be successful reconciliation requires the establishment of what de la Rey calls a human rights culture.

Full participation and power sharing by different groups within a society is crucial if social justice is to exist (Wessells et al., 2001). This includes gender justice and the full participation by women within political, economic, and social institutions at all levels including leadership roles. Because of the breadth of issues this encompasses, gender equality and empowerment will be discussed next in its own section.

Gender Equality and Empowerment

Despite the large number of women who have been active and influential in the practice of nonviolent social action (Chambliss, 2002), the gendered thinking that considers the perspectives and behaviors of both men and women has not characterized peace psychology (McKay, 1996; McKay & Mazurana, 2001). Gender issues are not routinely considered in peace psychology and the study of nonviolence even today (de la Rey & McKay, 2006).

The harsh reality is that "there is no society in the world where women enjoy the same opportunities as men, whether measured by enrollment in school, literacy, preparation for careers, political participation, earned income, or any other measure that reflects quality of life (Schwebel & Christie, 2001, p. 121)." Gender inequalities that exist from conception oftentimes result in an untimely death. In India billboards encourage prospective parents to weigh the economic costs of giving birth to a little girl. Mazurana and McKay (2001) report the dowry price is over 1,000 times the price of an in utero sex determination test and abortion. This leads to selective female abortions. Son preference, leading to female infanticide and selective abortions, exists in India, China, and many other countries resulting in over 100 million girls and women "missing" worldwide. Mazurana and McKay also report many other inequalities between males and females that result from structural violence perpetrated by a wide range of economic, political, and religious systems and institutions. While women perform 66% of the work across the globe, they earn only 10% of the world's income. They point out the invisible nature of much of "women's work" as it is not reflected in governmental and international economic indicators. Because of this and other marketplace factors, women do not have the same access to loans for business development. Even within highly developed societies, the glass ceiling affects many women in their careers. Male privilege in food and healthcare distribution in some countries results in higher rates of anemia in women, fewer visits to the doctor for girls, and less food given to girls. Women and girls are more likely to be refugees following armed conflict. Costin (2006) reports 80% of refugees are women and girls and the gender biases regarding cultural eating patterns often results in well fed men living in refugee camps next to their women and girls who are starving because the men eat first and there is not enough food for all.

The structure of most societies in today's world is patriarchal and this prevents gender equality in many ways. A patriarchal society values men over women and the sexism that is present subordinates and devalues women (Bommersbach, 2000). Just like colonialism, patriarchy advances one group (men) at the expense of another (women) (Sylvester, 1989). McKay and Mazurana (2001) illustrate the pervasiveness of patriarchal thinking by asking people to think about those who are injured or killed in war. When you think about the casualties of war, if you are like most people, you imagine soldiers and other military personnel who are mostly male. Of course, McKay and Mazurama remind us that well over 90% of those injured or killed in wars and armed combat in the last half century are civilians, the majority of which are women and girls. Similarly, when asked to ponder peacemakers and peacebuilders, most people think of male examples not female ones. Adhiambo-Oduol (1999) describes the ideology and values behind patriarchy as one that considers men to be superior to women and therefore the men should have control over the lives of women. According to her, this patriarchal world-view posits "man is the natural head and leader at all times. He is stronger than the women, is rational and courageous, and has the responsibility of protecting the woman and the children. A woman on the other hand, is man's helper. Although biologically weak, she has the responsibility of bringing up the children. She is the home manager and is patient, kind, loving, and committed to the well-being of the family…. A woman is thus a symbol of unity and sacrifice in the family (p. 182)." With these assumptions and beliefs about men and women it is easy to see how gender equality is so elusive.

Achieving gender equality requires cultures to move away from patriarchal gender stereotypes, yet there are clear obstacles that stand in the way of this type of societal change. Many men in patriarchal cultures fully expect the full privileges accorded to them and are not in the least interested in giving up their dominant roles. Brienes (1999) views the major challenge is to dissuade men from thinking that empowering women would subsequently disempower them. She believes men need to be convinced that gender equality with new types of sharing and partnerships is a rewarding win-win situation for men and women. Most gender research has focused on women's roles and issues and Brienes notes that very little have looked at the roles of men. She does report the work of an UNESCO conference in the late 1990s that identified the problems caused by "the so-called hegemonic masculinity" and the need to foster other masculinities more conducive to cultures of peace. Brienes does have some optimism as she interprets gender relations as both dynamic and malleable. Feminist psychological theory and practice can assist in the move from patriarchic oppression of women by addressing the power differentials between men and women, empowering women, and increasing the degree that diversity is embraced in society (Bommersbach, 2000).

Brienes (1999) cites the *UNESCO Statement on Women's Contribution to a Culture of Peace* to support her gender perspective on a culture of peace. "Only together, women and men in parity and partnership, can we overcome obstacles and inertia, silence and frustration and insure insight, political will, creative thinking and concrete actions needed for a global transition from a culture of violence to a culture of peace (Brienes, p. 33)." Others like Adhiambo-Oduol (1999) echo the need for women and men to work equally in concert with one another to bring about a more peaceful and nonviolent world.

Human Rights

Wessells et al. (2001) describe the adherence to the rule of law and to human rights standards as a basic component for the existence of a culture of peace. The Universal Declaration of Human Rights (United Nations, 1948) was formally adopted by the United Nations in December 10, 1948. Thus, just over 3 years after World War II, this historic document provided a framework for human rights worldwide that needed to be assured by rule of law. Article 6 specifies, "Everyone has the right to recognition everywhere as a person before the law." The rights specified in this important declaration also include freedom, justice, dignity, security, and peace.

It also indicates that no one shall suffer slavery, torture, or cruel, inhuman, or degrading treatment or punishment.

The violation of human rights may be viewed as structural violence (Lykes, 2001). Of course any form of structural violence could prevent the development and continuation of cultures of peace. Citing the writings of Salvadoran social psychologist and priest, Ignacio Martín-Baró, Lykes calls attention to detrimental aftereffects of political repression. Through examples from Argentina and Guatemala, she illustrates how the social injustice and marginalization perpetuated by repressive leaders on some segments of the population violated the rights of all citizens in those countries.

Rule of Law

Kritz (2001) distinguishes the "rule of law" from being "ruled by a set of laws." He notes that laws can be used by totalitarian regimes to wield power at the expense of its citizens and even perpetrate atrocities with a legal cover. The rule of law works to constrain governmental powers and may be viewed as a fundamental component of good government. The rule of law exists when a clearly defined set of laws are universally accepted and applied to all members of a society without special privilege or prejudice (United States Department of State, n.d.). Legal scholars have discussed aspects of the rule of law since the third century BCE (Bouloukos & Dakin, 2001). While the rule of law may exist outside of a democracy, the rule of law is an essential component of democratic societies and it depends on an independent judiciary, a free press, free elections, and checks and balances within different branches of government. Current conceptualizations of the rule of law can be traced back to the writings of A. C. Dicey from the late nineteenth century (Bouloukos & Dakin; Rose, 2004). Dicey viewed the rule of law to consist of the lack of far reaching governmental power whereby citizens may only be punished if specific laws are broken and the presence of laws that pertain to all citizens regardless of their position (Rose). Hayek, the great Austrian economist, viewed the rule of law as a means of controlling the government to protect human rights and these rules "make it possible to foresee with fair certainty how the authority will use its coercive powers in given circumstances, and to plan one's individual affairs on the basis of this knowledge (Hayek, cited in Bouloukos & Dakin, p. 148)." Thus, individuals may pursue their goals with known constraints.

The establishment of the rule of law within national and international contexts is not without problems and challenges. White (2007) describes maintaining the rule of law in the United States as an intensive undertaking that will take multiple generations with successes and setbacks to fully accomplish. White cites the mindsets that led to the regular use of extraordinary rendition, the rejection of international laws, treaties, and accepted codes of conduct, and the abuses at facilities like Abu Ghraib as indicative of some of the problems of achieving an international rule of law. He calls for reaffirmation of "the stature of the Geneva Conventions, the right of *habeas corpus*, the right to counsel, the right to examine evidence, and, indeed, the right to trial (p. 14)." Bouloukos and Dakin (2001) make the case for a "Universal Declaration of the Rule of Law" to move the international community forward.

The United States Institute of Peace (USIP, n.d.) maintains a *Rule of Law Center of Innovation* that assists policymakers and practitioners to endorse the rule of law through research and the promotion of best practices. USIP has summarized research on the rule of law and their Web site reports "Research suggests that societies based on the rule of law are more likely to be stable democracies and contribute to international order and less likely to be sources of conflict than other states (USIP, ¶ 1)".

The *Southern Poverty Law Center* (SPLC, 2008) was founded in the United State in 1971 and is one of many organizations that work to protect human rights through the rule of law. When it was first established, the small law office that had taken civil rights cases in the South *pro bono* during the sixties began to establish a national presence to fight discrimination throughout the United States. Strategic cases were taken to stop hate groups like the Ku Klux Klan and the Aryan Nations from discriminating against and violating the rights of others. Many cases ended up being successfully argued in the Supreme Court and resulted in diminishing the prestige and power of the plaintiffs in these civil suits. In addition heavy fines for some hate groups resulted in extensive loss of operating assets and in some cases bankruptcy. The SPLC monitors the activities of many hate groups and publishes the information in publications and posts the information on its Web site.

Violence Against Women as a Human Rights Issue

Raven-Roberts (1999) argues for the clear establishment of laws to protect women and girls from gender-based violence and the enforcement of these laws both in country and during times of exile. Unfortunately, the rule of law does not always extend to women and girls within patriarchal societies. Ethnonationalism and fundamentalist religious ideologies reaffirm the patriarchal hierarchies within societies further entrenching the lowered legal status for women and girls (Raven-Roberts).

The level of security experienced by (or afforded to) women and girls is not equal to men. The direct and structural violence aimed at women during war and armed conflict is profound and all too common. Raven-Roberts (1999) describes violence towards women and girls as an endemic problem in most societies and its use in armed conflict as a clear violation of rights. She notes how the use of rape as a strategy of war compounds other forms of domestic and gender based violence and has put women in fear of their safety in places like Bosnia, Rwanda, Myanmar, and Uganda. Avoiding these traumas is difficult since women in war torn countries often are primary care givers plus, with their husbands killed or off to war, they have to provide food and shelter for their families. Getting the needed food and water to feed themselves and their children can sometimes only be accomplished by entering into situations where rape, torture, and/or death are highly likely. Even as refugees, women and girls are very vulnerable to rapes and sexual assaults in transit to camps and while they are in the camps since the regular family and cultural institutions that protect them have vanished (Costin, 2006).

The immediate trauma of rape and sexual assault is not the only violence affecting victims of sexual violence. Costin (2006) lists unwanted pregnancies, sexually transmitted diseases, shame and humiliation as additional aspects of the trauma of rape. She points out how being forced to carry and give birth to the child of their aggressor can leave psychological and spiritual scars that deeply impact the social and cultural identities of the victims. The shame of the women who have been raped can have personal, spiritual, and collective cultural elements making treatment with techniques developed in other contexts and cultures insufficient. Costin notes that these psychological effects can prevent women from seeking medical treatment out of concern for the ways their families and communities will react to their situation. Traditional community-based cleansing rituals are oftentimes necessary to deal with the spiritual aspects of the sexual trauma for the women and girls who were raped and for their communities so they can be welcomed back (McKay, 1998). Psychosocial resources for these women are often inappropriate or unavailable, and as a result, suicide rates are high (Costin; Wessells, & Monteiro, 2001).

Armed Conflict and Human Rights

War and armed conflict have been shown to violate the human rights of children in other ways too. The effects of armed conflict on children have increased because of the changing nature of war since World War II (Wessells, 1998). Okorodudu (1998) reviewed the 1996 *Graça Machel UN Study on the Impact of Armed Conflict on Children* from a human rights perspective. She describes the findings and recommendations to be based on human rights law and international humanitarian law and indicates eight critical areas where the best interests of children are either directly or indirectly violated. Okorodudu explains how children in armed conflicts have their physical, intellectual, emotional, and social development impaired as a result of separation from parents and family, a breakdown in the educational institutions, and a general disintegration of the societal institutions and norms that traditionally guide children toward a productive and healthy adulthood. She challenges psychologists to assist children in armed conflict by reducing their suffering and promoting their psychosocial development.

The recruitment and forced conscription of child soldiers in many parts of the world is another real human rights issue. Mendelsohn and Straker (1998) indicate that there have been about a quarter of a million children who were or are soldiers in almost three-dozen conflicts over the last two decades. They add that most of these child soldiers are less than 15 years old with some as young as 8 years old. While few studies have assessed the psychosocial effects of children being forced to witness and participate in the violence of war, Mendelsohn and Straker describe the short-term and long-term implications for the psychological well being of soldiering on children. While they call for more research, being a child soldier seems to result in increased levels of violent talk and violent behavior as adults.

McKay (1998) stresses that these child soldiers include large numbers of girls as well, who in addition to the psychosocial problems experienced by boy soldiers, experience rape and sexual trauma plus inadequate or unavailable reproductive health care at a critical time in their development. McKay (2005) describes how witnessing and participating in the torture and killing of parents and other family members and friends, amputations and mutilation of body parts, and other violence seriously effects the girl child soldiers' gender identity and development.

Rights of Indigenous Peoples

Cooper (2003) summarizes efforts that have been made to restore the human rights of indigenous peoples throughout the world. Despite suffering genocides at the hands of European colonists, indigenous peoples such as the Maori of New Zealand, the Cayuga of Canada, and the American Indian Movement in the United States have used nonviolent approaches to obtain their dignity and equal treatment in the international legal realm. While it took nearly three decades, the UN adopted the nonbinding Declaration on the Rights of Indigenous Peoples in 2007 (http://www.un.org/esa/socdev/unpfii/en/declaration.html). While Australia, Canada, New Zealand, and the United States voted against the resolution, it was approved by 143 countries and outlines the individual, collective, cultural, language, employment, education, identity, economic, and other rights of indigenous peoples (United Nations adopts Declaration on Rights of Indigenous Peoples, 2007).

Nonviolence

Nonviolence and rejecting violence is a core element of cultures of peace (Adams, 2000; Anderson & Christie, 2001; Wessells et al., 2001). Wessells et al. view this element as including (1) institutionalized arrangements for nonviolent conflict resolution and reconciliation, (2) values and attitudes of civility, and (3) norms that promote human security, cooperation, interdependence, and harmonious relationships at all levels.

Interactive Problem-Solving Workshops

Brenes and Wessells (2001) indicate that in order to build and nurture cultures of peace, multidisciplinary approaches need to be followed to affect the necessary political, social, economic, and cultural transformations. One such approach is the interactive problem-solving workshops of Herb Kelman. For over three decades Kelman (1972, 1982, 1996, 1997, 1999) has developed, implemented, analyzed, and revised an interactive problem-solving workshop strategy to deal with the psychological perceptions and problems that exist between parties in intractable conflicts. Kelman (1999) views this interactive problem solving as a metaphor for conflict resolution with three assumptions. First, he assumes the conflict needs to be viewed as a shared problem of the parties involved. As a shared problem, the needs and interests of the other party must be recognized and addressed. Second, he assumes negotiations should be focused on solving the shared problem. The problem solving aspect of negotiation will transform the relationship between parties as underlying causes of the conflict and unmet needs are addressed. Third, Kelman assumes negotiations should be an interactive process. By engaging in a joint effort to generate solutions that take the other's perspective under consideration both parties become more responsive to each other's needs and are more likely to be committed to the agreed upon solution.

An intractable conflict is one in which the likelihood of resolution seems to be nearly impossible and therefore the conflict persists (Coleman, Vallacher, Nowak, & Bui-Wrzosinka, 2007). Intractable conflicts exist in Sri Lanka, Northern Ireland, Kashmir, and the Middle East (Bar-Tal, 2007). Bar-Tal characterizes intractable conflicts as protracted when they are violent, perceived as irresolvable and as a win–lose proposition, central to the lives of the people living in the societies involved, and span at least one generation. Specifically applied to the intractable Israeli–Palestinian conflict, Kelman and his colleagues have been bringing prominent members of Israeli and Palestinian communities together, usually at some neutral location in Europe, to discuss their concerns, perspectives, and needs of the shared conflict without the contextual pressures within their respective communities bearing down on them bearing down on them. Rouhana and Kelman (1994) presume protracted ethnic conflicts, like the Israeli–Palestinian conflict, are over unmet and nonnegotiable needs such as identity, security, and justice. Since these needs are not going to go away, the interactive workshops are designed to provide a mechanism for both sides to hear the other side and to develop a relationship with the other side as well. Kelman (1982, 2007) has provided a research– and theory-based blueprint for movement toward a resolution of the Israeli–Palestinian conflict in which the interactive problem solving workshops create a positive prenegotiation climate.

Cromwell and Vogele (2008) consider nonviolent actions to be much more flexible in their design and implementation to deal with conflict than violent approaches. Even in democracies, they view nonviolent actions as an important mechanism to balance the institutions of power. Because nonviolent actions do not seek a win–lose outcome in which the other party is eliminated, nonviolence has the positive dynamic of leaving the door open for social compromise even in quite contentious situations.

Social Norms

Norms are unwritten rules within a culture that inform us which behaviors are appropriate and which are not. Building a culture of peace that encourages nonviolence and rejects violence requires a systematic approach that looks at societal norms. Unfortunately, many norms encourage violent behavior and these are deeply entrenched in most societies today. Two prominent types of norms of violence that need to be lessened are retribution norms like "an eye for an eye" and the norms that maintain cultures of honor. These norms indicate that violent behavior is not only acceptable in some situations but it is the best behavior to use to solve problems and to fail to do so has dire consequences for the individual and family. Norms of nonviolence that need to be strengthened include norms like the "Golden Rule," norms of cooperation and prosocial behavior, and norms that break cycles of violence like Gandhi's *tapasya*.

The "eye for an eye" norm dates back to early religious texts of Jews, Christians, and Muslims and is found in the Old Testament of the Bible in Exodus 21:23–21:25. Although some believe that this passage sets specific levels of retribution that need to be acted upon when someone has been wronged, a careful reading shows that this norm places clear limits on the severity of retribution that one is permitted to deliver. If someone takes out your eye, you are told that you may not kill him or take both his eyes in revenge, but you must limit your retribution to the same level inflicted upon you. If someone scratches your car with a key, you are not permitted to burn down their house but you may inflict a similar level of damage on their car. While "an eye for an eye" reflects proportional retribution, it clearly condones violent behavior that keeps the cycle of violence in motion.

The culture of honor is discussed by Fiske (2004) as a set of norms that endorse violence to protect an individual's reputation for toughness and to retaliate to insults. This norm is strong among males in former southern slave owning states in the United States and has been correlated with higher homicide rates. Fiske also finds similar patterns of violent behavior and higher levels of acceptance of the use of violence to resolve problems by residents in some Western states that were settled by Southerners after the Civil War. If a man raised in a culture of honor has their masculine reputation threatened or challenged, they are expected to fight to reestablish it, and if they do not, they may lose respect from members of their family and community. Insults toward a family member or another man flirting with a date may trigger violent responses as well. Gangs in the United States have similar honor norms that push members to respond to insults with violence (Horowitz & Schwartz, 1974). Similarly, the dynamics of bullying in the schools point to the norms that perpetuate high levels of violence among teenagers by creating expectations for students to fight back (Sherman, 1999). Hawkins, Farrington, and Catalano (1998) find many youth today behave violently to maintain their status. They report that peers and families operate under the norm that violence is both justified and necessary in certain circumstances and a failure to respond to provocations leads to rejection and a loss of standing in the group. If someone hits them, the pressures from friends and family to hit back can be very strong in order to "look tough" or "save face." Hawkins et al. see this norm of violent reciprocation to be quite strong among today's adolescents. Colburn (1985) has examined ice hockey games and found fistfights and violence on the ice also to be a function of respect and honor.

Honor killings and honor-related torture and violence have been found around the globe in a wide variety of societies (Hossain & Welchman, 2005). George Piro, FBI interrogator of Saddam Hussein, said that the Iraqi leader's decision to invade

Kuwait in 1990 was based on an insult that became an honor issue (Pelley, 2008). Saddam told his interrogator that the Kuwaiti Amir boasted to Iraq's foreign minister that he would neither stop taking oil from a field that Saddam thought was Iraqi nor stop demanding Iraq repay its loans until the Amir had turned every Iraqi women into a $10 whore. After Saddam was informed of the Amir's statement the decision for Iraq to invade Kuwait was sealed so Saddam could punish the Amir.

Honor-related violence has primarily, but not exclusively, been directed towards women. Honor killing of women or femicide has been found in Brazil (Pimentel, Pandjiarjian, & Belloque, 2005), Egypt (Centre for Egyptian Women's Legal Assistance, 2005), Great Britain (Gill, 2007), Greece (Safilios-Rothschild, 1969), Iraq (Begikhani, 2005), India (Abdo, 2006), Israel (Abdo), Jordan (Faqir, 2001), Lebanon (Hoyek, Sidawi, & Mrad, 2005), Mexico (Pimentel et al.), Pakistan (Warraich, 2005), and Uruguay (Pimentel et al.) to name a few. Premarital sex or extramarital sex (even when a woman was raped) are the behaviors that regularly precipitate murder to restore family honor but even lesser "honor crimes" like seeking divorce or suspicion of infidelity are violently punished (Begikhani). In one case a woman was killed for simply announcing she planned to marry someone without the permission of a male in the family (Centre for Egyptian Women's Legal Assistance). The availability of cell phones with cameras have played a role in increasing the vulnerability of women to honor killings as some take pictures of out of wedlock couples and have placed them on the internet. When discovered, the families use the pictures as a reason to kill those involved. Abdo makes the case that these honor-killings are part of patriarchal cultures where women are considered property and not rooted in any religious beliefs per se. In addition to these honor-killings honor-based violence towards women includes a range of the domestic violence, sexual torture, and female genital mutilation (Centre for Egyptian Women's Legal Assistance; Coomaraswamy, 2005). Changing the norms that perpetuate these practices and strengthening legal statutes that can protect women from these human rights violations are clearly required to achieve cultures of peace.

Norms of nonviolence are not nearly as strong as norms of violence in most modern societies and need to be strengthened. One nonviolent norm endorsed by all major religions is the "Golden Rule" (Gensler, n.d.). Traditional Biblical versions are "Do unto others as you would have them do unto you." More modern interpretations are "Treat others only in ways that you're willing to be treated in the exact situation (Gensler, ¶ 3)" or "What goes around comes around (Côté, Plickert, & Wellman, 2006, p. 2)." The "Golden Rule" is a positive reciprocity norm whereby an individual is expected to treat others in a positive fashion so that others will reciprocate. Some philosophical problems do exist in assuming the use of the "Golden Rule" is a good thing. For instance, sadomasochists might behave violently since this is the treatment they would prefer but it would not be culturally good (Shafer-Landau, 2004). While there are some exceptions, the "Golden Rule" is generally supportive of cultures of peace and its broad based support by so many religions make it easier to strengthen across cultures.

Just as there are norms that push men in a culture to behave violently in certain situations, there are competing nonviolent norms. As a boy, I distinctly remember my father telling me that it is not appropriate to hit girls. It was just the way things should be. It was not "manly" to hit girls and I was not to do it. This "family norm" did not mean that I could not defend myself but there was no reason, even if hit by a girl, to hit back. I was expected to use nonviolent means to respond to and interact with girls and the norm was modeled. Although this was not even a community norm let alone a societal one, it is a reasonable norm to foster in boys. Given the widespread violence directed toward girls and woman documented above, this seem to be a good place to start. There are many campaigns to instill norms against violence toward girls and women. The Canadian-based White Ribbon Campaign is an international effort that focuses on getting men to stop violence by men against women.

Many peaceful societies possess the nonviolent norm of cooperation. Studies have shown that repeated cooperative experiences build norms of cooperation (Bettenhausen & Mernighan, 1991). Since competition and competitive experiences can work against the establishment of cooperative group norms and many social institutions are based on competition, it is important to establish and nurture social institutions that provide sufficient cooperative opportunities for norm building. Schools, churches, and community organizations can integrate cooperative approaches at many levels to develop the norm of cooperation.

Other norms might also help in rejecting violence and encouraging nonviolence in cultures of peace. Two prosocial norms that are relevant are the norm of equity (people who are "haves" should help the "have nots") and the norm of social responsibility (people need to help others who need assistance) (Kassin, Fein, & Markus, 2008). These moral norms encourage people to initiate helping behavior, and while they are not the sole reason for prosocial actions, research has shown that they do play a role in encouraging positive behaviors (Staub, 1972). These norms are associated with helping behaviors and are consistent with nonviolence. Gandhi's *tapasya* or self-suffering was important in breaking the cycle of violence. The norms of self-sacrifice and self-discipline in certain situations might reflect the needed behaviors for *tapasya* to become accepted and practiced on a larger scale. Naess (2005) describes several norms of nonviolence that are relevant for nonviolent patterns of communication. Based on the philosophy of Gandhi, the norms of nonviolence of Naess reflect honest and direct communication with clearly articulated nonviolent goals that are formulated to establish cooperation. Naess also presents the norm of admitting to mistakes when they are made to best facilitate nonviolent communication between parties in a conflict.

Inclusiveness

Inclusiveness involves respect for differences, the participation by different groups, meeting the identity needs of different groups in a society, and cultural sensitivity (Wessells et al., 2001). Many groups have been and are still marginalized within many communities and nations to the benefit of those in power. Women have been marginalized in many cultures (Mazurana & McKay, 2001). Similarly, minority and nondominant cultural, ethnic, and religious groups are marginalized around the world (Barany, 1998; Branch, 1998; de la Rey, 2001). This marginalization can lead to loneliness and can impact identity needs (Unger, 1998).

The values inherent in democracies are very important to this aspect of cultures of peace, as is the push to franchise citizens around the world. Likhotal (2007) believes democracy is in fact the only governmental system that has a legitimate claim to addressing critical issues for cultures of peace to emerge in today's world. However positive a democracy might be, its value can be compromised. Gandhi said, "There is no human institution without its dangers. The greater the institution, the greater the chances for abuse. Democracy is a great institution and therefore is liable to be greatly abused. The remedy, therefore, is not avoidance of democracy but reduction of possibility of abuse to a minimum (Attenborough, 1982, p. 39)."

Within democracies, voting is clearly an important activity. Those in power oftentimes disenfranchise women, minorities, and nondominant groups. This was done in the United States with African Americans even after slaves were freed and the 14th and 15th Amendments to the US Constitution were passed in the last half of the nineteenth century (Valelly, 2006). Jim Crow laws and practices effectively segregated the South under erroneously "separate but equal" policies and disenfranchised African Americans into the 1960s. It took the efforts of Martin Luther King Jr. and his many supporters to demonstrate in Selma Alabama and other parts of the South for voting rights along with discussions in Washington, DC with President Johnson and lawmakers to obtain rights that were already granted by the constitution (Kotz, 2005; Tuck, 2006). Efforts to register African Americans in Alabama, Georgia, and Mississippi brought the disenfranchised plight of African Americans to the public's attention and helped remove exclusionary practices (McClain, Brady, Carter, Perez, & Soto, 2006). The eventual passage of the Voting Rights Act in 1965 and subsequent renewals began the process of enfranchising African Americans back to levels of the nineteenth century. South African apartheid disenfranchised all "colored and Indians" until 1984 and all Blacks until 1994 (Kagee, Naidoo, & Van Wyk, 2003; Jones, 2006).

Another group that has been disenfranchised involves ex-felons (Hull, 2006). Despite serving time for a crime and "paying one's dues to society," many states in the United States do not allow ex-felons to vote. Hull reports that almost all states prevent incarcerated felons from voting, 36 prevent felons on parole from voting, 31 prevent felons on probation from voting, and 13 states prohibit all or some ex-felons from ever voting after parole or probation. During the US 2000 presidential elections, over 2% of the total voting-age population were disenfranchised with the largest percentages in the states of Georgia, Texas, Delaware, Idaho, and Louisiana (Hull). Given the inordinately high percentage of minorities who enter the US criminal justice system, the effect of voting restrictions hits African Americans and Hispanic Americans more than other groups. For instance, one in seven African American males have been disenfranchised by laws prohibiting ex-felons to vote and in some states the rate reaches one in four (Manza & Ugggen, 2006).

Comparatively speaking, the disenfranchisement laws of the United States regarding ex-felons are viewed as unjust by almost all other democracies and only totalitarian regimes like Pinochet's Chile were similar to the United States. In fact Canada, Israel, Japan, Kenya, Peru, South Africa, Zimbabwe, and 18 European countries allow felons in prison to vote and this is a trend (Hull, 2006; Lieberman, 2006).

Women in most societies have had limited rights and were disenfranchised until the twentieth century. New Zealand granted women the right to vote in 1893 and is the first country to do so (Crowley, 2001). Most Scandinavian countries granted voting rights to women prior to World War I. Other European countries like Austria, Belgium, Germany, the Netherlands, Soviet Russia, and Sweden granted suffrage a few years after World War I (Lewis, 2007). While women received the right to vote in some individual states earlier, women did not universally receive the right to vote in the United States until 1920 (Baker, 2002). French women were not franchised and until the end of World War II (Trumblety, 2003) and Swiss women not until 1971. Independence from colonial rule allowed many African and Asian nations to grant suffrage in the 1960s and 1970s (Lewis). Kuwaiti women did not become franchised until 2005 (Fattah, 2005). In many cases early voting rights had limitations associated with them. In some cases women needed to be 30 while men could vote if they were younger or women needed to have completed elementary school to vote while men did not. While suffrage may have been granted, it was also often the case that countries did not allow women to run for office for years after being franchised.

The inclusion of women in leadership positions may be viewed as essential in the pursuit of cultures of peace (Brienes, 1999; Breines, Gierycz, & Reardon, 1999). Even though women make up roughly half of the adult population across the globe, a very small percentage of women participate fully in governments and businesses and hold positions of leadership or power. "There are only 1% of women elected heads of state and government, 7% of women ministers (with very few women heading powerful departments such as ministries of foreign affairs, defense, the interior or finance) and some 11% of women parliamentarians (Brienes, p. 41)." Mazurana and McKay (2001) also note that when women rise to cabinet posts their appointments tend to be in the areas of family and community concerns that have less power than the posts given to their male counterparts. Brienes goes on to report that during the twentieth century 99% of the world's political power was in the hands of men and only 30 women have been president or prime minister of their countries. Thus the patriarchal biases also can be seen in the number of women in governmental leadership positions worldwide although there are some exceptions. Women's representation in national governmental leadership positions have been reported to be as high as 46% in the Seychelles and are relatively high in the Scandinavian countries (Finland 39%; Norway 36%; Sweden 34%). Marurana and McKay also found the relatively high levels of women in government of the countries of East Central Europe have dropped dramatically during democratization because quotas for women office holders have been abandoned. These findings are unfortunate as women can serve as sources of innovation in peacebuilding if given leadership opportunities (Brienes).

Enhancing the participation of women in economic and political decision making was a concern addressed by the *Women and a Culture of Peace Programme* of

UNESCO (Brienes, 1999). The priorities set by this organization include "(1) strategies to enhance women's full participation in the democratic process, notably women's access to decision-making positions, and (2) networking among "empowered" women, notably parliamentarians, mayors, and local leaders, to strengthen their roles as promoters of a culture of peace (Brienes, p. 51)."

Martin Luther King Jr. probably captured the essence of this inclusivity dimension of cultures of peace best in his memorable "I Have a Dream" in Washington, DC during the summer of 1963. He said, "I have a dream that one day…sons of former slaves and sons of former slave owners will be able to sit down together at the table of brotherhood…. I have a dream my four little children will one day live in a nation where they will not be judged by the color of their skin but by the content of their character…. I have a dream that one day…little black boys and little black girls will be able to join hands with little white boys and white girls as sisters and brothers. I have a dream today! (cited in Washington, 1962, pp. 104-105)." That is still the dream of inclusivity today.

Civil Society

The strength and diversity of civic groups in sectors such as health, business, religion, education, and community action, along with full citizen participation in government, makes for a civil society according to Wessells et al. (2001). The functioning of any society involves government and business activities and these have been discussed earlier in this chapter in the section on inclusivity. Civil society involves an important third sector of society.

Civil society is a concept that dates back to city-states in ancient Greece (Ehrenberg, 1999). The classical thought about civil society considered the interconnectedness between political life and private life with an eye to the common good. Later St. Augustine and his writings dichotomized the world into the "City of God" and the "City of Man" (Khondker, 2001b). While noting no universally accepted definition for a civil society exists, Hauss (2003) describes civil society as the voluntary participation by citizens in the affairs of society outside of the workings of government and business. Civil society includes the actions of individuals and civil society organizations and nonprofit organizations including religious groups, professional associations, labor unions, civic advocacy organizations, neighborhood associations, and other nongovernmental organizations. Eberly (1994) considers civil society to be "the realm of volunteer networks and informal associations in which individuals conduct much of their lives (p. xxx)." Eberly incorporates the concept of mediating structure, which he attributes to Berger and Neuhaus, into the full understanding of civil society. Mediating structures are social institutions such as families, neighborhoods, voluntary associations, and churches, temples, mosques, and synagogues that are critical for the functioning of a vibrant democracy. Civil society may be considered to be a necessary but not a sufficient condition for a democracy (Khondker, 2001a). Given the associations between democracy and civil society, it is tempting to assume that democracies foster civil society, however, when safety and survival needs are challenged, civil society will often become subordinate to day-to-day existence (Warfield, 1997). Mediating structures empower citizens and need to be protected and fostered to assure the health of communities and societies. Civil society is not a political entity and it transcends the state (Eberly).

Salamon, Haddock, Sokolowski, and Tice (2007) document that in monetary terms the nonprofit institutions sector of eight national economies average to be about 5% of Gross National Product and that figure is larger than expected. They add that for the eight countries studied, the economic contributions of nonprofit institutions outdistanced or equaled that of major industries like electricity, gas, and water, construction and financial institutions. Beyond an economic impact, Hauss (2003) sees the functions of civil society are to strengthen democracy and assists in resolving conflicts. He makes the case that strong civil societies build bridges between citizens with different views, interests, and backgrounds and thus create the trust and tolerance important for democracies. Bridging activities could include participating in recreational sports leagues, like bowling, softball, or basketball, volunteering to deliver "Meals on Wheels," doing yard work for an elderly couple, being a member of the League of Women Voters, and coaching a Boys and Girls Club soccer team. In fact, Putnam (2000) argues that the decline of bowling leagues, bridge clubs, and other similar activities in the United States has paralleled the collapse of many aspects of civil society since no comparable bridging activities have taken their places. Volunteering in one's community and participating in civic society organizations also helps to build social networks that make more people feel like they belong and feel included within their communities and society (Hauss). All bridging activities put people together who share the immediate concern at hand and the values relevant to that concern, yet the people are diverse in a multitude of ways. It is the mix of diverse viewpoints and backgrounds in informal interactions around a common goal that works to build trust, tolerance, and friendships and to foster a propensity for nonviolent conflict resolution.

United States President John F. Kennedy exemplified the essence of the power of civil society in his 1961 inaugural address when he said, "Ask not what your country can do for you – ask what you can do for your country." Civil society is a needed characteristic of society that liberals, moderates, and conservatives can generally agree upon (Eberly, 1994). However, the intensification of partisan politics in the United States during the last decade of the twentieth century and the first decade of the twenty-first century has seriously hampered civil society in Washington, DC and it has had negative effects on civil society across the country as well. Instead of developing relationships and bridging with those who are from a different party outside of the halls of government, too often members of the US Congress spend time with their colleagues who believe as they do. Presently, congressional representatives do not have the depth of relationships that existed even a few decades ago across party lines and across branches of government that resulted in the compromises needed for positive legislative work. Former Press Secretary for President Ronald Reagan lamented, "It's gotten to be a nasty business with so much divisiveness. Ronald Reagan and Tip O'Neill could disagree totally on issues and then get together for a social event. We need to moderate on both sides (Brady & Brady, 2006, ¶ 7)." This has been associated with little or no input accepted by the party in power from the minority party, with little or no compromises on legislation, and with an "earmarks as entitlement" mentality. Unfortunately, these behavioral patterns and expectations seem to have been adopted by many civil society organizations and civil advocacy organizations as well.

The discussion earlier in this chapter makes it clear that considerable work needs to be done to achieve inclusivity for women in government. Brienes (1999) makes the point that, in addition to governmental positions, women do not make up a sizable proportion of policy makers in industry, finance, the military, and the church either. However, women have assumed important leadership roles in civil society organizations such as grassroots peacebuilding organizations in many countries and their work in nongovernmental organizations is significant and growing even if it has also been limited by patriarchal structures (McKay & Mazurana, 2001).

The presence of a civil society can be very influential in nonviolent conflict resolution and peacebuildng (Barnes, 2006). Lederach (2001) illustrates how civil society makes reconciliation more likely to be successful as civil society provides a safe space where truth, mercy, justice, and peace can flourish. Lederach provides examples of the positive role of civil society from Nicaragua, Liberia, and South Africa. It has also been linked to positive outcomes in Northern Ireland (McCartney, 1999), Sierra Leone (Turay, 2000), Somalia (Warfield, 1997), and Tajikstan (Mullojanov, 2001) to name just a few places. McCartney's analysis of the Troubles in Northern Ireland points out the difficulty civil society groups have in coming to an agreed upon plan of action to reduce violence even when there is agreement on the ultimate goal of peace. Nonetheless, he notes that, though stressed by the process, civil society is energized and is moving in the direction of peace. In Sierra Leone, Turay documents the involvement of civil society groups like the Inter-Religious Council of Sierra Leone (IRCSL) that consisted of Muslim and Christian leaders from the country. While separating out the impact of the IRCSL from other players in the peace process is problematic, Turay does make the case that the IRCSL's actions played a significantly role in building confidence between the rebels and the society at large during the peace talks. Warfield reports that even in the anarchy and disarray of Mogadishu, merchants in conducting commerce were able to set up a local peace committee to develop some level of interclan management for the seaports and airports. Another neighborhood instituted a rudimentary form of crime watch to deter criminals to some success. Whereas Northern Ireland and Sierra Leone benefited from religions civil organizations, Mullojanov indicates that NGOs and women's organizations assisted in the peacebuilding processes in Tajikistan. In fact, he points out that over a third of the NGOs are headed by women too. Mullojanov notes there are challenges ahead for the NGOs to adapt conflict resolutions methods to the constraints of modern Tajik society but linking the NGO efforts to local grassroots networks has promise.

Barnes (2006) synthesizes the findings of the Global Partnership for the Prevention of Armed Conflict with regard to civil society. Civil society is seen as a force for people-centered security whereby individuals are agents of their security and not passive recipients. Since it is extremely difficult to force peace on those committed to using violence to reach their goals, civil society and an effective dialog between individuals in the conflict can contribute depth and robustness to peacebuilding. Civil society organizations may constructively address conflicts plus develop and encourage the use of proactive strategies to create the social change needed to promote peace and reduce suffering. These organizations help to develop a better vision for the future, to reframe attitudes and perceptions about conflicts, to mobilize constituencies for peace, and to promote security and reduce violence. While there needs to be more research on the relationship between civil society and violence, the preliminary studies and observations show that a strong civil society may mediate violence (Stacey & Meyers, 2005).

The notion of a global civil society that extends beyond national borders has emerged over the last decade (Bowden, 2006; Ho, Baber, & Khondker, 2002; Khondker, 2001a, 2001b). Bowden warns that the notion of extending the concept of a national civil society to a global civil society has serious limitations. He advises caution in seeing a global civil society as a vehicle to rid the world of problems in the same way civil society within a country helps promote nonviolent conflict resolution among its citizens. This is because the unique interdependency between a nation's civil society and its government does not have an analog on the world stage. There may be global civil society organizations but there is no world government. Despite these concerns, some see the potential for global civil society to have an impact in certain area like the environment (Khondker, 2001a, 2001b).

One civil society issue that has been recently developed at the international level is referred to as the Global Marshall Plan. Based on the idea of the Marshall Plan developed and implemented by the United States in conjunction with its European allies immediately following World War II to help war torn Europe rebuild its infrastructure and civil society, the use of this model has been discussed since the 1990s (Gore, 1992). Currently, there are at least three initiatives that follow the same principles today. The first Global Marshall Plan is sketched out by former US vice president Al Gore. The second Global Marshall Plan has been developed and supported by noted economists, political scientists, environmentalists, and other professionals primarily from European Union countries. The third plan has been supported by a group of spiritual progressive religious leaders from a range of religious orientations. Since there is considerable overlap between the positions, the second plan will be discussed in depth and the first and third plans mostly in terms of the differences in their goals and structure.

The Global Marshal Plan Initiative began in 2003 and aims at a "World in Balance." It emerged from ethical concerns about the level of poverty on this planet and the struggle for human dignity that those in poverty experience on a daily basis (Global Marshall Plan, n.d.c). Since 3.2 billion people are surviving on less than US $2 per day, half the world's population is in poverty and the implications of a plan to reduce poverty is critical for humanity (Lorentz, 2006). Like the original Marshall Plan, the Global Marshall Plan is viewed as a symbol of hope, solidarity, and peace (Global Marshall Plan, n.d.b). The overarching goal requires better-designed globalization along with a redesigned worldwide Eco-Social Market Economy (Global Marshall Plan, n.d.c). This requires an improved global structural framework, sustainable development, environmental protection and equity, and the eradication of poverty, altogether resulting in a new global "economic miracle." The Global Marshall Plan considers the realization of the United Nations Millennium Development Goals, which were signed by 189 nations in 2000, to be an important first step. The following Millennium Development Goals would ideally be achieved by 2015:

1. Eradicate extreme poverty and hunger
2. Achieve universal primary education
3. Promote gender equality and empower women
4. Reduce child mortality
5. Improve maternal health
6. Combat HIV/AIDS, malaria, and other diseases
7. Ensure environmental sustainability
8. Develop a global partnership for development

The Global Marshall Plan is designed to address these goals within a new market economy "in which markets and competition are inseparably linked to high standards – maybe development state dependent – regarding the welfare of all human beings (Radermacher, 2004, p. 38)." The shift to an ecosocial global market economy would assist in eliminating poverty that has been created or exacerbated by a global market that currently has emerged without adequate regulations. Radermacher, a German economist, and others involved in the Global Marshall Plan Initiative see the European Union as taking the lead role in this world-wide movement to integrate the activities of nations, the World Trade Organization, World Bank, International Monetary Fund, the International Labor Union, the United Nations, and numerous NGOs to systematically reduce poverty in the world. The developed world will need to invest in this process, which it has not done consistently up to this point in time, and the investment will be substantial but not prohibitive. Costs would be significantly less than the amount currently spent on military weapons and hardware.

The five strategic cornerstones for the Global Marshall Plan Initiative are (1) rapidly implementing the Millennium Development Goals of the United Nations as an intermediate step for a just world order and sustainable development; (2) raising a minimum of an additional US $100 billion per year for development from 2008 to 2015. This is in addition to the comparable financing necessary to implement the Millennium Development Goals, (3) establishing fair mechanisms for the raising of necessary funds with the target of 0.7% of national budgets. Additional money will be raised through levies on global transactions and on the consumption of global public goods, (4) gradually realizing a worldwide Eco-Social Market Economy and overcoming the market fundamentalism through a fair global contract that establishes a better regulatory framework for the world economy, and (5) establishing a workable regulatory framework with a reasonable collaborative partnership on all levels without corruption and with an coordinated flow of resources (Global Marshal Plan, n.d.a).

The Global Marshall Plan is designed to encourage multiple segments of civil society, business, and government to participate. Specifically, the hope is that individuals, churches and other religious organizations, interest groups, NGOs, the scientific community, business leaders, governments and parliaments, the G8, the European Union, and the United Nations will all address the goals. The goal to shape the process of globalization based on mutual respect, empathy, and tolerance is clearly consistent with cultures of peace. By linking funding to environmental and social standards concrete recommendations can be made to regulate the global economy to benefit more people. These recommendations include (1) limiting the risk of speculation against national economies and currencies, (2) implanting a worldwide tax system that abolishes tax havens and offshore banking to realize the $50–60 billion in lost revenue to use for the common good, (3) creating a worldwide policy of cooperation between countries and regions, (4) developing a system where the environmental costs of production are a core element of ecosocial market economy (i.e., polluters pay for their actions), and (5) establishing a world competition commission to prevent overpowering monopolies and cartels (Global Marshall Plan, n.d.b).

Gore (1992) has outlined five strategic goals for his Global Marshall Plan and these are (1) stabilizing the world population, (2) creating and fully developing environmentally appropriate technologies, (3) comprehensively changing the "economic rules of the road" so our decisions are based on environmental impact, (4) negotiating and approving a new generation of international agreements, and (5) establishing a cooperative environmental education plan for the citizens of the world. The overarching goal is to establish the social and political conditions throughout the world, and especially in the developing world, which are conducive to the development of sustainable societies. These goals all have some counterpart in the Global Marshall Plan Initiative discussed above.

The Network of Spiritual Progressives (NSP) developed the third Global Marshall Plan (Network of Spiritual Progressives, 2007). The Network of Spiritual Progressives includes religious leaders from diverse persuasions who have been active to bring more social justice into the world and is co-chaired by Rabbi Michael Lerner, Sister Joan Chittister, a Benedictine nun, and Cornel West, a professor of religion at Princeton University. This NSP Global Marshall Plan is designed to move from the security through domination paradigm to a national security strategy of generosity and care. The overarching goal is to mobilize the world's people to eliminate poverty and restore the health of the environment. As would be expected considering the backgrounds of the developers of this plan, the foundation for this approach is ethical and spiritual (Network of Spiritual Progressives, n.d.).

Like the other Global Marshall Plan, the NSP plan addresses some of the same problems inherent in the world market-based economy yet it goes further in addressing the problems of poverty and sustainability than the other plan (Lerner, 2006). The NSP plan encourages the United States to take a leadership role by example by dedicating at least 1% of its gross domestic product (GDP) toward eliminating global poverty, homelessness, and hunger while providing good health care, good education, and restoring global environments. The intent is to get all industrialized nations to dedicate 1–2% of their GDP as well and these funds would be administered by a newly created international NGO governed by ethicists, religious leaders, social and natural scientists, activists, and others who have demonstrated they place the welfare of the common person above the welfare of corporations or the wealthy (Network of Spiritual Progressives, n.d.). The NSP approach also calls for eliminating debt repayments by the world's poorest countries to the wealthier countries and for changing trade agreements so the privileged countries are not privileged at the expense of the poorer countries. In addition, the NSP plan encourages governmental initiatives in the United States and in other countries as well to ensure hands-on involvement by requiring every citizen to spend two years in national service conducting activities consistent with the Global Marshall Plan goals (Lerner; Network of Spiritual Progressives).

The NSP Global Marshall Plan also has strong educational and training components. First, it seeks to retrain military units in countries to become skilled in construction methods that are environmentally sensitive. In this way a country's military would be better able to provide relief and reconstruction of infrastructure and other important areas. Second, the NSP plan calls for all citizens of the world to be educated in "techniques of nonviolent communication, diversity, environmental sustainability, family and parental support, stress reduction, emergency health techniques, diet and exercise, and caring for others who are in need of help (Network of Spiritual Progressives, n.d., ¶ 16)." The underlying context of this effort requires a respect of native cultures and the empowerment of local people with the intent to "embody and foster love, caring, kindness, generosity, nonviolence, ethical and environmental sensitivity, and the ability to respond to the universe with awe and wonder (Network of Spiritual Progressives, 2007, ¶ 3)."

The Network of Spiritual Progressives is aware that others may view their plan as unrealistic, but nonetheless, consider their plan to be very reasonable. The realization of the vision outlined in the NSP Global Marshall Plan is eventually estimated to cost 3–5% of the world's GDP, but starting at 1% is considered as a good starting point to begin achieving their goals. Not only is the plan viewed as realistic but it is ethically the right thing to do since it is in every one's own best interest to assure that the well-being of everyone else in the world is taken care of too (Network of Spiritual Progressives, n.d.). Lerner (2008) differentiates the NSP plan from previous failed plans to alleviate poverty by pointing to the changes in infrastructure that directly reaches the poor and the caring, spiritual components that will provide affirming bonds to be accomplished by this plan.

Education and Peace Education

Nobel Peace Prize winners in a 1997 manifesto described the best method of ending violence is with nonviolence through education (Harris, 2002b). Wessells et al. (2001) note that both formal and informal education is important for peace at all levels. While in the education system, children and adolescents learn the values, attitudes, and behaviors conducive to peace and social justice. Education is a positive approach to raise people out of poverty and reduce many types of structural violence associated with low socioeconomic status. McGranahan (1995) analyzed longitudinal data from 46 countries and found the ten fastest growing countries based on GDP had invested more in education. Investment in the educational system is significantly associated with positive economic development. "Education has proven the most effective means to address poverty, malnutrition, and poor health conditions that affect one-fifth of the world's population. Throughout the world, education is a means to a better and longer life (Mazurana & McKay, 2001, p. 133)." Education is also a key to the decision making that makes democracies successful (Brienes, 1999).

Not only is a commitment to education in general an important component in achieving cultures of peace, but also the education of girls and women has particularly positive societal benefits. When girls and women receive more education and have higher literacy rates, countries have (1) lower population growth, (2) lower infant mortality rates, (3) women who marry later, (4) women who bear children later in life, (5) women who have fewer children, and (6) better family nutrition (Schwebel & Christie, 2001). Unfortunately, there is gender bias in education rates as women receive only about half the education of men and two-thirds of the nearly one billion illiterate adults in the world are women (Mazurana & McKay, 2001; Schwebel & Christie). Efforts aimed at increasing the number of girls and women who are educated and literate would be very beneficial. Building schools to educate girls where they have not had opportunities in the past is a first step. Greg Mortenson has been building schools for girls in Pakistan and his dedication and tenacity in making education for girls a reality in remote mountainous regions of Asia is a beacon of hope for peace in that part of the world even in these volatile times (Mortenson & Relin, 2006).

One of the fundamental components of global education outlined by UNESCO is learning to live together (Brienes, 1999). Brienes considers "learning to live together" as a type of literacy that is necessary for a culture of peace. Incorporating peace education and the study of nonviolent actions into the educational system of a country is an important step in building cultures of peace (Cromwell & Vogele, 2008). Peace education in its many variations has already been discussed in a previous chapter. While many schools have included peace education into their local curricula, Costa Rica is a country that has integrated many components of peace education into its national curricula (Brenes & Ito, 1994). Since Costa Rica has dissolved its military, it is in a unique position for such action. Costa Rica's commitment to cultures of peace played a role in it becoming the site for the United Nations University for Peace established in the 1980 (Osborn, 2000). Funding and staff consistency has limited the impact of the United Nations University for Peace, however multiple cadres of international graduate students have received several different masters degrees over the years. In addition throughout the 1990s numerous short-term (2–4 weeks) workshops have been offered to leaders in business, government, opposition parties, labor, religious institutions, and civic organizations to encourage values and actions consistent with cultures of peace. The initiative to establish a *Culture of Peace and Democracy* has been developed to make the values of peace and democracy integral to the countries of Central America (Osborn).

Sustainability

The preservation of global resources and meeting the needs of the current generation without compromising the ability to meet the needs of future generations is another component of culture of peace (Wessells et al., 2001). The environmental problems facing our planet have been widely discussed with the prominent voices of Rachel Carson (1962), Lester Brown (1981), and Al Gore (1992, 2006) and this has led to the concern about sustainable development. Sustainable development, as defined by the World Commission on Environment and Development, is "development that meets present needs without compromising the ability of future generations to meet their own needs (Kimmel, 1995, p. 108)." The dimensions of sustainability include natural resources, environment, transportation, population, recreation, and culture along with health, education, political involvement, and government involvement (Corson, cited in Kimmel).

Sustainability has been viewed as the number one priority facing humankind (Likhotal, 2007). Brenes and Winter (2001) regard global environmental security as a critical component in the development of cultures of peace and the task of protecting our global environment to provide this security as one that requires a supreme effort. They note humanity must reduce the threats to survival created by global warming, loss of the earth's ozone, the exhaustion of agricultural land and fisheries, destruction of water supplies, pollution and acid rain, and overconsumption of natural resources. Adelson (2000) stresses the interconnectedness between sustainable human development and the other components of cultures of peace including human rights, women's equality, and respect for diversity. If sustainability is to be reached, she rightfully notes that these other aspects of cultures of peace need to be modified as well.

Brenes and Winter (2001) depict the trends in environmental degradation as leading to increased human suffering on a very large scale. They also remind us how often environmental factors have precipitated or contributed to armed conflicts like the genocides in Rwanda and Cambodia following agricultural disasters. War may be caused by environmental crises, like access to water or other natural resources like oil in the Middle East. Klare (2001) describes the concept of resource wars where national security now depends on the continued availability of needed natural resources and goods. Resource wars have been fought when the real or potential disruption in the flow of needed resources occurs. Klare points to US military actions in the Persian Gulf and Caspian Sea Basin over oil. He also illustrates resource conflicts over water in the Nile, Jordan, Tigrus-Euphrates, and Indus river basins along with mineral and timber rights in Africa and Asia. War can also precipitate environmental pollution and degradation. For instance, the 1991 Persian

Gulf War released many toxins and radiation into the air and into the water and food supply for human consumption through fire and munitions casings made from depletes uranium (McKay, 1996).

The United Nations has recognized the link between environmental issues and sustainability and world peace for some time. The UN Conference on Environment and Development (UNCED) released the *Agenda 21* document in 1993; the Earth Charter was released in 1997 and both documents present approaches to sustainability for the planet. Brenes and Winter (2001) provide a nice historical context and analysis of these two documents. The *Agenda 21* is an over 800-page document developed to guide governments toward principles, goals, policies, and actions that can restore and protect the global environment (http://www.un.org/esa/sustdev/documents/agenda21/index.htm). Agenda 21 deals with (1) the social and economic dimensions of consumption, sustainability, and survival, (2) conservation and resource management, (3) strengthening the role of women, children, workers and farmers, businesses, scientists, and other major groups in working for sustainability, and (4) financial and international mechanisms of implementation. Despite the good intentions behind the Agenda 21, Brenes and Winter point out that it has not resulted in the implementation of government actions needed to restore spoiled environments. The Earth Charter is a much shorter, parallel document to *Agenda 21* and is directed more toward private citizens, humanitarian groups, and nongovernmental organizations and more indirectly toward government leaders. While it is also a soft law document, like *Agenda 21*, the Earth Charter is more of a consciousness-raising document designed to develop a sense of personal, ethical responsibility with the intent that binding, hard law treaties will soon be negotiated.

The Earth Charter was formulated in over a decade of discussions and numerous conferences with significant support from Mikhail Gorbachev, former head of state of the Soviet Union and chair of Green Cross International, and Maurice Strong, Canadian businessman, environmentalist, and Chair of the Earth Council, and the organizations they represented (Likhotal, 2007). The 16 principles of the Earth Charter within four general areas are as follows:

1. Respect and care for the community of life:
   (a) Respect Earth and life in all its diversity
   (b) Care for the community of life with understanding, compassion, and love
   (c) Build democratic societies that are just, participatory, sustainable, and peaceful
   (d) Secure Earth's bounty and beauty for present and future generations
In order to fulfill these four broad commitments, it is necessary to:

2. Ecological integrity:
   (a) Protect and restore the integrity of Earth's ecological systems, with special concern for biological diversity and the natural processes that sustain life
   (b) Prevent harm as the best method of environmental protection and, when knowledge is limited, apply a precautionary approach
   (c) Adopt patterns of production, consumption, and reproduction that safeguard Earth's regenerative capacities, human rights, and community well-being

(d) Advance the study of ecological sustainability and promote the open exchange and wide application of the knowledge acquired

3. Social and economic justice:
    (a) Eradicate poverty as an ethical, social, and environmental imperative
    (b) Ensure that economic activities and institutions at all levels promote human development in an equitable and sustainable manner
    (c) Affirm gender equality and equity as prerequisites to sustainable development and ensure universal access to education, health care, and economic opportunity
    (d) Uphold the right of all, without discrimination, to a natural and social environment supportive of human dignity, bodily health, and spiritual well-being, with special attention to the rights of indigenous peoples and minorities

4. Democracy, nonviolence, and peace:
    (a) Strengthen democratic institutions at all levels, and provide transparency and accountability in governance, inclusive participation in decision making, and access to justice
    (b) Integrate into formal education and life-long learning the knowledge, values, and skills needed for a sustainable way of life
    (c) Treat all living beings with respect and consideration
    (d) Promote a culture of tolerance, nonviolence, and peace. (Earth Charter Initiative (n.d.); Earth Charter Principles, 2007)

In addition to the principles that directly relate to ecological concerns and sustainability issues, an inspection of these 16 principles again demonstrates the interrelationships between sustainability and the other aspects of cultures of peace. For instance, principle 16 deals with nonviolence and principle 13 addresses democracy and inclusiveness while gender equity is part of principle 11. Likhotal (2007) summarizes the impact of the Earth Charter well when he characterizes it as a blueprint of relevant ethical principles that are designed to serve as a bold and creative stimulus for the transformation of the world toward a sustainable future. Vilela (2007) considers the Earth Charter to be more than a document in that it is a process whereby the capacity of civil society can be tapped to bring about a significant social change.

Brenes and Winter (2001) point out one advantage of the brief Earth Charter over *Agenda 21* is that it incorporates the psychological concepts of responsibility, interdependence, shared identity, and values. In so doing it may be more readily taken up by nongovernmental organizations that may be better able to affect the positive change needed to achieve sustainability. The notion of people needing to define themselves as members of an international family, instead of only being citizens of a particular country, implies an interdependent identity needed to broach a broader or universal responsibility to human kind and the whole planet.

Moving toward sustainable development throughout the world is a positive goal and, as argued above, it is an imperative goal for human kind and the development of cultures of peace. There are many strategies that can move humanity toward sustainability and many should be implemented simultaneously to complement each other. Methods that increase sustainability, once imagined, can be implemented in the daily lives of people at a local level (Lipschutz, 2002). Likhotal (2007) identifies more societal recommendations based upon the Earth Charter and the findings of Green Cross International's Earth Dialogue initiative. Poyyamoli (2003) sees ecotourism as a positive activity to put pressure on different cultures to maintain environmental integrity within their regions of the world. Using India as an example, Poyyamoli delineates the advantages of ecotourism while noting the pitfalls of mass tourism with respect to the environment.

In a 1946 telegram to a group of fellow scientists Einstein warned us that "The unleashed power of the atom has changed everything save our modes of thinking, and we thus drift toward unparalleled catastrophe (cited in Hauss, 1996, p. 9)." Kimmel (1995) alludes to this in the context of sustainability, as the perils faced by this potential human disaster are akin to those faced by irresponsible nuclear policies. Brenes and Winter (2001) conclude that the attainment of the environmental health of the planet requires a psychological solution and a shift in the way people conceptualize our global environment. They describe the real task is to develop behavioral changes so that human greed, selfishness, and hedonism are overcome to restore environmental health and to maintain a sustainable world. Likhotal (2007) sees the resolution of the sustainability question as an ethical issue and Brenes and Winter as a moral issue. Kimmel points to the need for clear reasoning and moral judgments. Brenes and Winter demonstrate the moral aspect of environmental behaviors with the familiar example of recycling. People do not recycle because it saves them money, is personally beneficial, or is easy to do. Recycling is time consuming and generally inconvenient. It is done because it is moral and the right thing to do.

"Sustainable cultures will require changed thoughts, beliefs, feelings, and behaviors of billions of people making daily choices, as well as the education of local, state, and national leaders whose decisions will affect the environmental health for generations to come (Brenes & Winter, 2001, p. 169)." Businesses and economic institutions like the World Bank and the International Monetary Fund are oftentimes working against the shift in thinking and behaving, as the status quo is better for their monetary bottom lines. Major international firms and conglomerates of local and regional companies are encouraged and funded to implement projects that pollute the environment, destroy habitats and natural resources, and disrupt or destroy local and indigenous cultures to turn larger profits (Kimmel, 1995). The task in building cultures of peace is to reorient from thinking of the monetary profits as the driving force. The sustainable bottom line is not about money; the real bottom line should be a moral line. This notion is captured nicely in the preamble to the Earth Charter that states "We must realize when basic needs have been met, human development is primarily about being more, not having more (Earth Charter Initiative, n.d., p. 1)."

Conclusion

I have described several dozen peaceful societies or peaceful cultures and the characteristics of these are informative to understanding how we might move from a culture of violence and war to a culture of peace. These peaceful societies favor cooperative interactions and oppose competition in most forms. Members of peaceful societies do not view conflict and violence as a normal occurrence and when the potential for conflict emerges, they often try to avoid it initially and are seldom inclined to directly deal with the other parties without third party involvement. Nonviolence, harmony, and the well being of the community are integral parts of a peaceful society's worldview. Child rearing practices build and reinforce these societal norms in a consistent fashion.

The notion of a culture of peace that has been outlined and delineated by the United Nations is a potentially powerful concept. On a societal level a culture of peace encompasses many of the components discussed in terms of intrapersonal and interpersonal peace as well as some new concepts. Nonviolence and norms to sustain nonviolent behavior are certainly in common with all three types of peace. The values associated with intrapersonal nonviolence and interpersonal nonviolence, such as being forgiving, tolerant, and broadminded relate to inclusiveness in society at large. The priority placed on the value of self-control and the value type of conformity impact human rights standards and the rule of law. Universalism values may be seen as the basis for sustainability and social justice. The self-transcendence values of benevolence and universalism are relevant to building and maintaining a civil society.

A culture of peace might take many forms depending on the specific societal and cultural constraints in the location in which it is developed. Therefore, there are many potential cultures of peace that could replace the cultures of violence that dominate societies in today's world. The Manifesto 2000 and the United Nations work on cultures of peace provide individuals, groups, communities, societies, and nations with a positive blueprint to use in peacebuilding and developing a more nonviolent world. It is important that efforts to create cultures of peace are not imposed otherwise the potential for a new type of imperialism might undermine any progress made (Brenes & Wessells, 2001). As in any peacebuilding endeavor, there are many societal institutions that will make changes from a culture of violence to a culture of peace difficult. However, there are many concrete recommendations that have been proposed including peace education and the Global Marshall Plans that appear to be able to move society in the direction of peace and nonviolence sooner than later if they are adopted with reasonable resources. As Brenes and Wessells point out, "The construction of cultures of peace is an inherently multidisciplinary task because it requires political, social, economic, and cultural transformation (p. 102)." This multidisciplinary effort will take time, energy, resources, and perseverance.

Recommended Readings

Bonta, B. D. (1993). *Peaceful peoples: An annotated bibliography*. Metuchen, NJ: Scarecrow.
    Bonta has identified and annotated a considerable amount of books, articles, and chapters that discuss and analyze the many peaceful cultures from around the world. This volume will be very helpful to peace scholars, peace researchers, and peace activists in locating information on 47 societies that foster peacefulness.
Boulding, E. (2000b). *Cultures of peace: The hidden side of history*. Syracuse, NY: Syracuse University Press.

Boulding presents the development of the cultures of peace movement and from the perspective of someone who was intimately involved at many levels. Her easily read book reviews the history of cultures of war and peace movements before presenting the peace cultures in action today. She outlines the feminist perspectives along with the importance of partnerships between men and women and between children and adults. Boulding also analyzes how existing conflict structures might be transformed into cultures of peace.

Brenes, A., & Wessells, M. (Eds.). (2001). Entire issue of *Peace and Conflict: Journal of Peace Psychology, 7*(2).

This entire Millennium II issue of *Peace and Conflict: Journal of Peace Psychology* looks at the psychological contributions to cultures of peace. Separate articles address political obstacles, democratization, solidarity, nonviolence, sustainability, and policies.

Christie, D. J. (1997). Reducing direct and structural violence: The human needs theory. *Peace and Conflict: Journal of Peace Psychology, 3*(4), 315–332.

In this classic paper, Christie presents the case for having human needs theory replace the theory of power politics in peace psychology. He outlines how human needs theory can be used to reduce direct and structural violence. Human needs theory has clear implications for more social justice in the world.

de Rivera, J. H. (Guest Ed.). (2004). Assessing cultures of peace [Special issue]. *Peace and Conflict: Journal of Peace Psychology, 10*(2).

In this special issue methods to assess whether a particular culture is a culture of peace are conceptualized and tested in several contexts. The UN definition and components of cultures of peace are used by de Rivera in a template for assessing cultures of peace. Fernández-Dols et al. provide an alternative definition with different measurement recommendations. Other authors specifically apply the concept of cultures of peace with Spain and Brazil.

de Rivera, J. H., & Perez, D. (Eds.). (2007). Emotional climate, human security, and culture of peace. An entire issue of *Journal of Social Issues* devoted to cultures of peace, *66*(2).

In this special issue of the Journal of Social Issues, de Rivera and Páez have assembled a range of articles that address cultures of peace and the role of psychosocial processes and emotional climate. A secondary theme that cuts across the articles is human security and the effect of terrorist attacks with a focus on South America and Europe.

Norsworthy, K. L., & Gerstein, L. H. (Eds.). (2003). Counseling and building communities of peace. An entire issue of the *International Journal for the Advancement of Counselling, 25*(4).

In this special issue counselors and therapists address a variety of structural and systemic counseling approaches that can impact the establishment and reinforcement of cultures of peace. Both theory and practice are scrutinized across nine articles. Specific topics considered are counseling's role in community based projects, racism, reconciliation, human rights for lesbian, gay, bisexual, and transgendered people, bullying, and child soldiers.

Sponsel, L. E., & Gregor, T. (Eds.). (1994). *The anthropology of peace and nonviolence.* Boulder, CO: Lynne Rienner.

This edited volume by Sponsel and Gregor includes several articles that analyze peaceable cultures from an anthropological perspective. The relevant dynamics of culture that make the people in peaceful societies behave nonviolently are discussed. Many illustrative examples are presented from the Inuits in Canada, the Semai of Malasia, and the Meninaku and Yanomami in South America. A case is made for a pedagogy of the anthropology of peace and nonviolence.

Recommended Web Sites

Culture of Peace News Network, http://cpnn-usa.org/

The Culture of Peace News Network (CPNN) is a global network of interactive Internet sites for readers to exchange information about events, experiences, books, music, and Web news that promotes a culture of peace. This is a project sponsored by the United Nations for the

International Decade for a Culture of Peace and Non-Violence for the Children of the World. There are many useful links on this site including links to articles relevant to each of the Manifesto 2000's eight keys to peace.

Earth Charter Initiative, http://www.earthcharter.org/

This Web site is devoted to the Earth Charter and its implementation worldwide. In addition to the complete text of the charter in over 30 languages plus FAQ and background material on its development, this Web site has a means for individuals to personally endorse the charter. Recent news about the Earth Charter Initiative in general and the specific initiatives for youth are also linked on the Web site. It is also possible to download primary, secondary, and higher education lesson plans and resource materials on aspects of the Earth Charter and the book *Toward a Sustainable World: The Earth Charter in Action*. In addition to the typical organizational requests for money, this Earth Charter Initiative provides those interested in volunteering their time concrete examples of what the organization needs. Another related and worthwhile Web site that links to *Agenda 21* is http://www.un.org/esa/sustdev/documents/agenda21/index.htm

Education for a Culture of Peace, UNESCO, http://www.unesco.org/education/ecp/index.htm

This Web site is part of the United Nations and UNESCO's work to improve the education of people of the world. The mandate for the organization behind this site is in article 26 of the Universal Declaration of Human Rights that stated, "Everyone has the right to education... Education shall be directed to the full development of the human personality and to the strengthening of respect for human rights and fundamental freedoms. It shall promote understanding, tolerance, and friendship among all nations, racial and religious groups, and shall further the activities of the United Nations for the maintenance of peace."

Global Marshall Plan: Balancing the World, http://www.globalmarshallplan.org/

The first Web site for the Global Marshall Plan Initiative brings together individuals from many disciplines to develop a fairer globalization process and a better balance in the world. Within this integrative organizational platform an alliance of positive energy from politics, business, science, and civil society seek to bring their special skills and access diverse social networks to the Initiative. This page links to a treasure trove of information that is relevant to students, professionals, researchers, and activists interested in helping those in poverty and in improving the global economy by creating balance between the economy, environment, society, and culture. Another Web site (http://www.spiritualprogressives.org/article. php?story=20070226095019665) by the *Network of Spiritual Progressives* provides an alternative Global Marshall Plan. Both sites deserve a look.

Let's Talk America, http://www.letstalkamerica.org/

Let's *Talk America* is a nationwide movement designed to bring Americans from diverse political points of view together in multiple venues from homes to churches to restaurants and cafes for lively and spirited dialog to consider important questions facing our democracy. This "town hall" meeting process is being encouraged to rekindle what used to be viewed as the lifeblood of our democracy. Within *Let's Talk America* sessions, everyone is encouraged to talk about America's promise and the meaning of freedom, democracy, unity, and equality to "we the people." *Let's Talk America* is a safe place for people to come together to listen, speak, ask, and learn – without being forced to agree, change, or bite our tongues.

Manifesto 2000, The United Nations Cultures of Peace. Retrieved April 24, 2008, from http:// www3.unesco.org/iycp/uk/uk_sum_cp.htm

This page will link you to the page where you can still sign the Manifest 2000 pledge electronically. You will need to click on the *Manifesto 2000* button in the column on the left and then click on the Manifesto and Sign It buttons on the top of subsequent pages to read and then electronically sign the Manifesto.

Open Society Institute, Retrieved June 2, 2008, from http://www.soros.org/

The Open Society Institute (OSI) was founded by investor and philanthropist George Soros as a private grant making foundation to effect policy that promotes democracy in general plus human rights and economic, legal, and social reform at the local through international levels. OSI has funded initiatives in Africa, Asia, Europe, North and South America to deal with may aspects of cultures of peace and specifically covering topics from public health to education to business development. The Web site includes information about the past and current initiatives, about applying for grants, scholarships, and fellowships, and about events relevant to open societies around the world. The resources links on the Web site include video and multimedia presentations about a range of human rights issues.

Southern Poverty Law Center, Retrieved May 4, 2008, from http://www.splcenter.org/

From its beginnings in 1971 as a small civil rights law firm the Southern Poverty Law Center has grown into an internationally known organization that has developed tolerance education programs, provided legal support for people threatened and attached by white supremists and hate groups. The legal victories it has won have stopped and forced the bankruptcy of many hate groups including the Aryan Nation.

United Nations CyberSchoolBus. (1995). *Peace Education*. Retrieved September 13, 2007, from http://www.un.org/cyberschoolbus/peace/home.asp

United Nations CyberSchoolBus is a most interesting Web site that tailors to the "learner as teacher" or the "teacher as learner." From the beginning this Web site differentiates the differences in peace education for what role the individual plays in society. Learner as teacher entails of five units that represent critical themes in educating others about "a culture of peace" and allow for creativity, whereas the teacher-as-learner consists of a more broad selection to choose from on the theory of peace education. Therefore, this Web site is great for a breakdown of the roles common in school systems today and some parts of the world.

The UN Universal Declaration of Human Rights. (1948). http://www.un.org/Overview/rights. html; http://www.unesco.org/shs/humanrights/udhr_60anniversary

The first link takes you to the text of the UN's Universal Declaration of Human Rights that was adopted by the General Assembly of the Unites Nations on December 10, 1948. The second link takes you to the UNESCO Web page that commemorates the 60th anniversary of the Universal Declaration. This page links to analyses of the steps needed and the hurdles that must be jumped to make this declaration a real universal around the world in the twenty-first century.

White Ribbon Campaign: Men Working to End Men's Violence Against Women, http://www. whiteribbon.ca/about_us/

The White Ribbon Campaign claims to be the world's largest effort to get men to end violence directed towards women and exists in over 50 different countries. The emphasis is on educating men and boys to be aware of the problems women experience and to take an active role in ending violence against women. Curricular materials for middle school and high school may be ordered through their Web site.

Women and Cultures of Peace, http://www.unesco.org/cpp/uk/projects/gender.htm

While this page primarily focuses on women and cultures of peace in the Caribbean Region of the world, the concepts and information presented are very relevant to gender and peace issues regardless of location. In addition the Publication button and Exemplary Actions button link to reports and information about women and cultures of peace from around the world.

Chapter 7
Nonviolent Perspectives Within the Abrahamic Religions

> *Religions are different roads converging upon the same point.*
> *What does it matter that we take different roads so long as we*
> *reach the same goal?*
>
> Gandhi, cited in Attenborough, 1982, p. 75

While Allport (1950) noted that empirical psychology and religion separated early in the history of psychology, he recognized that "there is inherent absurdity in supposing that psychology and religion, both dealing with the outward reaching of man's mind, must be permanently and hopelessly at odds" (p. x). Religion is a significant aspect in the lives of billions of people. As was shown in Chap. 4, Eastern religions have much to offer in our understanding of intrapersonal nonviolence. Over half of the world's population follow one of the four Abrahamic religions of Judaism, Christianity, Islam and Bahá'í so these faiths can undoubtedly assist us in our grasp of nonviolence and peace psychology.

This chapter looks carefully at the religious texts of Judaism, Christianity, Islam and Bahá'í to better understand the views on nonviolence of these four Abrahamic faiths. In addition to looking at the holy texts the discussion includes remarkable members of each faith that championed and used nonviolence in their writings and in their life works. Both historically important and contemporary proponents of nonviolence will be highlighted. An annotated bibliography of classic and recent books on this topic as well as websites will be provided at the end.

Judaism, Christianity, Islam, and Bahá'í are monotheistic religions that have their origins in the cradle of western civilization or what is generally referred to today as the Middle East. All four religions share the story of Abraham and his sons Isaac and Ishmael (Solomon, Harries, & Winter, 2005). In fact much of the early writings and prophets in each faith are shared. Because the dates of the beginning of each religion are sequential, Judaism overlaps the least with the other three and Bahá'í overlaps the most with the other three in terms of common stories.

In this chapter I will present the major teachings, beliefs and practices of each of the four Abrahamic religions in chronological order of their emergence on the world scene. While limited space does not allow for a complete discussion of each belief system, the summaries are designed to provide a minimally sufficient knowledge base to understand how nonviolence is conceptualized within each religious

D.M. Mayton II, *Nonviolence and Peace Psychology*, 167
DOI 10.1007/978-0-387-89348-8_7, © Springer Science+Business Media, LLC 2009

context, and to begin to see similarities and differences in the religious perspectives. After discussing the tenets of each religion, I will describe two individuals in that religion who have championed nonviolence in a major way. The chapter will end with an outline of commonalities among the religions in their approaches to peace and nonviolence.

Judaism

While Judaism may refer to a group of people and their ancient and rich culture with its songs, literature, social institutions, and other trappings of culture, Judaism also refers to the religion of this group (Steinberg, 1947). Therefore, when speaking of Judaism, one may be referring to the Jewish people and culture or the Jewish religion. The number of Jews in the world today is hard to determine because of this. It is estimated that there are about 17 million Jews in the world today with between a quarter and a third of that number being secular Jews who are not practicing and unaffiliated with a synagogue. In this chapter I will be exploring Judaism from its religious connotation.

Jewish Beliefs and Rituals

Judaism has been described as the "Mother of Monotheism" and its history goes back four millennia (Steinberg, 1947). The Jewish religion contains seven strands that are:

1. A doctrine concerning God, the universe and man
2. A morality for the individual and society
3. A regimen of rite, custom, and ceremony
4. A body of law
5. A sacred literature
6. Institutions through which the foregoing find expression
7. The people, Israel – central strand out of which and about which others are spun (Steinberg, pp. 3–4)

While distinct in some respects, Steinberg describes these strands or threads as woven together over the centuries such that it is impossible to separate any one of them from the others.

Judaism worships one God, initially referred to as Yahweh, not many gods as there were in other religions of the time (Monroe, 1995). God is seen as the creator and is not synonymous with the world in a pantheistic way but is seen as being in the world (Hertzberg, 1961). Judaism believes that God reveals himself to significant people or prophets who have special talents and are inspired by God (McCasland et al., 1969). In this manner God, the creator of man and the universe, has communicated to the Jewish people that they are the "Chosen People" and will bring the rule of order, law, and peace to the world when the time is right (Monroe). Within Judaism, a special covenant or contract between God and man exists and this spells out the relationship between man and God. Obedience to God, and only God, will be rewarded with freedom and salvation from personal and collective sins. God is seen as omniscience and omnipresent (McCasland et al.). Monroe indicates that for Jews, sin and morality have an individual aspect as well as a social one, but the responsibility of finding the path to redemption from sin is with the individual. He also points out that Judaism views people as basically good and that the earth is for them to enjoy during their lives and looking toward enjoyment with an afterlife in heaven is not a focal point.

Sacred Jewish Texts

The sacred literature of Judaism includes several texts. The early oral tradition began to be written down around 1000 B.C.E. and continued as more and more scholars put the stories to scroll. The Hebrew Bible includes much of the writings of the Christian Old Testament and its twenty-four books are divided into three parts: the *Torah* or Law, the *Prophets*, and the *Writings*. The *Torah*, which includes Genesis, Exodus, Leviticus, Numbers, and Deuteronomy, covers the tradition on Moses and was probably written over seven centuries beginning after his lifetime around 1200 B.C.E. (McCasland et al., 1969). While synagogues may take many architectural forms and may have no symbolism displayed or have considerable ornamentation, the presence of the *Torah* and a Jewish congregation define a place of worship for Jews (Steinberg, 1947). "Every synagogue possesses, enshrines, and makes accessible at least one copy, in scroll form, of the book known as the *Torah*. With this book go almost unfailing appurtenances: robes and adornments with which it is draped, an Ark or cabinet in which it is housed, a lectern from which it is read, and even an ever-burning lamp reminiscent of that which illuminated the Tabernacle and Temple in ancient times, but symbolic equally of the unquenchable light of the book" (Steinberg, pp. 18–19). The contents of the *Torah* provide a history of the Jewish people, God's interactions with humanity, and prescriptions about how to obey God's laws and earn his blessings (Monroe, 1995). The *Prophets*, or second section, includes the writings about the earliest prophets, except for Moses, through the prophets from the sixth century B.C.E. This section preached obedience to God, the idea that Jews needed to be "suffering servants" of God, and that God would send a messiah or military hero to save them (Monroe). The *Writings* are the last books of the Jewish Bible and this canon became recognized around 100 C.E. (McCasland et al.). Monroe describes the *Writings* as the wisdom books since the authors of the books in this section infused philosophical concepts from Egypt and Greece into their text. Thus, the *Writings*, which included Psalms, Job, Proverbs, and Ecclesiastes, explored ultimate truth and knowledge for the Jewish people (Monroe).

Another important text for Jews is the *Talmud*. McCasland et al. (1969) describe the Talmud as an encyclopedic work of interpretations by religious scholars of the Torah and the codes of law that Jews need to live by. The first section of the *Talmud* is the *Mishnah* that analyzes problems and rules concerning family life and the position of women, sexual behavior, civil law, agriculture, sanitation, and festivals and rites (Monroe, 1995). The remainder of the *Talmud*, the *Gemara*, is commentaries and interpretations of the *Mishnah*. The *Talmud* is required study for all Jewish scholars (McCasland et al.).

Jewish Dogma and Holy Days

Whether there is a dogma, or set of beliefs, in Judaism has been a topic debated by Jewish scholars for centuries at least (Steinberg, 1947). McCasland et al. (1969) warn that it is important to realize ancient Hebrews viewed religion as an integral aspect of life in the broadest sense and not as a philosophical or even theological system. Steinberg describes Judaism as having "a very definite religious outlook" and not a dogma, precise propositions, or a formal creed. Among the many rites, rituals, and customs, the oldest ritual is male circumcision. On the eighth day after birth all males are to be circumcised as a sign of the covenant with God. Failure to do so breaks the covenant (Hertzberg, 1961). Marriage is considered a basic unit of Jewish society and it is expected that men and women will marry and have children. Sex within marriage is to be enjoyed as part of the good life God has provided, however, premarital sex and adultery are viewed as evil (Monroe). While Judaism is patriarchal, the role of women in the family has typically been strong in raising and educating the children as well as running the household. Children celebrate coming of age at thirteen with a bar mitzvah for boys or a bat mitzvah for girls. The observation of the Sabbath begins on Friday evening and continues through Saturday. During the Sabbath, work is not permitted. Traditionally, families are together at home, special blessings are observed, and special food is served following religious principles. The Kashruth, or dietary requirements and restrictions, involves eating kosher foods and avoiding certain foods or combinations of foods. While pork and shellfish are forbidden and milk and meat cannot be consumed together, animals must be slaughtered in a special way and with special tools under the supervision of a rabbi for the meat to be kosher (Hertzberg, Monroe).

There are many holy days that are celebrated throughout the year that mark significant events in the history of the Jewish people. The Passover feast of unleavened bread in the springtime celebrates the renewal of life and commemorates the night when the Jews were exiled in Egypt and God spared them from the ravages of a plague. Rosh Hashanah is the first two days of the Jewish New Year and marks the day of creation and the Day of Judgment. The Day of Judgment is the highest holy day when Jews ask for repentance for their sins. Yom Kippur is the tenth day after Rosh Hashanah and is a time of fasting and repentance. Hanukah, an eight-day festival of lights, commemorates the successful resolution of a siege of a group of

Jewish people and the rededication of their temple when the lights were relit. During Hanukah, candles are symbolically lit each evening, starting with one and adding another each subsequent evening, until all are burning the last night. Presents are exchanged each day during this happy time. Other holy days include Sukkoth, a festival celebrating fall harvests, and Purim, commemorating the role played by Queen Esther in winning the release of her Jewish people held captive in Persia (Monroe, 1995).

Branches of Judaism

Modern Judaism in the western world includes Orthodox, Conservative, and Reform divisions as the major branches. The Orthodox Jew attaches the utmost importance to the *Torah*, all commandments, and all scripture. These texts are considered to be infallible and unchanging. "A good [Orthodox] Jew is expected to pray three times a day, eat only kosher food, observe the Sabbath, refrain from sexual intercourse for two weeks each month, avoid interracial and interreligious marriages, and devote much time to the study of Scripture" (Monroe, 1995, pp. 156–157). The role of women among Orthodox Jews is more traditional with less freedom. About 40% of the Jews in the United States follow Orthodox practices. Hasidic Jews make up a more conservative subbranch of Orthodox Jews. The Conservative Jew is less extreme than those who are Orthodox. While Conservative Jews follow the Torah and practice the traditional rites and ceremonies, they are more tolerant of other groups than the Orthodox tend to be. Women are treated as equals in the synagogue and languages other than Hebrew may be used during worship services. About 30% of the Jews in the United States are Conservative and the remaining 30% are in the Reformed branch. The Reformed Jew follows the most liberal practices and recognizes the effects of modernity in their religious practices. Strict interpretations of sacred texts are rejected and dietary laws, dress codes, and rituals are relaxed. Reformed Jews downplay supernatural aspects of their religion and put more of their time and resources into social and political causes. Equality for women in the Reformed tradition extends to the right to hold official positions in the synagogue. Reconstructionist Jews make up a more liberal sub branch of Reformed Jews (Monroe).

Jewish Views of Nonviolence

Judaism is not a pacifistic religion and, given a long history of persecution because of anti-Semitic attitudes, the Jewish people have regularly used violence to assure their survival. While Semite originally referred to the people from southwestern Asia who spoke any of many Semitic languages including Arabic, Aramaic and Hebrew, the term has come to be a derogatory one for a Jew. Anti-Semitism involves discrimination and hostility directed toward Jews as a religious or ethnic group. Throughout history anti-Semitism has had a profound impact on the psyche of the Jewish people. Whether it involved prejudice, discrimination, or persecution at the community level or whether it involved large-scale strategies like the Spanish Inquisition of the fifteenth century, pogroms in Central and Eastern Europe in the last two centuries, and the Holocaust in the twentieth century, thousands and thousands of Jews have been killed each century of their latest exile. During the twentieth century the death toll was exponentially higher as at least one in five Jews worldwide was killed. The last half of the twentieth century and the beginning of the twenty-first century has been a much more positive time for Jews with the establishment of Israel (Eizenstat, 2008). However, while Israel has provided incredible opportunities for its Jewish citizens, the survival of the state has depended on them successfully waging a string of wars against neighboring states and the maintenance of a strong military.

It is possible to use Judaism to justify the use of violence and this has been done (Milgrom, 1998). The Talmud and the rest of the Hebrew Bible and other Jewish sacred texts have numerous passages where extreme violence occurs and is enacted, commanded, and approved of by God. As examples, Milgrom points to Genesis where sinners are killed in the flood along with innocents, to Exodus where Egyptians are drowned in the Red Sea even though it is not necessary for the survival of the Israelites, and to Deuteronomy where God demands the eradication of idolaters and political enemies. These and other texts portray a God that requires followers to perform terrifying acts of violence and cruelty in order to satisfy Him or to obtain His approval.

Violence, as an act of self-defense, is permitted under Jewish law (Lichton, 2001). Gendler (1981) sees Judaism as placing self-defense as a primary duty for Jews. Interpretations of the Talmud do allow for people to kill another, as a type of preemptive self-defense, if the other person is coming to kill them (Kimelman, 2005). However, self-defense should not result in killing, unless there are no other alternatives. When self-defense does result in killing, Judaic texts provide relatively little solace to the defender (Kimelman). It is also not appropriate to attribute one's success to one's ability to use physical force and violence. This belief would undermine a person's faith and understanding in God. God also sanctions capital punishment (Milgrom, 1998). While Jewish law allows for the killing of animals, this killing must be done humanely and only for food to sustain human life (Lichton).

Even with these violent aspects in Judaic writing, many have elaborated on accounts that support nonviolence from a Jewish perspective (Fisher, 1990; Kimelman, 2005; Milgrom, 1998; Solomonow, 1981). Murder is not allowed and this admonition is stated in Exodus as a commandment (Kimelman). The Torah also rejects someone striking another person (Grunblatt, 1981). Evil behavior is not appropriate in Judaism and, even when confronted with evil, people should not respond with evil, otherwise evil will remain with them (Kimelman).

Jewish law also stresses the nourishment and protection of human life too, and this can support nonviolence (Lichton, 2001). Lichton notes the Torah indicates it is important to proactively save an endangered life except when so doing requires murder, adultery, or idolatry. Kimelman points out that the Hebrew Bible does not explicitly require or expect a person to live a nonviolent life, yet in Proverbs it says "Do not envy a man of violence and do not choose any of his ways" (p. 29). The need to love our neighbor as our self, found in Leviticus 19:18 of the Talmud, is another example of a nonviolent aspiration. Lerner (2006) sees Isaiah as supporting this life nourishing aspect of Judaism. "Learn to do good, seek justice, aid the oppressed, uphold the rights of the orphan, defend the cause of the widow" (Isaiah 1:17, cited in Lerner, p. 215). Kimelman also identifies the phrase of "*Gadol Hashalom*" from many major rabbinic texts that places peace as the most important value for Jews. *Shalom*, or peace, can be referred to at an interpersonal or at a collective level and it is often viewed as an inclusive concept that must be shared with others.

Kimelman (2005) describes how in Proverbs the expectation is to give food and drink to your enemy if they are hungry or thirsty. Assisting one's enemy in this way or other ways is important to change the enemies perception of you, and you are better off as your assistance curbs your hate for the enemy. Kimelman's analysis of the Talmud also revealed the need to avoid hate. "You shall not hate your brother in your heart" (Leviticus, cited in Kimelman, 1981, p. 26). This view of hate is also reflected in some Judaic phrasing of the golden rule when it is stated as "That which is hateful unto you, do not do to your comrade" (Milgrom, 1998, p. 128). Kimelman (1981, 2005) also finds a parallel to Gandhi's self-suffering in the Talmud. The Talmud also asserts "Who is a hero? He who turns his enemy into a friend" (Groves, 2008, p. 79).

Judaic writings and traditions do support many aspects of cultures of peace. These can be seen in the Messianic vision of peace from Isaiah (Kimelman, 2005; Milgrom, 1998) and in the many interpretations of the sacred texts (Gendler, 1981; Lichton, 2001; Milgrom; Schwarzschild, 1981). Judaism addresses social justice, human rights, and issues of poverty, oppression, and sustainability.

Notable Jewish Advocates of Nonviolence

Many Jewish people have advocated peace through nonviolent means and devoted their time to activist causes. Rabbi Heschel walked with Martin Luther King Jr. during Civil Rights Marches in the American South and spoke out against racism. Morton Deutsch and Milt Schwebel are two people identified as "Pioneers in Peace Psychology" by the Society for the Study of Peace, Conflict, and Violence. While neither was an absolute pacifist as both served in the military during World War II, both were deeply concerned about social injustice and devoted their life to making the world more just and less violent. Deutsch's work on cooperation and conflict resolution has already been discussed in earlier chapters. Although not a religious person, being Jewish is a part of his identity, and Deutsch did personally experience anti-Semitism as a youth (Deutsch, personal communication, June 13, 2008). These personal experiences and his awareness of anti-Semitism in the world sensitized

Deutsch to prejudice and discrimination toward Jews and other people as well. During his illustrious academic career he conducted groundbreaking research on peace, conflict resolution, cooperation, and a range of social issues. He served as president of the Society for the Psychological Study of Social Issues, International Society of Political Psychology and the Society for the Study of Peace, Conflict, and Violence (Roe, Wessells, & McKay, 2006). Schwebel grew up in a relatively orthodox Jewish home and experienced anti-Semitism from the age of 8 or 9 when he recalls seeing a sign on a playground that said, "No Dogs or Jews Allowed." He quickly realized he was part of a group being targeted for discrimination and his concerns about equality and justice grew during this time in his life. His early experiences were a combination of religious wisdom and family teaching, and these instilled a humanism and liberalism in him even though during his college years he became an atheist and socialist (Schwebel, personal communication, June 13, 2008). Like Deutsch, even though Schwebel had anti-war sentiments, he joined the military and fought in World War II. Two months before D-Day in England he had two American soldiers "spit out the words, Nigger lover" at him. Early in his career Schwebel was a youth counselor and coach who racially integrated teams for the first time and worked for sexual equality in hiring. After receiving his doctorate, his concerns led him into teaching, research, and activism for the cause of peace and social justice with his wife, Bernice. He published pioneering empirical research on the impact of the nuclear threat on children in the 1960s and was founding editor of the journal *Peace & Conflict: Journal of Peace Psychology*. His activism was typified by his decades' long involvement in Psychologists for Social Action and then Psychologists for Social Responsibility (Roe, McKay, & Wessells, 2003).

Joseph Abileah has been described as the "Jewish Gandhi" and spent decades in the Middle East engaging in activities designed to obtain reconciliation between Arabs and Jews (Bing, 1990). Abileah was born in Austria in 1915 into a family with strong musical roots. While his father was not religious in the traditional sense, he was a spiritual Zionist and a pacifist. The Abileah family immigrated to Haifa in the 1920s and young Joseph had many opportunities to interact and play with both Arabs and Jews in a cosmopolitan city that allowed for a free mixing of diverse groups and faiths. Joseph developed friendships within the Arab community and he continued to refer to Arabs as his brothers throughout his life. From a young age, Joseph had the expectation that he would become a professional musician and he did. He performed professionally throughout most of his life but music was not his only love, as peace and reconciliation became a dominant activity too (Bing).

Abileah's view that Jews and Arabs could live in peace together was reinforced by his early life in Palestine where in fact Jews and Arabs lived together peacefully. He reasoned that it had happened before in Haifa so why not again. Throughout the time before Israel's emergence as a nation, Abileah was a strong advocate for peaceful and nonviolent means to establish a place for Jewish immigration. Others in the Zionist movement began to move away from his position and approved and acted with violent means to establish the Jewish state of Israel. The conflict and turmoil of the 1930s and 1940s did not deter him from his beliefs. He worked hard to encourage the formation of a federation of nations that would be a united Middle

East. He repeatedly presented his ideas and reports to the United Nations Special Committee on Palestine (UNSCOP) in the 1940s. His plan was ultimately rejected and a more nationalistic one was implemented and this led to conflict between himself and many in his family, as well as many prominent Jews (Bing, 1990).

Shortly after the establishment of Israel, Abileah was put on trial for failing to report for mandatory service in the Israeli military or in a nonmilitary capacity for the nation. During his trial he argued the effectiveness of nonviolence using his own life experiences and, though he expected to be convicted, the court judgment required him to perform nonmilitary service without other punishment. Even though he rejected this outcome the court managed to have him declared unfit and therefore he was exempt from serving and the outcome was mute.

During the 1950s and 1960s, Abileah became active in a wide range of peace organizations. He learned about the Quaker peace movement and was impressed with the work of early Quakers like William Penn, so much so that he joined the Wider Quaker Fellowship in 1950. Other groups he joined included War Resisters International, Israeli League for Human and Civil Rights, and the Service Civil International. He worked hard as a nonviolent advocate for Arab rights (Bing, 1990).

Following the 1967 war, Abileah was much more optimistic about peace and developed and presented a plan to solve the Arab-Jewish problem to the United Nations. He became a spokesperson for many organizations and lectured on peace and nonviolence in academic and nonacademic settings throughout the region and the world. As his biographer, Bing (1990), notes Abileah is better known outside of Israel than within it. His involvement in peace demonstrations was either totally ignored or not publicized by the press and despite being invited to lecture at Oxford, Cambridge, Harvard, and Columbia University, the university in Haifa never asked him to speak even though he lived there for sixty years. In 1994 Abileah died at the age of 79 in Israel.

Another prominent Jewish advocate for peace and nonviolent action is Rabbi Michael Lerner. Born in 1943, Rabbi Lerner has been actively involved in issues of human rights and social justice at least since his teenage years as a student of Rabbi Abraham Joshua Heschel in New York. After earning his B.A. from Columbia University in 1964, Lerner began his graduate studies at UC Berkeley where he became a student activist in the "free speech movement" of the 1960s and the anti-war movement as well. Lerner's activism is fueled by his Jewish values and his strong concerns for the psychological and spiritual welfare of humankind (Lerner, personal communication, February 12, 2007). His anti-war activities in Seattle led to his arrest for his role in a demonstration against US involvement in the Vietnam War and although the charges against him were appealed and later dropped, he did serve time in prison over this. After his release, Lerner returned to Berkeley where he earned a Ph.D. in philosophy in 1972. While pursuing an academic career, Lerner began looking for ways to be more productive in changing society for the better. Working as a therapist with underprivileged minorities and white working class families in California followed a second PhD in social/clinical psychology. During this time he studied for the rabbinate under the direction of a Hasidic Rabbi Zalman Schachter-Shalomi and cofounded the magazine TIKKUN to create a voice for Jewish liberals and progressives. His rabbinic ordination was in 1995 (*Biographical notes on Rabbi Lerner*, 2008).

Currently, TIKKUN, the magazine, is part of an international interfaith organization called The TIKKUN Community. The TIKKUN Community is dedicated to inspiring "compassion, generosity, non-violence and recognition of the spiritual dimensions of life" (TIKKUN Community, 2008, ¶1). Rabbi Lerner has continued to serve as editor of TIKKUN, to work within the American Jewish community as rabbi of Beyt Tikkun synagogue in San Francisco, and a leader in the interfaith community of spiritual progressives. His two books, *Healing Israel/Palestine: A path to peace and reconciliation* (Lerner, 2003) and *The left hand of God: Taking back our country from the religious right* (Lerner, 2006), have advocated a peace through nonviolence and repentance. In his work he calls for ending Palestinian oppression while "ensuring Israel's survival and security and eliminating terror as a daily reality of life in Israel" (Lerner, 2003, p. 143). These works and other publications have created considerable controversy for Rabbi Lerner inside and outside the Jewish community. He has been banned from speaking at peace rallies for being pro-Israel and he has been attacked by Jewish groups for being a "self-hating Jew and an enemy of Israel." His provocative writing calls for people to orient their actions "toward a world of love, nonviolence, social justice, ecological responsibility, openheartedness, and generosity" (Lerner, 2006, p. 23). His writings and speeches demonstrate a compassion for an Israeli mother mourning for her daughter who was killed by a Palestinian suicide bomber and also for a Palestinian mother mourning for her daughter killed in an Israeli air strike. Rabbi Lerner presents a nonviolent spiritual covenant that is based on Judaic values and principles and that he thinks will help heal the planet from conflict and destruction. While some challenge his underlying intentions, his concrete strategies for peace in the Middle East and the world are well presented and challenge entrenched policies that have not succeeded to date.

Christianity

Christianity had its beginnings about two millennia ago. There are about two billion Christians in the world and its membership is the largest of any religion today (Monroe, 1995). While it is a minority faith in Asia and Africa, it is the dominant religion of Europe, North America, and South America (McCasland et al., 1969).

Christian Beliefs and Rituals

Christianity started as a small movement within Judaism (McCasland et al., 1969). This linkage can be seen in the fact that early Christians only allowed Jews into their worship services, they adopted the Jewish Bible as the first part, or Old

Testament, of their Bible, and they developed a new scripture of their own, the New Testament, in Judaic tradition (McCasland et al.). In addition to incorporating many Judaic aspects into their faith Christians also included many pagan practices as well (Monroe, 1995).

Life of Jesus

Jesus, son of a carpenter who lived outside of Jerusalem in Nazareth, is considered to be the founder of Christianity even though he never refers to himself in this way and seems to have considered himself as a Jew his entire life (McCasland et al., 1969). Little is know about the life of Jesus outside of the first four books of the New Testament of the Christian *Bible* (Mathew, Mark, Luke, and John) except that a Jewish historian does mention that he was crucified (Monroe, 1995). According to Biblical accounts, Jesus was born to Joseph and Mary in Bethlehem during the time of a census in Roman occupied Palestine. The sketchy details surrounding the birth of Jesus and his very early experiences are further muddled as the accounts in the Gospels of Mathew, Mark, Luke, and John are often inconsistent and contradictory. Without elucidating the inconsistencies in the description of the life of Jesus, the following overview will report generally agreed upon events. Jesus was baptized as an adult by "John the Baptist" in the Jordan River. He spent forty days and forty nights alone in the wilderness and was tempted by the devil. He performed many deeds that were described as miracles including the healing or curing of blindness, epilepsy, fever, leprosy, paralysis and a withered hand. He is said to have walked on water, to have withered a fig tree, and to have fed a very large crowd of people with a few baskets of fish and bread that never ran out despite containing insufficient quantities for the task (McCasland et al.).

Jesus was born to Jewish parents and his training was in the Judaism of the time. As a young man he studied in the synagogues of Nazareth and Jerusalem and he traveled as a teacher. Much that is written about what Jesus said and taught is consistent with Judaic writings and principles. People were expected to love God and their neighbor as themselves and Jesus reinforced this. In many instances Jesus was critical of temple priests because they were lax in following Jewish law and practices such as the observance of the Sabbath, food regulations, and tithing. He was particularly angered, and even violent, when some were allowing moneychangers to do their business in the sacred temple. At several points in the New Testament Jesus made statements that proclaimed his belief that he was the Jewish Messiah even though the sacred texts indicated that meant he would be killed. When his disciples treated him as the Messiah and crowds received him in Jerusalem as the Messiah, the already troubled Jewish leaders plotted to have him executed. After a trial, the Roman occupiers of Jerusalem had Jesus executed by crucifixion. Three days after his death and burial, his tomb was empty and his disciples spread the news that he had arisen from the dead. The belief in the resurrection of Jesus is a cornerstone in the Christian faith (McCasland et al., 1969).

Sacred Christian Texts

The sacred text of Christianity is the *Bible*. The first part of the Christian *Bible* is the Old Testament and this is essentially drawn from the Jewish sacred texts of the *Torah*, the *Prophets*, and the *Writings*. The second part of the *Bible* is the New Testament. While the Old Testament represents the covenant between God and man for both Jews and Christians, the New Testament represents a second covenant between God and man (McCasland et al., 1969). This second part describes the life and teachings of Jesus and interpretations of his teachings by his disciples and followers. Very little of the New Testament was written by people who had met Jesus during his lifetime (Monroe, 1995). The first complete list of the books of the New Testament, as it appears today, appeared in the Festal Letter of Athanasius in 367 C.E., however, there are indications that most of the chapters were already set by around 200 C.E. (McCasland et al.). It was not until the fourth century that the New Testament, as a canon and legitimate book of guidance for the church, became available (Monroe).

Christian Tenets and Holy Days

The basic beliefs of Christianity have evolved over two millennia. In the first few centuries after the death of Jesus, multiple methods of Christian beliefs and styles of worship were prominent throughout the Mediterranean region. Early Christians tended to worship in the Judaic tradition with just a few modifications. The sacraments of baptism and the recognition of the last supper of Jesus through a communion were added (Monroe, 1995). Baptism was an act of repentance and a commitment to faith and was practiced to gain entrance into the church, while communion represented a symbolic "breaking of bread" in the way that Jesus did with his disciples (McCasland et al., 1969). Worship occurred on Sunday, instead of the Jewish Sabbath, as commemoration of the day of the resurrection of Jesus. In 325 C.E. Constantine, emperor of the Roman Empire, called Christian leaders and scholars together in Nicene to develop a formal creed. The Council of Nicea developed the first official statement of Christian dogma with five basic tenets. These are "(1) the concept of the Holy Trinity, the idea that God the father, Jesus the son, and the Holy Spirit are all of one substance, (2) Christ came to earth to save the souls of mankind, (3) the Resurrection of Christ gave all mankind the promise of eternal life, (4) the promise that Christ will return to earth gave hope all Christians will enjoy eternal life, (5) there is only one Catholic and Apostolic Church into which one can be baptized to secure remission of sins" (Monroe, p. 235). This Nicene Creed was designed to clarify the nature of Christ and settle disputes among Christians as to whether Jesus was a man or God's son. The concept of the Holy Trinity resolved this question and became the official position of the Christian faith and those who disagreed were, from this point on, heretics (McCasland et al.). Different denominations of Christianity have added sacraments and the rites and ceremonies vary but most Christians adhere to the beliefs outlined above. Today, Christians view salvation as obtaining eternal life in heaven and this is gained by believing in Jesus as the Son of God and one's personal savior. This is expressed in the passage John 3:16, "For God so loved the world, that he gave his only begotten Son, that whosoever believeth in him should not perish, but have everlasting life (King James Version of the Bible)."

Christian Holy Days generally are associated with the life of Jesus. Christmas is the celebration of the birth of Jesus. During the Christmas celebration Christians attend special church services and exchange gifts with friends and family. While the exact day of the birth of Jesus is no longer known, the Christian church chose to celebrate it on and around the time of the winter solstice probably to assist in the conversion of believers of pagan rituals to Christianity. Christmas is generally celebrated on December 25 or December 26 in Western Europe, the Americas, and many countries of the British Commonwealth. In some places Christmas is celebrated in January. Easter Sunday commemorates the day of the resurrection of Jesus and it is celebrating roughly on the first Sunday after the first full moon after the spring equinox. Easter is associated with special church services and these are preceded by a week of related ceremony (Palm Sunday, Maundy Thursday, Good Friday). The forty days prior to Easter many, but not all, Christians honor as the period known as lent. Lent is a period where Christians are to reflect on the suffering and sacrifice of Jesus and to undergo a time of fasting or moderation as a manifestation of repentance and spiritual discipline. Another Christian holy time revolves around the Pentecost or the time when the Holy Spirit descended to earth. Pentecost is celebrated on the 49th day after Easter.

Christian Denominations

Like Judaism, Christianity and its beliefs and practices have evolved over time from its beginnings after the crucifixion of Jesus. The followers of Jesus or his disciples were the nucleus of the first church or assembly of Christians in Jerusalem. The number of followers grew quickly and as disciples left Jerusalem, their travels spread the ideas of Jesus and Christianity with them. Peter was reportedly executed by Nero in Rome and is considered the patriarch of the Roman Catholic Church, which once established, dominated Christian theology for centuries. The Roman emperor, Constantine, adopted Christianity as the religion of the empire and this precipitated the Eastern Orthodox branches of Christianity. Martin Luther and John Calvin led the Protestant Reformation in the 1500s because of their concern about the laxity and corruption in the Catholic Church, and Protestant branches of Christianity were founded. A range of theological, political, and social concerns and pressures led to many more denominations of Christianity to develop over the last five centuries. Some of the major Christian denominations include the Lutherans and Presbyterians who emerged in the 1500s, Episcopalians, Baptists, and Quakers in the 1600s, Methodists in the 1700s, Mormons, Jehovah's

Witnesses, and Christian Scientists in the 1800s, and the Disciples of Christ and Unitarians in the 1900s (McCasland et al., 1969).

Christian Views of Nonviolence

Because the Christian religious tradition is built upon Judaism, the views of violence from the Hebrew Bible apply directly to Christianity as well, since the Old Testament of the Christian Bible includes Genesis, Exodus, and Deuteronomy. The God of the Old Testament is regularly violent in action and requires sacrifice from believers by having them engage in atrociously violent and cruel acts. However, the New Testament and the teachings of Jesus, provide another characterization of God and another set of behavioral expectations of humanity that are distinctly more nonviolent for Christianity than Judaism.

Jesus proclaimed that nonviolence was appropriate and at the same time renounced war (Wink, 1992). Smith-Christopher (1998c, 2003) argues that Jesus was not proposing something new to his time but was extending existing Judaic notions of nonviolence and expanding on it. Both Wink and Smith-Christopher concur that Jesus' fervent admonitions against violence and war were much stronger and less equivocal than in the Judaism of his day. Hauerwas (2004) links Christian nonviolence with truthfulness. Numerous Biblical citations can be drawn upon to highlight the anti-violence and pro-nonviolence beliefs and practices of Jesus. Jesus preached, "All who take the sword will perish by the sword" (Mathew 26:52, cited in Aspey, 1990, p. 28). Expanding on Judaic teachings, Jesus also stated, "You have heard that it was said, 'An eye for an eye and a tooth for a tooth.' But I say to you, do not resist an evildoer. But if he strikes you on the right cheek, turn the other also; and if anyone wants to sue you and take your coat, give him your cloak as well; and if anyone forces you to go a mile, go also the second mile" (Mathew 5:38–41, cited in Wink, 2003, p. 10). Wink points out that Jesus' statement about the right cheek has particular cultural significance. If someone has hit another on the right cheek, it was typically done with their left hand that was used for "unclean tasks." Because there were laws against using one's left hand in public and so doing had other cultural implications, turning the other cheek changed the dynamic of the conflict in a provocative way for the original aggressor. Therefore, when a person turns their other cheek, they have engaged in nonviolent direct action. Wink also points out that giving a person your cloak (undergarment), when they sue for your coat, is another power shifting behavior. Nakedness was more an embarrassment and a humiliation to the person who created the nakedness than it was for the person who was made naked. Perhaps the most important statement advocating nonviolence is a version of the golden rule or "Do to others as you would have them do to you" (Mathew 7:12, cited in Wink, p. 127). Jesus expanded the notion of loving your neighbor to loving all of humanity. He said, "You have heard that it was said, 'You shall love your neighbor and hate your enemy.' But I say to you, love your enemies and pray for those that persecute you" (Mathew 5:43–44, cited in Aspey, p. 28). Jesus also taught that "If your enemy is hungry, feed him; if he is thirsty, give him drink; for by so doing you will heap burning coals on his head. Do not be overcome by evil, but overcome evil with good" (Romans 12:20–21, cited in Aspey, p. 28).

Jesus delivered his most famous declaration about peace and nonviolence during the "Sermon on the Mount." "Blessed are the peacemakers, for they will be called the children of God" (Mathew 5:9, cited in Smith-Christopher, 1998c, p. 146). The Sermon on the Mount was a very powerful set of blessings and guidelines for living a good spiritual life. Christians and non-Christians have been moved by its meaning. Gandhi was very much taken by its implications. In fact, when asked why he did not become a Christian himself, he declared that he would if all Christians really lived their lives by the true teachings within the Sermon on the Mount (Fischer, 1954).

Jesus taught his followers to eschew violence and to embrace nonviolence through his teaching and through the way he lived his life. During his life, he spoke out against violence around him. When a follower cut off the ear of the high priest's slave he reprimanded the aggressor never do something like that again (Wink, 1992). Jesus used nonviolent approaches to the point of accepting his impending execution by the Romans without fighting back. There are at least two places where Jesus' actions have been viewed as being violent. On one occasion Jesus witnessed moneylenders doing business in the temple and in a rage he threw the tables upside down spilling the money on the floor and chasing out the transgressors in this holy place. While no person seems to have been physically hurt, this instance is oftentimes cited as an example of how Jesus was out of control and not an absolute pacifist (Smith-Christopher, 1998c). On another occasion Jesus said, "Think not that I am come to send peace on earth: I came not to send peace, but a sword" (Mathew 10:34). He goes on to explain this statement and while many point to the peaceful prescriptions at the end of this dialogue (Smith-Christopher; Wink), it does appear to contradict the messages of peace and nonviolence found elsewhere in the New Testament. However, the vast majority of conversations, stories told, and actions of Jesus depict a nonviolent man.

Many of the values that Jesus stressed to his followers are consistent with the components of cultures of peace. Wallis (2006) identifies several social issues that are referenced in the Bible including poverty, the environment, and the stewardship of the earth. In a content analysis of the Old Testament, Wallis found poverty was the second most mentioned theme behind idolatry. "One of every sixteen verses in the New Testament is about the poor or the subject of money.... In the first three (Synoptic) gospels it is one out of ten verses, and in the book of Luke, it is one in seven!" (Wallis, p. 212). Poverty is a very important concern for Christians and working to reduce the hardship and trauma the poor experience is prescribed over and over in the teachings of Jesus. Jesus speaks of tolerance, equality, and ethnocentrism, plus he challenges the domination system (patriarchy) of the day in advocating for better treatment for women (Wink, 1992). Within the Beatitudes (Mathew 5:3–12), Jesus speaks to the importance of social justice, self-control, humility, virtuousness, mercy, nonviolence, and a love of God and humankind.

By taking the decree to refrain from acting violently toward a person that is evil, Jesus offered the way for Christians to oppose evil without mirroring it (Wink, 2003). Based on an analysis of Jesus' teachings, Wink has delineated over a dozen nonviolent approaches or actions Jesus used or described in a parable. These extrapolated guidelines include: "(1) seize the moral initiative, (2) find a creative alternative to violence, (3) assert your own humanity and dignity as a person, (4) meet force with ridicule or humor, (5) break the cycle of humiliation, (6) refuse to submit or to accept the inferior position, (7) expose the injustice of the system, (8) shame the oppressor into repentance, (9) force the Powers to make decisions for which they are not prepared, (10) recognize your own power, (11) be willing to suffer rather than to retaliate, (12) cause the oppressor to see you in a new light, (13) deprive the oppressor of a situation where a show of force is effective, and (14) be willing to undergo the penalty for breaking unjust laws" (pp. 27–28). Some of these guidelines are full strategies for nonviolent conflict resolution while others are useful components of a strategy to integrate with others into a full plan.

Notable Christian Advocates of Nonviolence

As the early Christian church evolved in the first few centuries after the death of Jesus, the followers took Jesus, proclamations to refrain from violence and to be nonviolent and peaceful very seriously (Akers, 2000). Members of the early Christian church were mostly pacifists who refused to engage in violence regardless of the circumstances (Akers). Aspey (1990) reports that, "During this period, Christians refused service in the army; and there is no direct evidence that they ever used force against the bloodthirsty persecutions to which they were subjected. While paying lip service to the ancients, most people in the Empire at the time of Jesus recognized no responsibility to a divine power beyond themselves and their rulers spared no cruelty in the ten major persecutions, which were launched against the Christians…. Christians were happy without resistance by force, to share the martyrdom of Jesus; and this had a tremendous effect in converting those who witnessed their suffering" (p. 27). Those who observed the persecutions of the Christians must have wondered what God would offer his followers the strength and serenity to accept the torture and executions with nonviolence and peaceful acceptance. The refusal to fight in the military and the commitment to nonviolence changed dramatically, not because of religious reasons, but because of the politics in the fourth century C.E. when the Roman Emperor made Christianity the state religion and placed the cross on the shields his soldiers carried into battle. With this change Christian doctrine began to shift away from pacifism and nonviolence (Akers). By 436 the shift was so complete that a man needed to be a Christian to serve in the Roman legion (Smith-Christopher, 1998c).

Over the last century there have been many Christians who have spoken out in favor of the use of nonviolence and have been nonviolent activists in responding to important social issues of the day. Some Christian writers and theorists include people like the Trappist monk Merton (2000), pacifist Muste (2000), theologian Rienhold Niebuhr (Steger, 2003), and Catholic sister Prejean (1995). King (2000/1958, 1990/1963, 1992/1967) is the most notable example of a nonviolent activist in the USA during the twentieth century. Some other Christian activists include Palestinian Christian Awad (1990), Lutheran pastor Dietrich Bonhoeffer (Hauerwas, 2004), Benedictine sister Joan Chittister (Chittister, Chishti, & Waskow, 2007), Catholic peacemaker Dorothy Day (Forrest, 2000), Jesuit priest Dear (2008), progressive evangelical minister Wallis (2006), and environmentalist Kelly (1994). In addition some denominations of the Christian faith address nonviolence and peace more directly than others. The Anabaptists, who originated in Switzerland, include the Amish, Mennonites, and Hutterites and were discussed previously under peaceful societies (Smith-Christopher, 1998a). The Quakers or Society of Friends, founded by George Fox, are another Christian denomination that places peace and nonviolence in a central position in their faith. Notable Quakers who wrote about nonviolence and/or acted in nonviolent ways to further a cause and improve society include John Naylor, William Penn, and John Woolman (Chernus, 2004).

Martin Luther King Jr

While some of the specifics in the life and activism of Martin Luther King Jr. were discussed in Chap. 2, they will not be repeated here. However, the factors that King (2000/1958) viewed as moving him toward the use of nonviolence are illuminating and these will be presented. It was during his teenage years that the injustices in the segregated south and the brutality and barbarous nature of the Ku Klux Klan became a stark reality to King. Even though he felt economically secure in his own home, the poverty he saw around him resulted in his making the connections between racial and economic injustice. As a freshman at Morehouse College in Atlanta, King read Thoreau's *Essay on Civil Disobedience* for the first time and found it moving. When he was a seminary student, his concern to rid the world of social injustice led him to a wide range of authors in theology and philosophy. The works of Plato, Aristotle, Rousseau, Hobbes, Mill, Locke, Marx, and Rauschenbusch were read and many of the ideas were integrated or rejected as he developed his personal social philosophy. Even though he strongly rejected communism as a Christian on many grounds, the analysis of the economic gulf between the wealthy and poor by Marx resonated as a concern for King. After listening to a lecture by pacifist A. J. Muste and listening to a sermon about the work of Gandhi, King began to read about and seriously consider the nonviolent views and approaches of Gandhi. His readings of Gandhi and the critique of pacifism by Christian ethicist Reinhold Niebuhr helped him understand his own perspectives on nonviolence from a Christian point of view. While at Boston University for his doctoral studies, King was able to meet many proponents of nonviolence and his faculty mentors introduced him to the phenomenological views of Hegel and personalistic philosophy.

When he moved to Montgomery Alabama to assume a ministry, he had an integrated social philosophy that viewed nonviolent resistance as "one of the most
potent weapons available to oppressed people in their quest for social justice"
(King, p. 70). At the time he had no expectation about using this method in his own
life, but when Rosa Parks refused to move from her seat, King was moved to
answer the call for a spokesperson for the nonviolent resistance that became known
as the Montgomery bus boycott. The rest of King's tragically short life was then set
in motion.

Dorothy Day

Dorothy Day, co-founder of the Catholic Worker movement, was born in 1897 in
New York. She grew up primarily in Chicago where a family friend introduced her to
Catholicism and she experienced poverty first hand when her father was unemployed.
As a young girl, Day read books like Sinclair's *The Jungle* that made her ponder
social and personal morality and her relationship to other human beings. Even in
college she found herself reading about radical social movements and this passion
resulted in her dropping out of college (Forrest, 1994).

Chernus (2004) has described her work as a reporter as that of a radical political
journalist. Stints at various reporter jobs found her working for the magazine called
The Masses during World War I. Because her magazine opposed the war, the magazine
was seized and five editors were charged with sedition. When she demonstrated for
women's suffrage with forty other women in 1917 in front of the White House, she
was imprisoned and was part of a hunger strike for treatment as political prisoners
(Forrest, 1994).

After World War I, Day held a number of journalist positions with newspapers
and magazines in Chicago, New Orleans, and New York. She reported on the plight
of the poor and downtrodden, on Hunger marches, and other demonstrations.
During this time period she became a devout Catholic (Forrest, 1994). With the aid
of Peter Maurin, a French priest, Day created and served as editor of the publication
Catholic Worker in 1933. The newspaper soon expanded into a magazine that
included articles about love, pacifism, and charity while promoting nonviolence
from a Roman Catholic perspective (Chernus, 2004). Day's writing was inspirational
and encouraged volunteerism to help the poor and homeless. This message
resonated with her readers and as interest grew, the Catholic Worker movement
was able to establish a series of hospitality houses and farming communes.
By 1936 the number of Catholic Worker houses approached three dozen. All needy
people were welcome to the houses where the volunteer staff received only room
and board (Forrest).

Forrest (2000), Day's biographer, described Dorothy Day as "a patron saint of
conscientious objectors" (p. 106). She was a pacifist who spoke out against World
War I, The Spanish Civil War, World War II, and the Cold War. Her pacifistic
writing in the *Catholic Worker* during World War II did result in some backlash by

her readers and donors but she persevered on principle. During the 1950s, 1960s, and the early 1970s, Day demonstrated and fasted against nuclear war, and civil defense drills and for civil rights, farm worker rights, church policy, and the rights of conscientious objectors serving time in prison many times up to the age of 75. She received many honors for her work including the opportunity to receive communion from Pope Paul VI and a special recognition from Mother Teresa. She died in 1980 (Forrest, 1994).

Islam

Islam is a fast growing religion with about 1.3 billion followers (Miller & Kenedi, 2002). As the second largest religion, Islam accounts for one fifth of the world's religious population. Islam is another Abrahamic religion that has its roots in Judaism (Monroe, 1995). Islam means "the willing and active recognition of and submission to the Command of the One, Allah" (Waines, 1995, p. 3). Followers of Islam refer to themselves as Muslims (McCasland et al., 1969).

Islamic Beliefs and Rituals

Islam is a monotheistic religion that began on the Arabian Peninsula about six centuries after the life of Jesus based on the teachings of the prophet Muhammad. Theologically speaking, Islam denounces polytheism and idolatry while affirming the worship of one God in a brevity and clarity that is easily understood by the masses (McCasland et al., 1969). Allah is the Arabic word for "the God" and is used by Muslims when they refer to the one God (Drummond, 2005).

Life of Muhammad

Muhammad was born on or around 570 C.E. in Mecca of present day Saudi Arabia (McCasland et al., 1969). Both his parents died by the time he was six years old and his intelligent, religious, and influential relatives of the Quraysh tribe raised him (Monroe, 1995). During his youth, he traveled the region with his uncle who was a trader. As an adult, Muhammad worked as a trader on these same routes. Khadija, a widow, hired him to manage her trading company and he eventually married her (Waines, 1995). Muhammad married Khadija at the age of 25 at her proposal, even though she was 15 years his elder, and it was a happy marriage of 26 years as evidenced by the fact he took no other wives until after her death (Drummond, 2005). During his time on the trade routes through the Fertile Crescent from Egypt to India, Muhammad was an astute observer of the beliefs and customs where he traveled and he became very interested in and knowledgeable of the Jewish, Zoroastrian, Christian, and Hindu religions (Monroe).

In 611, when about forty, Muhammad began to withdraw from social life in Mecca and to meditate about religious issues (McCasland et al., 1969). During this time period of relative isolation, Muhammad began to have visions in which the archangel, Gabriel, appeared and spoke to him. In these visions Gabriel told him that he was receiving a message from God and he was supposed to spread the word of the one and only Allah to the citizens of Mecca (Monroe, 1995). Initially, few listened to his message, but over time the message for the renunciation of the popular polytheistic religion and the adoption of a monotheistic view did get through. Instead of believing Muhammad's religious approach, many in Mecca were hostile as this message threatened their prosperous way of life (McCasland et al.). Feeling imminent danger for himself and his family, Muhammad moved to Medina in 622 for refuge and this date signified the birth of Islam. Tradition has it that Muhammad traveled by white horse to Jerusalem with Gabriel where they prayed to the Jewish prophets, he ascended to heaven from what is now the Dome of the Rock, and then returned back to earth in Medina. (Monroe).

Muhammad initially saw his religious views as an extension of Judaism and thought Jews might accept him as the Messiah but they did not (Busse, 1998; McCasland et al., 1969). Because he accepted the holy standing of Abraham, Moses and other Jewish prophets, and Jesus, Muhammad expected Jews and Christians to readily convert to Islam, but this also did not happen. Leaving Mecca did not quell the hostility toward him by powerful interests in Mecca, and when these interests plotted to mount a military campaign against Muhammad in Medina, Muhammad raised an army in Medina to defeat them. Muhammad's military forces easily prevailed and he conquered Mecca and established it as the most holy site in Islam in 630 (Monroe, 1995).

Following his military victory in Mecca, Muhammad was able to garner the support of most Arabs and nearly all of Arabia viewed him as The Prophet (McCasland et al., 1969). He died in 632 in Medina. Given his statesmanship, leadership, and religious impact, he "passed from the scene of human history the greatest man Arabia has produced" (Drummond, 2005, p. 52).

Islamic Tenets and Holy Days

There are five basic tenets or "Pillars of Islam." These are:

1. Basic creed (*Shahadah*)
2. Prayer (*Salat*)
3. Alms (*Zakat*)
4. Fasting (*Saum*)
5. Pilgrimage (*Hajj*) (McCasland et al., 1969)

The basic creed is the proclamation or confession that Allah is the true God and Muhammad is the greatest prophet and messenger of Allah. The *shahadah* is said in the form of the prayer, "There is no God but the one God, and Muhammad is his prophet" (Monroe, 1995, p. 218).

Prayer or *salat* should be daily and both public and private. It should occur five times a day at specific times answering the call of the muezzin or crier. How to wash and prepare for prayer is also specified for Muslims so that the body is purified. Prayer is done while facing the holy city of Mecca. Charity or alms are expected of all Muslims to assist the poor, to aid travelers, to pay for missionary work, and to support other Islamic causes and functions. Fasting or *saum* occurs each year during the month of Ramadan that commemorates the time that the Qur'an was sent to Muhammad from Allah in 614. During the entire month, all Muslims over fourteen years old do not drink, eat, or have sexual relations during the daylight hours. Ramadan is also a time of prayer, reading the Qur'an and self-reflection. All Muslims, who have the monetary means and physical stamina, are expected to travel to Mecca for their hajj or pilgrimage at least once in their lifetime during the first half of the last month of the lunar year (McCasland et al., Monroe).

Islamic holy days and times include Ramadan, Eid ul-Fitr, the Islamic New Year, and the birthday of Muhammad. Ramadan is the month long time of fasting and was discussed previously. The end of Ramadan is celebrated with the three day Islamic holiday of Eid ul-Fitr. During Eid ul-Fitr, Muslims show their appreciation to Allah for the strength given to them during Ramadan and the blessings they have received too. Special prayers and services occur and charity for the poor is stressed. Islamic New Year or Muharram starts on the day that Muhammad moved from Mecca to Medina. Most but not all Muslim sects celebrate Muhammad's birthday.

In many respects Islam is a way of life and more than a religion. Besides obedience to the Qur'an and its principles and rules, marriage and the family are very important (Monroe, 1995). While Muhammad had a revelation that men might have no more than four wives, common practice is for only one wife. All wives are to be treated equally.

Many interpret the Qur'an and the teachings of Muhammad to require all women to be secluded, covered, and protected from the sexual advances of men (Monroe, 1995). While the importance of the Muslim norm of chastity for women is not disputed, some Muslim scholars challenge the requirement of *purdah* or the veil for women. Engineer (1996) argues that the Qur'an does not require *purdah* but simply requires women to "not display their sexual charms, but dress in a dignified manner" (p. 14). He posits that, as the veil was used as a means to assist in maintaining honor and a woman's inviolable feminine chastity, the veil and morality became synonymous among some Muslims. He challenges the practice that the *purdah* is necessary to protect a women's chastity and honor in this day and age and he provides support for his position from the Qur'an and the canon law of Islam. Many Muslim women today who wear the veil do feel pressure to do so although many others do so by choice.

By present day feminist standards the treatment of Muslim women may seem backward and overly restrictive with limited rights to move through society and with restrictions in dress, however in Muhammad's time his views for the treatment of women were advanced in many ways (Engineer, 1996; Monroe, 1995). Engineer indicates, "the Qur'an was the first scripture to have conceded so many rights to women and that too in a period when women were very oppressed in the major civilizations" (pp. 12–13). While acknowledging the Qur'an does contain verses that speak to the superiority of man over woman and other inequalities, Engineer's analysis points to Islamic jurists in the centuries after Muhammad's death who drew from pre-Islamic traditions within the Arab world to curb many women's rights discussed by the Prophet. For instance, he notes the "Qur'an demanded of women a reasonable degree of submission to their husbands as they maintain them and spend their wealth on them, but the juristic formulations require them to submit totally to their husbands" (p. 13).

Islamic Sacred Text

The Islamic holy book is the Qur'an, Qurãn, or Koran depending on how the Arabic name is transliterated. Allah revealed the contents of the Qur'an to Muhammad in 614 through the angel Gabriel, and Muhammad in turn revealed these sacred truths through his sermons, sayings, writings, and conversations. "The text of the Koran is considered by Western Scholars to be one of the most reliable of sacred texts in the entire history of religions" (Drummond, 2005, p. 53). Because Muhammad was not a man of letters and because he died unexpectedly, the Qur'an was primarily written by those around him and much of it was written after his death based on the oral tradition of Muhammad (McCasland et al., 1969). Zaid ibn Thabit, a close Medinan follower of Muhammad, collected and edited all written statements and sermons of Muhammad into book form. The Qur'an is organized into 114 chapters or *suras*. The Qur'an, like Jewish sacred texts, is about laws and rules for followers to conduct their life. The Qur'an speaks to all aspects of life including family, sex, children, charity, business, government, war, and peace (Monroe, 1995). McCasland et al. reports that many Western readers of the Qur'an find its style confusing and unengaging, however, Muslims and Arabic speakers find it a poetic and eloquent classic in Arabic literature.

Despite the breadth of topics addressed in the Qur'an, many followers realized more guidance was needed to explain the Qur'an and to elaborate on areas of human existence where the Qur'an did not provide direction. Initially, this was done with an oral tradition or *sunnahs*, however these explanations were eventually written down forming the Hadiths. The Hadiths codified and organized the *sunnahs* and are useful for Muslims and Muslim scholars, but they are not part of the Islamic canon and are rejected by some fundamentalist believers (Monroe, 1995).

Islamic Sects

Like Judaism and Christianity before it, Islam also has developed divisions of belief. The two most prominent sects of Islam are the Sunnis and the Shiites.

The differences can be traced back to the time immediately after the death of Muhammad and the controversy over who was to be his heir. The Sunnis, who are more liberal in their interpretation of the Qur'an, thought the elected caliph and friend of Muhammad, Abu Bakr, should be the head of the Islamic faith. The Sunnis accept the oral traditions surrounding Muhammad and the Hadiths, plus they believe the head of the faith ought to be elected. The Shiites considered the husband of Muhammad's daughter, Fatima, to be leader of the Islamic faith after The Prophet's death. Initially, bloodlines to Muhammad were the way to determine Muhammad's successor. In 656 Fatima and Ali's son, Hussein, unsuccessfully led an army against the Sunnis and he was tortured and executed.

While the doctrinal differences between Sunnis and Shiites are not great, the early history has driven a wedge between the two sects and it was not until 1959 that the Sunnis recognized Shiites as true Muslims (Monroe, 1995). Today, 85–90% of Muslims worldwide are Sunnis with between 10 and 15% being Shiites (Blanchard, 2008). Iran, Iraq, Bahrain, Azerbaijan, and Palestine are the countries with majority Shiite populations (Blanchard; Monroe).

Islamic Views of Nonviolence

The general non-Muslim public does not typically place Islam and nonviolence in the same sentence (Harris, 1998). Academic research and writing also tends to hold similar views (Abu-Nimer, 2001). The views of Islam as a violent religion may stem from Moorish and Ottoman conquests over Medieval Christendom (Harris), the tales of the Christian crusaders in the Holy Lands (Muhaiyaddeen, 1987), the legacy of colonial subordination of Islamic nations (Abu-Nimer, 2003), the recent conflicts in the Middle East, and the attacks against the USA on September 11, 2001. Despite these biases or stereotypes, Islam is a religion with a deep theme of peace and nonviolence that can be drawn from its sacred texts and practices (Abu-Nimer, 2003; Muhaiyaddeen; Paige & Gilliatt, 2001; Paige, Satha-Anand, & Gilliatt, 1993).

A reading of the Qur'an and the Hadith can locate passages to support the use of violence in a variety of situations just like the sacred texts of Judaism and Christianity might be used (Abu-Nimer, 2003). The knowledge that the Prophet Mohammad did spend a considerable amount of time battling his enemies in war also works to support the view that Islam is only a religion of violence. One Islamic concept that has helped to create considerable confusion in understanding the roles of violence and nonviolence for Muslims is *jihad*. *Jihad* does not translate to holy war, murder, or other violent attack as is commonly done (Satha-Anand, 1993). It is better understood as a "struggle or effort" (Harris, 1998). Harris delineates the two aspects of *jihad* as the inner struggle to control oneself and the outer struggle to reduce social injustice and oppression to actively pursue cultures of peace. The inner struggle is the greater of the two as it is a personal one to become a better person in the worship of God. This inner struggle also implies patience in seeking to improve oneself in developing a greater awareness of God (Siddiqui, 2005).

The outer struggle is the "lesser struggle" and it may take many forms including armed or unarmed struggle (Harris). The focus of *jihad* is to stop structural violence in the community and world (Satha-Amand). While *jihad* may be violent, because Mohammad used armed struggle, it need not be since the Prophet also used nonviolence to work against oppression and injustice. Abu-Nimer points out that Mohammad adopted nonviolent methods for his thirteen year Meccan period. An example is his response to the dominant religious group in Mecca when he was accused of blasphemy and was tortured and humiliated. He did not speak ill of his tormenters and he simply prayed for their understanding (Ahmad, 1993). Even when an armed struggle is chosen over an unarmed one, the Qur'an and the Hadith put limitations on how much violence is permitted. The Qur'an forbids the killing of noncombatants in war like women, children, and the elderly and murder is a major sin (Satha-Anand).

Just as the Qur'an endorses violence in certain circumstances, it also calls its followers to use nonviolence and to seek peace. Abu-Nimer (2003) specifically points to many Qur'anic verses that stipulate the need for nonviolent actions. He cites, "Whenever they kindle the fire of war, God extinguishes it. They strive to create disorder on earth and God loves not those who create disorder (5:64). God commands you to treat (everyone) justly, generously, and with kindness (16:90). Repel evil with that which is best [not evil]: We are well acquainted with things they say (23:96).... But if the enemy incline toward peace, do thou (also) incline toward peace, and trust in Allah: for He is the One that heareth and knoweth all things (8:61)" (p. 60).

Many Islamic values and principles are also consistent with peacebuilding and cultures of peace (Abu-Nimer, 2003; Ahmad, 1993; Satha-Anand, 1993). Ahmad lists the values of equality, brotherhood, love, forgiveness, mercy, and purity of character. Muhammad is quoted as saying, "You will not enter paradise, until you have faith, and you will not complete your faith until you love one another" (Groves, 2008, p. 167). Abu-Nimer points out that Abdul Ghaffar Khan lists service, faith, and love as important values and that other Muslims reference the Muslin values of social justice, beneficence, compassion, wisdom, tolerance, submission to God, and the recognition of the rights of others. The linkage of these Islamic values to the components of cultures of peace discussed in the previous chapter should be clear. Abu-Nimer and others have documented these values within the Qur'an and in the Prophet's tradition nicely. The Qur'an has around a hundred expressions that capture the notion of justice and there are over two hundred admonitions against injustice (Abu-Nimer). The Qur'an points to the sacredness of human life (15:29, Satha-Anand), the unity of all existence including humanity, animals, and the environment (Siddiqui, 2005), equality (49:13, Abu-Nimer), brotherhood (3:103, Satha-Anand), kindness (2:263, Ahmad), forgiveness (42:40, 24:43, Abu-Nimer), love (3:103, Ahmad), and tolerance (3:64, Abu-Nimer, 2001).

Satha-Anand (1993) has developed eight theses for Muslim nonviolence that underlie the true meaning of nonviolence within Islam. These are

1. For Islam, the problem of violence is an integral part of the Islamic moral sphere.
2. Violence, if any, used by Muslims must be governed by rules prescribed in the Qur'an and Hadith.

3. If violence used cannot discriminate between combatants and noncombatants, then it is unacceptable in Islam.
4. Modern technology of destruction renders discrimination virtually impossible at present.
5. In the modern world, Muslims cannot use violence.
6. Islam teaches Muslims to fight for justice with the understanding that human lives – as all parts of God's creation – are purposive and sacred.
7. In order to be true to Islam, Muslims must utilize nonviolent action as a new mode of struggle.
8. Islam itself is fertile soil for nonviolence because of its potential for disobedience, strong discipline, sharing and social responsibility, perseverance and self-sacrifice, and the belief in the unity of the Muslim community and the oneness of mankind (p. 23).

As these points indicate, Islam is not an absolute pacifistic religion, yet it provides its adherents with values, principles, and beliefs that allow for nonviolent approaches to life and conflict (Abu-Nimer, 2003). The Qur'an emphasizes the freedom of conscious necessary for Muslims to follow the path indicated by Satha-Anand when it says, "Let there be no compulsion in religion. Truth stands out, clear from error (2:256)" (Ahmad, 1993, p. 40). Abu-Nimer (2001) makes a good case that Islam, because of its rituals and traditions, is conducive to nonviolence and peacebuilding.

Notable Muslim Advocates of Nonviolence

Over the fourteen hundred years of Islam, there have been many Muslims who have been nonviolent activists in places like India, South Africa, Egypt, Israel, the United States, and Sudan, as well as many others. In this section I will focus on two. The first is Abdul Ghaffar Kahn who was born into a prominent Muslim family in British occupied India at the end of the nineteenth century and the other is Mohammed Abu-Nimer who was born in Israel in the latter half of the twentieth century.

Abdul Ghaffar Kahn

Perhaps the greatest Muslim nonviolent activist to have ever lived was Abdul Ghaffar Kahn. Abdul Ghaffar Kahn was born in Utmanzai, India in 1890 into a devout Muslim family who belonged to the Mohammadzais tribe of the Pashtun people. Utmanzai is about twenty miles north of Peshawar and west of the Indus River in the shadow of the all-important Khyber Pass, key to the trade routes between the Middle East and India. As the youngest child of four, young Ghaffar was a good and respectful child who was somewhat of a free spirit and grew up on the family farm on the Swat River. His father, Berham Kahn, was the trusted village chief who did not miss his *namaz* or daily prayers no matter where he was. His mother was very devout as well and was known to extend her daily *namaz* for hours from time to time (Easwaran, 1984).

The Pashtun people have a strong ethic of honor that is extremely important to men regardless of their position in the tribe or community. The importance of *badal* or revenge among the Pashtuns extends from generation to generation as blood for blood is expected in order to maintain justice and honor. While the Pashtuns were notoriously violent, the Mohammadzais tribe was generally peaceful, although *badal* was still important. However, Ghaffar's father did not have a taste for *badal* and he avoided feuds, bore no grudges, and did not make enemies. His penchant to forgive went against Pashtun qualities and resulted in some ridicule, but his trustworthiness and fair treatment of the villagers worked in his favor. Berham believed forgiveness was a better way to please God and this belief had a positive effect on young Ghaffar. His father's fairness and forgiveness rubbed off on his son who tended to make friends with laborers and craftsmen (Easwaran, 1984).

As a young boy, Ghaffar Kahn watched as the British occupiers of his land brutally thwarted a Pashtun rebellion. That experience, and an accumulated set of personal experiences with some British occupiers, helped form his psyche so that independence of India from British rule became his driving cause. However, not all his interactions with the British were negative. He attended a mission high school in Peshawar and the head of the school was a positive role model. He also made British friends, respected his teachers and was a good student. Being six foot three and over two hundred pounds, it is not surprising he was tapped for service in an elite military unit, but when he saw how bigoted the British soldiers were to their Indian counterparts, he immediately resigned (Easwaran, 1984).

As a young man, Ghaffar Kahn came to the realization that many of his fellow Pashtuns' problems were a function of high levels of poverty, inadequate education or no education at all, apathy, and a culture that was full of violence. While his Muslim faith was strong, Ghaffar was a progressive man and he decided that the best way to serve God was to help his children, the Pashtun people, by educating them. In 1901, he opened his first of what was to be dozens and dozens of new schools. Education was perceived to be a threat to the British occupiers and to the Muslim clerics. Despite pressure and harassment from both directions, Ghaffar Kahn persisted in his efforts to educate his people. As he traveled throughout his frontier region, he visited every village between 1915 and 1918. In a meeting in one frontier village he was labeled as "Badshah Kahn" which means king of the kahns or chiefs. As his new name spread, his power as a leader in the region grew. While his notoriety was spreading, so was that of Mohandas Gandhi to the east (Easwaran, 1984).

When Gandhi called for a national day of fasting and prayer, Ghaffar Kahn convinced the villagers he had met in his travels to do the same. As elsewhere in India, the Peshwar was nearly deserted. After a meeting in which he spoke out against the British rule, Ghaffar Kahn was arrested and imprisoned without trial.

Following his release from prison, he toured more villages and started new schools. The British efforts to get him to stop eventually resulted in his arrest for "spreading education among impoverished and illiterate people" (Easwaran, 1984, p. 84).

During the 1920s, Ghaffar Kahn spent his time out of jail meeting with the Pashtun people and trying to improve their lot in life. Besides schools, he founded the Pashtun Youth League, and a magazine in the Pashtun language. He worked against the traditional but restrictive system of *purdah* that kept women from being full participants in society. His magazine spoke openly against *purdah* while educating readers about hygiene, social issues, and Islamic law. It was during this time that a discussion with a concerned villager led to the idea of the development of an army of nonviolent soldiers and Ghaffar decided to see if it could be done (Easwaran, 1984).

Ghaffar Kahn tried to develop an army of nonviolent soldiers from a people with a strong violent reputation and culture. He reasoned that perhaps the Pashtuns might be reckless enough to make it work. His army was called the Khudai Khidmatgans that means "Servants of God." Like the regular military, recruits were drilled and disciplined and had officers and a chain of command. They also had uniforms and a flag and even a bagpipe corps. All in the Khudai Khidmatgens were required to take a strict oath. They had to pledge,

I am a Khudai Khidmatgar, and as God needs nor service, but serving his creation is serving him, I promise to serve humanity in the name of God.
I promise to refrain from violence and from taking revenge. I promise to forgive those who oppress me or treat me with cruelty.
I promise to refrain from taking part in feuds and quarrels and from creating enmity.
I promise to treat every [Pashtun] as my brother and friend.
I promise to refrain from antisocial customs and practices.
I promise to live a simple life, to practice virtue and to refrain from evil.
I promise to practice good manners and good behavior and not to lead a life of idleness.
I promise to devote at least two hours a day to social work (Easwaran, 1984, p. 111).

This oath requires those that take it to reject their beliefs in *badal* that is a significant part of their identity as a Pashtun. Amazingly, Ghaffar Kahn was able to initially recruit a few thousand into the ranks of the Khudai Khidmatgens. They were trained, donned uniforms of a red-dyed tunic, and armed with "their discipline, their faith, and their native mettle" (Easwaran, p. 113). The weapons of the Prophet they bore were patience and righteousness.

The heroics of the Khudai Khidmatgens began in conjunction with Gandhi's Salt March in 1930. After Gandhi called for all of India to make salt in defiance of British law, Ghaffar Kahn and his followers joined the nationwide civil resistance. Badshah and other leaders were arrested but the Khudai Khidmatgens continued to organize the villagers in the frontier. When troops were ordered to disperse a crowd that was protesting the arrests at the Kissa Kahni Bazaar, the confrontation with the protesters turned bloody. When the protesters held their ground, the troops opened fire. The Khudai Khidmatgens did not run but held their ground without retaliating. Repeatedly, unarmed Khudai Khidmatgens bared their chests to the soldiers and were shot in cold blood. Over a six-hour period, the troops fired again and again until the bodies of the dead and the wounded lay in piles. As word of the actions of the Khudai Khidmatgens reached the rest of the country, this became an inspiration for nonviolent action across all of India. This incident and the British harassment of the Khudai Khidmatgens to embarrass and humiliate them resulted in the recruitment growing exponentially until the ranks of the Khudai Khidmatgens were 80,000 strong (Easwaran, 1984).

The success of his army of nonviolence led to Ghaffar Kahn being dubbed the "Frontier Gandhi," a name he did not approve. His continued efforts in the 1930s to educate the illiterate, feed and clothe the poor, and expand the freedoms of women led to more prison time and also banishment from the frontier region. This enabled Kahn to spend time with Gandhi at his ashram where the two men's mutual respect and friendship grew strong. Gandhi and Kahn supported each other in principle and in action many times until the British agreed to allow Indians to have home rule. The Khudai Khidmatgens were effective in many more campaigns designed to convince the British to leave, despite the atrocities brought upon them. Ghaffar Kahn was as disappointed as Gandhi about the partitioning of India (Easwaran,).

Back in his native Utmanzai of the frontier, Ghaffar Kahn worked for a united Pashtun province within newly independent Pakistan. Shortly after a radical Hindu assassinated Gandhi, because he was too pro-Muslim, Ghaffar Kahn was imprisoned by Pakistani authorities for being too pro-Hindu. The Frontier Gandhi ended up spending half of the first three decades of Pakistan's existence in prison. He died in Peshawar in 1988 after proving nonviolent actions in the name of Islam are very possible and can be quite successful. Abdul Ghaffar Khan, the man also known as Badshah Kahn and the Frontier Gandhi, followed the teachings of Muhammad who taught him "that man is a Muslim who never hurts anyone by word or deed, but who works for the benefit and happiness of God's creatures. Belief in God is to love one's fellowmen" (Easwaran, 1984, p. 55).

Mohammed Abu-Nimer

Mohammed Abu-Nimer was born in 1962 and was the first child in a large Muslim family in a town in northern Israel. He grew up in a mixed village among Muslims, Christians, and Druze, with his eight siblings. As a young man of 19, Abu-Nimer worked as a facilitator in an Arab-Jewish dialogue focused on coexistence. While in Jerusalem he was confronted by many who did not support this type of interaction. During the ten-year period in which he worked as a peace educator, he also completed his bachelor's degree and a master's degree at Hebrew University. Abu-Nimer is the first member of the Muslim community in his hometown to have received a master's degree. As a peace educator, he designed the first Arabic peace curriculum for Arab educators to use in his native Israel.

During the first Intifada, Abu-Nimer left Israel to work with several NGOs. During his time out of country, he enrolled at George Mason University and received his doctorate in conflict resolution in 1993 (another first for his Muslim community in Israel). His dissertation evaluated the Arab-Jewish dialogue and coexistence models in Israel and it has been used by fifteen organizations. He has worked with people in conflict zones around the world in places like Northern Ireland, Sri Lanka, Bosnia, Sierra Leone, as well as Palestine and Israel, to assist others in conducting dialogues, to train people in the dialogue process, and to conduct interfaith dialogues too.

Abu-Nimer's work has reflected a balance between activism, theory building, research, and policy. He brings strong cultural and religious perspectives and understanding to his work on nonviolence and peace that has been fostered by his living within multiple cultures in a conflict zone. During the 2006 war between Israel and Lebanon, he had one relative living in Lebanon killed by bombs dropped by Israeli planes and another relative living in Israel killed by a Hezbollah missile (Abu-Nimer, 2006). During this war, Abu-Nimer and others fasted outside the US State Department in Washington DC to bring attention to the refusal of the USA to encourage the two sides in the conflict to meet and begin to negotiate a cease fire and peace. Today Abu-Nimer continues his contributions of advocacy, practice, and teaching that led to his being the fourth recipient of the international Morton Deutsch Conflict Resolution Award.

Bahá'í

The fourth Abrahamic religion to be presented here is the Bahá'í faith that had its beginnings in Iran during the middle of the 1800s (Hatcher & Martin, 1985). There are estimated to be between five and six million Bahá'ís in the world today who reside in countries on all continents.

Beliefs and Rituals of Bahá'í

A central belief of the Bahá'í faith is the oneness of humankind. Bahá'í grew out of the Islamic faith much like Christianity did out of Judaism. The Bahá'í faith not only accepts the validity of Islam, it recognizes all the other great faiths including Judaism, Christianity, Buddhism, and Zoroasterism as well. The prophets of these other religions are viewed as real messengers of God so the teachings of Abraham, Buddha, Moses, Jesus, Muhammad, and Zoroaster are considered important in finding paths to salvation (Hatcher & Martin, 1985).

Life of Bahá'u'lláh

Bahá'u'lláh is the name taken by an Iranian nobleman who is the founder of the Bahá'í faith. Born Mírzá Husayn' Alí in Tehran on November 12, 1817, he was an early convert to the Bábí religion at the age of 27. Despite beliefs that called for peaceful behaviors, the Bábí religion was viewed as a serious challenge to the Shiite majority clergy. While the founder of that religion and hundreds of followers had been persecuted, tortured, and killed under the direction of the Shiite leadership, Bahá'u'lláh had escaped death despite his role as a teacher and leader of the Bábí faith. His social position and friends in high places worked in his favor and influenced those who imprisoned and tortured him to exile him and not execute him. Weakened and permanently scarred by his torture, Bahá'u'lláh was exiled without trial in 1852 (Hatcher & Martin, 1985).

During Bahá'u'lláh's time in prison in Tehran, he had a vision in which God revealed to him that he was a man of special religious significance and would fulfill a prophecy in the Bábí religion. After pondering and meditating on this vision and other religious issues in seclusion in Kurdistan, he returned to the Bábí religious community in Iraq and regained his role as spiritual leader. In 1863, in a Baghdad island garden in the Tigris River of present day Iraq, Bahá'u'lláh proclaimed to some of his close followers that he was a universal messenger of God and "He Whom God Will Make Manifest." Because of political pressures and actual banishment, Bahá'u'lláh and his supporters moved throughout the region. It was in 1868 in Edirne, Turkey that Bahá'u'lláh made the public announcement that he was the messenger of God in the Bábí prophesy. This announcement resulted in support from the vast majority of the Bábí community and is widely viewed as the beginning of the Bahá'í faith. (Esslemont, 1970; Hatcher & Martin, 1985).

Bahá'u'lláh wrote many letters to kings, sultans, presidents, prime ministers, and other heads of state in addition to writing the pope and other religious leaders informing them of his mission and new religion. These letters resulted in little direct response from the leaders of the world but they did strike fear about the power Bahá'u'lláh seemed to have. Bahá'u'lláh and about seventy of his follower were therefore imprisoned in the city of Acre in present day Israel. It was a time of great hardship as the city was dangerous due to crime, disease, and poor sanitation. Bahá'u'lláh and his fellow Bahá'í prisoners maintained a positive outlook and expectations for release. After his release, Bahá'u'lláh lived in the Acre region. Here he wrote about his mission and its implications for humanity, met with Bahá'ís and those interested in the Bahá'í faith, and lived with his family until his death in 1892 at the age of 75 (Esslemont, 1970; Hatcher & Martin, 1985).

Bahá'í Tenets and Holy Days

Believers in the Bahá'í faith follow the three fundamental principles of (1) the oneness of God, (2) the oneness of humankind, and (3) the fundamental unity of religion (Hatcher & Martin, 1985). The oneness of God reflects the monotheistic traditions of the other Abrahamic religions already discussed. The oneness of God implies the single omnipotent and omniscience being who created the universe, all creatures, and all forces in it. The oneness of humankind reflects the view that the human race is a single unit with the same God-given capacities. Along this vein, Bahá'ís need to embrace diversity and reduce prejudice, discrimination, power seeking, and other aspects that negate the oneness of the human race to allow for the optimal development of all people. This oneness of humankind "implies not only a new individual consciousness, but the establishment of the unity of nations, of world government, and ultimately of a planetary civilization" (Hatcher & Martin, p. 77). The oneness of religion reflects the belief that humankind is searching for spiritual understanding and the collective revelations of major religions advance this understanding. While various religions view God and their faith differently, Bahá'ís believe the religion of God is the only religion. The prophets of other religions (e.g., Abraham, Buddha, Moses, Jesus, Muhammad) advanced our knowledge of God and his world with each new revelation. The teachings of Bahá'u'lláh are therefore the latest stage in this progression of religion (Bahá'u'lláh, 1976; Hatcher & Martin).

These three fundamental Bahá'í principles, with the universal theme of unity, are supplemented by other moral and spiritual principles endorsed by the Universal House of Justice (2008), an international Bahá'í advisory and governing body. Some of these other principles include:

1. Women and men are equal.
2. All prejudice – racial, religious, or economic – is destructive and must be overcome.
3. We must integrate truth for ourselves, without preconceptions.
4. Science and religion are in harmony.
5. Our economic problems are linked to spiritual problems.
6. The family and its unity are very important.
7. World peace is the crying need of our time (Universal House of Justice).

Bahá'ís strive to put these principles into practice throughout their daily lives. This includes at home, at work, and in the wider community.

The Bahá'í faith assumes that human beings innately possess good qualities and these need to be developed so people can live a life of spiritual and moral strength. "The purpose of God in creating man hath been, and will ever be, to enable him to know his creator and to attain His Presence" (Bahá'u'lláh, 1976, p. 70). Bahá'ís believe a person needs to engage in a continual process of spiritual discovery and development during their life, and after their death their soul will continue to grow in the spiritual world (Hatcher & Martin, 1985). The teachings of Bahá'u'lláh and the Bahá'í faith can provide guidance for spiritual growth, but knowing who Bahá'u'lláh was, is not necessary as "The man who lives the life according to the teachings of Bahá'u'lláh is already a Bahá'í" ('Abdu'l-Bahá cited in Esslemont, 1970, p. 71).

There are eleven Bahá'í holy days and a nineteen-day fasting period for all adult Bahá'ís during each year. The holy days generally center around events in the lives of prominent Bahá'í and Babí leaders of both religions. The most sacred is the twelve-day Festival of Ridvan that commemorates the anniversary of Baha'u'llah's declaration that he was the universal messenger of God. It is celebrated from April 21 to May 2. The nineteen-day Bahá'í fasting period occurs in March. Like Ramadan this fast does not allow Bahá'í s to eat or drink between sunrise and sunset. It is a time of self-reflection, prayer, and meditation. On March 21 at the end of the fasting period, The Feast of Naw-Rúz is held to celebrate the Bahá'í New Year. Some of the other Bahá'í holidays include Bahá'u'lláh's birthday in November, Bahá'u'lláh's Ascension Day in May, and a gift giving time of Ayyám-i-Há at the end of February.

Bahá'í Sacred Texts

Hatcher and Martin (1985) indicated that Bahá'ulláh wrote over one hundred books and tablets and these are collectively viewed as expressing the essence of Bahá'í. His successors as keepers of the Bahá'í faith, 'Abdu'l-Bahá and Shoghi Effendi, have written and interpreted additional aspects of the religion. While Bahá'ís view all these as generally equal authorities for their faith, the *Kitab-i-Ahd*, the Covenant of Bahá'u'lláh, and the Will and Testament of 'Abdu'l-Bahá are the two central documents of the Bahá'í revelation (Universal House of Justice, 2008). Hatcher and Martin delineate the four categories of Bahá'í writings as (1) basic concepts and progressive revelations, (2) principles of human life and conduct, (3) binding and obligatory laws and ordinances, and (4) social and administrative organizations.

Bahá'í Views of Nonviolence

From its early beginnings the Bahá'í religion has made strong statements against the use of violence. For instance, Bahá'u'lláh spoke out against the use of *jihad* or violence in response to religious persecution at a time when they were violently threatened and attacked for their beliefs on a regular basis (Hatcher & Martin, 1985). Many Bahá'ís have also used Bahá'í teachings to reduce the amount of violence in the world and to bring about world peace (Danesh, 1979; Porkorny, 1984).

Many Bahá'í writers have also advocated the pursuit of many components of cultures of peace (Gandhimohan, 2000; Huddleston, 1998; Lee, 1986). More specifically, Schoonmaker (1984), the Universal House of Justice (1985), and Gandhimohan show how the Bahá'í perspective relate to the issues of social justice and inclusiveness for women. The Universal House of Justice states that full equality for women is a necessary prerequisite for peace and addresses this in Bahá'í principle 6 above. Gandhimohan cites the metaphor of humanity as a flying dove used by 'Abdu'l-Bahá to highlight the importance of the equal partnership of the sexes. If one wing is male and the other female, then the dove can only fly if both wings are strong and working together with a common purpose. The importance of social justice and inclusiveness for racial groups is stressed in Bahá'í principle 7 and explained by Brown (1984) and Thomas (1984b). Human rights from a Bahá'í perspective is elucidated by Cole (1984), the rule of law by Hatcher and Martin (1985) and Huddleston, civil society by Thomas (1984a), and education by Danesh (1979) and Huddelston, and sustainability by Pelle (2001) and Huddleston.

A close look at the statements and teachings of Bahá'u'lláh can show why Bahá'ís have been active in seeking nonviolent means for developing world peace. Pelle (2001) cites many instances where Bahá'u'lláh and other leaders specifically speak out against violence and advocate nonviolent actions instead. "Spread not disorder in the land, and shed not the blood of anyone" (Bahá'u'lláh, cited in Pelle, p. 15). 'Abdu'l-Bahá, son of Bahá'u'lláh and second guardian of the Bahá'í faith, stated, "Fighting and the employment of force, even for the right cause, will not bring good results, the oppressed who have right on their side must not take the right by force... the evil will continue. Hearts must be changed" (cited in Pelle, pp. 15-16).

The Universal House of Justice (1985) has adopted and published a Bahá'í vision for world peace. *The Promise of World Peace* is a letter to the peoples of the world, and in it, this Bahá'í body acknowledges difficulties and obstacles that keep humanity from achieving world peace, but also challenge many common assumptions that stop people from investing time and energy in moving in the direction of peace. *The Promise* calls for a people to embrace moral actions through their religion and other positive social institutions and to reject materialism, nationalism, and prejudice. It also calls for the fostering of selfless love as a realization of the Bahá'í belief in the oneness of humankind. Their vision is designed with a theme of strong unity to transcend the end of war and help to develop agencies of international cooperation that can lead to the demilitarization of the world and a long lasting peace. This would lead to the ultimate goal of optimal social development for humanity and "the unification of all the peoples of the world in one universal family" (p. 13).

Notable Bahá'í Advocates of Nonviolence

Bahá'u'lláh, the founder and prophet of the Bahá'í faith, lived a nonviolent life while facing considerable violence toward himself and those around him. He was born into a position of wealth yet he chose to follow a path in life that led to the erosion of his position of privilege and to his persecution for his beliefs. During his lifetime, thousands of Bahá'ís were martyred and thousands more were persecuted, imprisoned, tortured, and exiled (Pelle, 2001). Despite this violent and unjust treatment, Bahá'u'lláh advocated nonviolence for himself and his followers and did not engage in or call for violence at any time. His advice to his followers was "if ye be slain, it is better for you than to slay" (cited in Gandhimohan, 2000). He viewed murder and killing as wrong and was extremely pained when some Bahá'ís killed a rival leader of the faith (Hatcher & Martin, 1985). Bahá'u'lláh also spoke out against nonlethal forms of violence as well. He proclaimed, "Sanctify your ears from idle talk of them that are the symbols of denial and the exponents of violence and anger" (cited in Pelle, p. 15).

Bahá'u'lláh advocated many types of nonviolent responses to resolve conflicts and to respond to violence. He declared, "He [God] hath moreover, ordained that His Cause be taught through the power of men's utterance and not through resort to violence" (cited in Pelle, 2001, p. 15). Bahá'u'lláh used the religious message of oneness or unity as an important tool in conflict resolution. He told his followers that "people need no weapons of destruction, inasmuch as they have girded themselves to reconstruct the world. Their hosts are the hosts of goodly deeds, and their arms the arms of upright conduct, and their commander the fear of God. Blessed that one that judgeth with fairness" (cited in Gandhimohan, 2000).

Because of the true nature of the Bahá'í faith, most practicing Bahá'ís engage in actions that are consistent with activism for the components of cultures of peace (Rhett Diessner, elected member of the Regional Bahá'í Council of the Northwestern States, personal communication, June 12, 2008). In addition many Bahá'ís work together with others in their advocacy work so the collective often makes the names of individual activists less prominent. Having said that, many Bahá'í activists can be identified for their nonviolent work to build cultures of peace.

Richard St. Barbe Baker was born in 1889 in England. At boarding school St. Barbe Baker developed interests in botany and forestry and these interests were the focus of his life's work. After serving in World War I, St. Barbe Baker studied forestry at Cambridge and plied his trade in North Africa, Kenya, Nigeria, the Gold Coast, Palestine, and the United States. His work addressed the mismanagement of the environment and forests and his work to save and restore native trees and forests in many areas of the world resulted in the establishment of the organization, Men of the Trees. This international green organization has worked to reforest Kenya, Palestine, and Nigeria, to save the redwood trees in California, and to plant trees to reclaim the Sahara Desert. St. Barbe Baker planted his last tree in Canada in 1982 just days before his death (Bahá'í World Centre, 1986).

Layli Miller-Muro is a Bahá'í woman who was raised in Atlanta. Her mother was an assistant to Coretta Scott King and her family was involved in civil rights issues. After receiving her bachelor's degree at Agnes Scott College in 1993, she received her law degree in 1996 from American University's Washington College of Law. Miller-Muro has been a champion of women's rights in many ways. During law school, she worked on behalf of a young woman from Togo who sought refuge status to avoid the tribal practice of female genital mutilation (FGM). This was a landmark case in establishing FGM as a basis for asylum. Following law school, Miller-Muro helped establish the Tahirith Justice Center that works to protect women from civil rights abuses by providing legal assistance, and where she is currently the executive director. Miller-Muro's energies and pro-bono work have dealt with violence toward women and girls and addressed human and sex trafficking, domestic and dating violence, refugee status issues, and international marriage brokers (Atlanta Bahá'í, 2008).

Implications of the Abrahamic Religions for Nonviolence and Peace

None of the four Abrahamic religions are absolutely pacifistic, and Judaism, Christianity, and Islam specify situations in which violence is a legitimate response. People who wish for sanctions for violent acts may find support in the sacred texts and those who want to characterize one of these religions as a religion of violence can cite verses to do so as well. However, all four religions also encourage or require nonviolent responses in dealing with other people in certain contexts.

Abu-Nimer (2003) reminds us that the specific implementation of a faith occurs within the unique cultural context of the followers. Because Israel is culturally different from Australia, Judaism practiced in Israel may have some differences from Judaism in Australia. Similarly, Islam in Syria will have some variations in its practice from Islam in Indonesia since believers experience the faith through their distinctive cultural lenses. Therefore, it is imperative that any particular faith not be viewed as a monolithic entity but should be viewed as a more heterogeneous grouping with essential commonalities.

Wessells and Strang (2006) stress that religion can be a double-edged sword in that it may either entice a person to violence or push them toward a nonviolent response. They warn that religion should not be considered totally positive or negative in the way it influences believers. Religion is an important aspect of a group's identity and "religious feelings can mobilize people faster than any other element of their identity" (Kadayifçi-Orellana, 2003, p. 26). The personalities of leaders, political agendas, the power brokers, and situations unique to any culture may transform any religion into an extreme instrument of violence and oppression (Wessells & Strang). Religious fundamentalism can result in an ultra-strict or rigid interpretation of beliefs and practices that may predispose a person to focus on differences between believers and nonbelievers and may reduce levels of tolerance. Whether it is Jewish fundamentalism, Christian fundamentalism, or Islamic fundamentalism, the potential that the fundamentalist will adopt a violent stance to a conflict needs to be studied. All three seem to be playing a negative role in the conflicts within Israel today.

Jews, Christians, Muslims, and Bahá'ís all have a belief system that promotes nonviolent thinking and behavior. The common teaching of the golden rule, love for God and humanity, forgiveness and repentance, and a preference for nonviolent means are found in each religion within the Abrahamic tradition. These parallels are encouraging as followers of each of these religions should be able to experience part of their own faith in the other three.

Recommended Readings

Abu-Nimer, M. (2003). *Nonviolence and peace building in Islam: Theory and practice.* Gainesville, FL: University of Florida Press.
Mohammed Abu-Nimer presents a strong case for nonviolence and peacebuilding from an Islamic base. As the title implies, Abu-Nimer provides a theoretical framework for nonviolence in Islamic religion and culture. He then carefully analyzes the social, political, and cultural applications of nonviolent methods in Muslim communities. He devotes considerable time to the analysis of the Palestinian Intifada as a case study. The scholarship in this book reflects the many awards (e.g., 2005 Morton Deutsch Conflict Resolution Award) that this author has received for his work on peace and conflict resolution. This book presents an important perspective that is not regularly heard in either the popular or academic press.

Easwaran, E. (1984). *A man to match his mountains: Badshah Khan, nonviolent soldier of Islam.* Petaluma, CA: Nilgiri Press.

This is a biography of Abdul Ghaffar Khan, from what is today Pakistan, and known as the "Frontier Gandhi" and as Badshan Kahn or the "king of kahns." This devout Muslim Pashtun man, who grew up near the Khyber Pass, was able to build an army of nonviolent soldiers to work to end the tyranny of British occupation in the first half of the twentieth century and his story is captivating. The author not only brings the nonviolent activism of Badshah Kahn alive to the reader but the historical context for this man's life is also informative. This is an excellent biography of the life of a great man.

Hatcher, W. S., & Martin, J. D. (1984). *The Bahá'í Faith. The emerging global religion.* San Francisco: Harper & Row.

This book is written somewhat like a textbook on the Bahá'í religion by two well-respected Bahá'í s. Hatcher and Martin provide the historical context for the development of the Bahá'í faith and explain the historical events and people that influenced the beliefs of the religion, as we know it today. The basic teachings, administration, and laws of the Bahá'í religion are presented clearly, along with the changes in the world order called for by the founder, Bahá'u'lláh. This is a good starting book for someone unfamiliar with the Bahá'í faith.

Lerner, M. (2006). *The left hand of God: Taking back our country from the religious right.* San Francisco: Harper Collins.

In this book Rabbi Michael Lerner presents his prescription for spiritual people who are progressive in their political views to assert themselves in politics without having to join the religious right. Rabbi Lerner makes the case that spirituality is an important human need and it must be valued and acknowledged. He draws out a Spiritual Covenant with America based upon religious values of a loving God who is merciful, compassionate, and kind. His covenant calls for people to become committed to the "traditional spiritual values of love, generosity, kindness, responsibility, respect, gratitude, humility, awe, and wonder at the grandeur of the world" (p. 229) whether they are secular or non-secular. Rabbi Lerner also discusses the Global Marshall Plan.

Solomon, N., Harries, R., & Winter, T. (Eds.) (2005). *Abraham's children: Jews, Christians, and Muslims in conversation.* New York: T & T Clark.

This edited book presents the writings of religious scholars and theologians as they discuss the great prophets that Judaism, Christianity, and Islam have. Jewish, Christian, and Muslim perspectives are presented on Abraham, Moses, Jesus, and Mohammad, along with a summative essay by the editors. The images and views of God, pluralism, gender, the environment and life after death are also explored.

Wallis, J. (2006). *God's politics: Why the right gets it wrong and the left doesn't get it.* New York: Harper Collins.

Jim Wallis describes himself as a progressive evangelical Christian minister and in this book he clearly explains how this label is not as outrageous as it might sound. Wallis outlines how he thinks religion and politics should relate to each other in an easily understood fashion with numerous examples. His premise is that God is neither a Republican nor a Democrat and that neither party in the United States has integrated the Christian values expressed in the Bible into their platforms or agenda accurately or effectively. His writing does not directly address cultures of peace from a Christian perspective but it does so indirectly by discussing Christian values and the priorities presented in the Bible.

Wink, W. (2003). *Jesus and nonviolence: A third way.* Minneapolis, MN: Fortress Press.

This little book analyzes several of the stories Jesus told about nonviolent solutions to problems and also relates them to problems in today's world. Wink presents a series of nonviolent strategies that can be extrapolated from the parables and statements of Jesus. In addition to this analysis of what he calls Jesus' third way, Wink also makes connections with contemporary nonviolent actions and demonstrations over the last few decades.

Recommended Web Sites

The Bahá'í Chair for World Peace: Scholarship and Spirituality in Service to Peace, http://www.bahaipeacechair.org/index.htm
The Bahá'í Chair for World Peace is housed at the University of Maryland and is dedicated to developing and applying material and spiritual knowledge in cooperative pursuits of peace, social justice, economic justice, and security. This is accomplished through empirical study, objective presentation, reflective analysis, and pragmatic application of ethical and spiritual principles.

Fellowship of Reconciliation for a World of Peace, Justice, and Nonviolence, http://www.forusa.org/
The Fellowship of Reconciliation (FOR) is a Christian interfaith organization founded in 1914 in Switzerland and has worked to replace a culture of violence (violence, war, racism, and economic injustice) with a culture of peace (nonviolence, peace, and justice). The FOR website links you to descriptions of many peace activist initiatives including Interfaith Initiatives in Israel and Palestine, the Campaign of conscience for Iraqi People, Peace and Disarmament, and Nonviolence Training. A wide range of articles and resources that can be downloaded and books and peace related gifts may be purchased through the website.

Jewish Voices for Peace, http://www.jewishvoiceforpeace.org/
Jewish Voices for Peace (JVP) is a diverse community of activists that supports peace activists in Palestine and Israel, and works in broad coalition with other Jewish, Arab-American, faith-based, peace and social justice organizations to bring peace to the Middle East. The JVP efforts are guided by the Jewish tradition to work together for peace, social justice, and human rights.

Muslim Peace Fellowship, http://muslimpeacefellowship.wordpress.com/about/
This organization was founded in 1994 and was the first Muslim group specifically focused on Islamic nonviolence. Its goals include the exploring and deepening of the understanding of peace and nonviolence within Islamic teachings, plus working against injustice and for peace from an intrapersonal through a global level. The Muslim Peace Fellowship also has an outreach function to other religious traditions.

Sojourners: Faith, Politics, and Culture, http://www.sojo.net/index.cfm
Sojourners was founded in 1971 by Jim Wallis as an organization devoted to social justice from a biblical perspective. The specific pursuits were intended to build hope by transforming individuals, communities, the church and the world. Sojourners uses its website, an email newsletter, and a hard copy magazine to get its message out to interested people. While primarily Christian, this Washington DC based organization is open to all who are interested in furthering the stated mission. Good resource links are on the website for community activists and Sunday school teachers to subscribe and download discussion topics and lesson ideas. This is a great site to visit.

Tikkun (to heal, repair, and transform the world), http://www.tikkun.org/
Tikkun (pronounced tick-coon) is an international community, a magazine, and a website designed to heal, repair, and transform the world. Established and led by Rabbi Michael Lerner, the Tikkun community includes people of many faiths who are concerned about social justice and political freedom. The website and magazine provides current information and in depth analyses about world events that impact people in their homes and communities. The vision of Tikkun is to influence public dialogue and to influence policy "in order to inspire compassion, generosity, non-violence and recognition of the spiritual dimensions of life." The website links to position papers on many pressing issues of the day, the Global Marshall Plan, and the Network of Spiritual Progressives. This is another excellent site worth visiting for good and timely information.

Chapter 8
Situational Influences on Nonviolent Action

Our behavior is purposeful; we live in a psychological reality
or life space that includes not only those parts of our physical
and social environment that are important to us but also
imagined states that do not currently exist

Lewin, 1997/1951

While holding personal beliefs in support of nonviolent behavior is very important, any analysis of nonviolence requires the careful consideration of the situational constraints from the micro- through the macro-level. This analysis will incorporate the framework of Ross and Nisbett (1991), which builds on the powerful and pioneering work of Kurt Lewin and casts light on many causes of social behavior. From Ross and Nisbett's perspective, social behavior is a function of three variables: (1) the nature of the situation, (2) the way individuals construe the situation, and (3) the dynamic systems of tension across levels of human experience from individual psyches, through small groups, to national levels.

Accordingly, this chapter is organized around these three dimensions. The first dimension, the situation, involves the social reality surrounding a person or group, as well as, the actual grievance that is to be addressed by the nonviolent action itself. The nature of grievances may be categorized according to the human rights, needs, or values that are violated or frustrated and thereby activating nonviolent political action. While Ross and Nisbett (1991) note the influence of early behaviorists like John Watson in focusing on the importance of the situation in determining behavior, the behaviorist position, unfortunately, did not adequately attend to the next two aspects of the situation. The second dimension involves the psychological factors that affect the construal processes and refers to the ways in which individuals engaged in nonviolent action interpret and understand the situation within which they are embedded. The third dimension involves the tension system and it encompasses the organizational, group, and individual tensions with which individuals engaged in nonviolent action are confronting. This dimension also reflects conflicting norms and personal values in addition to their cultural and national values (Schwartz, 1990).

D.M. Mayton II, *Nonviolence and Peace Psychology,*
DOI 10.1007/978-0-387-89348-8_8, © Springer Science+Business Media, LLC 2009

Situational Dimension of Nonviolent Political Action

The social situation is more influential in determining human behavior than individual personality (Fiske, 2004). This does not mean that personal characteristics are unimportant, but in understanding and predicting a social behavior like nonviolence, there is a need to consider the characteristics of the person in conjunction with the situation in which the person is operating. Both the person and the situation must be included in the prediction process and the situation plays the more significant role.

From the early social psychological research of Triplett's cyclists in 1898 and Chen's ants in 1937 to more contemporary social psychological research, the presence of others has been shown to facilitate performance when the action needed to complete a task is well learned or highly accessible and to lower performance for new behaviors or less accessible ones (Smith & Mackie, 2000; Zajonc, 1966). Whether co-acting with others performing the same task or competing with others for the same goal, social facilitation has been found to be consistent in favoring dominant responses. Within cultures of violence, the scripts we have internalized are much more likely to be violent. Since the typical child spends 40 h watching television per week and an estimated 60% of television programs include violence, it is not surprising that heavy watchers of violence, both male and female, are more likely to engage in violence in their families and communities (Baumeister & Bushman, 2008). Because violent scripts are better learned and more salient, they are more likely to be used during conflicts and nonviolent responses may be overshadowed. After September 11, many groups in the United States supported military action. Even the minority party in the US Congress did not want to look weak so they authorized the president to use military force against Iraq in order to compete for votes in the next election. Before social facilitation effects can work in favor of nonviolent action, nonviolent ways to deal with conflict and hostilities need to be learned well until they become the dominant behavior within a culture of peace.

Channel Factors

Ross and Nisbett (1991) view the power of situationism as necessitating attention to the Lewinian concept of channel factors. Channel factors are relatively minor aspects of a situation that have what seems to be uncharacteristically large influence on behaviors (e.g. Gladwell, 2000). When present, a channel factor can result in a large behavioral change or might thwart what might otherwise be expected to be an inevitable behavioral change. Small channel factors include the negative effect an impending deadline has on helping behavior or the positive effect of direct personal requests for charitable giving. When in a rush to complete a task, even very altruistic individuals ignore those in need (Darley & Batson, 1973). Identifying channel factors and using them to move people to nonviolent action should be a productive approach. The effect of making a small concession on future concessions has been documented and called the "foot in the door" technique using a metaphor from door-to-door salespersons. Small requests granted by potential clients make people more likely to comply with larger requests. Using this channeling factor might involve initially encouraging small investments or commitments in nonviolent activism and only after that would a person be asked to participate in a large-scale nonviolent intervention.

Terror Management Theory

Situations that activate the unconscious awareness that death is inevitable can have a powerful impact on human behavior. This idea is part of a relatively new theory in psychology referred to as terror management theory (TMT) (Greenberg, Pyszczynski, & Solomon, 1986; Pyszczynski, Greenberg, & Solomon, 1999; Solomon, Greenberg, & Pyszczynski, 1991). TMT was originally developed over the last two plus decades by Jeff Greenberg, Tom Pyszczynski, and Sheldon Solomon and the growing research base for the theory is impressive. The foundation for TMT was the work of Ernest Becker, a cultural anthropologist, who wrote about how the awareness of one's mortality and eventual death serves as a motivational force for human beings (Cohen, Solomon, Maxfield, Pyszczynski, & Greenberg, 2004).

TMT is an interdisciplinary theory that is grounded in evolutionary theory and has the potential to be used to improve the social conditions needed to maximize the well-being of humanity (Pyszczynski, Solomon, & Greenberg, 2002). The terror reflected in the name of the theory refers to the terror of one's inevitable death. Since human beings are able to understand our place as members of the animal kingdom and are able to anticipate the future, we are aware of the fact that we will someday die, decompose, and return to be the dust we once were. TMT posits that this realization creates a terror that must be controlled so we can function in our day-to-day lives. If we believe that our lives are important and meaningful, the terror of death may be under reasonable control. To uphold these beliefs TMT suggests we must endorse "(1) faith in a culturally derived worldview that imbues reality with order, stability, meaning, and permanence, and (2) belief that one is a significant contributor to this meaningful reality (pp. 16–17)." The cultural worldviews that we develop are critically important in providing a way to transcend our own deaths with an alternative path to immortality. Our cultural worldview may give us literal immortality through an afterlife or a symbolic immortality through our contributions and connections to society. For some of us our symbolic immortality may be through our children (biological), while for others it may be through our work, teaching, or societal contributions (creative). For others still, it may be as part of the eternal natural universe (natural), or a higher plane of existence (spiritual and religious attainments), or through intense peak experiences (experiential). Regardless of the type(s) of immortality our worldview provides, it functions to give us a sense of meaning and to reduce our anxiety about our death (Pyszczynski et al.).

The fear of our own demise is not something we are conscious of all the time as it is often repressed or at least out of our immediate awareness. Terror management involves working to maintain a strong worldview and, when our mortality is made salient, we must work to defend our worldview. We try to maintain our sense of security and our sense of death transcendence in the face of our knowledge of our eventual death. We might disparage, attack, or even kill those who hold worldviews that conflict with ours. These negative responses toward those who challenge our worldviews are coupled with more positive evaluations of people who validate us. We might incorporate the appealing aspects of an opposing worldview into our own or we might even convert to a new worldview to alleviate our death anxiety (Pyszczynski et al., 2002).

Greenberg, Pyszezynski, Solomon, former and current students, and other colleagues have conducted dozens of studies in support of TMT and have demonstrated its wide applicability. (An excellent bibliography of TMT compiled and maintained by Jamie Arndt can be found at http://www.tmt.missouri.edu/publications.html.) In a typical TMT experiment the treatment group is placed in a situation that makes them think about their own mortality. The condition of mortality salience (MS) may accomplish this overtly (asking participants to imagine their body's decay after their death) or more subtly (conducting the study with a cemetery in the background) with the subtle approaches being more effective. Those in MS conditions have been found to positively evaluate others who validate their worldview and to negatively evaluate those who challenge their worldviews (Pyszczynski et al., 2002). In addition to attitude changes, those whose mortality was made salient also behaved differently toward the person they believed challenged their worldview. Using the administration of hot sauce as a form of aggression, McGregor et al. (1998) and Lieberman, Solomon, Greenberg, and McGregor (1999) found MS participants to be more aggressive toward those challenging their worldview than the control group. McGregor et al. also demonstrated the MS resulted in more aggression toward someone who challenged the participants' worldviews than toward someone who was aggressive toward the participants.

While mortality salience can precipitate negative evaluations and aggression without people realizing it, TMT can also be applied to elicit prosocial behaviors. When terrorist attacks occur anywhere in the world and are reported in the press, mortality salience is a natural outcome. After the events of September 11 in 2001, Yum and Schenck-Hamlin (2005) investigated the reactions of college students in the Midwestern section of the United States and determined that almost four of five respondents engaged in altruistic and prosocial behavior including donating blood or money, showing empathy for the victims, and communication with others to do the same. Jonas, Schimel, Greenberg, and Pyszczynski (2002) also found mortality salience for American participants to increase charitable giving when the charities support an American cause but not for international ones. The prosocial giving was not enhanced for charities outside of one's own culture. If a person's worldview contains strong prosocial components, as is the case for liberals who embrace tolerance, mortality salience increases evaluations consistent with those views. Greenberg et al. (1992) found that dislike for dissimilar others increased for conservatives but decreased for liberals. In addition, they found priming people for the value of tolerance, prior to the MS condition, counteracts the tendency for mortality salience to elicit negative reactions to others who hold worldviews different than us.

TMT has implications for the political world. Cohen, Ogilvie, Solomon, Greenberg, and Pyszczynski (2005) studied the effect of MS on preferences for US presidential candidates in the 2004 election. College students who were registered voters within the MS condition overwhelmingly preferred George Bush over John Kerry while the control condition preferred John Kerry to the same degree. Cohen et al. hypothesize that the Osama bin Laden videotape that was shown on television news a week before the election may have created a fear of mortality among the American electorate that may have changed the outcome of the close election. Willer (2004) investigated the impact of government-issued terror warnings on the approval ratings of President Bush and found a consistent positive relationship. The president's approval ratings went up after terror warnings (mortality salience) during his first term in office. Cohen et al. (2004) found MS to impact the electorate's evaluation of charismatic and relationship-oriented political candidates. The MS condition resulted in more positive evaluations of the charismatic candidate and more negative evaluations of the relationship-oriented candidate.

TMT has many implications for conflict resolution and peace. Dechesne, van den Berg, and Soeters (2007) studied Dutch peacekeeping troops while they were either stationed in Europe or in Afghanistan. While in a combat zone in Afghanistan with high mortality salience, the soldiers were less supportive of international collaborative efforts to resolve the conflict than soldiers outside a combat zone. Pyszczynski et al. (2002) have presented a process whereby TMT explains the psychological aspects of the ethnopolitical hatred that led to the terrorism of 9/11. According to their analysis, religion is not the root of the problem. The difficulties in managing the existential terror of death are the root of the problem at the psychological level. While the 9/11 terrorists were Muslims, Pyszczynski et al. argue that the terrorists rigid worldview, that does not include the tolerance taught in the Qur'an and is exacerbated by low self-esteem and identity needs that are not being met, creates the conditions whereby terrorist acts may in fact reduce death anxiety. So TMT provides a parsimonious explanation for why the radical Islamic views held by some are related to a dislike of modernity, the United States, and much of the Western world and why this and many US actions have moved these individuals to engage in violent acts against those who challenge their worldview. Unfortunately, the same TMT dynamics that elucidates the actions of terrorists can also explain why responses to terrorist events by Americans are counterproductive (Pyszczynski et al.). Terrorism creates mortality salience and, when those involved hold different worldviews, people with the same worldviews as the terrorists are hated and attacked in many ways. After 9/11, many Americans began expressing bigoted statements about Arabs and Muslims (Yum & Schenck-Hamlin, 2005) and support for going to war with Muslim Iraq soared even though links between Iraq and 9/11 did not exist.

Pyszczynski et al. (2002) also see a hope for the pursuit of peace in TMT. First, the need to change the worldview of people toward tolerance would go a long way to avoid the violent responses between people when mortality salient events occur. While this is easier said than done, they call for the nourishing of more moderate religious elements. Whether it is Judaism, Christianity, or Islam, encouraging the moderates to be more vocal and involved within communities can mitigate the negative aspects of ultraorthodox Judaism, fundamentalist Christianity and radical Islam. A liberal education system that prepares students to be successful and to lead a productive life would bolster self-esteem, meet identity needs, and also help in building tolerance into worldviews. Besides changing worldviews to include tolerance, Pyszczynski et al. also encourage efforts to reduce the mortality salience in the world. In too many places mortality salience is a near continuous reality. Meeting the physical needs of people by reducing poverty, improving health care, and resolving armed conflicts are difficult challenges but they would help if addressed. In addition the needs for meaning and value in the lives of many people are not being met, and if they were, peace would be more likely. The components of a culture of peace discussed in Chap. 6 are all relevant either to the issues of physical needs or personal meaning and identity needs. While TMT may foster violent or nonviolent responses, other situational contexts may be more likely to be the precursor to nonviolent action.

Situational Contexts That Foster Nonviolence

Certain situations are often linked with nonviolent political movements. Sharp (1973) noted that a considerable number of nonviolent actions throughout history have been poorly documented, if documented at all. Despite this propensity, hundreds of nonviolent struggles can be identified throughout recorded history and dozens of nonviolent campaigns initiated around the world during the twentieth century were discussed in Chap. 2 (Ackerman & DuVall, 2000; Ackerman & Kruegler, 1994; Holmes, 1990; Lynd & Lynd, 1995; Sharp; Zunes, Kurtz, & Asher, 1999). Situations that are marked by social injustices often precipitate nonviolent political action. These include situations that limit freedoms, maintain inequalities, sustain economic oppression, or threaten security and safety on both individual and societal levels.

Many nonviolent actions have taken place in the interest of bringing about more democratic forms of government. For instance between 1905 and 1906, Russian workers engaged in marches, general strikes, the withdrawal of funds from banks, and the nonpayment of debts in order to get the Tsar to act on their demands for a more representative government.

Similarly, during the 1920s, German citizens initiated nonviolent actions to establish the freedoms they thought were implicit in a democratic society by thwarting an attempted coup d'état with noncooperative acts (Sharp, 1973). In addition nonviolent actions are often undertaken to reestablish personal freedoms as was done by the Danish people against their Nazi occupiers during the 1940s (Ackerman & Kruegler, 1994).

Grievances over inequality have been another major concern leading to nonviolent political action as typified by the Suffragette-Hunger Strike (Lynd & Lynd, 1995). The satyagraha in the early 1920s on behalf of the untouchable caste in India to obtain access to the Vykom Temple Road is another example (Bondurant, 1965).

Many of the nonviolent activities of Martin Luther King Jr and his colleagues in the 1950s and 1960s were meant to eliminate inequalities in the United States. Economic oppression has been cited as a cause of nonviolent political action many times during the twentieth century as was the case for the strikes and boycotts pursued by Cesar Chavez and the United Farm Workers in the USA (Eppler, 1990). Another set of grievances resulting in nonviolent political actions can be categorized as security and safety issues. One example that was precipitated by fear for the safety of their husbands is the successful street protests in front of Gestapo Headquarters in Berlin by the Aryan wives of Jewish men in Germany (Stolzfus, 1996). The nonviolent noncooperation by the Druze of Golan Heights between 1981 and 1982 is another (Kennedy, 1990).

Construal Dimension of Nonviolent Political Action

A fundamental axiom of social psychology is that people construct their own reality (Smith & Mackie, 2000). The construction of reality is shaped by both cognitive and social processes and ultimately defines any situation for each person. One's constructed reality is a better predictor of behavior for a person than any objective analysis of situational components by outside observers. Ross and Nisbett (1991) assert, "that much, if not most, everyday human behavior, especially social behavior, becomes explainable and predictable only when we know, or can accurately guess the subjective interpretations and beliefs of the people involved (p. 60)." The construal dimension encompasses the psychological processes employed by individuals in conjunction with an awareness of the situation's components to interpret the situation as one that calls for nonviolent political action. These psychological processes influence each individual's understanding of the group and individual tensions facing them. Input from individuals and groups who are actually present or whose presence is imagined also is encompassed by this dimension.

The constructs relevant to this construal dimension for nonviolent individuals include their beliefs, their perceived individual and group efficacy, their values, their scripts and schemas, as well as their perceptions of the perpetrators of injustices in their lives. Knowing the unique combinatory set of situational, organizational, and individual psychological factors and constraints experienced by those who decide to engage in the nonviolent political action is also crucial if we are to begin to understand how interpretations of a situation precipitate subsequent nonviolent action. While some are idiosyncratic to a particular situation, many factors are more generic such as framing effects, social comparisons, the attribution process and attribution errors, and communicator credibility,

Leung et al. (2002) have outlined and developed a measure to determine a set of pan-cultural general beliefs that can guide an analysis of the construal process. These beliefs are "generalized beliefs about oneself, the social and physical environment, or the spiritual world, and are in the form of an assertion about the relationship between two entities or concepts (Leung et al., p. 289)." Leung et al.

assessed: (1) beliefs and principles that guide interactions with others, and beliefs about everyday matters, (2) beliefs with regard to the self, other people, social relations, social groups, the environment, and the supernatural, and (3) beliefs with regard to issues on health, love, marriage, society, politics, religion, entertainment/ recreation, work, family, sports, and life in general. These beliefs can be reduced to five factors: cynicism, social complexity, reward for application, spirituality, and fate control. Cynicism represents a negative or biased view of human nature, groups of people, and social institutions. Social complexity represents beliefs in multiple ways of achieving a given outcome and that human inconsistency is prevalent. Reward for application represents a general belief that effort, knowledge, and careful planning leads to positive outcomes. Spirituality assesses beliefs about the existence of supernatural forces and the functions of religion. Fate control represents beliefs in the pre-determination of life events and the ways people influence them.

These pan-cultural general beliefs can be a useful tool in understanding how some individuals and groups might construe a situation as one in which nonviolent action is a realistic option and others in the same situation might not. Individuals and groups that are high in cynicism and fate control should have more difficulty seeing the potential for nonviolent political actions to be successful, whereas those higher in social complexity, reward for application, and spirituality should be more likely to see the positive potential for nonviolent actions and would pursue nonviolent alternatives to resolve conflicts and to reduce social injustice. Individuals and groups low in fate control would exhibit high levels of efficacy and would again be more likely to interpret situations as appropriate for nonviolent action. The Bolsheviks' bloody revolution and the nonviolent strikes led by Father Gapon both occurred in Russia at the beginning of the twentieth century but the differences in the beliefs of the leadership is clearly reflected in these pan-cultural beliefs (Ackerman & DuVall, 2000). High cynicism and low spirituality reflected the Bolshevik beliefs while more positive views of human nature and spirituality reflected the beliefs of the nonviolent strikers. In fact spirituality beliefs have been repeatedly demonstrated to be associated with nonviolent movements. From Gandhi's Hindu *Bhagavad-Gita* to Martin Luther King's Christian Bible to the Talmud and Qur'an, it is the spirituality beliefs that are associated with nonviolent construal tendencies (Holmes, 1990). Although extreme fundamentalist religious beliefs seem to be a negative force, the lower social complexity and higher levels of fate control may be mediating the effect of spirituality beliefs in this case.

Human values are transsituational goals that serve as guiding principles in people's lives (Schwartz, 1992, 1994a). An individual's value system can help explain his or her actions in a range of social and political situations (Rokeach, 1973, 1979). Schwartz (1994a) identified ten value types that have implications for understanding the construal dimension of nonviolent political action. Mayton, Diessner, and Granby (1996) demonstrated that higher predispositions to act nonviolently are positively related to more emphasis on universalism, benevolence, and conformity values. Their value findings are consistent with the goals and principles which Gandhi considered important. The two self-transcendent value types of universalism and benevolence correspond to the notion of the welfare of all (*sarvodaya*) and the concern about truth and wisdom (*satya*). The value type of conformity reflects the emphasis placed on self-discipline. When people, who place a high priority on theses value types, see human suffering and injustice, they are more inclined to construe the situation in a way that moves them to nonviolent action. However, people who place a low priority on these values and instead place a high priority on power and hedonism construe the situation very differently.

Cognitive structures like schemas and scripts can be viewed as the "tools of construal" (Ross & Nisbett, 1991, p. 12). A schema is a cognitive structure that individuals use to organize their experiences in a particular domain, while a script is a learned, normative sequence of events for a particular situation (Moghaddam, 1998). By categorizing people and situations into learned and available schemas and scripts, individuals are able to interpret their social reality more quickly and with less effort. Unfortunately, the advantages of time and energy efficiency in using cognitive representations are lost if interpretive mistakes are made (Ross & Nisbett). Numerous cognitive structures are relevant in the construal of situations as either appropriate or inappropriate for nonviolent political action. Aggressive scripts that have been internalized from movies and television programs are often-times more accessible than scripts containing nonviolent actions. For instance, after the terrorist attacks on September 11, the predominant script or plan of action involved a violent military response. Likewise, the violent actions of the British, as in the massacre perpetrated by General Dyer on peaceful Indian demonstrators, moved many Indians to want to respond with violence but Gandhi insisted that nonviolent schemas be applied and his influence prevailed (Fischer, 1954).

Tension System Dimension of Nonviolent Political Action

Ross and Nisbett (1991) have described the importance of the dynamic systems of tension involving individual psyches and the collectivities from the small group to national levels. This Lewinian notion is powerful and complex but very difficult to totally pin down due to its fluidity and truly dynamic qualities. Within a tension system one may expect to find restraining factors that prevent changes from happening yet may find that a seemingly stable situation is very close to changing in major ways with minimal intervention (Ross & Nisbett). Restraining factors may be strong cultural norms like the norm of reciprocity where violence is responded to by violence. This "eye for an eye" norm can make things very difficult to change. An example of seemingly stable systems that fell apart with relatively small efforts based on the perceptions of most throughout the world occurred in the Soviet Union and the Soviet Bloc countries in the late 1980s (Ross & Nisbett). Communist governments in East Germany, Hungary, and Czechoslovakia fell relatively quickly without the need for military intervention.

A range of tensions that are particularly relevant to the decision to develop and implement nonviolent political actions can be delineated. The general cultural context(s) within which a grievance is experienced is a crucial factor that can create enormous pressures for particular courses of action. Attempts to define and delineate cultures have focused on the value differences at a national level (Hofstede, 1980; Schwartz, 1990). While the labels for the value differences may vary across cultures, the values that reflect the dimensions of culture are essentially the same. Schwartz has demonstrated at the country level of analysis that several levels of values explain the distinctions effectively. The first is collectivism vs. individualism. Within a collectivist society, individuals define their identity by the nature of the groups to which they are attached. The Indian actions during the 1920s at the Temple Road in Vykom and the Bardoli Peasants versus Bombay activities are examples of nonviolent political actions within a collectivist culture (Bondurant, 1965). Within an individualistic society, individuals define their identity by personal choices and achievements. The civil rights movement in the 1950s and 1960s and the Vietnam War protests in the USA are relevant examples within individualistic cultures (Lynd & Lynd, 1995). The values of hierarchy vs. social concern reflect the amount of respect and deference between those in superior and subordinate positions with examples of nonviolent political action in Germany during the 1920s (Sharp, 1973) at the hierarchy end of the continuum and in Thailand during 1992 at the other end (Zunes et al., 1999). The values of mastery vs. harmony reflect the notions of success vs. caring and quality of life. The United Farm Workers movement in the USA in the 1970s (Ackerman & DuVall, 2000) is indicative of the mastery values (ambitious, independent, capable) while the People Power Revolution in the Philippines (Ackerman & Kruegler, 1994) was more concerned with quality of life (Zunes et al.).

Although the classical studies on cultural values made cross-country comparisons, it is useful to search for cultural variations between national subgroups, divided along ideological, ethnic, and/or religious lines, and separated from each other by asymmetric power positions. The culture of the group creating a grievance and of the group experiencing that grievance may be similar, as was the case in the Vorkuta labor camps actions in the Soviet Union in 1953 (Sharp, 1973) or the Vietnam War protests in the USA from 1966 to 1973 (Lynd & Lynd, 1995). On the other hand, there may be power asymmetries that divide by culture as was the case in the Salt Act Reform actions in India in 1930 and 1931 (Bondurant, 1965). In this set of actions the British with their individualistic culture and politico-economic interests, aggravated and clashed with the Indian people who formed a collectivist culture with fewer resources. Along with the character of the general culture(s) in which the grievances and the nonviolent action occurs, tensions exist as a function of the informal and formal groups that are involved with the grievance. The unique subjectivities, collectivities, and organizational dynamics must be analyzed to understand how the pluralities of oppressed or marginalized individuals attempt to control and direct a nonviolent response to a conflict situation to their advantage.

Just as there may be dissonance between individual attitudes, values, and behaviors, there may also be tensions among social norms. A situation may activate several norms at the same time. For instance, a norm for reciprocity or the "you scratch my back and I'll scratch yours" norm may be activated at the same time that the norm within a culture of honor is triggered. This might happen when a person has received a favor from someone and then realizes this person has wronged a close friend. The tension and the norm eventually acted upon may be difficult to predict.

Military–Economic–Governmental–News Complex

One tension creating dynamic in the United States and many nations with a strong military capability throughout the world is what I refer to as the Military–Economic–Governmental–News complex (Mi–EGo News complex, pronounced my ego news complex). This is the twenty-first century version of the military–industrial complex that President Eisenhower warned about during his presidential farewell address in 1961. Eisenhower cautioned, "In the councils of government, we must guard against the acquisition of unwarranted influence, whether sought or unsought, by the military–industrial complex. The potential for the disastrous rise of misplaced power exists and will persist" (Pilisuk, 2008, p. 100). He went on to advise, "We must never let the weight of this [military–industrial complex] endanger our liberties or democratic processes. We should take nothing for granted. Only an alert and knowledgeable citizenry can compel the proper meshing of the huge industrial and military machinery of defense with our peaceful methods and goals." If Eisenhower were alive today, he probably would not commend Americans for heeding his warning, but would undoubtedly amend his comments to address the expanded power of this complex with its new components and increased dangers. The military–industrial complex has expanded to include more aspects of our economy such as investment firms, the stock market, and divested global corporations. The government and the news media need to be added to this complex today as these two institutions are now intertwined with the workings of the military and economic interests in ways that result in the exercise of the misplaced power Eisenhower warned about. The government is linked with the military in that it engages our military personnel in conflicts across the globe, funds proxy armies and proxy wars, approves and encourages arms sales, and sets the military budget. The movement of military personnel into the government creates a revolving door that parallels another revolving door between the military and related aspects of the economy that includes arms dealers, defense contractors, and security contractors. When these revolving doors are combined with the revolving door between government positions and lobbying and military aspects of the economy, a labyrinth of interconnections often hides intentions and interests of the people involved. A free press is an essential component of a strong democracy, but a manipulated and controlled press can work to support, maintain, and enhance the linkages between military, economic, and governmental interest. The US news media's failure to ask hard questions and the lock-step fashion in which it supported President Bush in the lead up to the US invasion of Iraq in 2003 is an example of a compromised "free press." Corporate media ownership of many news outlets, the growth of opinion programming that looks like news, talk radio news/opinion programming, and the profit driven aspect of news organizations all have combined over the last decade to produce this

Mi-EGo News complex. Each of the four components of the Mi-EGo News complex depends on each of the others for their political and financial well-being.

Each component of the Mi-EGo News complex serves a useful function within today's world. While not all would agree, a case can be made that a capable military, a strong economy, a responsible government, and free press are important institutions with clear functions. The institutions in the Mi-EGo News complex do include selfish and self serving people, but what makes it so powerful and difficult to control, or at least keep it in check, is the fact that many of those that help to perpetuate it are good people who do so inadvertently with very good intentions. The reasons given for the invasion of Iraq in 2003 demonstrate the complex dynamics and power of the Mi-EGo News complex. Oil, armament industry, weapons of mass destruction, poor intelligence, fear because of 9/11, Bush family dynamics concerning Saddam Hussein, politicians who feared looking weak, US-Israeli interests, desire for a military base in the region, media as cheerleader, and an unengaged electorate are just some of the reasons the Mi-EGo News complex pushed the case for war forward. There were people who supported each one of these reasons. Some wanted to secure oil reserves, some to bolster sales of military hardware, some for military contracts, some for a military base, some for fear, some for a show of strength, and so on. The *Project for the New American Century* attests to the fact that many in the government were eager to establish a major military base in that part of the world outside of Saudi Arabia. The staff, signatories and supporters of this document included many in the Bush administration (i.e., Dick Cheney, Donald Rumsfeld, Paul Wolfowitz, John Bolton, and Richard Armitage), in the news media (i.e., William Kristol), and the economic world (i.e., Steve Forbes). Some in the oil industry and some in the military probably believed their interests would be aided by a permanent military base to protect US economic interests in the region. Certainly, it was not the norm, but undoubtedly some in the defense industry viewed the Iraq war as a way to sell their deadly widgets. Because of the revolving doors between the components of the Mi-EGo News complex, some in the defense industry supported the invasion to support their friends in the military or the government, some in the government to support their connections to industry, and so on. Because the post 9/11 climate created fear among many members of Congress, members of the news media, and the general citizenry, people feared appearing weak and to be blamed if there were another attack on the USA. Some in the news media supported the administration's position because they believed it to be the best approach to take in stopping a future terrorist attack in the USA, but others probably did so to maintain access to the administration. If tough questions are asked in a news conference too many times, reporters may not be called on in the future and this might jeopardize their job status. During this time period, some publishers and editors were probably concerned about impending FCC regulations and did not want to rock the administrations boat. Due to these and other reasons, a generally uncritical media supported President Bush in his invasion of Iraq. While many other interconnections between the military, economic, governmental, and news media regarding the invasion of Iraq can be added to the above list, it is clear that the interrelationships within the Mi-EGo News complex provided a multifaceted push toward an Iraq invasion and a very difficult momentum to stop.

An awareness of the involvement of social scientists in the Mi-EGo News complex has also been growing. The ethics of including uniformed cultural anthropologists with US troops in Afganistan has been raised in professional anthropology circles. Psychologists have been dealing with the ethics and appropriateness of psychologists involved in the interrogation and torture of detainees at Guantanamo Bay. This has been a difficult and divisive topic resulting in heated emotional debate in the American Psychological Association (APA) fueled in part by the Mi-EGo News complex since 2003. Elements of the MI-EGo News complex may be seen in the very large number of psychologists, including some in APA leadership, who are employed by the military, intelligence agencies, the defense industry, or work as contractors for the Department of Defense. If the APA adopts a strong statement about psychological ethics on this topic, it may directly affect the livelihood of this group and/or their friends and acquaintances. Other psychologists do not support a strong statement because of the potential to antagonize an administration that may grant prescription privileges to psychologists in the near future. Angering this administration could result in no prescription privileges and fewer behavioral science research dollars plus other actions supportive of psychology may not be in the offing. So even at the professional level within one discipline, aspects of the Mi-EGo News can be observed in all its complexity.

The Mi-EGo News complex is a clear example of the tension dynamic within the situation. There is a need to reduce the power of the Mi-EGo News complex. Many avenues might be pursued to begin to accomplish this and there are many approaches that might be extrapolated from nonviolence theory and nonviolent activism. Approaches might address (1) avoiding conflicts of interest between the four institutional components, (2) dealing with revolving door issues between the four components, (3) making connections between the four components transparent, (4) establishing a stronger "balance of power" between the four components, and (5) reducing groupthink tendencies enhanced by the revolving doors.

Conclusion

The characteristics of the situation that people find themselves in is a large determinant of behavior and nonviolent behavior is no exception. Some situations may encourage nonviolent actions and others may work against them. While very little research has been completed on the situational factors influencing nonviolence, this chapter highlighted the general model of Ross and Nisbett (1991) that incorporates the characteristics of the situation, how the situation is construed, and the dynamic systems of tension across the complexities of human experience. A special emphasis was given to TMT at the interpersonal level and the Mi-EGo News complex at the societal level.

At the time President Eisenhower issued his warning about the situational factor of the military-industrial complex, he also provided hope when he said, "I like to believe that people in the long run are going to do more to promote peace than our governments. Indeed, I think that people want peace so much that one of these days governments had better get out of the way and let them have it." The important situational factor for this to happen is the presence of a fully functioning democracy and the free flow of news and information to the people. Efforts to build cultures of peace throughout the world would support this hopeful vision.

Recommended Readings

Pilisuk, M. (2008). *Who benefits from global violence and war: Uncovering a destructive system.* Westport, CT: Praeger Security International.

Marc Pilisuk has written an in-depth analysis of the people and corporations that have profited and continue to profit from war. Based on a long standing concern, Pilisuk shows us the painful costs of war and globalization today as he documents many players in the military-industrial complex as well as many in what he refers to as the "elite clubs" that build, maintain, and wield networks of power. Pilisuk ends by addressing the values inherent in the Western worldview and argues why these need our attention.

Pyszczynski T., Solomon, S., & Greenberg, J. (2002). *In the wake of 9/11: The psychology of terror.* Washington, DC: American Psychological Association.

This book by the major architects of TMT provides a clear and in depth description of this fresh theory. Pyszczynski et al. summarize a large amount of the research on TMT conducted up to 2001 in an easily accessible way. In addition to their explanation of TMT the authors use the theory to address issues of terrorism, responses to terrorism, and possible methods to bring the world closer to a peaceful existence. Highly recommended place to start to learn about this important theory.

Ross, L. & Nisbett, R. E. (1991). *The person and the situation: Perspectives of social psychology.* Philadelphia, PA: Temple University Press.

This book outlines the ways in which the situation is so powerful in determining social behavior. Ross and Nesbitt draw on many classic experiments in social psychology to show how the nature of the situation, the way individuals construe the situation, and the systems of tension across levels of human experience all work in a dynamic way to influence human behavior. The authors do a nice job weaving classic social psychological theories with more contemporary approaches in this very readable text.

Chapter 9
Measurement Tools for Research on Nonviolence and Related Concepts

Before high-quality empirical research may advance our understanding of nonviolence, sound measures of nonviolence and related concepts must be available and utilized. This chapter first reviews the assessments of nonviolence reported in the social science research literature to date. Nonviolent measures discussed include the Teenage Nonviolence Test (TNT) (Mayton et al., 1998), the Pacifism Scales (Elliott, 1980), the Gandhian Personality Scale (GPS) (Hasan & Khan, 1983), Nonviolence Test (NVT) (Kool & Sen, 1984), Multidimensional Scales of Nonviolence (MSN) (Johnson et al., 1998) and a couple other scales that assess nonviolence. These measures are reviewed to draw attention to their strengths and weaknesses.

In addition to the measures of nonviolence, brief analyses of measures of related concepts that are relevant to the characteristics of a peaceful person (e.g., empathy, forgiveness, materialism, need for cognition, self-control, spirituality), to human values, and to the characteristics of cultures of peace are provided. Reference books and websites for additional measures are also mentioned. Recommendations are made for the use of these assessments as outcome measures in future nonviolence and peace psychology research, as well as an outline of additional measures that need to be developed by peace psychologists.

The TNT (Mayton et al., 1998) is highlighted and its psychometric properties are explained in depth. While the TNT has been described elsewhere (Mayton et al., 2002), this discussion includes the full instrument and a considerable amount of unpublished material from a variety of sources that document the internal consistency, stability, and validity of the measure in a variety of contexts. This not only demonstrates the strengths and usefulness of the TNT but also serves as a guideline for others who are developing related measures. Thus, the underlying goals for the chapter are to increase the awareness of peace researchers to an array of sound measures and to provide guidelines for the conduct of research on new measures related to nonviolence and nonviolence research.

D.M. Mayton II, *Nonviolence and Peace Psychology*,
DOI 10.1007/978-0-387-89348-8_9, © Springer Science+Business Media, LLC 2009

The Teenage Nonviolence Test

Mayton et al. (1998) developed the TNT to measure the nonviolent tendencies of adolescents and young adults. The TNT was designed to be used by psychologists, other mental health professionals, and educators concerned with developing nonviolent behaviors in teenagers and to assess the impact of interventions with their clients or students. The TNT is based on the philosophy of Mohandas K. Gandhi (1951, 1957/1927). and is centered around the concepts of *ahimsa* (nonviolence), *satyagraha* (search for wisdom and truth), and *tapasya* (willingness to accept suffering). The TNT is also based on the conceptualization of pacifism of Elliott (1980) and the writings on nonviolence of Kool (1990).

The TNT contains 55 Likert items divided into six subscales and is presented in the Appendix. The first two subscales were designed to measure *ahimsa* and are labeled physical nonviolence and psychological nonviolence. The labels and general descriptions of these subscales are drawn from the applications of Elliott (1980). The physical nonviolence subscale has 16 items and it measures the conscious rejection of behaviors or the threat of behaviors intended to inflict bodily injury on another person in an attempt to coerce, curtail, or eliminate their behavior in favor of alternate forms of conflict resolution. The psychological nonviolence subscale also has 16 items and it measures the conscious rejection of behaviors or the threat of behaviors intended to humiliate, intimidate, or in other ways demean the human dignity of another person or group in an attempt to coerce, curtail, or eliminate their behavior in favor of alternate forms of conflict resolution. The third subscale, also based upon the research work of Elliott, is the four item subscale labeled active value orientation. Active value orientation measures the willingness to perform behaviors designed to achieve a situation commensurate with one's own norms, values, and goals. The fourth subscale is labeled empathy and helping and it measures the willingness to assist others with minor levels of need. The last two subscales, more directly related to Gandhian principles, are the ten-item satyagraha subscale and the four-item tapasya subscale. The satyagraha subscale measures the active search for wisdom and the willingness to change one's own conception of truth. The tapasya subscale measures the willingness to endure hardship or suffering rather than to inflict harm on others.

Responses to each statement on the TNT are definitely true, probably true, probably not true, or definitely not true for the respondent. The most nonviolent response for each item on the TNT is coded as a four, the next most nonviolent response is coded as a three, the next most nonviolent response is coded as a two, and the least nonviolent response is coded as a one for analysis purposes. Subscale scores are computed by summing the scores for each item in the subscale and dividing by the number of items in the subscale. Therefore, scores above 2.5 are indicative of nonviolent tendencies and those below 2.5 are indicative of more violent tendencies. The scoring for each subscale is presented in the Appendix to this chapter.

In the sections that follow, I will present data concerning the psychometric characteristics of the TNT. Initially, I will discuss reliability and validity data for using the TNT with 12–19 year olds. This information is drawn from a variety of papers previously presented at conferences but not published (Konen et al., 1999; Mayton et al., 1998; Mayton, Weedman, Sonnen, Grubb, & Hirose, 1999) and other data not available elsewhere. After the psychometrics of the TNT are presented for adolescents, the psychometrics of the TNT for usage with college students will be presented.

Reliability of the TNT

Internal Consistency of TNT

A sample of 376 junior high adolescents from Northern Idaho, approximately equal number of males and female, were used to assess internal consistency of the subscales. The seventh graders (23.1%), eighth graders (40.7%), and ninth graders (36.2%) had a mean age of 13.5 with a standard deviation of 0.91. The predominantly Caucasian (86.4%) sample also included 5.7% Latino/Hispanics and 2.2% Native-American Indians.

Alpha coefficients were computed for each subscale for the entire sample and are presented in Table 9.1. Alpha coefficients were also calculated for males and females separately and are presented in Table 9.1 too. The TNT appears to have high internal consistency for five of the six subscales with alpha coefficients ranging from a high of 0.904 on the physical nonviolence subscale to a low of 0.772 on the Satyagraha subscale for the total sample. The active value orientation subscale only had an alpha coefficient of 0.322 which is inadequate. The same patterns were found when male and female data was analyzed separately. All of the six subscales except the active value orientation subscale were identified to be internally consistent.

Test–Retest Reliability

The samples for this part of the study included 87 junior high students from Northern Idaho, 21 eleventh graders from Southern Idaho, and 16 Native American Indian adolescents from Southern Idaho. Males made up about 55% of the three samples that were predominantly Caucasian except for the last one.

Table 9.1 Internal consistency of the TNT

TNT subscales	Alpha coefficients		
	Total sample	Males	Females
Physical nonviolence	0.904	0.901	0.877
Psychological nonviolence	0.863	0.853	0.838
Active value orientation	0.322	0.397	0.193
Helping/empathy	0.801	0.733	0.811
Satyagraha	0.772	0.775	0.754
Tapasya	0.776	0.782	0.756

Table 9.2 Stability of the TNT across groups

| | Test-retest reliability coefficients | | | |
TNT subscales	Males (*n* = 46)	Females (*n* = 38)	Total (*n* = 84)	American Indian (*n* = 16)
Physical nonviolence	0.868	0.872	0.880	0.947
Psychological nonviolence	0.701	0.866	0.795	0.938
Active value orientation	0.483	0.464	0.477	0.422
Helping/empathy	0.711	0.863	0.789	0.939
Satyagraha	0.833	0.800	0.818	0.847
Tapasya	0.608	0.697	0.645	0.853

Table 9.3 Stability of the TNT across grade levels

| | Test-retest reliability coefficients | | | |
TNT subscales	7th Grade	8th Grade	9th Grade	11th Grade
Physical nonviolence	0.928	0.811	0.924	0.877
Psychological nonviolence	0.916	0.761	0.762	0.911
Active value orientation	0.583	0.618	0.272	0.734
Helping/empathy	0.865	0.766	0.805	0.745
Satyagraha	0.938	0.753	0.790	0.798
Tapasya	0.858	0.492	0.707	0.708

Teachers administered the TNT to their students who volunteered to participate. The time period between the first and second administration of the TNT was 10–15 days. Test–retest reliability coefficients for the first sample are presented in Table 9.2 along with test–retest coefficients for males and females computed separately and the results for the Native American Indian sample. The test–retest coefficients for the physical nonviolence, psychological nonviolence, helping empathy, and satyagraha subscales were all in between 0.701 and 0.880 which are strong. The test–retest coefficients for tapasya were all above 0.60 which is adequate for group research usage. The active value stability values were not adequate. The breakdown by grade level is presented in Table 9.3. Similar patterns were generally identified by grade level with five subscales showing adequate stability and the active value orientation subscale stability being quite poor. Values across the eighth grade sample were generally lower than other grades.

The test–retest coefficients appear to be quite adequate for nonviolence research on groups of teenagers with the exception of the deficient active value orientation subscale.

Concurrent Validity of the TNT

The concurrent validity of the TNT was assessed with four different comparison measures across three separate samples. The first measure to be correlated with the TNT was the 65-item NVT by Kool and Sen (1984) that was developed to assess nonviolent predisposition of college students and adults. The instrument will be discussed in more detail later in this chapter. The second measure, the Aggression Questionnaire (AQ), was developed by Buss and Perry (1992). The AQ is a 29-item scale that uses five point Likert items for respondents to rate how characteristic each statement is for them. The four subscales of physical aggression, verbal aggression, anger, and hostility are scored so higher AQ subscale scores indicate higher levels of aggressive behaviors. The third measure was the English transla-tion of the BAMED Teacher Rating Form where teachers must indicate on a five point scale whether a student is above or below average on different behaviors (Baker, Mednick, & Hocevar, 1991). The BAMED subscales of aggression (three items), adult relations (two items), and peer relations (seven items) were used in this study with higher scores indicating a student is above average on the behaviors as compared to normal same-aged peers. The fourth measure was a student self-rating of their aggressive tendencies. For this self-rating students indicated their self-perceptions to five questions on aggressive dispositions (i.e., Would you consider yourself aggressive?) using a scale of 1 (never) to 10 (always). Five questions were posed to determine the degree to which adolescents viewed themselves as aggressive.

The samples ranged in size from 129 to 479 and had roughly an equivalent number of males and females. The larger sample included junior high students and all included senior high students. The vast majority of adolescents reported they were Caucasian.

The correlations between the five reliable TNT subscales and the NVT total scale plus the subscales of the Aggression Questionnaire are presented in Table 9.4. Positive correlations between the TNT subscales and the scores on the NVT were expected and negative correlations were expected between the TNT subscales and the AQ subscores. All five correlations with the NVT were positive and significant at the 0.01 level. Three of the TNT subscales (physical nonviolence, psychological nonviolence, and satyagraha) had significant, negative correlations with physical aggression, verbal aggression, anger, and hostility at the 0.01. Helping/empathy yielded no significant correlations while tapasya was only significantly correlated with hostility.

Negative correlations were hypothesized between the TNT subscales and the aggression scale of the BAMED teacher ratings as well as the self-rating of aggression.

Table 9.4 Validity data for the TNT

| TNT subscales | NVT | Aggression questionnaire | | | |
		Physical aggression	Verbal aggression	Anger	Hostility
Physical nonviolence	0.57**	−0.85**	−0.54**	−0.64**	−0.37**
Psychological nonviolence	0.53**	−0.74**	−0.56**	−0.60**	−0.33**
Helping/empathy	0.42**	−0.15	−0.14	−0.15	−0.08
Satyagraha	0.39**	−0.38**	−0.30**	−0.38**	−0.28**
Tapasya	0.34**	−0.03	−0.07	−0.01	−0.21*

$*p < 0.05$; $**p < 0.01$

Table 9.5 Self-and teacher-rated validity data for the TNT

TNT subscales	Self-rating	Teacher rating		
		Aggression	Adult relations	Peer relations
Physical nonviolence	−0.71**	−0.33**	0.32**	0.06
Psychological nonviolence	−0.72**	−0.38**	0.23*	0.02
Helping/empathy	−0.46**	−0.12	0.01	0.03
Satyagraha	−0.46**	−0.16	0.15	0.17
Tapasya	−0.21*	−0.21*	−0.14	−0.17

$*p < 0.05; **p < 0.01$

The correlations between the TNT subscales and the BAMED rating subscales and the self-rating of aggression are presented in Table 9.5. The self-rating aggression scale is negatively correlated with all five reliable TNT subscales. The highest correlations are with physical nonviolence −0.71 ($p < 0.01$) and psychological nonviolence −0.72 ($p < 0.01$). Teacher ratings of aggression significantly correlated in a negative direction with physical and psychological nonviolence at the 0.01 level too. Tapasya was the only other significant, negative correlation with teacher rated aggression levels.

Known Groups Validity

Small groups of adolescents in a residential facility for troubled youth ($n = 8$) and adolescents in a juvenile detention facility ($n = 18$) completed the TNT as did members of a religious youth group ($n = 21$). The troubled youth were expected to have lower average scores on the TNT than the public school samples and the religious youth group. Five independent t tests were computed between the youth church group and the combined residential youth facility and the juvenile detention groups. Significant differences were found for three of the subscales of the TNT. The youth church group scored more nonviolent on the physical nonviolence and psychological nonviolence subscales at the 0.01 level. The youth church group also scored significantly higher on the helping/empathy subscale at the 0.05 level.

Buddhist youths were solicited to complete the TNT through their temple's Web site over the Internet and 121 agreed to do so. A relatively equal number of adolescent males and females completed the TNT. Each Buddhist adolescent received the TNT through the postal service, completed the survey, and returned it via the postal service. The Buddhist scores for the physical nonviolence, psychological nonviolence, and the satyagraha subscales were higher than the comparable sample from the public schools used in determining concurrent validity of the TNT. There was no significant difference between the Buddhist sample and the public school adolescents on the other two subscales.

Psychometrics of TNT with College Students

While the TNT was originally intended to be used with adolescents, the possibility of its usage with college students was tested. Material reported in this section is drawn from Mayton, Richel, Susnjic, and Majdanac (2002). Their samples for calculating the alpha coefficients and concurrent validity were 160 and 129 traditional age college students who were primarily Caucasian, with little less than two-thirds of the sample being female. Their sample for calculating test-retest reliability was similar to the other two and numbered 62.

Reliability

The alpha coefficients and the test–retest correlations are presented in Table 9.6. The internal consistency and the stability of the physical and psychological nonviolence subscales were high and all values are adequate for conducting group research.

Validity

The concurrent validity was assessed by correlating the TNT with the NVT (Kool & Sen, 1984), the Pacifism Scale (Elliot, 1980), and the AQ (Buss & Perry, 1992). The NVT and the Pacifism Scale will be discussed later in this chapter and the AQ was previously described. The correlations between the TNT and the other three measures are presented in Tables 9.7 and 9.8. The five subscales of the TNT significantly

Table 9.6 Reliability of the TNT for college students

TNT subscales	Alpha coefficients[a]	Test-retest coefficients[b]
Physical nonviolence	0.857	0.871
Psychological nonviolence	0.878	0.867
Helping/empathy	0.701	0.694
Satyagraha	0.612	0.756
Tapasya	0.764	0.706

[a]$n = 160$
[b]$n = 62$

Table 9.7 Concurrent validity of TNT with Pacifism scale

		Pacifism scale		
TNT subscales	NVT	Physical nonviolence	Psychological nonviolence	Activism
Physical nonviolence	0.69***	0.45***	0.33***	0.13
Psychological nonviolence	0.63***	0.33***	0.33***	0.22**
Helping/empathy	0.21*	0.09	0.14	0.13
Satyagraha	0.35***	0.13	0.18*	0.18
Tapasya	0.23*	−0.07	0.20*	0.12

$*p < 0.05; **p < 0.01; ***p < 0.001$

Table 9.8 Concurrent validity of TNT with Aggression Questionnaire

TNT subscales	Aggression questionnaire			
	Physical aggression	Verbal aggression	Anger	Hostile
Physical nonviolence	−0.78***	−0.51***	−0.40**	−0.16
Psychological nonviolence	−0.66***	−0.40**	−0.38**	−0.26*
Helping/empathy	−0.11	0.16	0.18	−0.09
Satyagraha	−0.16	−0.02	−0.12	−0.02
Tapasya	0.03	−0.01	−0.10	−0.09

*$p < 0.05$; **$p < 0.01$; ***$p < 0.001$

correlated with the total score of the NVT with the strongest relationships for the physical nonviolence, psychological nonviolence, and the satyagraha subscales. The physical nonviolence and psychological nonviolence on the TNT and Pacifism Scales were significantly correlated, as they should be. The TNT satyagraha and tapasya subscales were significantly correlated with Pacifism psychological nonviolence but not the other pacifism scales.

Overall Assessment of the TNT

These overall results reveal that the TNT is a generally valid and reliable measure of nonviolent tendencies for adolescents and college students. Five of the six subscales of the TNT appear to be internally consistent and stable while the other should not be scored. The TNT is a reliable instrument for Native American Indian adolescents as well. The physical nonviolence, the psychological nonviolence, the helping/empathy subscales, and the satyagraha subscales seem to be strongest in terms of validity for adolescents. The physical nonviolence and the psychological nonviolence reflected valid assessments for college students too. The satyagraha and tapasya subscales have showed some concurrent validity with minimal validity support for the empathy subscale for college students. The TNT seems to have potential in determining nonviolent tendencies in teens and college students across the country, however more cross-cultural reliability and validity research is needed to substantiate the breadth of potential applications for the TNT.

Other Measures of Nonviolence

Mayton, Susnjic et al. (2002) reviewed five measures of nonviolence and nonviolent dispositions that were located via searches of the PsycINFO database between 1974 and 2001. A subsequent search of PsycINFO up to May 2008 yielded one new assessment of nonviolence. An Internet search located three other measures of nonviolence.

Pacifism Scales

The Pacifism Scale is a 57-item assessment that was developed by Elliott (1980). Elliott subjected the items to item analysis and factor analytic techniques to confirm three subscales of pacifism. The physical nonviolence scale measures the conscious rejection of physical violence in all its forms in favor of alternate methods of conflict resolution. Likewise, psychological nonviolence is a rejection of psychological violence. The third subscale of the Pacifism Scale is active value orientation whereby the will to behave in a way that corresponds to one's norms, values, and goals in life is measured. Mayton, Susnjic et al. (2002) considered the subscales of the Pacifism Scale to have adequate internal consistency and some encouraging validity data for Western samples, plus the concurrent validity data for the TNT reported earlier in this chapter may be considered positive validity data for the Pacifism Scales as well. However, Heaven, Rejab, and Bester (1984) did find reliability problems when the Pacifism Scale was used with nonwestern samples.

Nonviolence Test

The NVT is a 65 forced-choice item scale that was developed by Kool and Sen (1984). With 36 scored items and 29 filler items, the NVT yields a single total score for nonviolent predispositions within a variety of situations and is based on the theory of nonviolence of Kool (1993b). The total score ranges from 0 (not at all nonviolent) to 36 (extremely nonviolent). Both the internal consistency and the stability coefficients for the NVT total score are above 0.8 so the scale has good reliability. Kool and Sen as well as Kool and Keyes (1990) provide evidence of concurrent validity as the NVT was found to negatively correlate with the Buss–Durkee Aggression Inventory (Buss & Durkee, 1957) and the Machiavellian V Scale. The correlations between the NVT and TNT subscales reported earlier in Tables 9.4 and 9.7 are additional evidence of the validity of the NVT. Kool and Keyes aiso provide known group data to further document the validity of the NVT. As expected, they found Buddhists and Quakers to have very high total scores while violent youths had very low scores on the NVT.

Kool (2008) reports the results of a factor analysis of the NVT that identified seven interpretable factors. The factors of the NVT were "(1) self-control including understanding and negotiation, (2) antipunitiveness including compassion and forgiving, (3) forbearance including tolerance and judging the intentions of others, (4) equity of justice including equality of adjudicating justice, (5) self-defense, (6) constructive reform, and (7) affective control including emotional control in the face of irritation (p. 130)." While little is provided as to the psychometric strength of these subscales nor the methods of scoring them, Kool does provide the full NVT along with the scoring key in his book.

Gandhian Personality Scale

The GPS, developed by Hasan and Khan (1983), was designed to assess important aspects of Gandhi's philosophy of life and his teachings. This 29-item measure was reduced from 129 items through a factor analysis. The six factors of the GPS are (1) Machiavellianism/anti-Machiavellianism, (2) authenticity, (3) cynicism/anticynicism, (4) openness to experience and tolerance, (5) tenderness and generosity, and (6) trust in human nature. Mayton, Susnjic et al. (2002) found the GPS wanting, as less than adequate psychometric information is available for the GPS.

Multidimensional Scales of Nonviolence

Johnson and a cadre of her students developed the MSN for use with adults (Johnson et al., 1998). This 80-item measure included items from six domains however a principle components analysis identifies the best solution to have five components. In order of strength these are (1) spirituality, (2) international nonviolence, (3) dominance, (4) domestic nonviolence, and (5) Gandhi's ahimsa. While subscale internal consistency is positive and concurrent validity is provided for the MSN total score, test–retest reliability and concurrent and other validity data would be helpful for the five subscales.

The Nonviolent Relationship Questionnaire

The Nonviolent Relationship Questionnaire (NVRQ, Eckstein & La Grassa, 2005) is a 24-item assessment that is based on the principles of nonviolent communication developed by Rosenberg (2003) and discussed in Chap. 5. Respondents to the NVRQ indicate on a ten-point Likert scale their agreement with statements about their own communication patterns with their partner and their perceptions of the communication patterns as a couple. The NVRQ measures eight variables (nonthreatening, respect, honesty, parenting together, equal responsibility, economic partners, fairness, and trust) within nonviolent communication and scores can range from 3 to 30 for each subscale. Respondents are asked to predict their ratings on each subscale, after they have answered the questions and before they score their questionnaire. Eckstein and La Grassa provide a scoring key and indicate what constitutes a low, medium, and high score for the subscales, however no reliability or validity data are provided. While the NVRQ is based on an interesting theory and the suggestions for using the results in a therapeutic relationship to increase nonviolent communication between couples are consistent with Rosenberg's work, there is a real need to establish the reliability and validity of the NVRQ.

"Self-Assessments" of Nonviolence

Internet searches have identified three "self-assessments" of nonviolence. Each of these self-administered scales is designed for use as a means of self-reflection about nonviolent tendencies in one's own behavior patterns. Given a lack of psychometric data on these self-assessment scales, each is probably better utilized as an intervention than as an outcome measure in a study of nonviolence until proper test development is forthcoming.

Nonviolence Self-Inventory

French (2004) developed the Nonviolence Self-inventory to encourage people to engage in a self-analysis about their nonviolent and violent behaviors. No scores are computed for the Nonviolence Self-inventory nor are there any data provided about the characteristics of the inventory. Respondents are simply asked to read and answer the 34 questions that cover a wide range of topics about risky driving and road rage, corporal and capital punishment, meat in one's diet, abortion, nuclear weapons, recycling, nonviolent activism, and euthanasia to name a few.

Self-Test on Nonviolence

The Self-Test on Non Violence was developed by Diamond (2001). Respondents initially are asked to complete ten Likert items about their beliefs and actions concerning violence, war, and nonviolence. Once completed, respondents are asked to reflect on the items they disagree with to try to identify patterns about themselves. After they reflect on potential patterns for the items they agree with, respondents are then encouraged to share their assessments with family, friends, colleagues, and other social groups to discuss the results and the questions and concerns they may have about their views and actions relative to violence and nonviolence. As for the Nonviolence Self-inventory, there are no scores computed, nor any psychometric data reported.

Nonviolence Inventory of Your Home and Family

The Nonviolence Inventory of Your Home and Family is another self-assessment developed by Diamond (2001). As the name implies, this self-assessment asks respondents to consider how often the choice is made to use violent or nonviolent responses in the home with one's family. In this assessment respondents are asked to estimate how often they or other members of the household hit, shame, watch violence on television, play violent video games, and get angry, as well as whether there are norms against violence and how often family members discuss issues related to nonviolence and violence. This self-assessment of family life style is then used for discussion. Again, no total score is computed and no psychometric data is presented.

Selected Measures for Assessing the Peaceful Person

The underlying variables reflecting a peaceful person at the intrapersonal and interpersonal levels were discussed in Chaps. 4 and 5. Agreeableness, anger control, cooperativeness, empathy, forgiveness, happiness, materialism, mindfulness, need for cognition, optimism, positive orientation to democratic principles, satisfaction with life, self-control, social dominance orientation, spirituality, tolerance, trust, the values of equality, forgiveness, freedom, tolerance, and trust, and the value types of universalism, benevolence, conformity, and power have all differentiated peaceful from nonpeaceful persons or have been predicted to do so. The conduct of sound empirical research on the characteristics of a peaceful person necessitates strong measures of these personality traits, values, and attitudinal variables along with any other variables added to the profile.

Fortunately, several psychometrically sound measures exist for most of these variables and some have been discussed already. These variables are oftentimes part of large personality assessments and more and more they may be the sole focus of a shorter assessment. For instance, the *California Personality Inventory* contains the subscales of empathy, responsibility, self-control, and tolerance. Also, measures for many of these variables, including happiness, mindfulness, optimism, self-control, and satisfaction with life relate to positive psychology, and may be located through the Positive Psychology website at the University of Pennsylvania (http://www.ppc.sas.upenn.edu/ppquestionnaires.htm) or through a positive psychology handbook (Lopez & Snyder, 2003; Ong & Van Dulmen, 2007; Peterson & Seligman, 2004). Agreeableness, as one of the big five personality traits, has many good assessments available within the field of personality testing. Empathy may be measured by a number of good scales like the ones developed by Davis (1994) or Zhou, Valiente, and Eisenberg (2003). Forgiveness might be assessed as a value (see discussion on values to follow) or as a positive psychology construct (Thompson & Snyder, 2003). Maio, Thomas, Fincham, and Carnelley (2008) provide a comprehensive discusion of forgiveness at the interpersonal level. Robinson, Shaver, and Wrightsman (1991) review a number of measures for trust, self-esteem, and control, plus a range of measures related to life satisfaction. In a later volume Robinson, Shaver, and Wrightsman (1999) review a number of measures for equality, racial attitudes, democratic values and attitudes, political tolerance, and trust in government. Materialism may be approached as an attitude (Richins & Dawson, 1992) or as a political value (Inglehart, 1991). Both need for cognition (Cacioppo, Petty, & Kao, 1984), and social dominance orientation (Pratto, Sidanius, Stallworth, & Malle, 1994) have well researched and psychometrically strong measures.

The previous discussion about the Abrahamic religions in Chap. 7 and Eastern religions in Chap. 4 demonstrate the importance of religious beliefs and one's spirituality to being a peaceful and nonviolent person. There is an abundance of measures within the psychology of religion dealing with religiousness and spirituality (Hill & Pargament, 2003; Tsang & McCullough, 2003). However, most measures have a Western focus. For instance, in assessing religious values Rokeach (1973) found the value of salvation worked well for Christianity but did not resonate well with all religious orientations. Likewise, when Schwartz (1992) developed his ten value types, he had difficulty identifying a religious value type with cross-cultural relevance due to the marked differences between religious beliefs around the world. Spirituality is a multidimensional construct that has a very large number of assessments available for research usage (Allport & Ross, 1967; Piedmont, 1999). From Allport's (1950) conceptualization of intrinsic and extrinsic orientations toward religion to the hierarchical approach to spirituality of Tsang and McCullough, many scales have been developed and continue to be developed. Gorsuch (1984) recognized, that despite many sound measures being available to assess a range of multidimensional issues of religiosity, new measures assessing the same constructs are not needed, but new measures following a different paradigm are. A scale that captures the nonviolent aspects of religions from Abrahamic to Zen would be extremely helpful in assessing the spiritual aspect of a peaceful person. The Body–Mind–Spirit Well-Being Inventory developed by Ng, Yau, Chan, Chan, and Ho (2005) appears to be a scale that is designed with this direction in mind.

There are three first-rate measures of values that are available for research. The Rokeach Value Survey (Ball-Rokeach, Rokeach, & Grube, 1984; Rokeach, 1973) reliably and validly assesses individual value priorities for 18 terminal values and 18 instrumental values including equality, forgiveness, freedom, tolerance, and trust. The Schwartz Values Survey (Schwartz, 1992, 1994a) and the Portrait Values Questionnaire (Schwartz, 2003; Schwartz et al., 2001) both assess the ten value types and have extensive cross-national reliability and validity data to attest to the psychometric strength of the scales. These two instruments assess the value types of universalism, benevolence, conformity, and power.

Selected Measures for Assessing Cultures of Peace

de Rivera (2004a, 2004b, 2004c) and his colleagues have made an excellent start in identifying methods to assess cultures of peace at the societal level. This group of researchers was discussed in Chap. 6 and, as their work continues, more thorough methods of assessment will emerge. To complete the determination of cultures of peace, additional avenues for assessing cultures of peace might be developed at both the individual and community level.

As a culture of violence moves toward becoming a culture of peace, it is hoped that changes at the individual level might be achieved. In some instances the individual changes may even precede the societal changes. It would be enlightening to document trends in peoples' perception of improvements in human rights, gender equality, racial and ethnic discrimination, and inclusivity in the community and government. It would also be useful to see if attitudes and behaviors toward environmental sustainability and education are shifting. Perhaps there are a critical number of people that need to shift their beliefs and behaviors before a culture of peace emerges. Whether this is true or not, the assessment of the culture of peace components would help answer this type of question.

Communities likely will find themselves moving from a culture of violence to a culture of peace at different rates within a society. Identifying the pockets within a larger society that adopt the components of a culture of peace might be helpful in understanding the dynamics of the changes that need to take place. There should be ways of adapting the indicators identified by de Rivera (2004a, 2004b, 2004c) and his colleagues for nations to communities within nations. This will obviously depend on the data gathering systems that are in place within a particular country, however this could be informative in determining the variables that precipitated shifts in some areas and that might be mobilized in areas that are slow to change.

Concluding Comment

There are several sound measures of nonviolence that are appropriate for use with various age groups as outcome measures in interventions designed to reduce violence and/or to increase nonviolent dispositions and behaviors. Peace education, conflict resolution programs, and other preventative implementations are often designed to impact participants on the variables assessed by these measures of nonviolence. The intention of reviewing these scales was to encourage their use in empirical research.

Appendix

Social and Personal Opinion Survey

This is the Teenage Nonviolent Test and is reprinted from (Mayton et al., 1998) with the permission of the first author. Requests to use the TNT should be made to the author at dmayton@lcsc.edu

This is a chance to look at yourself and see how you feel about things. Be sure that your answers show **how YOU feel** about each statements. **PLEASE DO NOT TALK ABOUT THE STATEMENTS OR YOUR ANSWERS WITH ANYONE ELSE**. We will keep your answers private and not show them to your teachers, principal, parents, or anyone else.

Please read each statement and decide whether it is true or not for you. Circle the response which best describes how you feel about the statement. If the statement is definitely true or nearly always true for you, circle the response "definitely true for me." If the statement is generally true for you but not always true, circle the response "usually true for me." If the statement is occasionally true for you but generally not true, circle the response "usually not true for me." If the statement is definitely false or nearly always not true for you circle the response "definitely not true for me."

If you have any questions raise your hand. Once you have started, **PLEASE DO NOT SAY YOUR ANSWERS OUT LOUD OR TALK**.

Appendix

1. Reasoning helps me avoid fights.
   definitely true for me   usually true for me   usually not true for me   definitely not true for me
2. I am open minded.
   definitely true for me   usually true for me   usually not true for me   definitely not true for me
3. When someone is rude to me, I am rude back.
   definitely true for me   usually true for me   usually not true for me   definitely not true for me
4. If people talk the talk, they should walk the walk.
   definitely true for me   usually true for me   usually not true for me   definitely not true for me
5. If someone insulted me in front of my friends, I would smack them.
   definitely true for me   usually true for me   usually not true for me   definitely not true for me
6. Yelling at someone makes them understand me.
   definitely true for me   usually true for me   usually not true for me   definitely not true for me
7. I'll argue for what I believe despite what others say.
   definitely true for me   usually true for me   usually not true for me   definitely not true for me
8. Some people respect me because they fear me.
   definitely true for me   usually true for me   usually not true for me   definitely not true for me
9. If someone dropped their books, I'd help them pick them up.
   definitely true for me   usually true for me   usually not true for me   definitely not true for me
10. Life is what you learn from it.
    definitely true for me   usually true for me   usually not true for me   definitely not true for me
11. I'd give the person in front of me my extra change if they didn't have enough for lunch.
    definitely true for me   usually true for me   usually not true for me   definitely not true for me
12. I don't get mad, I get even.
    definitely true for me   usually true for me   usually not true for me   definitely not true for me
13. I try to tell people when they do a good job.
    definitely true for me   usually true for me   usually not true for me   definitely not true for me
14. Sometimes I make fun of others to their face.
    definitely true for me   usually true for me   usually not true for me   definitely not true for me
15. I try to learn from others mistakes.
    definitely true for me   usually true for me   usually not true for me   definitely not true for me
16. I like helping new students find their classes.
    definitely true for me   usually true for me   usually not true for me   definitely not true for me
17. Everyone has the right to injure another to protect their property.
    definitely true for me   usually true for me   usually not true for me   definitely not true for me
18. If someone got in my face, I'd push them away.
    definitely true for me   usually true for me   usually not true for me   definitely not true for me

(continued)

Appendix (continued)

19. I can scare people into doing things for me.

    definitely true for me usually true for me   usually not true for me   definitely not true for me

20. I would let my friend buy the last shirt in a store even if I wanted it a lot.

    definitely true for me usually true for me   usually not true for me   definitely not true for me

21. When I am arguing with someone, I always try to see their side of it.

    definitely true for me usually true for me   usually not true for me   definitely not true for me

22. I like the look of defeat on people's faces when I beat them in competition.

    definitely true for me usually true for me   usually not true for me   definitely not true for me

23. I often do things without having a good reason.

    definitely true for me usually true for me   usually not true for me   definitely not true for me

24. Violence on television bothers me.

    definitely true for me usually true for me   usually not true for me   definitely not true for me

25. I don't like to make fun of people.

    definitely true for me usually true for me   usually not true for me   definitely not true for me

26. I won't fight if people call me names.

    definitely true for me usually true for me   usually not true for me   definitely not true for me

27. I attempt to learn from all my experiences.

    definitely true for me usually true for me   usually not true for me   definitely not true for me

28. If someone shoves me in the hall, I would just keep walking.

    definitely true for me usually true for me   usually not true for me   definitely not true for me

29. I often call people names when they make me angry.

    definitely true for me usually true for me   usually not true for me   definitely not true for me

30. I try to do what I say I am going to do.

    definitely true for me usually true for me   usually not true for me   definitely not true for me

31. I have been known to pick fights.

    definitely true for me usually true for me   usually not true for me   definitely not true for me

32. I would give up my seat on the bus for someone else.

    definitely true for me usually true for me   usually not true for me   definitely not true for me

33. I don't pay attention to people with different opinions.

    definitely true for me usually true for me   usually not true for me   definitely not true for me

34. I humiliate people who make me feel bad.

    definitely true for me usually true for me   usually not true for me   definitely not true for me

35. I often think about developing the best plan for the future.

    definitely true for me usually true for me   usually not true for me   definitely not true for me

36. If someone cuts in front of me in the cafeteria, I want to shove them out of line.

    definitely true for me usually true for me   usually not true for me   definitely not true for me

37. My actions can influence others.

    definitely true for me usually true for me   usually not true for me   definitely not true for me

(continued)

Appendix (continued)

38. When someone calls me a name, I ignore it.

definitely true for me usually true for me   usually not true for me   definitely not true for me

39. I like to laugh when others make mistakes.

definitely true for me usually true for me   usually not true for me   definitely not true for me

40. If someone pushes me, I push them back.

definitely true for me usually true for me   usually not true for me   definitely not true for me

41. I sometimes bring weapons to school.

definitely true for me usually true for me   usually not true for me   definitely not true for me

42. I try to make decisions by looking at all the available information.

definitely true for me usually true for me   usually not true for me   definitely not true for me

43. It is ok to carry weapons on the street.

definitely true for me usually true for me   usually not true for me   definitely not true for me

44. If someone spit on me, I would hit them.

definitely true for me usually true for me   usually not true for me   definitely not true for me

45. If there was only one dessert left, I would let my friend eat it even if I really wanted it.

definitely true for me usually true for me   usually not true for me   definitely not true for me

46. I don't like to watch people fight.

definitely true for me usually true for me   usually not true for me   definitely not true for me

47. It is often necessary to use violence to prevent violence.

definitely true for me usually true for me   usually not true for me   definitely not true for me

48. If someone disagrees with me, I tell them they are stupid.

definitely true for me usually true for me   usually not true for me   definitely not true for me

49. I enjoy saying things that upset my teachers.

definitely true for me usually true for me   usually not true for me   definitely not true for me

50. Starting a nasty rumor is a good way to get back at someone.

definitely true for me usually true for me   usually not true for me   definitely not true for me

51. I'd give up my coat if a friend was cold.

definitely true for me usually true for me   usually not true for me   definitely not true for me

52. If I can find out why people are arguing, I can help them solve their problem.

definitely true for me usually true for me   usually not true for me   definitely not true for me

53. Sometimes people get me to fight by teasing me.

definitely true for me usually true for me   usually not true for me   definitely not true for me

54. If my friend and I both wanted the same pair of shoes in a store, I would let them buy it and do without.

definitely true for me usually true for me   usually not true for me   definitely not true for me

55. I tease people I don't like.

definitely true for me usually true for me   usually not true for me   definitely not true for me

Teenage Nonviolence Test (TNT): Scoring Key

Physical Nonviolence (alpha = 0.91)

- Conscious rejection of all forms of physical violence in favor of alternate forms of conflict resolution (due to a professed moral or ethical belief structure)

[physical violence – behaviors or the threat of behaviors intended to inflict bodily injury on another person in an attempt to coerce, curtail, or eliminate their behavior]

5	Physical nonviolence – not true nonviolent
12	Physical nonviolence – not true nonviolent
17	Physical nonviolence – not true nonviolent
18	Physical nonviolence – not true nonviolent
24	Physical nonviolence – true nonviolent
26	Physical nonviolence – true nonviolent
28	Physical nonviolence – true nonviolent
31	Physical nonviolence – not true nonviolent
36	Physical nonviolence – not true nonviolent
40	Physical nonviolence – not true nonviolent
41	Physical nonviolence – not true nonviolent
43	Physical nonviolence – not true nonviolent
44	Physical nonviolence – not true nonviolent
46	Physical nonviolence – true nonviolent
47	Physical nonviolence – not true nonviolent
53	Physical nonviolence – not true nonviolent

Psychological Nonviolence (alpha = 0.91)

- Conscious rejection of all forms of psychological violence in favor of alternate forms of conflict resolution (due to a professed moral or ethical belief structure)

[psychological violence – behaviors or the threat of behaviors intended to humiliate, intimidate, or in other ways demean the human dignity of another person or group in and attempt to coerce, curtail, or eliminate their behavior]

1	Psychological nonviolence – true nonviolent
3	Psychological nonviolence – not true nonviolent
6	Psychological nonviolence – not true nonviolent
8	Psychological nonviolence – not true nonviolent
14	Psychological nonviolence – not true nonviolent
19	Psychological nonviolence – not true nonviolent
22	Psychological nonviolence – not true nonviolent
25	Psychological nonviolence – true nonviolent
29	Psychological nonviolence – not true nonviolent
34	Psychological nonviolence – not true nonviolent
38	Psychological nonviolence – true nonviolent
39	Psychological nonviolence – not true nonviolent
48	Psychological nonviolence – not true nonviolent
49	Psychological nonviolence – not true nonviolent
50	Psychological nonviolence – not true nonviolent
55	Psychological nonviolence – not true nonviolent

Active Value Orientation (alpha = 0.65)
– Willingness to perform behaviors designed to achieve a situation commensurate with one's own norms, values, and goals

4	Active value orientation – true nonviolent (active)
7	Active value orientation – true nonviolent (active)
30	Active value orientation – true nonviolent (active)
37	Active value orientation – true nonviolent (active)

Helping/empathy (alpha = 0.78)

9	Helping/empathy – true nonviolent (prohelping)
11	Helping/empathy – true nonviolent (prohelping)
13	Helping/empathy – true nonviolent (prohelping)
16	Helping/empathy – true nonviolent (prohelping)
32	Helping/empathy – true nonviolent (prohelping)

Satyagraha (alpha = 0.75)
– Active search for wisdom, because the truth is based upon the subjective perceptions of individuals, a person needs to be willing to change his or her conception of truth. [literally "holding on to the truth"]

2	Satyagraha – true nonviolent
10	Satyagraha – true nonviolent
15	Satyagraha – true nonviolent
21	Satyagraha – true nonviolent
23	Satyagraha – not true nonviolent
27	Satyagraha – true nonviolent
33	Satyagraha – not true nonviolent
35	Satyagraha – true nonviolent
42	Satyagraha – true nonviolent
52	Satyagraha – true nonviolent

Tapasya (alpha = 0.73)
– Willingness to endure hardship or suffering rather than to inflict harm on others. [literally "self-suffering"]

20	Tapasya – true nonviolent
45	Tapasya – true nonviolent
51	Tapasya – true nonviolent
54	Tapasya – true nonviolent

Chapter 10
New Directions for Research on Nonviolence

> *If it is true, in general, that 'ideas have consequences,' then man's ideas about man have the most far-reaching consequences of all. Upon them may depend the structure of government, the patterns of culture, the purpose of education, the design of the future, and the human or inhuman uses of human beings.*
>
> Watson, cited in Danesh, 1979, p. 3.

Like the elephant being approached by the group of blind men for investigation, nonviolence is a concept with many dimensions and many levels that has been approached by many disciplines with their unique methods and theoretical orientations. Anthropologists, historians, political scientists, psychologists, sociologists, and theologians have added insights and knowledge to our understanding of nonviolence and nonviolent action. Much remains for study within each discipline, however more can be learned if interdisciplinary approaches are pursued.

This chapter provides a unified look at the conceptualization of nonviolence presented in this book. In addition specific recommendations for research on nonviolence and cultures of peace are delineated with recommendations for topics for student research and dissertation projects. In this chapter I also address the need for networking and collaboration across traditional disciplinary boundaries either informally or under the umbrella of interdisciplinary organizations. It is also important for researchers and theorists to partner with activists in designing studies.

Nonviolence and Nonviolent Action into the Twenty-First Century

Nonviolence is more complex than it seems. Nonviolence is not the absence of violence but is an action that uses power and influence to reach a goal without direct injury to the persons working against that goal achievement. Nonviolence is sometimes a principled action based upon an underlying belief system that desires to understand the truth within a conflict, believes in the noncooperation with evil, considers violence as something to be avoided, and shows a willingness to accept

D.M. Mayton II, *Nonviolence and Peace Psychology*,
DOI 10.1007/978-0-387-89348-8_10, © Springer Science+Business Media, LLC 2009

the burden of suffering to break the cycle of violence. The ultimate intent of principled nonviolence is to confront injustice in order to increase social justice without using direct violence. However, nonviolence may be used as a practical approach to achieve ones goals without a principled belief system to support it. This pragmatic nonviolence considers nonviolent behavior to be an effective method to resolve conflict and uses it to confront a conflict situation without using direct violence but does not maintain a belief system held by those who practice principled nonviolence.

Despite a surprising lack of attention and reporting in the news, as well as academic outlets, nonviolence has been used widely and oftentimes successfully over the last two millennia. Even during the twentieth century, described by many as one of the bloodiest centuries in terms of military and civilian casualties of war, many nonviolent movements impacted history by positive means to positive ends. From the USSR to the USA, from Cambodia to Czechoslovakia, from the Greensboro sit-ins to the Green Movement, from the Orange Hats in Washington DC to the Orange Revolution in Ukraine, nonviolent activism was regularly successful across the planet. From voting rights to human rights, from safety to Salt Laws, and from dictators to democracies, nonviolence addressed many grievances in a variety of contexts. The dawn of the twenty-first century continued the momentum created in the twentieth century.

While social scientists have spent relatively little time developing theories on nonviolence, some promising theories have emerged and their robustness needs to be assessed. In Chap. 3 theories of nonviolence were discussed from philosophical, anthropological, sociological, psychological, political and interdisciplinary perspectives. The sociological theory of Ritter (2005), psychological theories of Brenes (1999) and Kool (1993b, 2008), political theories and paradigms of Ackerman and Kruegler (1994), Sharp (1999), and Sharp and Paulson (2005), and the interdisciplinary strategies and theories of Burrowes (1996) and Sharp (1985), all have provocative elements, are based on historical precedent, and seem to have the potential to explain the dynamics and effectiveness of principled and pragmatic nonviolent actions and methods. Unfortunately, data to support these theories and paradigms is either nonexistent or just starting to emerge in the research literature.

Nonviolence and a range of related concepts may be studied across a spectrum from the intrapersonal to the interpersonal to the societal or cultural levels. At the intrapersonal level the conception of self is important for understanding inner peace. The personality characteristics of a peaceful person generally point to lower levels of materialism and to higher levels of agreeableness, anger control, cooperativeness, empathy, forgiveness, need for cognition, optimism, spirituality, tolerance, and trust. The values of a peaceful person reflect higher priorities on conformity (self-control) and the self-transcendent values of benevolence and, in some instances, universalism. Peaceful persons tend to place lower priorities on power and hedonistic values. Religious beliefs can play an important role in the experience of inner peace. While the Eastern religions of Buddhism, Jainism, and Hinduism are discussed in Chap. 4 in terms of their impact on inner peace, the Abrahamic religions of Judaism, Christianity, Islam, and Bahá'í also have relevance to inner peace. At the interpersonal level, communication plays a significant role in nonviolent behavior. The compassionate or nonviolent communication process of Rosenberg (2003) can diffuse a potentially violent situation and can precipitate nonviolent behavior when interpersonal conflicts occur. There is a continuum of strategies for resolving conflict from the more informal, private and voluntary to the more formal, public, and involuntary. This continuum moves from negotiation to mediation, conciliation, arbitration, and finally to adjudication (Picard, 2002). Many preventative approaches to dealing with interpersonal conflict have been developed and implemented within schools and communities. These approaches include conflict resolution education that consists of social and emotional learning and peer mediation, nonviolence education, peace education, and violence prevention programs. While research support across all of these programs is not even, the empirical support in some areas, particularly conflict resolution education, is very positive and the empirical support seems to be growing across the board for prevention programs with only a few exceptions.

Even as most societies in today's world function as cultures of violence, there are pockets of peaceful societies in Africa, Asia, and North and South America. Moving the majority of nations and societies toward cultures of peace is as vital a task as it is daunting. The United Nations, with its Manifesto 2000 and its cultures of peace initiatives, has set some excellent goals for changing societies toward cultures of peace. To become a culture of peace, a society needs to address human rights, gender equality, democratic participation, tolerance, and solidarity among all their people, participatory communication and the free flow of information, international peace and security, general education and peace education, and sustainable development (de Rivera, 2004c). Regrettably, few nations have heeded this call and acted with the energy and resources that are needed for systemic change from a culture of war to a culture of peace. Nonetheless, the goals have hastened some action especially regarding the development of strategies to assess cultures to determine the degree that they have achieved cultures of peace (de Rivera, 2004a, 2004b).

The way people interpret or construe the situation is an important determinant of behavior in general and nonviolent behavior is no exception. The situational constraints that specifically encourage or inhibit nonviolence are not well understood but some universal issues were discussed in Chap. 8. Social facilitation, channeling factors, scripts, societal norms, and cultural values all play a role in the construal process that determines whether a nonviolent response will be used or not. How people construe their world is an interaction of the situation, their unique experiences and worldview, and general human tendencies. One situational factor with strong relevance to the construal process is the awareness of one's mortality and terror management theory. The military–economic–governmental–news complex readily highlights the individual situational tensions that exist to maintain a culture of violence and prevent a culture of peace from being implemented. Research leading to a better understanding of the dynamics of construal underlying the constituents within the Mi–EGo news complex would be very timely.

Religion and religious faith is a nearly universal component of the human experience. Each of the major religions, reviewed in Chaps. 4 and 7, contains beliefs and teachings that are highly supportive of nonviolent behaviors and lifestyles. Whether you are a Buddhist, Jaina, Hindu, Jew, Christian, Muslim, or Bahá'í, your faith values tolerance and nonviolence. It is certainly the case that Hinduism and the three largest Abrahamic religions have tenets that also support violence and war. For instance, within Ecclesiastes of the Hebrew and Christian Bibles, it is said, "To every thing there is a season, and a time to every purpose under the heaven; A time to be born, and a time to die; a time to plant, and a time to pluck up that which is planted; A time to kill, and a time to heal; a time to break down, and a time to build up;… A time to love, and a time to hate; a time of war, and a time of peace." Even though this passage places healing actions and peace at the same level of inevitability as killing and war, peacefulness is a cherished belief. The key for nonviolence to emerge from all religions is the focal point of the nonviolent teaching within the worldview espoused by its followers. Jewish, Christian, or Islamic fundamentalism may all ignore the nonviolent teachings of their religion and embrace the aspects that result in intolerance and violence toward out groups. Followers of other religions, even Buddhists, may embrace nonviolence but may withdraw from society so the goodness of their beliefs will not be felt as fully by society because of their disengagement or neglect. Whether nonviolent beliefs are negated by indifference, neglect, or violence, the outcome is not the best possible one. The key for religion to affect peace and promote nonviolence in the world is to encourage more moderate and balanced clergy and followers of any religion to impact their believers.

Some Research Questions on Nonviolence and Nonviolent Action

Throughout this book, I have alluded to areas where research has not been done, is sketchy, or contains conflicting results. In this section I will specifically point to areas where research on nonviolent behavior and action is clearly needed to advance this aspect of peace psychology. I will generally follow the outline of the book in advancing ideas for future research, however some suggestions will be discussed outside of this sequence. The intent is to encourage peace researchers, whether academics, clinicians, or activists, to focus their energies on some of the crucial matters in our understanding of nonviolence and nonviolent action. These research suggestions may also be fruitful for undergraduate, masters, and doctoral students to investigate.

Validating Theories of Nonviolence

The need for more and better research on nonviolent theory has been noted by many academics in several disciplines (Martin, 2005; McCarthy & Kruegler, 1993). While it is important that research on nonviolence be oriented to scholars specifically interested in nonviolence, as well as scholars in related disciplines, Martin sees the value in orienting research on nonviolent theory to activists, policy makers, and governments too.

Ritter (2005) proposes that principled nonviolence that utilizes nonviolent means to achieve nonviolent ends is superior to strategic nonviolence. Ritter makes the case that the coercive action within the pragmatic use of strategic violence will lead to short-term successes and only the conversion of the other in any conflict would enable a long-term solution. This coercive/conversion dimension needs to be investigated (McCarthy & Kruegler, 1993). Ritter suggests that this would require a way to reliably classify large-scale conflict resolution actions in terms of violent and nonviolent means in addition to violent and nonviolent ends. Developing a reliable and valid classification system is another methodological hurdle that must be negotiated and is an area of needed research.

Burrowes (1996) has proposed another two-dimensional theory of nonviolence that would benefit from empirical validation. Within Burrowes' theory, the principled pragmatic axis and the reformist revolutionary axis form four quadrants of nonviolent action. Developing a sound methodology to classify nonviolent movements into the two dimensional space defined by these axes would be helpful. The use of case studies of various nonviolent movements with this new classification methodology could then advance this theory.

McCarthy and Kruegler (1993) express concern for a progressive research program to build the knowledge base and theory related to nonviolent action. They suggest that the assumptions of nonviolent approaches to conflict resolution need to be empirically verified as necessary, and if they are not necessary, they should be abandoned. McCarthy and Kruegler raise issues reflected in the following questions:

1. Is it necessary for leaders and activists in nonviolent struggles to be committed to nonviolence as a way of life or can they view it as a technique?
2. Does the leadership of a nonviolent action need to be highly centralized and charismatic?
3. What are the most productive leadership tasks, organization types, means of recruitment, and communication systems for nonviolent movements?
4. What are the necessary components of a nonviolent movement that induce the intended changes? Is it the self-suffering and the accompanying moral contradictions it creates in one's adversaries that achieves change? How much sacrifice are people willing to make to achieve a more nonviolent world?

McCarthy and Kruegler are critical of the inductive case-study approach and call for a theory driven program of research whereby the generalizations of specific theories are tested using critically analyzed case studies of historical nonviolent movements. McCarthy and Kruegler advocate for research on the theory of nonviolent action that identifies and differentiates the strongly supported and poorly supported aspects of the theory. In addition this research should identify areas where gaps and absences exist while developing a conceptual framework open to full discussion and criticism. McCarthy and Kruegler call for "a serious effort to inventory the propositions stated in the theory of nonviolent action, subject them to criticism, and restate the theory in a fully specified form that can support coming decades of research on this important aspect of group conflict (p. 29)."

Research on the Peaceful Person Across Intrapersonal and Interpersonal Levels

Inner peace and nonviolence, interpersonal nonviolence, and nonviolence in groups and society at large have been discussed separately in Chaps. 4–6. While this served an organizational function, the interrelationships between intrapersonal, interpersonal, and societal nonviolence remains unknown. Are these three levels of nonviolence independent of one another? Black Elk, the great Oglala Sioux medicine man and leader who experienced the Battle of the Little Big Horn and the massacre at Wounded Knee during the late nineteenth century, describes inner peace as a necessary requirement for interpersonal peace, and peace between nations. He said "The first peace, which is the most important, is that which comes within the souls of men when they realize their relationship, their oneness, with the universe and all its Powers, and when they realize that at the center of the universe dwells Wakan Tanka, and that this center is everywhere, it is within each of us. This is the real Peace, and the others are but reflections of this. The second peace is that which is made between two individuals, and the third is that which is made between two nations. But above all you should understand that there can never be peace between nations until there is first known that true peace which, as I have often said, is within the souls of men (Brown, 1989, p. 115)." The preeminent position Black Elk gives to intrapersonal peace and nonviolence needs to be empirically assessed. Do people need to have inner peace to practice interpersonal peace? While exceptions do come to mind, how prevalent are these exceptions? Does one need to possess inner peace in order to practice principled nonviolence? How successful are activists involved in a large-scale nonviolent movement if they have difficulty being nonviolent on an interpersonal level? Are there other models that better explain the interrelationships of these three levels of nonviolence? These and many related questions about the relationships between intrapersonal, interpersonal, and societal nonviolence need to be empirically studied.

The research on the characteristics of a peaceful person is encouraging but it definitely needs to be extended across age groups from childhood through late adulthood. Currently, most of the research on the characteristics of a peaceful person has been conducted on college students and young adults. What are the characteristics of peaceful children? What are the characteristics of peaceful adolescents? What are the characteristics of peaceful middle aged and elderly adults? In addition not all personality variables that have been hypothesized to characterize peaceful persons have been studied. With the emergence of positive psychology and the identification of 24 character virtues, there is the new question concerning how many of these are associated with being a nonviolent or peaceful person.

While most societies today reflect cultures of violence, people do exhibit nonviolent tendencies. As new and psychometrically sound assessments of nonviolence have become available, data concerning the prevalence of nonviolent children, adolescents, and adults can now be drawn within many societies. Normative studies of children, adolescents, and adults from different ethnic backgrounds and different countries would be very helpful to develop a picture of current percentages of nonviolent people. These normative data would also serve as baseline information as communities and societies implemented strategies to move toward cultures of peace. A related issue would be to assess what people really think about nonviolent actions designed to achieve a political goal. Do people view nonviolent activism as a successful option for achieving political goals or do they view nonviolent movements as less efficacious than violent approaches?

Another useful focus for future research on nonviolence would be to investigate the causal factors for people to develop nonviolent predispositions or to become peaceful persons. Longitudinal and cross-lagged studies from childhood through adulthood would be optimal although exploratory studies of potential causal factors have not been conducted and would be a good place to begin this line of research. Because nonviolent behavior is oftentimes based on rational choices, the theory of reasoned action (Ajzen & Fishbein, 1980) and the theory of planned behavior (Ajzen, 1991; Shapiro & Watson, 2000) might be fruitful theories to apply here as situational issues concerning norms and motivations to comply with relevant norms have been shown to influence intentions to behave in a wide variety of contexts.

Research on Nonviolence and Cultures of Peace

Cultures of peace are communities and societies in which social justice, human rights, and inclusiveness exist within a civil society characterized by nonviolence and a good educational system with sustainable development. Some peaceful societies have been identified and were discussed in Chap. 6. It would be interesting to assess the values of these cultures using the methodology of Schwartz described in Chap. 8.

As de Rivera (2004c) has pointed out, there is a need to document the degree to which nations possess the characteristics of cultures of peace in order to establish a baseline for efforts to move societies in that direction. Intervention strategies to change cultural attitudes, norms, and behaviors would benefit by following the lead of Bandura and others (Bandura, 2002; Kohn, Hasty, & Henderson, 2004; Mohammed, 2001) who used social cognitive theory to develop media strategies called entertainment education. This strategy incorporates educational messages into soap operas and other media programming on the television and radio to change the attitudes and behaviors of the audience. For instance, in sub-Saharan Africa writers for a radio soap opera in conjunction with researchers incorporated condom use and the effects of failures to use them into the story line in a very realistic way consistent with social cognitive theory. Long distance truck drivers, who often engaged in unprotected sex, were one of the major targets of this large-scale intervention. Condoms, distributed free of charge by health clinics, were dispersed at a rate of one million per year prior to intervention and afterwards the figure was 30 million. The effects of entertainment education have been documented in Latin America, Africa, Asia and the United States. Positive outcomes have been related to gender equality, adult literacy, family planning, and health issues like HIV/AIDS prevention. These methods could be adapted to address most aspects of cultures of peace.

Efforts to infuse nonviolence instruction into the education curricula needs to continue and the impact empirically studied. A few questions to evaluate include:

1. How best can objectives concerning nonviolence, nonviolent actions, and cultures of peace be included into social studies curricula?
2. Can teaching history from a culture of peace perspective, instead of a culture of war perspective, be effective?
3. To what degree do textbooks perpetuate a culture of war? A culture of peace?
4. Does the training of students to be nonviolent activists as a classroom activity impact their predispositions to behave nonviolently?
5. Does children's literature effect their nonviolent predispositions? What books do this?

Gerstein and Moeschberger (2003) suggest that qualitative methodologies would be well suited to conduct research on cultures of peace. They recommend ethnographic procedures to investigate levels of tolerance, solidarity, and the process of reconciliation.

There are many activist organizations that focus on specific aspects of cultures of peace and research on the effectiveness of their activities is relevant here too. For instance, gender equity, racism, inclusivity, and sustainability are culture of peace concerns plus they are subspecialties within social science disciplines too. The advantage of this overlap is important for academicians who need to publish in a mainstream field like gender studies yet want to impact an even wider issue like cultures of peace.

Religion, Worldviews, and Nonviolence Research

Religion does not need to be interpreted as absolutely pacifist to justify nonviolent actions and nonviolent methods of conflict resolution (Abu-Nimer, 2003). While speaking about Islam, Abu-Nimer's comments are applicable to other faiths as well when he says that just because certain policymakers and factions have chosen a violent path does not mean others need to follow. To encourage nonviolent choices Abu-Nimer calls for research and theory building on the following guiding principles. "(1) Islamic religious identity provides an effective basis for recruiting people to join a nonviolent campaign by nurturing strong identity and discipline; (2) Islamic religious values provide a strong basis for nonviolent activists' goals of serving others and implementing broad social, economic, and political reforms; (3) Reinterpretation of religious values can mitigate violent tendencies in a conflict, encourage activists to avoid intolerance toward other people, and enable them to overcome their time-honored inclination to use violence against adversaries, both in interpersonal and intergroup conflicts; (4) Nonviolent actions enable many Muslims to be politically more effective than they were when using violent tactics; (5) Muslim religious teachings and discourse can provide a basis for enabling people to question the meaning of their own tradition; and (6) Muslim religious commitments have sustained the determination and courage of their nonviolent leadership (p. 182)." These guiding principles provide excellent routes for research on nonviolence and Islam to proceed. Similar guidelines for Judaism, Christianity, and other religions would be useful to focus nonviolence research too.

Since any religion can promote violence or nonviolence, it is the responsibility of the faithful to concentrate on the nonviolent principles in their holy texts (Abu-Nimer, 2003).

Research into the ways that are most effective in integrating the nonviolent principles of religion into one's dominant worldview would also be helpful. Nonviolent and tolerant values and worldviews might diminish the negative aspects of fear and mortality salience that is usually associated with terror management. Pyszczynski, Vail, and Motyl (In press) report how research is now building at the University of Colorado at Colorado Springs that shows how mortality salience in some situations results in behaviors consistent with peacefulness and nonviolence. When making both compassionate scripture and mortality salient, both Christians and Muslims become less supportive of war and harbor less hostile attitudes. Pyszczynski et al. also discuss research that links mortality salience with construals of violence as animalistic, with reminders of one's values of a common humanity, and with feelings of secure attachment in such a way that peaceful attitudes resulted. More research on this vein would advance our understanding of nonviolence.

Dialogue between people of different faiths would be another topic for research. How can more interfaith dialogue be encouraged and what might be the best methods of organizing it to maximize mutual understanding?

Interdisciplinary Research Approaches to Nonviolence

Kool (2008) rightfully stresses the importance of interdisciplinary approaches to nonviolence research and theory development. One informal approach might involve teams of researchers from different disciplines working on the same research project. Several organizations might facilitate this process because of their interdisciplinary membership and orientation. Examples of such interdisciplinary professional organizations include the International Peace Research Association (IPRA) and the International Society of Political Psychology (ISPP). Both IPRA and ISPP comprise social scientists of all types interested in peace and nonviolent action. Psychologists for Social Responsibility and the Society for the Study of Peace, Conflict, and Violence have a majority of their membership in psychology but are open to and encourage members from all related fields to join. All these organizations would help to facilitate cooperative research teams and their Web sites are reported at the end of the chapter.

Many research ideas and creative scholarship of a interdisciplinary flavor are worth addressing but I will only describe a few. Case studies of individuals raised in peaceful cultures would be one topic that could generate a range of different questions from many disciplines. The effect of children's literature on the nonviolent attitudes and behavior has already been discussed. How about writing a children's story with a theme of peace and nonviolence and then testing the impact on children? Soldiers have a unique perspective on nonviolence and peace that is often ignored. The conduct of interviews and ethnographic studies of soldiers' views of violence and nonviolence would be an enlightening way to test theories from different disciplines. Another ethnographic study might look at the impact of field trips and study abroad programs to peaceful cultures.

Nonviolence for the Twenty-First Century

Reading and studying about nonviolence and the exemplary people who have championed nonviolent actions to achieve humanitarian goals has been an enjoyable and invigorating journey for me. Being able to "meet" Joseph Abileah, Mohandas Gandhi, Badshah Khan, Martin Luther King Jr., and others, even if only vicariously, challenges me to do more for humanity through nonviolent means. As I have tried to show, there are hundreds more people like these who are inspiring role models but toil in relative obscurity in societies that report violence and relegate nonviolent news to a passing mention at best.

When I was early in the writing process and told people I was writing a book, I was invariably asked about the topic. Often the response was surprise. "Oh really, that's interesting" or "Oh, that is a topic that we need to better understand" were typical responses. As soon as I indicated I was writing a textbook on nonviolence to one professional person, without batting an eye, he queried if I was writing fiction (with a smirk). That type of comment reflects the uphill trek that nonviolent researchers, theorists, and activists need to traverse to bring nonviolence into the forefront of human experience as a mainstream conflict resolution option. While the journey may be long and we are only a relatively short distance from the trailhead, it is a trek that is worth making.

Despite what some say, I believe nonviolent behavior is the norm for human beings. Throughout a typical day, people overwhelmingly behave nonviolently. This does not mean that being a peaceful or nonviolent person, as discussed in Chaps. 4 and 5, is the norm either though. A friend repeatedly challenges me to give an example of a truly nonviolent person. When I cannot identify anyone who is always nonviolent, he believes this proves that everyone is violent. It is an interesting argument. Of course, if we use this line of reasoning, no one is violent either since I am unable to find someone who is perfectly violent all the time. Even Adolph Hitler was kind to his dog and his mistress, Eva Braun. I do not think anyone would argue that means he was not a violent man.

While we tend to behave in nonviolent ways throughout our lives, our societies with their cultures of violence push us to develop worldviews that predispose us to act violently when presented with many types of conflict. Whether conflict is intrapersonal, interpersonal, societal, or international in scope, we have learned an overwhelming number of violent scripts to follow and all too few nonviolent scripts. Gandhi provided an optimistic interpretation when he said, "When I despair, I remember that all through history the way of truth and love has always won. There have been tyrants and murderers and for a time they seem invincible but in the end, they always fall – think of it, ALWAYS!" The under emphasis on nonviolent actions can be changed but the time and effort needed to steer societies toward cultures of peace to do so is significant.

The growing body of research and theories of nonviolence and the growing number of activists encourage me. However, as Eleanor Roosevelt reminded us, "It isn't enough to talk about peace. One must believe it. And it is not enough to believe in it. One must work at it (Groves, 2008, p. 143)." In this same spirit Gandhi cautioned us "We may never be strong enough to be entirely nonviolent in thought, word and deed. But we must keep nonviolence as our goal and make strong progress towards it."

I hope you are willing and motivated to bring nonviolence into the mainstream of your discipline, your life, and our world. In other words follow Gandhi's charge and "Be the change that you want to see in the world." Our world will be better for it!

Recommended Readings

McCarthy, R. M., & Kruegler, C. (1993). *Toward research and theory building in the study of non-violent action* (Monograph Series Number 7). Cambridge, MA: The Albert Einstein Institute.
  This little monograph is an excellent analysis of the purpose of theory building within the social sciences in general and more specifically in the study of nonviolent activism. The authors provide many recommendations with concrete examples throughout the book. Anyone interested in conducting research on nonviolent activism should consider this a must read.
McCarthy, R. M., & Sharp, G. (1997). *Nonviolent action: A research guide*. New York: Garland Press.
  This book is based on the assumption that researchers who want to advance the field of nonviolent action in an efficacious manner need to carefully study the methods of nonviolent action used in conflicts around the world. The book is divided into two parts. The first section is a compilation of references to nonviolent actions from the social sciences and government sources organized by region and country. The second part of the book is a compilation of references to the nature, theory, and perspectives on nonviolent action. This part is organized by methods, dynamics, pacifism, conflict, power, violence, and collective action.

Recommended Web Sites

Christie, D. J., Wagner, R. V., & Winter, D. D. (Eds.) (2001). *Peace, conflict, and violence: Peace psychology for the 21st century*. Upper Saddle River, NJ: Prentice Hall.

This is a groundbreaking book in the field of peace psychology. The editors have brought together over two dozen experts in the field who have developed theory and reported research under their 2 × 2 rubric of violence (direct vs. structural) and peace (peacemaking vs. peacebuilding). This book may be downloaded at no cost from the following Web site: http://academic.marion.ohio-state.edu/dchristie/Peace%20Psychology%20Book.html

International Peace Research Association, http://soc.kuleuven.be/iieb/ipraweb/index.php?action = home&cat = home

IPRA is a network of scholars, practitioners and decision makers from all continents that strive to stay at the cutting edge of the state of the art of peace. Established in 1964, IPRA has been pursuing interdisciplinary research into the most pressing issues related to sustainable peace. It has working groups on development and peace, the Earth Charter, evaluation of development and peace activities, knowledge and peace, Middle East, peace negotiations and mediation, peace psychology, sport and peace, and world governance and peace.

International Society of Political Psychology, http://ispp.org/

ISPP is a scientific, educational, and nonpartisan organization that is concerned about political and psychological phenomena. Membership includes a community of scholars and other concerned individuals in universities, government, the communications media, etc that are supportive of each other. Its purpose is to support scientific research, theory, and practice across disciplinary, national, and ideological boundaries, both among members of the Society and those outside the Society and to increase the theoretical and practical significance of political psychology both inside and outside academia. Political psychology covers a many different approaches and theories including social and cognitive psychology, political science, neuroscience, philosophy, psychoanalysis, history, sociology, communications, international relations, and political economy. Annual meetings are held across the globe.

Peace History Society, http://www.peacehistorysociety.org/

Founded in 1964, the Peace History Society encourages and coordinates national and international scholarly work designed to explore and articulate the conditions and causes of peace and war, and to communicate the findings of scholarly work to the public.

Peace, War, and Social Conflict, A Section of the American Sociological Association, http://www.peacewarconflict.org/

This is the Web page for a section of a professional organization of sociologists designed to encourage the application of sociological methods, theories, and perspectives to the study of peace, war, and social conflict. Topics studied by the group include: causes and dynamics of war, conflict resolution, peace movements, military institution, nonviolence, race and ethnic conflict, gender and violence, and war refugees

Psychologists for Social Responsibility, http://www.psysr.org/

Psychologists for Social Responsibility is a multidisciplinary community of members and supporters that share a commitment to the application of psychological knowledge in addressing today's pressing societal challenges and in building cultures of peace with social justice.

Society for the Study of Peace, Conflict, and Violence, http://www.webster.edu/peacepsychology/

Established within the American Psychological Association (APA) in 1990 as the Division of Peace Psychology, this Society is a growing organization consisting of psychologists, students, and professional affiliates from diverse disciplines. The purpose of the Society is to increase and apply psychological knowledge in the pursuit of peace where peace is defined to include both the absence of war and the creation of positive social conditions that minimize destructive conflicts and promote human well-being. The Society has working groups that address Children, Families, and War; Ethnicity and Peace; Feminism and Peace; Environmental

Justice and Protection; Globalization, Structural Violence, and Disarmament; and Conflict Resolution.

Suggestions for Research Projects in Peace Psychology, by Rachel MacNair (2003), http://www.rachelmacnair.com/research-ideas.html

This Web site provides suggestions for research projects that are relevant to nonviolence and peace. MacNair also has links to her consulting service in this area.

References

Abdo, N. (2006). Sexual violence, patriarchy, and the state: Women in Israel. *Pakistan Journal of Women's Studies*, *13*(2), 39–63.

Abu-Nimer, M. (2001). A framework for nonviolence and peacebuilding in Islam. *Journal of Law and Religion*, *15*(1/2), 217–265.

Abu-Nimer, M. (2003). *Nonviolence and peace building in Islam: Theory and practice*. Gainesville, FL: University of Florida Press.

Abu-Nimer, M. (2006, August). *Invited address as recipient of the Morton Deutsch Conflict Resolution Award*. Presented at the Annual Meeting of the American Psychological Association, New Orleans, LA, USA.

Ackerman, P., & DuVall, J. (2000). *A force more powerful: A century of nonviolent conflict*. New York: St Martin's Press.

Ackerman, P., & Kruegler, C. (1994). *Strategic nonviolent conflict: The dynamics of people power in the twentieth century*. Westport, CT: Praeger.

Adams, D. (Ed.). (1991). *The Seville Statement on Violence: Preparing the ground for the constructing of peace*. Paris: UNESCO.

Adams, D. (2000). Toward a global movement for a culture of peace. *Peace and Conflict: Journal of Peace Psychology*, *6*(3), 259–266.

Adams, D. (2003). Early history of the culture of peace: A personal memoire. Retrieved April 24, 2008, from http://www.culture-of-peace.info/history/introduction.html

Adelson, A. (2000). The culture of peace and the evolution of human beings. *International Journal of Humanities and Peace*, *16*(1), 23–33.

Adhiambo-Oduol, J. (1999). Traditional mediating techniques and women's contribution to a culture of peace. In I. Breines, D. Gierycz, & B. A. Reardon (Eds.), *Towards a women's agenda for a culture of peace* (pp. 181–190). Paris: UNESCO.

Agger, I. (2001). Reducing trauma during ethno-political conflict: A personal account of psycho-social work under war conditions in Bosnia. In D. J. Christie, R. V. Wagner, & D. D. Winter (Eds.), *Peace, conflict, and violence: Peace psychology for the 21st century* (pp. 240–250). Upper Saddle River, NJ: Prentice-Hall.

Ahmad, R. (1993). Islam, nonviolence, and global transformation. In G. D. Paige, C. Satha-Anand, & S. Gilliatt (Eds.), *Islam and nonviolence* (pp. 27–52). Honolulu, HI: Center for Global Nonviolence, Inc. Retrieved June 17, 2008 fromhttp://www.globalnonviolence.org/islam.htm

Ajzen, I. (1991). The theory of planned behavior. *Organizational Behavior and Human Decision Processes*, *50*, 179–211.

Ajzen, I., & Fishbein, M. (1980). *Understanding attitudes and predicting social behavior*. NJ: Prentice-Hall.

Akers, K. (2000). *The lost religion of Jesus: Simple living and nonviolence in early Christianity*. New York: Lantern Books.

Allport, G. W. (1950). *The individual and his religion*. New York: The MacMillan Company.

Allport, G. W., & Ross, J. M. (1967). Personal religious orientation and prejudice. *Journal of Personality and Social Psychology, 5*, 432–443.

Allport, G., Vernon, P., & Lindzey, G. (1960). *The study of values* (3rd ed.). Boston, MA: Houghton Miflin.

Altman, N. (1980). *Ahimsa: Dynamic compassion*. Wheaton, IL: Quest Books.

Ambrose, S. A. (2003). *To America: Personal reflections of an historian*. New York: Simon and Schuster.

Anderson, A. (2000, August). *Orange Hats: Nonviolent community action in Washington, D.C.* Paper presented at the Annual Meeting of the American Psychological Association, Washington, DC.

Anderson, J. (2007). Forgiveness – a relational process: Research and reflections. *European Journal of Psychotherapy and Counseling, 9*(1), 63–76.

Anderson, A., & Christie, D. J. (2001). Some contributions of psychology to policies promoting cultures of peace. *Peace and Conflict: Journal of Peace Psychology, 7*(2), 173–185.

Antonioni, D. (1999). Relationship between the big five personality factors and conflict management styles. *International Journal of Conflict Management, 9*(4), 336–355.

Aristophanes (1944). Lysistrata. In W. J. Oates & C. T. Murphy (Eds.), *Greek literature in translation* (pp. 370–405). York: Longmans, Green, & Co.

Aspey, L. S. (1990). How transforming power was used in the past by early Christians. In R. L. Holmes, (Ed.), *Nonviolence in theory and practice* (pp. 27–28). Long Grove, IL: Waveland Press.

Aspey, L. S. (2005). How transforming power was used in modern times – Against race prejudice in America. In R. L. Holmes & B. L. Gan (Eds.), *Nonviolence in theory and practice* (2nd ed., pp. 95–100). Long Grove, IL: Waveland Press.

Atlanta Bahá'í (2008). *Layli Miller-Muro, Esq.* Retrieved June 20, 2008, from http://www.atlanta-bahai.org/profile-miller-muro.php

Attenborough, R. (1982). *The words of Gandhi*. New York: Newmarket Press.

Audi, R. (1971). On the meaning and justification of violence. In J. A. Shaffer (Ed.), *Violence: Award-winning essays in the Council for Philosophical Studies Competition* (pp. 45–99). New York: David McKay Company, Inc.

Avery, P., Johnson, D. W., Johnson, R. T., & Mitchell, J. M. (1999). Teaching an understanding of war and peace through structured academic controversies. In A. Raviv, L. Oppenheimer, & D. Bar-Tal (Eds.), *How children understand war and peace: A call for international peace education* (pp. 260–280). San Francisco, CA: Jossey-Bass.

Awad, M. (1990). Nonviolent resistance: A strategy for the occupied territories. In R. L. Holmes (Ed.), *Nonviolence in theory and practice* (pp. 155–163). Belmont, CA: Wadsworth Publishing Company.

Bahá'í World Centre. (1986). *The Bahá'í world: An international record (Vol. XVIII)*. Haifa, Israel: Author

Bahá'u'lláh. (1976). *Gleanings from the writings of Bahá'u'lláh* (2nd ed.). (S. Effendi, Trans.). Wilmette, IL: Bahá'í Publishing Trust. (Original work ca. 1860–1890; translation by Shoghi Effendi first published 1935)

Baker, J. H. (Ed.). (2002). *Votes for women: The struggle for suffrage revisited*. New York: Oxford University Press.

Baker, R. L., Mednick, B. R., & Hocevar, D. (1991). Utility of scales derived from teacher judgements of adolescent academic performance and psychosocial behavior. *Educational and Psychological Measurement, 51*, 271–286.

Bales, R. F. (1968). Interaction process analysis. In D. L. Sils (Ed.), *International encyclopaedia of the social sciences*. New York: MacMillan.

Ball-Rokeach, S. J., Rokeach, M., Grube, J. W. (1984). *The Great American values test: Influencing behavior and belief through television*. New York: The Free Press.

Bandura, A. (1997). *Self-efficacy: The exercise of control*. New York: W. H. Freeman and Company.

Bandura, A. (2002). Environmental sustainability by sociocognitive deceleration of population growth. In P. Schmuch & W. Schultz (Eds.), *The psychology of sustainable development* (pp. 209–238). Dordrecht, The Netherlands: Kluwer.

Barany, Z. (1998). Ethnic mobilization and the state: The Roma in Eastern Europe. *Ethnic and Racial Studies, 21*(2), 308–327.

Barnes, C. (2006). *Agents for change: Civil society roles in preventing war and building peace.* Issue Paper 2. Den Haag, Netherlands: European Centre for Conflict Prevention.

Baron, R. A., & Richardson, D. R. (1994). *Human aggression.* New York: Plenum Press

Baron, R. A., Byrne, D., & Branscombe, N. R. (2007). *Mastering social psychology.* Boston, MA: Pearson Education, Inc.

Basabe, N., & Valencia, J. (2007). Culture of peace: Sociostructural dimensions, cultural values, and emotional climate. *Journal of Social Issues, 63*(2), 405–419.

Bar-Tal, D. (2002). The elusive nature of peace education. In G. Salomon & B. Nevo (Eds.) *Peace education: The concept, principles, and practices around the world* (pp. 27–36). Mahwah, NJ: Lawrence Erlbaum Associates.

Bar-Tal, D. (2007). Sociopsychological foundations of intractable conflicts. *American Behavioral Scientist, 50*(11), 1430–1453.

Baumeister, R. F., & Bushman, B. J. (2008). *Social psychology and human nature (Brief version).* Belmont, CA: Thomson/Wadsworth.

Beer, M. A. (1999). Violent and nonviolent struggle in Burma: Is a unified strategy workable? In S. Zunes, L. R. Kurtz, & S. B. Asher (Eds.), *Nonviolent social movements: A geographical perspective* (pp. 174–184). Malden, MA: Blackwell Publishers.

Begikhani, N. (2005). Honour-based violence among Kurds: The case of Iraqi Kurdistan. In S. Hossain & L. Welchman (Eds.), *'Honour': Crimes, paradigms, and violence against women* (pp. 209–229). London: Zed Books.

Berkowitz, L. (1993). *Aggression: Its causes, consequences, and control.* Philadelphia, PA: Temple University Press.

Bettenhausen, K. L., & Mernighan, J. L. (1991). The development of an intragroup norm and the effects of interpersonal and structural challenges. *Administrative Science Quarterly, 36*(1), 20–35.

Bickmore, K. (1999). Teaching conflict and conflict resolution in school: (Extrea-) curricular considerations. In A. Raviv, L. Oppenheimer, & D. Bar-Tal (Eds.), *How children understand war and peace: A call for international peace education* (pp. 233–259). San Francisco, CA: Jossey-Bass.

Bing, A. G. (1990). *Israeli pacifist: The life of Joseph Abileah.* Syracuse, NY: Syracuse University Press.

Biographical notes on Rabbi Lerner. (2008). Retrieved June 16, 2008 from http://www.tikkun.org/rabbi_lerner/bio

Bjerstedt, A. (1997). Educate for peace: Desirable? possible? how? *Peace and Conflict: Journal of Peace Psychology. 3*(4), 395–397.

Blake, S. M. (2002). *A step toward violence prevention: Nonviolent communication as part of a college curriculum.* Unpublished master's thesis, Florida Atlantic University, Boca Raton, FL.

Blanchard, C. M. (2008). Islam: Sunnis and Shiites. A CRS Report for Congress. (Order code RS21745) Retrieved June 10, 2008 from http://www.fas.org/sgp/crs/misc/RS21745.pdf

Blumberg, H. H. (1968). Accounting for a nonviolent mass demonstration. *Sociological Inquiry, 38*(1), 43–50.

Blumberg, H. H., Hare, A. P., & Costin, A. (2006). *Peace psychology: A comprehensive introduction.* Cambridge, UK: Cambridge University Press.

Bodine, R., Crawford, D., & Schrumpf, F. (1994). *Creating the peaceable school: A comprehensive program for teaching conflict resolution.* Champaign, IL: Research Press.

Bommersbach, M. L. (2000). *The role of nonviolence in psychology: Multidisciplinary perspectives and integration with community and feminist psychology.* Unpublished doctoral dissertation, California School of Professional Psychology, Los Angeles, CA.

Bondurant, J. V. (1965). *Conquest of violence: The Gandhian philosophy of conflict* (Rev. Ed.). Berkeley, CA: University of California Press.

Bonta, B. D. (1993). *Peaceful peoples: An annotated bibliography.* Metuchen, NJ: Scarecrow Press.

Bonta, B. D. (1996). Conflict resolution among peaceful societies: The culture of peacefulness. *Journal of Peace Research, 33*(4), 403–420.

Bonta, B. D. (1997). Cooperation and competition in peaceful societies. *Psychological Bulletin*, *121*(2), 299–320.

Bose, A. (1987). *Dimensions of peace and nonviolence: The Gandhian perspective*. Delhi: Gian Publishing House.

Boston University. (2006). *The anger quiz*. Retrieved November 15, 2006, from http://www.bu. edu/fsao/html/fyi_anger.html

Boulding, E. (1996). Toward a culture of peace in the twenty-first century. *Social Alternatives*, *15*(3), 38–40.

Boulding, E. (2000a). New chance for human peaceableness. *Peace and Conflict: Journal of Peace Psychology*, *6*(3), 193–215.

Boulding, E. (2000b). *Cultures of peace: The hidden side of history*. Syracuse, NY: Syracuse University Press.

Boulding, K. E. (1977). The power of nonconflict. *Journal of Social Issues*, *33*, 22–33.

Boulding, K. E. (1989). *Three faces of power*. Newbury Park, CA: Sage Publishing.

Bouloukos, A. C., & Dakin, B. (2001). Toward a universal declaration of the rule of law: Implications for criminal justice and sustainable development. *International Journal of Comparative Sociology*. *42*(1/2), 145–162.

Bowden, B. (2006). Civil society, the state, and the limits to global civil society. *Global Society: Journal of Interdisciplinary International Relations*, *20*(2), 155–178.

Brady, J., & Brady, S. (2006, March 30). Reagan assassination attempt: 25 years later. The Washington Post. Retrieved May 30, 2008, from http://www.washingtonpost.com/wp-dyn/content/discussion/2006/03/29/DI2006032901373.html

Branch, T. (1998). *Pillar of fire: America in the King years, 1963–65*. New York: Simon & Schuster.

Brehm, S. S., Kassin, S., & Fein, S. (2005). *Social psychology* (6th ed.). Boston, MA: Houghton Mifflin.

Brienes, I. (1999). A gender perspective on a culture of peace. In I. Breines, D. Gierycz, & B. A. Reardon (Eds.), *Towards a women's agenda for a culture of peace* (pp. 33–56). Paris: UNESCO.

Breines, I., Gierycz, D., & Reardon, B. A. (Eds.) (1999). *Towards a women's agenda for a culture of peace*. Paris: UNESCO

Brenes, A. C. (1999, July). *Peaceful selfhood*. A paper presented at the 6th International Symposium for Contributions of Psychology to Peace, San Jose, Costa Rica.

Brenes, A. C. (2004). An integral model of peace education. In A. L. Wenden (Ed.), *Educating for a culture of social and ecological peace* (pp. 77–98). Albany, NY: State University of New York Press.

Brenes, A. C., & Ito, T. (1994). Peace education: Perspectives from Costa Rica and Japan. Peace Education Miniprints No. 62. Malmo School of Education, Lund University, Malmo, Sweden. (ERIC Document Reproduction Service No. ED 377111)

Brenes, A. C., & Wessells, M. (2001). Psychological contributions to building cultures of peace. *Peace and Conflict: Journal of Peace Psychology*, *7*(2), 99–107.

Brenes, A. C., & Winter, D. D. (2001). Earthly dimensions of peace: The Earth Charter. *Peace and Conflict: Journal of Peace Psychology*, *7*(2), 157–171.

Briggs, J. L. (1994). "Why don't you kill your baby brother?" The dynamics of peace in Canadian Inuit camps. In L. E. Sponsel, & T. Gregor (Eds.), *The anthropology of peace and nonviolence* (pp. 155–181). Boulder, CO: Lynne Rienner Publishers.

Brown, C. E. (1984). The continuing struggle against racial injustice in the United States. In A. A. Lee (Ed.), *Circle of unity: Bahá'í approaches to current social issues* (pp. 67–89). Los Angeles, CA: Kalimát Press.

Brown, J. E. (1989). *The sacred pipe: Black Elk's account of the seven rights of the Oglala Sioux*. Norman, OK: University of Oklahoma Press.

Brown, L. R. (1981). *Building a sustainable society*. New York: Norton Books.

Buck, L. A. (1984). Nonviolence and satyagraha in Attenborough's Gandhi. *Journal of Humanistic Psychology*, *24*, 130–141.

Bunker, B. B., & Rubin, J. Z. (Eds.) (1995). *Conflict, cooperation, and justice: Essays inspired by the work of Morton Deutsch*. San Francisco, CA: Jossey-Bass.

Burrowes, R. J. (1996). *The strategy of nonviolent defense: A Gandhian approach*. Albany, NY: State University of New York Press.

Buss, A. H., & Durkee, H. (1957). An inventory for assessing different kinds of hostility. *Journal of Consulting Psychology, 21*, 343–349.

Buss, A. H., & Perry, M. (1992). The Aggression Questionnaire. *Journal of Personality and Social Psychology, 63*(3), 452–459.

Busse, H. (1998). *Islam Judaism, and Christianity: Theological and historical affiliations*. (A. Brown, Trans.). Princeton, NJ: Markus Wiener Publishers. (Original work published 1988)

Cacioppo, J. T., & Petty, R. E. (1982). The need for cognition. *Journal of Personality and Social Psychology, 42*(1), 116–131.

Cacioppo, J. T., Petty, R. E., & Kao, C. E. (1984). The efficient assessment of need for cognition. *Journal of Personality Assessment, 48*, 306–307.

Cairns, E., & Hewstone, M. (2002). Northern Ireland: The impact of peacemaking in Northern Ireland on intergroup behavior. In G. Salomon & B. Nevo (Eds.), *Peace education: The concept, principles, and practices around the world* (pp. 217–228). Mahwah, NJ: Lawrence Erlbaum Associates.

Cardella, L. A., & Van Slyck, M. (1999, August). *Peace education and conflict resolution curricula for middle school students*. Paper presented at the 107th Annual Convention of the American Psychological Association, Boston, MA.

Carson, R. (1962). *Silent spring*. Boston, MA: Houghton Mifflin Company.

Center for Disease Control and Prevention (2007). *Violence prevention at CDC*. Retrieved February 2, 2008 from http://www.cdc.gov/ncipc/dvp/dvp.htm

Centre for Egyptian Women's Legal Assistance (2005). 'Crimes of honour' as violence against women in Egypt. In S. Hossain & L. Welchman (Eds.), *'Honour': Crimes, paradigms, and violence against women* (pp. 137–159). London: Zed Books.

Chambliss, B. B. (2002). *Contemporary women peacemakers: The hidden side of peacemaking*. Dissertation, Fielding Graduate Institute. Ann Arbor, MI: Proquest Information Learning Company.

Chapple, C. K. (1992). Nonviolence to animals in Buddhism and Jainism. In K. Kraft (Ed.), *Inner peace, world peace: Essays on Buddhism and nonviolence* (pp. 49–62). Albany, NY: State University of New York Press.

Chapple, C. K. (1998). Jainism and nonviolence. In D. L. Smith-Christopher (Ed.), *Subverting hatred: The challenge of nonviolence in religious traditions* (pp. 13–24). Cambridge, MA: Boston Research Center for the 21st Century.

Chatfield, C. (1999). Nonviolent social movements in the United States: A historical overview. In S. Zunes, L. R. Kurtz, & S. B. Asher (Eds.), *Nonviolent social movements: A geographical perspective* (pp. 283–301). Malden, MA: Blackwell Publishers.

Chernus, I. (2004). *American nonviolence: The history of an idea*. Maryknoll, NY: Orbis Books.

Chittister, J., Chishti, M. S. S., & Waskow, A. (Eds.) (2007). *Tent of Abraham: Stories of hope and peace for Jews, Christians, and Muslims*. Boston, MA: Beacon Press.

Christie, D. J. (1997). Reducing direct and structural violence: The human needs theory. *Peace and Conflict: Journal of Peace Psychology, 3*(4), 315–332.

Christie, D. J. (2001). Peacebuilding: Approaches to social justice. In D. J. Christie, R. V. Wagner, & D. D. Winter (Eds.), *Peace, conflict, and violence: Peace psychology for the 21st century* (pp. 277–281). Upper Saddle River, NJ: Prentice-Hall.

Christie, D. J. (2003, August). *To promote positive peace, add affect to White's realistic empathy*. A paper presented at the annual meeting of the American Psychological Association, Toronto, Canada.

Christie, D. J., Wagner, R. V., & Winter, D. D. (Eds.). (2001). *Peace, conflict, and violence: Peace psychology for the 21st century*. Upper Saddle River, NJ: Prentice-Hall. Available at http://academic.marion.ohio-state.edu/dchristie/Peace%20Psychology%20Book.html

Cohen, F., Ogilvie, D. M., Solomon, S. Greenberg, J., & Pyszczynski, T. (2005). American roulette: The effect of reminders of death on support for George W. Bush in the 2004 presidential election. *Journal of Social Issues and Public Policy, 5*(1), 177–187.

Cohen, F., Solomon, S., Maxfield, M., Pyszczynski, T., & Greenberg, J. (2004). The effects of mortality salience on evaluations of charismatic, task-oriented, and relationship-oriented leaders. *Psychological Science, 15*(12), 846–851.

Colburn, K. (1985). Honor, ritual and violence in ice hockey. *Canadian Journal of Sociology, 10*(2), 153–170.

Cole, J. R. (1984). Human rights and the Bahá'í faith. In A. A. Lee (Ed.), *Circle of unity: Bahá'í approaches to current social issues* (pp. 117–133). Los Angeles, CA: Kalimát Press.

Coleman, P. T., & Deutsch, M. (2001). Introducing cooperation and conflict resolution into schools: A systems approach. In D. J. Christie, R. V. Wagner, & D. D. Winter (Eds.), *Peace, conflict, and violence: Peace psychology for the 21st century* (pp. 223–239). Upper Saddle River, NJ: Prentice-Hall.

Coleman, P. T., Vallacher, R. R., Nowak, A., & Bui-Wrzosinka, L. (2007). Intractable conflict as an attractor: A dynamical systems approach to conflict escalation and intractability. *American Behavioral Scientist, 50*(11), 1454–1475.

Coomaraswamy, R. (2005). Violence against women and "crimes of honour." In S. Hossain & L. Welchman (Eds.), *'Honour': Crimes, paradigms, and violence against women* (pp. xi–xiv). London: Zed Books.

Cooper, J. (2003). Persistent resistance: UN and the nonviolent campaign for the human rights of indigenous peoples. *Social Alternatives, 22*(3), 17–22.

Cortright, D. (2006). *Gandhi and beyond: Nonviolence for the age of terrorism.* Boulder, CO: Paradigm Books.

Costin, A. (2006). The feminist approach. In H. H. Blumberg, A. P. Hare, & A. Costin, *Peace psychology: A comprehensive introduction.* (pp. 37–43). Cambridge, UK: Cambridge University Press.

Côté, R. R., Plickert, G., & Wellman, B. (2006). *It's not who you know, it's how you know them: Who exchanges what with whom?* A paper presented at the annual meeting of the American Sociological Association, Montreal, Canada.

Cox, E., & Dannahy, P. (2005). The value of openness in e-relationships: Using Nonviolent Communication to guide online coaching and mentoring. *International Journal of Evidence Based Coaching and Mentoring, 3*(1), 39–51.

Cromwell, M., & Vogele, W. B (2009). Nonviolent action, trust, and building a culture of peace. In J. de Rivera (Ed.), *Handbook for cultures of peace.* (pp. 231–244). New York: Springer.

Crowley, V. (2001). Acts of memory and imagination: Reflections on women's suffrage and the centenary celebrations of suffrage in South Australia in 1994. *Australian Feminist Studies, 16*(35), 225–240.

Cultures of peace. (1997) UN Resolution A/RES/52/13, Retrieved April 24, 2008 from http://www.un.org/ga/documents/gares52/res5213.htm

Dajani, S. (1999). Nonviolent resistance in the Occupied Territories: A critical reevaluation. In S. Zunes, L. R. Kurtz, & S. B. Asher (Eds.), *Nonviolent social movements: A geographical perspective* (pp. 52–74). Malden, MA: Blackwell Publishers.

Danesh, H. B. (1979). *The violence-free society: A gift for our children* (2nd ed.). Ottawa: The Canadian Association for Studies on the Bahá'í Faith.

Darley, J. M., & Batson, C. D. (1973). From Jerusalem to Jericho: A study of situational and dispositional variables in helping behavior. *Journal of Personality and Social Psychology, 27*, 100–108.

Davis, M. (1994). *Empathy: A social psychological approach.* Madison, WI: Brown & Benchmark.

Dear, J. (2008). *Seeds of nonviolence.* Eugene, OR: Wipf and Stock.

Dechesne, M., van den Berg, C., & Soeters, J. (2007). International collaboration under threat: A field study in Kabul. *Conflict Management and Peace Science, 24*, 25–36.

de la Rey, C. (2001). In D. J. Christie, R. V. Wagner, & D. D. Winter (Eds.), *Peace, conflict, and violence: Peace psychology for the 21st century* (pp. 251–261). Upper Saddle River, NJ: Prentice-Hall.

de la Rey, C., & McKay, S. (2006). Peacebuilding as a gendered process. *Journal of Social Issues, 62*(1), 141–153.

Derfner, L. (2006, April 17). Brother in arms? *Jerusalem Post: Online Edition.*

de Rivera, J. H. (2004a). Assessing cultures of peace. *Peace and Conflict: Journal of Peace Psychology, 10*(2),95–100.

de Rivera, J. H. (2004b). A template for assessing cultures of peace. *Peace and Conflict: Journal of Peace Psychology, 10*(2), 125–146.

de Rivera, J. H. (2004c). Assessing culture of peace in contemporary societies. *Journal of Peace Research, 41*(5), 531–548.

de Rivera, J. H., Kurrien, R., & Olsen, N. (2007). The emotional climate of nations and their culture of peace. *Journal of Social Issues, 63*(2), 255–271.

de Rivera, J. H., & Páez, D. (2007). Emotional climate, human security, and cultures of peace. *Journal of Social Issues, 63*(2), 233–253.

Deutsch, M. (1973). *The resolution of conflict: Constructive and destructive processes.* New Haven, CT: Yale University Press.

Deutsch, M. (1994). Constructive conflict resolution: Principles, training, and research. *Journal of Social Issues, 50*(1), 13–32.

Deutsch, M. (1995). William James: The first peace psychologist. *Peace and Conflict: Journal of Peace Psychology. 1,* 27–35.

Deutsch, M. (2000). Cooperation and competition. In M. Deutsch & P. T. Coleman (Eds.), *The handbook of conflict resolution: Theory and practice* (pp. 21–40). San Francisco, CA:Jossey-Bass.

Deutsch, M., & Coleman, P. T. (Eds.) (2000). *The handbook of conflict resolution: Theory and practice.* San Francisco, CA: Jossey-Bass.

Devaney, E., O'Brien, M. U., Tavegia, M, & Resnik, H. (2005). Promoting children's ethical development through social and emotional learning. *New Directions for Youth Development, 108,* 107–116.

Diamond, L. (2001). The peace book: 108 simple ways to create a more peaceful world. Newburyport, MA: Conari Press.

Diwakar, R. R. (1948). *Satyagraha: The power of truth.* Hinsdale, IL: Henry Regenery Co.

Drevdahl, D., Kneipp, S. M., Canales, M. K., & Dorcy, K. S. (2001). Reinvesting in social justice: A capital idea for public health nursing? *Advances in Nursing Science, 24*(2), 19–31.

Drummond, R. H. (2005). *Understanding Muhammad and the Koran: Islam for the western mind.* Charlottesville, VA: Hampton Roads Publishing Company, Inc.

Earth Charter Initiative. (n.d.) *Earth charter in action.* Retrieved May 27, 2008, from http://www.earthcharterinaction.org/read_charter.html

Earth Charter Principles (2007). *Social Alternatives, 26*(3), 38–40.

Easwaran, E. (1984). *A man to match his mountains: Badshah Khan, nonviolent soldier of Islam.* Peteluma, CA: Nilgiri Press.

Eaton, J., & Struthers, C. W. (2006). The reduction of psychological aggression across varied interpersonal contexts through repentance and forgiveness. *Aggressive Behavior, 32,* 195–206.

Eberly, D. E. (1994). *Building a community of citizens: Civil society in the 21st century.* Lanham, MD: University Press of America, Inc.

Eckstein, D., & La Grassa, L. (2005). The non-violent relationship questionnaire (NVRQ). *The Family Journal: Counseling and Therapy for Couples and Families, 13*(2), 205–211.

Ehrenberg, J. (1999). *Civil society: The critical history of an idea.* New York: New York University Press.

Eizenstat, S. (2008). *Mega-trends in the next five years which will impact on world Jewry and Israel.* Jerusalem: The Jewish People Policy Planning Institute.

Elias, M. J., & Weissberg, R. P. (2000). Primary prevention: Educational approaches to enhance social and emotional learning. *Journal of School Health, 70*(5), 186–190.

Elliott, G. C. (1980). Components of pacifism. *Journal of Conflict Resolution, 24,* 27–54.

Engineer, A. A. (1996). *The rights of women in Islam.* London: C. Hurst & Company Publishers, Ltd.

Engler, B. (2003). *Personality theories: An introduction.* Boston, MA: Houghton Mifflin Company.

Eppler, K. (1990). Transforming power in the labor movement – Cesar Chavez. In R. L. Holmes (Ed.), *Nonviolence in theory and practice* (pp. 191–193). Belmont, CA: Wadsworth Publishing Company.

Erikson, E. G. (1963). *Childhood and society*. New York: W. W. Norton.

Esslemont, J. E. (1970). *Bahá'u'lláh and the new era: An introduction to the Bahá'í faith*. Wilmette, IL: Bahá'í Publishing Trust.

Ewan, R. B. (1998). *Personality: A topical approach*. Mahwah, NJ: Lawrence Erlbaum Associates.

Faqir, F. (2001). Intrafamily femicide in defence of honour: The case of Jordan. *Third World Quarterly, 22*(1), 65–82.

Fattah, H. M. (2005, May 17). Kuwait grants political rights to its women. *The New York Times*.

Fellman, G. (1998). *Rambo and the Dali Lama: The compulsion to win and its threat to human survival*. Albany, NY: State University of New York Press.

Fernández-Dols, J.-M., Hurtado-de-Mendoza, A., & Jiménez-de-Lucas, I. (2004). Cultures of peace: An alternative definition and its measurement. *Peace and Conflict: Journal of Peace Psychology, 10*(2), 117–124.

Feshbach, S., & Weiner, B. (1982). *Personality*. Lexington, MA: D. C. Heath and Company.

Fink, C. (1980). Peace education and the peace movement since 1815. *Peace & Change, 6*(1–2), 66–73.

Fischer, L. (1954). *Gandhi: His life and message for the world*. New York: Mentor Books.

Fisher, A. M. (1990). Opposition to violence: A Jewish perspective. In V. K. Kool (Ed.), *Perspectives on nonviolence* (pp. 178–84). New York: Springer.

Fisher, R., & Shapiro, D. (2005). *Beyond reason: Using emotions as you negotiate*. New York: Viking.

Fisher, R., Ury, W., & Patton, B. (1991). *Getting to yes: Negotiating agreement without giving in*. (2nd ed.). New York: Penguin Books.

Fiske, S. T. (2004). *Social beings: A core motives approach to social psychology*. New York: Wiley.

Flecknoe, M. (2005). What does anyone know about peer mediation? *Improving Schools, 8*(3), 221–235.

Fleischman, P. R. (2002). *The Buddha taught nonviolence not pacifism*. Seattle, WA: Pariyatti Press.

Flinders, T., & Easwaran, E. (2005). Nonviolent soldier of Islam. In R. L. Holmes, R. & B. L. Gan (Eds.), *Nonviolence in theory and practice* (2nd ed., pp. 309–317). Long Grove, IL: Waveland Press.

Folger, J. P., & Bush, R. A. B. (1996). Transformative mediation and third-party intervention: Ten hallmarks of a transformative approach to practice. *Mediation Quarterly, 13*(4), 263–278.

Forcey L. R., & Harris, I. M. (Eds.). (1999). *Peacebuilding for adolescents: Strategies for educators and community leaders*. New York: Peter Lang Publishing, Inc.

Forrest, J. (1994). *Love is the measure: A biography of Dorothy Day*. Mary Knoll, NY: Orbis Books.

Forrest, J. (2000). Remembering Dorothy Day. In W. Wink (Ed.), *Peace is the way: Writings on nonviolence from the Fellowship of Reconciliation* (pp. 104–108). Mary Knoll, NY: Orbis Books.

French, H. W. (2004, October). The Non-Violence Self Inventory. *Interreligious Insight*. Retrieved June 23, 2008, from http://www.worldfaiths.org/nonviolence.doc

Fried, G. (1999). Critiques of violence. In L. Kurtz (Ed.), *Encyclopedia of violence, peace, and conflict* (Vol. 2, pp. 507–515). New York: Academic.

Fry, D. P. (1994). Maintaining social tranquility: Internal and external loci of aggression and control. In L. E. Sponsel, & T. Gregor (Eds.), *The anthropology of peace and nonviolence* (pp. 133–154). Boulder, CO: Lynne Rienner Publishers.

Fry, D. P., & Bjorkqvist, K. (Eds.). (1997). *Cultural variation in conflict resolution: Alternatives to violence*. Mahwah, NJ: Lawrence Ehlbaum Associates.

Fry, D. P., & Fry, C. B. (1997). Culture and conflict resolution models: Exploring alternatives to violence. In D. P. Fry, & K. Bjorkqvist (Eds.), *Cultural variation in conflict resolution: Alternatives to violence* (pp. 9–23). Mahwah, NJ: Lawrence Ehlbaum Associates.

Galtung, J., & Tschudi, F. (2001). Crafting peace: On the psychology of the TRANSCEND approach. In D. J. Christie, R. V. Wagner, & D. D. Winter (Eds.), *Peace, conflict, and violence: Peace psychology for the 21st century* (pp. 210–222). Upper Saddle River, NJ: Prentice-Hall.

Gandhi, M. K. (1951). *Non-violent resistance*. New York: Schocken Books.

Gandhi, K. (1957/1927). *An autobiography: The story of my experiments with truth*. Boston, MA: Beacon Press.

Gandhi, M. K. (1999). *The way to God*. M. S. Dephande (Ed.). Berkeley, CA: Berkeley Hills Books.

Gandhimohan, M. V. (2000). *Mahatma Gandhi and the Bahá'ís: Striving towards a nonviolent civilization*. New Delhi:Bahá'í Publishing Trust of India. Retrieved June 12, 2008, fromhttp://bahai-library.com/books/gandhi/index.html

Gendler, E. (1981). Therefore choose life. In A. Solomonow (Ed.), *Roots of Jewish Nonviolence* (pp.7–16). Nyack, NY: Jewish Peace Fellowship.

Gensler, H. J. (n.d.) *The golden rule*. Retrieved May 22, 2008, from http://www.jcu.edu/philosophy/gensler/goldrule.htm#Es

Gerstein, L. H., & Moeschberger, S. L. (2003). Building cultures of peace: An urgent task for counseling professionals. *Journal of Counseling and Development, 81*, 115–119.

Gill, A. (2007, August 2). Root out honour killings. *Community Care, 1684*, 6.

Gladwell, M. (2000). *The tipping point: How little things can make a big difference*. New York: Back Bay Books.

Global Marshall Plan (n.d.a). *Five strategic cornerstones*. Retrieved June 2, 2008, from http://www.globalmarshallplan.org/infocenter/strategy/index_eng.html

Global Marshall Plan (n.d.b). *Global Marshall Plan: Balance the world with an eco-social market economy*. Retrieved June 3, 2008, from http://www.globalmarshallplan.org/infocenter/strategy/index_eng.html

Global Marshall Plan (n.d.c). *The Global Marshall Plan initiative* http://www.globalmarshallplan.org/the_initiative/strategy/index_eng.html

Goldschmidt, W. (1994). Peacemaking and the institutions of peace in tribal societies. In L. E. Sponsel, & T. Gregor (Eds.), *The anthropology of peace and nonviolence* (pp. 1–36). Boulder, CO: Lynne Rienner Publishers.

Goleman, D. (2006). *Social intelligence: The new science of human relationships*. New York: Bantam Books.

Gomez, L. O. (1992). Nonviolence and the self in early Buddhism. In K. Kraft (Ed.), *Inner peace, world peace: Essays on Buddhism and nonviolence* (pp. 31–48). Albany, NY: State University of New York Press.

Gore, A. (1992). *Earth in the balance: Ecology and the human spirit*. Boston, MA: Houghton Mifflin Company.

Gore, A. (2006). *An inconvenient truth: The planetary emergency of global warming and what we can do about it*. New York: Rodale Books.

Gorsuch, R. L. (1984). Measurement: The boon or bane of investigating religion. *American Psychologist, 39*, 228–236.

Gottfredson, D. C., & Gottfredson, G. D. (2002). Quality of school-based prevention programs: Results from a national survey. *Journal of Research in Crime and Delinquency, 39*(1), 3–35.

Graziano, W. G., & Eisenberg, N. (1997). Agreeableness: A dimension of personality. In R. Hogan, J. Johnson, & S. Briggs (Eds.), *Handbook of personality psychology* (pp. 795–824). San Diego, CA: Academic.

Graziano, W. G., & Tobin, R. M. (2002). Agreableness: Dimension of personality or social desirability artifact? *Journal of Personality, 70*(5), 695–727.

Greenberg, J., Pyszczynski, T., & Solomon, S. (1986). The causes and consequences of a need for self esteem: A terror management theory. In R. F. Baumeister (Ed.), *Public self and private self* (pp. 189–212). New York: Springer.

Greenberg, J., Simon, L., Pyszczynski, T., Solomon, S., & Chatel, D. (1992). Terror management and tolerance: Does mortality salience always intensify negative reactions to others who threaten one's worldview? *Journal of Personality and Social Psychology, 63*, 212–220.

Greenberg, M. T., Weissberg, R. P., O'Brian, M. U., Zin, J. E., Fredericks, L., Resnik, H., & Elias, M. J. (2003). Enhancing school-based prevention and youth development through coordinated social, emotional, and academic learning. *American Psychologist, 58*(6/7), 466–474.

Greene, M. B. (2005). Reducing violence and aggression in schools. *Trauma, Violence, and Abuse, 6*(3), 236–253.

Gregor, T. (1994). Symbols and rituals of peace in Brazil's Upper Xingu. In L. E. Sponsel & T. Gregor (Eds.), *The anthropology of peace and nonviolence* (pp. 1–36). Boulder, CO: Lynne Rienner Publishers.

Groves, J. W. (2000). Revisiting "self-suffering": From Gandhi to King to contemporary nonviolence. In G. S. Harak (Ed.), *Nonviolence for the third millennium* (pp. 201–227). Macon, GA: Mercer University Press.

Groves, E. (Ed.). (2008). *The anti-war quote book*. San Francisco: Quirk Productions, Inc.

Grunblatt, J. (1981). Violence and some aspects of Jewish tradition. In A. Solomonow (Ed.), *Roots of Jewish nonviolence* (pp.17–23). Nyack, NY: Jewish Peace Fellowship

Hagberg, J. (1984). *Real power*. Minneapolis, MN: Winston Press.

Hahn, T. N. (1987). *Interbeing: Fourteen guidelines for engaged Buddhism*. Berkeley CA: Parallax Press.

Hahn, T. N. (1991). *Peace is every step: The path of mindfulness in everyday life*. New York: Bantam Books.

Hahn, T. N. (1993). *Love in action: Writings on nonviolent social change*. Berkeley CA: Parallax Press.

Hahn, T. N. (2005). *Keeping the peace: Mindfulness and public service*. Berkeley CA: Parallax Press.

Hakvoort, I. (2002). Theories of learning and development: Implications for peace education. *Social Alternatives, 21*(1), 18–22.

Hall, R. (1999). Learning conflict management through peer mediation. In A. Raviv, L. Oppenheimer, & D. Bar-Tal (Eds.), *How children understand war and peace: A call for international peace education* (pp. 281–298). San Francisco, CA: Jossey-Bass.

Harak, G. S. (Ed.). (2000). *Nonviolence for the third millennium*. Macon, GA: Mercer University Press.

Hare, A. P. (1968a). Introduction to theories of nonviolence. In A. P. Hare, & H. H. Blumberg (Eds.), *Nonviolent direct action: American cases-social psychological analysis* (pp. 3–30). Washington CD: Corpus Books.

Hare, A. P. (1968b). Nonviolent action from a social-psychological perspective. In A. P. Hare, & H. H. Blumberg (Eds.), *Nonviolent direct action: American cases-social psychological analysis* (pp. 513–530). Washington CD: Corpus Books.

Hare, A. P., & Blumberg, H. H. (1968). *Nonviolent direct action: American cases-social psychological analysis*. Washington CD: Corpus Books.

Harris, I. M. (1988). *Peace education*. Jefferson, NC: McFarland & Company, Inc, Publishers.

Harris, R. T. (1998). Nonviolence in Islam: The alternative community tradition. In D. L. Smith-Christopher (Ed.), *Subverting hatred: The challenge of nonviolence in religious traditions* (pp. 95–113). Cambridge, MA: Boston Research Center for the 21st Century.

Harris, I. M. (1999a). Types of peace education. In A. Raviv, L. Oppenheimer, & D. Bar-Tal, (Eds.), *How children understand war and peace: A call for international peace education* (pp. 299–317). San Francisco, CA: Jossey-Bass.

Harris, I. M. (1999b). A summer institute on nonviolence. In L. R. Forcey & I. M. Harris (Eds.), *Peacebuilding for adolescents: Strategies for educators and community leaders* (pp. 309–329). New York: Peter Lang Publishing, Inc.

Harris, I. M. (2002a). Challenges for peace educators at the beginning of the 21st century. *Social Alternatives, 21*(1), 28–31.

Harris, I. M. (2002b). Conceptual underpinnings of peace education. In G. Salomon, & B. Nevo (Eds.), *Peace education: The concept, principles, and practices around the world* (pp. 15–25). Mahwah, NJ: Lawrence Erlbaum Associates.

Harris, I. M. (2004). Evaluating peace education. *Journal for the Study of Peace and Conflict*, 18–32.

Harris, I. M., & Morrison, M. L. (2003). *Peace education* (2nd. ed.). Jefferson, NC: McFarland & Company, Inc, Publishers.

Hasan, Q., & Khan, S. R. (1983). Dimensions of Gandhian (nonviolent) personality. *Journal of Psychological Researches, 2*, 100–106.

Hastings, T. H. (2005). *Power: Nonviolent transformation from transpersonal to the transnational*. Dallas, TX: Hamilton Books.

Hatcher, W. S., & Martin, J. D. (1985). *The Bahá'í faith: The emerging global religion*. San Francisco: Harper & Row.

Hauerwas, S. (2004). *Performng the faith: Bonhoeffer and the practice of nonviolence*. Grand Rapids, MI: Brazos Press.

Hauss, C. (1996). *Beyond confrontation: Transforming the new world order*. Wetport, CT: Praeger.

Hauss, C. (2003). Civil society. In G. Burgess & H. Burgess (Eds). *The beyond intractability knowledge base project*. Retrieved May 29, 2008, from http://www.beyondintractability.org/essay/civil_society/

Hawkins, J. D., Farrington, D. P., & Catalano, R. E. (1998). Reducing violence through the schools. In D. S. Elliott, B. A. Hamburg, & K. R. Williams (Eds.), *Violence in American schools: A new perspective* (pp. 188–215). New York: Cambridge University Press.

Heaven, P. C., Rejab, D., & Bester, C. L. (1984). Psychometric properties of Elliott's measure of Pacifism: Cross-Cultural comparison. *Journal of Cross-Cultural Psychology, 15*(2), 227–232.

Hedges, C. (2002). *War is the force that gives us meaning*. New York: Public Affairs Press.

Hertzberg, A. (Ed.). (1961). *Judaism*. New York: George Braziller Inc.

Heuchert, J. W. P. (2003, August). *Hawks and doves: The personality of peace*. A paper presented as a poster at the 111th Annual Convention of the American Psychological Association, Toronto, Canada.

Hicks, D. (Ed.). (1988). *Educating for peace: Issues, principles, and practice in the classroom*. London: Routledge.

Hill, P. C., & Pargament, K. I. (2003). Advances in the conceptualization and measurement of spirituality and religion. *American Psychologist, 58*, 64–74.

Ho, K. C., Baber, Z., & Khondker, H. H. (2002). 'Sites' of resistance: Alternative websites and state-society relations. *British Journal of Sociology, 53* (1), 127–148.

Hofstede, G. (1980). *Culture's consequences: International differences in work-related values*. Beverly Hills, CA: Sage.

Hofstede, G. (2001). *Culture's consequences: Comparing values, behaviors, institutions, and organizations across nations* (2nd ed.). Beverly Hills, CA: Sage.

Holmes, R. L. (1971). Violence and nonviolence. In J. A. Shaffer (Ed.), *Violence: Award-winning essays in the Council for Philosophical Studies Competition* (pp. 101–135). New York: David McKay Company, Inc.

Holmes, R. L. (Ed.). (1990). *Nonviolence in theory and practice*. Belmont, CA: Wadsworth Publishing Company.

Holmes, R. L., & Gan, B. L. (Eds.). (2005). *Nonviolence in theory and practice* (2nd ed.). Long Grove, IL: Waveland Press.

Homans, G. C. (1961). *Social behavior: Its elementary forms*. New York: Harcourt.

Horowitz, R., & Schwartz, G. (1974). Honor, normative ambiguity and gang violence. *American Sociological Review, 39*, 238–251.

Houar, M. A. (1984). Nonviolent societies and non-killing warfare: The case of American Indian tribal groups. *Social Alternatives, 4*(1), 49–54.

Hossain, S., & Welchman, L. (Eds.). (2005). 'Honour': Crimes, paradigms, and violence against women. London: Zed Books.

Hossner, R. M., Osterberg, L. D., Crea, J. A., Mayton, D. M., Ridinger, A. M., Smith, K. A., Boyer, A. A., & Dingman, R. M. (2004). *Adolescent values and nonviolence: Relationships in the new millennium*. Paper presented at the Annual Meeting of the American Psychological Association, Honolulu, HI, USA.

Hoyek, D., Sidawi, R. R., & Mrad, A. A. (2005). Murders of women in Lebanon: 'Crimes of honour' between reality and law. In S. Hossain & L. Welchman (Eds.), 'Honour': Crimes, paradigms, and violence against women (pp. 111–136). London: Zed Books.

Huddleston, J. (1998). *The search for a just society*. New Delhi: Sterling Publishers.

Hull, E. A. (2006). *The disenfranchisement of ex-felons*. Philadelphia, PA: Temple University Press.

Hunt, S. C. (2002). *The future of peace: On the front lines with the world's great peacemakers*. San Francisco: Harper Collins.

Hunter, D. (1990). On the Bhagavad-Gita. In R. L. Holmes (Ed.), *Nonviolence in theory and practice* (pp. 16–19). Belmont, CA: Wadsworth Publishing Company.

Inglehart, R. (1991). *Culture shift in advanced industrial society*. Princeton, NJ: Princeton University Press.

James, W. (1995/1910). The moral equivalent of war. *Peace and Conflict: Journal of Peace Psychology*. *1*, 17–26.

Jensen-Campbell, L. A., Gleason, K. A., Adams, R., & Malcolm, K. T. (2003). Interpersonal conflict, agreeableness, and personality development. *Journal of Personality*, *71*(6), 1059–1085.

Jensen-Campbell, L. A., & Graziano, W. G. (2001). Agreableness as a moderator of interpersonal conflict. *Journal of Personality*, *69*(2), 323–362.

Johnson, D. W. (1974). Communication and the inducement of cooperative behavior in conflicts: A critical review. *Speech Monographs*, *41*, 64–78.

Johnson, D. W. (2003). Social interdependence: Interrelationships among theory, research, and practice. *American Psychologist*, *58*, 934–945.

Johnson, D. W., & Johnson, R. T. (1979). Conflict in the classroom: Controversy and learning. *Review of Educational Research*, *49*, 51–70.

Johnson, D. W., & Johnson, R. T. (1995a). *Teaching students to be peacemakers*. Edina, MN: Interaction Book Company.

Johnson, D. W., & Johnson, R. T. (1995b). Teaching students to be peacemakers: Results of five years of research. *Peace and Conflict: Journal of Peace Psychology*, *1*(4), 417–438.

Johnson, D. W., & Johnson, R. T. (1995c). Social interdependence: Cooperative learning in education. In B. B Bunker, & J. Z. Rubin (Eds.), *Conflict, cooperation, and justice: Essays inspired by the work of Morton Deutsch* (pp. 205–251). San Francisco, CA: Jossey-Bass.

Johnson, D. W., & Johnson, R. T. (1996). Reducing school violence through conflict resolution training. *NASSP Bulletin*, *80*(579), 11–18.

Johnson, D. W., & Johnson, R. T. (2001). Peer mediation in an inner-city elementary school. *Urban Education*, *36*(2), 165–178.

Johnson, D. W., & Johnson, R. T. (2003). Field testing integrative negotiations. *Peace and Conflict: Journal of Peace Psychology*, *9*(1), 39–68.

Johnson, D. W., & Johnson, R. T. (2006). Peace education for consensual peace: The essential role of conflict resolution. *Journal of Peace Education*, *3*(2), 147–174.

Johnson, D. W., Johnson, R. T., Dudley, B., & Magnuson, D. (1995). Training elementary school students to manage conflicts. *The Journal of School Psychology*, *135*(6), 673–686.

Johnson, D. W., Johnson, R. T., Dudley, B., Ward, M., & Magnuson, D. (1995). The impact of peer mediation training on the management of school and home conflicts. *American Educational Research Journal*, *32*(4), 829–844.

Johnson, P., Adair, E., Bommersbach, M., Callandra, J., Huey, M., & Kelly, A. (1998, August). *Nonviolence: Constructing a multidimensional attitude measure*. Paper Presented at the Annual Meeting of the American Psychological Association, San Francisco, CA, USA.

Johnson, D. W., Johnson, R. T., & Tjosvold, D. (2000). Constructive controversy: The value of intellectual opposition. In M. Deutsch P. T. Coleman, (Eds.) *The handbook of conflict resolution: Theory and practice* (pp. 65–85). San Francisco, CA: Jossey-Bass.

Jonas, E., Schimel, J., Greenberg, J., & Pyszczynski, T. (2002). The scrooge effect: Evidence that mortality salience increases prosocial attitudes and behavior. *Personality and Social Psychology Bulletin*, *28*(10), 1342–1353.

Jones, J. M. (2006). From racial inequality to social justice: The legacy of *Brown v. Board* and lessons from South Africa. *Journal of Social Issues*, *62*(4), 885–909.

Jones, T. S. (2004). Conflict resolution education: The field, the findings, and the future. *Conflict Resolution Quarterly*, *22* (1–2), 233–267.

Jones, W. H., Couch, L., and Scott, S. (1997). Trust and betrayal. In R. Hogan, J. Johnson, & S. Briggs (Eds.) *Handbook of personality psychology* (pp. 465–482). San Diego, CA: Academic.

Kadayifçi-Orellana, S. A. (2003). Religion, violence, and the Islamic tradition of nonviolence. *The Turkish Yearbook*, *34*, 23–62.

Kagee, A., Naidoo, A. V., & Van Wyk, S. (2003). Building communities of peace: The South African experience. *International Journal for the Advancement of Counseling, 24*(4), 225–233.

Kalayjian, A. (1999). Forgiveness and transcendence. *Clio's Psyche, 6*(3), 116–119.

Karatnycky, A. (2005). Ukraine's Orange Revolution. *Foreign Affairs, 84*(2), 35–52.

Kassin, S., Fein, S., & Markus, H. R. (2008). *Social psychology* (7th ed.). Boston, MA: Houghton Mifflin.

Keashly, L. & Warters, W. C. (2000). Working it out: Conflicts in interpersonal context. In L. J. Fisk & J. L. Schellenberg (Eds.), *Patterns of conflict: Paths to peace* (pp. 35–65). Peterborough, ON: Broadview Press, Ltd.

Kelly, P. K. (1994). *Thinking green! Essays on environmentalism, feminism, and nonviolence.* Berkeley, CA: Parallax Press.

Kelman, H. C. (1972). The problem-solving workshop in conflict resolution. In R. L.Merritt (Ed.), *Communication in international politics.* (pp. 168–204). Urbana: University of Illinois Press.

Kelman, H. C. (1982). Creating the conditions for Israeli-Palestinian negotiations. *Journal of Conflict Resolution, 26*(1), 39–75.

Kelman, H. C. (1996). Negotiation as interactive problem solving. *International Negotiation: A Journal of Theory and Practice, 1*(1), 99–123.

Kelman, H. C. (1997). Group processes in the resolution of international conflicts: Experiences from the Israeli–Palestinian case. *American Psychologist, 52*, 212–220.

Kelman, H. C. (1999). Interactive problem solving as a metaphor for international conflict resolution: Lessons for the policy process. *Peace and Conflict: Journal of Peace Psychology, 5*(3), 201–218.

Kelman, H. C. (2007). The Israeli-Palestinian peace process and its vicissitudes: Insights from attitude theory. *American Psychologist, 62*(4), 287–303.

Keniston, A. H. (1990). Dimensions of moral development among nonviolent individuals. In V. K. Kool (Ed.), *Perspectives on nonviolence* (pp. 86–89). New York: Springer.

Kennedy, R. S. (1990). The Druze of the Golan: A case of nonviolent resistance. In R. L. Holmes (Ed.), *Nonviolence in theory and practice* (pp. 193–203). Belmont, CA: Wadsworth Publishing Company.

Khondker, H. H. (2001a). Environmental movements, civil society, and globalization: An introduction. *Asian Journal of Social Science, 29*(1), 1–8.

Khondker, H. H. (2001b). Environment and the global civil society. *Asian Journal of Social Science, 29*(1), 53–71.

Kimelman, R. (1981). Nonviolence in the Talmud. In A. Solomonow, (Ed.), *Roots of Jewish Nonviolence* (pp. 24–49). Nyack, NY: Jewish Peace Fellowship.

Kimelman, R. (2005). Nonviolence in the Talmud. In R. L. Holmes B. Gan (Ed.), *Nonviolence in theory and practice* (pp. 23–32). Belmont, CA: Wadsworth Publishing Company.

Kimmel, P. K. (1995). Sustainability and cultural understanding: Peace psychologyas public interest science. *Peace and Conflict: Journal of Peace Psychology, 1*(2), 101–116.

Kimmel, P. K. (2001). Conflict and culture. In M. Deutsch & P. T. Coleman (Eds.), *The handbook of conflict resolution: Theory and practice* (pp. 453–474). San Francisco, CA: Jossey-Bass.

King, C. S. (1969). *My life with Martin Luther King Jr.* New York: Holt, Rinehart, and Winston.

King, M. L. (1963). *Why we can't wait.* New York: Harper & Row.

King, M. L. (1990/1963). Letter from Birmingham jail. In R. L. Holmes (Ed.), *Nonviolence in theory and practice* (pp. 69–77). Belmont, CA: Wadsworth Publishing Company.

King, M. L. (1992/1967). A time to break silence. In J. M. Washington (Ed.), *I have a dream: Writings and speeches that changed the world* (pp. 135–152). Sunnyvale, CA: Scott Foresman.

King, M. L. (2000/1958). My pilgrimage to nonviolence. In W. Wink (Ed.), *Peace is the way: Writings on nonviolence from the Fellowship of Reconciliation* (pp. 64–71). Maryknoll, NY: Orbis Books.

King, M. L. (2002/1967). Declaration of independence from the war in Vietnam. In H. Zinn (Ed.), *The power of nonviolence: Writings of advocates of peace* (pp. 113–124). Boston, MA: Beacon Press.

King, S. B. (2000). Engaged Buddhism: Gandhi's ahimsa in practice. In G. S. Harak (Ed.), *Nonviolence for the third millennium* (pp. 101–119). Macon, GA: Mercer University Press.

Klare, M. T. (2001). *Resource wars: The new landscape of global conflict.* New York: Metropolitan Books.

Kluckholn, C. (1951). Values and value-orientations in the theory of actions. In T. Parsons & E. A. Shils (Eds.), *Toward a general theory of action* (pp. 388–433). Cambridge, MA: Harvard University Press.

Kluckholn, F. R., & Stodtbeck, F. L. (1961). *Variations in value orientations.* Westport, CT: Greenwood Press.

Kohn, C., Hasty, S., & Henderson, C. W. (2004, August 12). AIDS-related episodes on TV program increase calls to CDC AIDS hotline. [Electronic version] *Women's Health Weekly*, 10.

Kolko, G. (1995). *Century of war: Politics, conflicts, and society since 1914.* New York: New Press.

Konen, K., Mayton, D. M., Delva, Z., Sonnen, M., Dahl, W., & Montgomery, R. (1999, August). *The Teenage Nonviolence Test: Concurrent and discriminant validity.* Paper presented at the Annual Meeting of the American Psychological Association, Boston, MA, USA.

Kool, V. K. (Ed.). (1990). *Perspectives on nonviolence.* New York: Springer.

Kool, V. K. (Ed.). (1993a). *Nonviolence: Social and psychological issues.* New York: University Press of America, Inc.

Kool, V. K. (1993b). Toward a theory of the psychology of nonviolence. In V. K. Kool (Ed.), *Nonviolence: Social and psychological issues* (pp. 1–24). New York: University Press of America, Inc.

Kool, V. K. (2008). *Psychology of non-violence and aggression.* New York: Palgrave Macmillan

Kool, V. K. & Keyes, C. L. M. (1990). Explorations in the nonviolent personality. In V. K. Kool (Ed.), *Perspectives on nonviolence* (pp. 17–38). New York: Springer.

Kool, V. K. & Sen, M. (1984). The nonviolence test. In D. M. Pestonjee (Ed.) *Second handbook of psychological and social instruments.* Ahemdebad: Indian Institute of Management.

Kotz, N. (2005). *Judgment days: Lyndon Baines Johnson, Martin Luther King Jr., and the laws that changed America.* Boston, MA: Houghton Mifflin Company.

Kraft, K. (Ed.). (1992a). *Inner peace, world peace: Essays on Buddhism and nonviolence.* Albany, NY: State University of New York Press.

Kraft, K. (1992b). Prospects of a socially engaged Buddhism. In K. Kraft (Ed.), *Inner peace, world peace: Essays on Buddhism and nonviolence* (pp. 11–30). Albany, NY: State University of New York Press.

Kriedler, W. (1997). *Conflict resolution in the middle school.* Cambridge, MA: Educators for Social Responsibility.

Kriesberg, L. (2007). *Constructive conflicts: From escalation to resolution* (3rd ed.). Lanham, MD: Rowman & Littlefield.

Kritz, N. J. (2001). The rule of law in the postconflict phase: Building a stable peace. In C. A. Crocker (Ed.), *Turbulent peace: The challenges of managing international conflict* (pp.801–820). Washington, DC: United States Institute of Peace.

Krug, G. E., Dahlberg, L. L., Mercy, A. J., Zwi, A., & Lozano, R. (Eds.). (2002). *World report on violence and health.* Geneva: World Health Organization.

Lakey, G. (1968). Technique and ethos in nonviolent action: The Woman Suffrage case. *Sociological Inquiry, 38*(1), 37–42.

Leary, T. (1957). *Interpersonal diagnosis of personality.* New York: Ronald Press.

Lederach, J. P. (2001). Civil society and reconciliation. In C. A. Crocker (Ed.), *Turbulent peace: The challenges of managing international conflict* (pp. 841–854). Washington, DC: United States Institute of Peace.

Lee, A. A. (Ed.). (1986). *Circle of Peace: Reflections on the Bahá'í Teachings.* Los Angeles, CA: Kalimát Press.

Lerner, M. (2003). *Healing Israel/Palestine: A path to peace and reconciliation.* Berkeley, CA: Tikkun Books.

Lerner, M. (2006). *The left hand of God: Taking back our country from the religious right.* San Francisco: Harper Collins Publishers.

Lerner, M. (2008). *Global Marshall Plan FAQ.* Retrieved June 3, 2008, from http://www.spiritualprogressives.org/staticpages/index.php?page=20080102191329956

Leung, K., Bond, M. H., Carrasquel, S. R., Munoz, C., Hernandez, M., Murakami, F., Yamaguchi, S., Bierbrauer, G., & Singelis, T. (2002). Social axioms: The search for universal dimensions of general beliefs about how the world functions. *Journal of Cross-Cultural Psychology. 33*(3), 286–302

Lester, R. C. (1987). *Buddhism: The path to nirvana.* San Francisco: Harper and Row Publishers.

Leviton, S. C., & Greenstone, J. L. (1997). *Elements of mediation.* Pacific Grove, CA: Brooks/Cole Publishing.

Lewicki, R. J., & Bunker, B. B. (1995). Trust in relationships: A model of development and decline. In B. B Bunker, & J. Z. Rubin (Eds.), *Conflict, cooperation, and justice: Essays inspired by the work of Morton Deutsch* (pp. 133–173). San Francisco, CA: Jossey-Bass.

Lewicki, R. J., & Wiethoff, C. (2000). Trust, trust development, and trust repair. In M. Deutsch & P. T. Coleman (Eds.), *The handbook of conflict resolution: Theory and practice* (pp. 86–107). San Francisco, CA: Jossey-Bass.

Lewin, K. (1997/1951). *Resolving social conflicts & field theory in social science.* Washington, DC: American Psychological Association.

Lewis, J. J. (2007). *International woman suffrage timeline.* Retrieved June 3, 2008, from http://womenshistory.about.com/od/suffrage/a/intl_timeline.htm

Lichton, I. (2001). Jewish. In G. D. Paige & S. Gilliatt (Eds.), *Nonviolence in Hawaii's spiritual traditions* (pp. 13–27). Honolulu, HI: Center for Global Nonviolence, Inc.Retrieved June 11, 2008, from http://www.globalnonviolence.org/nv_hawaii_spirit.htm

Lidz, V. (1968). A note on "Nonviolence is two". *Sociological Inquiry, 38*(1), 31–36.

Lieber, C. M. (1998). *Making Choices About Conflict, Security, and Peacemaking: A High School Conflict Resolution Curriculum. Part I: Personal Perspectives.* Cambridge, MA: Educators for Social Responsibility.

Lieberman, R. C. (2006). Disenfranchisement and its impact on the political system. In R. M. Valelly (Ed.), *The Voting Rights Act: Securing the ballot* (pp. 21–36). Washington, DC: CQ Press.

Lieberman, J. D., Solomon, S. Greenberg, J., McGregor, H. A., (1999). A hot new way to measure aggression: Hot sauce allocation. *Aggressive behavior, 25*, 331–348.

Likhotal, A. (2007). Building a global culture of peace and sustainability. *Social Alternatives, 26*(3), 31–33.

Lindskold, S. (1986). GRIT: Reducing distrust through carefully introduced conciliation. In S. Worchel W. G. Austin (Eds.), *Psychology of intergroup relations* (2nd ed., pp. 305–322). Chicago: Nelson Hall.

Lipschutz, R. D. (2002). Sustainable development: Implications for world peace. *International Journal of Humanities and Peace, 18*(1), 32–37.

Little, D. (1995). Introduction. In Smock, D. R. (Ed.), *Perspectives on pacifism: Christian, Jewish, and Muslim views on nonviolence and international conflict* (pp.3–9). Washington, DC: United States Institute of Peace Press.

Looney, J. (1995). *Workbook for the Course in Peaceful Conflict Resolution "Alternatives to Violence"* Akron, OH: Peace Grows, Inc.

Lopez, S. J., & Snyder, C. R. (Eds.). (2003). *Positive psychological assessment: A handbook of models and measures.* Washington, DC: American psychological Association.

Lorentz, T. (2006). Developing a Global Marshall Plan: A blueprint for global economic renewal. *Journal of Globalization for the Common Good.* Retrieved June 1, 2008, from http://lass.calumet.purdue.edu/cca/jgcg/2006/fa06/jgcg-fa06-lorentz-gmp.htm

Lykes, M. B. (2001). Human rights violations as structural violence. In D. J. Christie, R. V. Wagner, & D. D. Winter (Eds.), *Peace, conflict, and violence: Peace psychology for the 21st century* (pp. 158–167), Upper Saddle River, NJ: Prentice-Hall.

Lynd, S. & Lynd, A. (Eds.) (1995). *Nonviolence in America: A documentary history* (2nd ed.). Maryknoll, NY: Orbis Books.

Macapagal, E. J., & Nario-Galace, J. (2003) Social psychology of People Power II in the Philippines. *Peace and Conflict: Journal of Peace Psychology, 9*(3), 219–233.

MacNair, R. M. (2003). *The psychology of peace: An introduction.* Westport, CT: Praeger.

Macy, J. (1983). *Despair and personal power in the nuclear age*. Philadelphia, PA: New Society Publishers.

Macy, J. (2000). Taking heart: Spiritual exercises from social activists. In W. Wink (Ed.), *Peace is the way: Writings on nonviolence from the Fellowship of Reconciliation* (pp. 135–142). Mary Knoll, NY: Orbis Books.

Maio, G. R., Thomas, G., Fincham, F. D., & Carnelley, K. B. (2008). Unraveling the role of forgiveness in family relationships. *Journal of Personality and Social Psychology, 94*(2), 307–319.

Manza, J., & Ugggen, C. (2006). *Locked out: Felon disenfranchisement and American democracy*. New York: Oxford University Press.

Martin, B. (2005). Researching nonviolent action: Past themes and future possibilities. *Peace & Change, 30*(2), 247–270.

Mathews, G., Deary, I. J., & Whiteman, M. C. (2003). *Personality traits* (2nd ed.). Cambridge: Cambridge University Press.

Mattis, J. F. (2004). Spirituality [religiousness, faith, purpose]. In C. Peterson & M. E. P. Seligman (Eds.), *Character strengths and virtues: A handbook and classification* (pp. 599–622). Washington DC: American Psychological Association.

May, R. (1972). *Power and innocence*. New York: Harper.

Mayor, F. (1995). How psychology can contribute to a culture of peace. *Peace and Conflict: Journal of Peace Psychology, 1*(1), 3–9.

Mayton, D. M. (1987a, July). *Value-attitude relationships regarding peace and national security in adolescents*. Paper presented at the Annual Meeting of the International Society of Political Psychology, San Francisco, CA, USA.

Mayton, D. M. (1987b). Values and nuclear freeze attitudes: Some value-attitude relationships in adolescents. *Contemporary Social Psychology, 12*(3),111–114.

Mayton, D. M. (1989a, April). *Spontaneous concern about nuclear war: Value priority differences in adolescents*. Paper presented at the Annual Meeting of the Western Psychological Association, Reno, NV. (ERIC Document Reproduction Service No. ED 312 178).

Mayton, D. M. (1989b, August). *Values, enemy images and political activist behavior*. Paper presented at the Annual Meeting of the American Psychological Association, New Orleans, LA, USA.

Mayton, D. M. (1992a). Value priority differences across levels of nuclear threat concern. *Journal of Social Psychology. 132*(4), 539–541.

Mayton, D. M. (1992b, August). *The value structure of nonviolent personality predispositions*. Paper presented at the Annual Meeting of the American Psychological Association, Washington, DC, USA. (ERIC Document Reproduction Service No. ED 353 194)

Mayton, D. M. (1994, August). *Values and nonviolent personality predispositions: A replication of correlational connections*. Paper presented at the Annual Meeting of the American Psychological Association, Los Angeles, CA, USA.

Mayton, D. M. (2000). Gandhi as peacebuilder: The social psychology of satyagraha. In D. Christie, R. Wagner, & D. D. Winter, *Peace, conflict, and violence: Peace psychology for the 21st century* (pp. 307–313). Englewood Cliffs, NJ: Prentice-Hall.

Mayton, D. M. (2001). Nonviolence within cultures of peace: A means and an ends. *Peace and Conflict: Journal of Peace Psychology, 7*(2), 143–155.

Mayton, D. M. (2009). Gandhian theory of non-violence. In N. Young (Ed.), *International encyclopedia of peace*. New York: Oxford University Press

Mayton, D. M., Ball-Rokeach, S. J., & Loges, W. E. (1994). Human values and social issues: An introduction. *Journal of Social Issues, 50*(4), 1–8.

Mayton, D. M., Craig, D. T., Solom, R. C., Cattron R. T., Buckner B. J., & Fukuchi, S. (2008, August). *Replicating and extending the profile of a peaceful person*. Paper presented at the Annual Meeting of the American Psychological Association, San Francisco, CA.

Mayton, D. M., Diessner, R., & Granby, C. A. (1993). Nonviolence and moral reasoning. *Journal of Social Psychology, 133*(5), 745–746.

Mayton, D. M., Diessner, R., & Granby, C. A. (1996). Nonviolence and values: Empirical support for theoretical relationships. *Peace and Conflict: Journal of Peace Psychology. 2*(3), 245–253.

Mayton, D. M., & Furnham, A. (1991, August). *Value underpinnings of antinuclear political activism: A cross national study*. Paper presented at the Annual Meeting of the American Psychological Association, San Francisco, CA, USA.

Mayton, D. M., & Furnham, A. (1994). Value underpinnings of antinuclear political activism: A cross-national study. *Journal of Social Issues, 50*(4), 117–128.

Mayton, D. M., Nogle, K. S., Mack, J. L., Maxcy, R. T., Weeks, R. G., Hamilton, D. L., Morton, C. M., Mineshita, T., & Nawata, A. (1998, August). *Teenage nonviolence test: A new measure of nonviolence*. Paper presented at the Annual Meeting of the American Psychological Association, San Francisco, CA, USA.

Mayton, D. M., Peters, D. J., & Owens, R. W. (1999). Values, militarism, and nonviolent predispositions. *Peace and Conflict: Journal of Peace Psychology, 5*(1), 69–77.

Mayton, D. M., Richel, T. W., Susnjic, S., & Majdanac, M. (2002, August). *Measuring the nonviolent tendencies of college students*. Paper presented at the Annual Meeting of the American Psychological Association, Chicago, USA. (ERIC Document Reproduction Service No. ED 468 267)

Mayton, D. M. & Sangster, R. L. (1992). Cross-cultural comparison of values and nuclear war attitudes. *Journal of Cross Cultural Psychology. 23*(3), 340–352.

Mayton, D. M., Solom, R. C., Wilder, A. M., Sawa, M., Stephens, A., Smith, H. L., & Garrison, M. T. (2007, August). *An view of a "peaceful person"*. Paper presented at the Annual Meeting of the American Psychological Association, San Francisco, CA.

Mayton, D. M., Susnjic, S., Palmer, B. J., Peters, D. J. Gierth, R., & Caswell, R. N. (2002). The measurement of nonviolence: A review. *Peace and Conflict: Journal of Peace Psychology, 8*(4), 343–354.

Mayton, D. M., Weedman, J., Sonnen, J., Grubb, C., & Hirose, M. (1999, August). *The Teenage Nonviolence Test: Internal structure and reliability*. Paper presented at the Annual Meeting of the American Psychological Association, Boston, MA, USA.

Mazurana, D., & McKay, S. (2001). Women, girls, and structural violence: A global analysis. In D. J. Christie, R. V. Wagner, & D. D. Winter (Eds.), *Peace, conflict, and violence: Peace psychology for the 21st century* (pp. 130–138.Upper Saddle River, NJ: Prentice-Hall.

McCartney, C. (1999). The role of civil society. *Conciliation Resources*. Retrieved May 30, 2008, from http://www.c-r.org/our-work/accord/northern-ireland/civil-society.php

McCarthy, R. M., & Kruegler, C. (1993). *Toward research and theory building in the study of nonviolent action*. (Monograph Series Number 7) Cambridge, MA: The Albert Einstein Institute.

McCarthy, R. M., & Sharp, G. (1997). *Nonviolent action: A research guide*. New York: Garland Press

McCasland, S. V., Cairns, G. E., & Yu, D. C. (1969). *Religions of the world*. New York: Random House.

McClain, P. D., Brady, M. C., Carter, N. M., Perez, E. O., & Soto, V. M. D. (2006). Rebuilding black voting rights before the Voting Rights Act. In R. M. Valelly (Ed.), *The Voting Rights Act: Securing the ballot* (pp. 57–75). Washington, DC: CQ Press.

McGranahan, D. (1995). Measurement of development: Research Institute for Social Development. *International Social Science Journal, 47*(1), 39–59.

McGregor, H. A., Lieberman, J. D., Greenberg, J., Solomon, S. Arendt, J., Simon, L., & Pyszczynski, T. (1998). Terror management and aggression: Evidence that mortality salience motivates aggression against worldview-threatening others. *Journal of Personality and Social Psychology, 74*(3), 590–605.

McKay, S. (1996). Gendering peace psychology. *Peace and Conflict: Journal of Peace Psychology, 2*(2), 93–107.

McKay, S. (1998). The effect of armed conflict on girls and women. *Peace and Conflict: Journal of Peace Psychology, 4*(4), 381–392.

McKay, S. (2005). Girls as "weapons of terror" in Northern Uganda and Sierra Leonean rebel fighting forces. *Studies in Conflict and Terrorism, 28*, 385–397.

McKay, S., & Mazurana, D. (2001). Gendering peacebuilding. In D. J. Christie, R. V. Wagner, & D. D. Winter (Eds.), *Peace, conflict, and violence: Peace psychology for the 21st century* (pp. 341–349). Upper Saddle River, NJ: Prentice-Hall.

McKnight, M. S. (1995). Divorce and child-custody mediation. In M. S. Umbreit, *Mediating interpersonal conflicts: A pathway to peace*. (87–113), West Concord, MN: CPI Publishing.

Mead, M. (1940). *Warfare is only an invention: Not a biological necessity*. ASIA, XL.

Mehrotra, R. (Ed.). (2005). *The essential Dalai Lama: His important teachings*. New York: Penguin Books.

Mendelsohn, M., & Straker, G. (1998). Child soldiers: Psychosocial implications of the Graça Machel/UN Study. *Peace and Conflict: Journal of Peace Psychology, 4*(4), 399–413.

Merton, T. (2000). Blessed are the meek: The roots of Christian nonviolence. In W. Wink, (Ed.), *Peace is the way: Writings on nonviolence from the Fellowship of Reconciliation* (pp. 41–45). Mary Knoll, NY: Orbis Books.

ME WE (2007). *Peace: The words and inspiration of Mahatma Gandhi*. Boulder, CO: Blue Mountain Press.

Milgrom, J. (1998). "Let your love for me vanquish your hatred for him": Nonviolence and modern Judaism. In D. L. Smith-Christopher (Ed.), *Subverting hatred: The challenge of nonviolence in religious traditions* (pp. 115–139). Cambridge, MA: Boston Research Center for the 21st Century.

Miller, R. B. (1971). Violence force, and coercion. In J. A. Shaffer (Ed.), *Violence: Award-winning essays in the Council for Philosophical Studies Competition* (pp. 9–44). New York: David McKay Company, Inc.

Miller, J., & Kenedi, A. (Eds.). (2002). *Inside Islam: The faith, the people, and the conflicts of the world's fastest growing religion*. New York: Marlowe & Company.

Moghaddam, F. M. (1998). *Social psychology: Exploring universals across cultures*. New York: W. H. Freeman and Company.

Mohammed, S. (2001). Personal communication networks and the effects of an entertainment-education radio soap opera in Tanzania. *Journal of Health Communication, 6*, 137–154.

Monroe, C. R. (1995). *World religions: An introduction*. Amherst, NY: Prometheus Books.

Morse, P. S., & Andrea, R. (1994). Peer mediation in the schools: Teaching conflict resolution techniques to students. *NASSP Bulletin, 78*(560), 75–82.

Montagu, A. (Ed.). (1978). *Learning non-aggression: The experience of non-literate societies*. New York: Oxford University Press.

Montiel, C. J. (2006). Political psychology of nonviolent democratic transitions in Southeast Asia. *Journal of Social Issues, 62*(1), 173–190.

Mortenson, G., & Relin, D. O. (2006). *Three cups of tea: One man's mission to promote peace... one school at a time*. New York: Penguin Books.

Muhaiyaddeen, M. R. B. (1987). *Islam and world peace: Explanations of a sufi*. Philadelphia, PA: Fellowship Press.

Mullojanov, P. (2001). Civil society and peacebuilding. *Conciliation Resources*. Retrieved May 30, 2008, from http://www.c-r.org/our-work/accord/tajikistan/civil-society-peacebuilding.php

Muste, A. J. (2000). Pacifism and class war. In W. Wink, (Ed.), *Peace is the way: Writings on nonviolence from the Fellowship of Reconciliation* (pp. 4–7). Mary Knoll, NY: Orbis Books.

Myers, D. G. (2001). *Psychology: Myers in modules* (6th ed.). New York: Worth Publishers.

Naess, A. (2005). Nonviolent communication in group conflicts: An intramural note. *The Trumpeter, 21*(1), 129–133.

Nagel Lechman, B. A. (1997). *Conflict and resolution*. New York: Aspen Law & Business Publishers.

Nakhre, A. W. (1982). *Social psychology of nonviolent action: A study of three satyagrahas*. Delhi, India: Chanakya Publications.

Nelson, L. L. (2003, August). *Perspective taking and empathic concern predict peaceful tendencies*. Paper presented at the Annual Meeting of the American Psychological Association, Toronto, Canada.

Nelson, L. L. (2005, August). *A framework for a peaceful person*. Paper presented at the Annual Meeting of the American Psychological Association, Washington, DC, USA.

Nelson, L. L. (2007, August). *Correlations between inner peace, interpersonal behavior, and global attitudes.* Paper presented at the Annual Meeting of the American Psychological Association, San Francisco, CA, USA.

Nelson, L. L., & Christie, D. J. (1995). Peace in the psychology curriculum: Moving from assimilation to accommodation. *Peace and Conflict: Journal of Peace Psychology, 1,* 161–178.

Nelson, L. L., Van Slyck, M. R., & Cardella, L. A. (1999a). Curricula for teaching adolescents about peace and conflict. *Peace and Conflict: Journal of Peace Psychology, 5,* 169–174.

Nelson, L. L., Van Slyck, M. R., & Cardella, L. A. (1999b). Peace and conflict curricula for adolescents. In L. R. Forcey & I. M. Harris (Eds.), *Peacebuilding for adolescents: Strategies for educators and community leaders* (pp. 91–117). New York: Peter Lang Publishing, Inc.

Network of Spiritual Progressives (2007). *The Global Marshall Plan.* Retrieved June 3, 2008, at http://www.spiritualprogressives.org/article.php?story=20070228183252814

Network of Spiritual Progressives (n.d.). *The Global Marshall Plan: A national security strategy of generosity and care.* Retrieved June 3, 2008, from link at http://www.spiritualprogressives.org/article.php?story=20070228183252814

Nevo, B., & Brem, I. (2002). Peace education programs and the evaluation of their effectiveness. In G. Salomon, & B. Nevo (Eds.), *Peace education: The concept, principles, and practices around the world* (pp. 271–282). Mahwah, NJ: Lawrence Erlbaum Associates.

Ng, S. M., Yau, J. K. Y., Chan, C. L. W., Chan, C. H. Y., & Ho, D. Y. F. (2005). The measurement of body-mind-spirit well-being: Toward multidimensional and transcultural applicability. *Social Work in Health Care, 41*(1), 33–52.

Niwano, N. (1977). *A Buddhist approach to peace.* Tokyo: Kosei Publishing Company.

Novaco, R. (1975). *Anger control: The development and evaluation of an experimental treatment.* Lexington, MA: Lexington Books.

Oishi, M. (2002) Creating a 'Ripe Moment' in the Burmese conflict through nonviolent action. *Social Alternatives, 21*(2), 52–60.

Okorodudu, C. (1998). A children's rights perspective on the Graca Machel study. *Peace and Conflict: Journal of Peace Psychology, 4*(4), 349–363.

O'Moore, M. (n.d.) *Defining violence: Toward a pupil based definition.* Retrieved October 24, 2008, from http://www.comune.torino.it/novasres/_private/Violencedefinition.PDF

Ong, A. D., & Van Dulmen, M. H. M. (Eds.). (2007). *Oxford handbook of methods in positive psychology.* New York: Oxford University Press.

Opotow, S. (1990). Moral exclusion and injustice: An introduction. *Journal of Social Issues, 46*(1), 1–20.

Osborn, W. S. (2000). United Nations University for Peace in Costa Rica: History and prospects. *Peace & Change, 25*(3), 309–338.

Osgood, C. E. (1962). *An alternative to war or surrender.* Urbana, IL: The University of Illinois Press.

Paige, G. D., Satha-Anand, C., & Gilliatt, S. (Eds.). (1993). *Islam and nonviolence.* Honolulu, HI: Center for Global Nonviolence, Inc. Retrieved June 17, 2008, from http://www.globalnonviolence.org/islam.htm

Paige, G. D., & Gilliatt, S. (Eds.). (2001). *Nonviolence in Hawaii's spiritual traditions.* Honolulu, HI: Center for Global Nonviolence, Inc. Retrieved June 11, 2008, from http://www.globalnonviolence.org/nv_hawaii_spirit.htm

Patfoort, P. (1987). *An introduction to nonviolence: A conceptual framework.* Nyack, NY: Fellowship of Reconciliation.

Patfoort, P. (2002). *Making transformations towards nonviolent conflict management concrete: The power in each of us.* Paper downloaded May 31, 2007 from http://www.patpatfoort.be/Article%201.pdf.

Payton, J. W., Wardlaw, D. M., Graczyk, P. A., Bloodworth, M. R., Tompsett, C. J., & Weissberg, R. P. (2000). Social and emotional learning: A framework for promoting mental health and reducing risk behavior in children and youth. *Journal of School Health, 70*(5), 179–185.

Pelle, T. (2001). Bahá'í. In G. D. Paige, & S. Gilliatt (Eds.), *Nonviolence in Hawaii's spiritual traditions* (pp. 13–27). Honolulu, HI: Center for Global Nonviolence, Inc. Retrieved June 11, 2008, from http://www.globalnonviolence.org/nv_hawaii_spirit.htm

Pelley S. (2008, January 27). CBS 60 Minutes interview with FBI Agent George Piro. New York: CBS News. Retrieved June 4, 2008, from http://search.cbsnews.com/?source=cbs&q=interrogation+of+Saddam+Hussein&x=21&y=17

Pelton, L. H. (1974). *The psychology of nonviolence*. New York: Pergamon Press.

Perkins, D. (2002). Paradoxes of peace and the prospects of peace education. In G. Salomon & B. Nevo (Eds.), *Peace education: The concept, principles, and practices around the world* (pp. 37–53). Mahwah, NJ: Lawrence Erlbaum Associates.

Petersen, R. L. (2001). A theory of forgiveness: Terminology, rhetoric, and the dialectic of interfaith relationships. In R. G. Helmick & R. L. Petersen (Eds.), *Forgiveness and reconciliation: Religion, public policy, and conflict transformation* (pp. 3–25). Philadelphia, PA: Templeton Foundation Press.

Peterson, C. (2006). *A primer of positive psychology*. New York: Oxford University Press.

Peterson, C., & Seligman, M. E. P. (Eds.). (2004). *Character strengths and virtues: A handbook and classification*. Washington, DC: American Psychological Association.

Phares, E. J. (1984). *Introduction to personality*. Columbus, OH: Charles E. Merrill Publishing Company.

Picard, C. A. (2002). *Mediating interpersonal and small group conflict*. Ottawa, ON: The Golden Dog Press.

Piedmont, R. L. (1999). Does spirituality represent a sixth factor of personality? Spiritual transcendence and the Five-Factor Model. *Journal of Personality, 67*, 985–1013.

Pilisuk, M. (2008). *Who benefits from global violence and war: Uncovering a destructive system*. Westport, CT: Praeger Security International.

Pimentel, S., Pandjiarjian, V., & Belloque, J. (2005). The 'legitimate defence of honour', or murder with impunity? A critical study of legislation and case law in Latin America. In S. Hossain & L. Welchman (Eds.). *'Honour': Crimes, paradigms, and violence against women* (pp. 245–262). London: Zed Books.

Plutchik, R. (1962). *The emotions: Facts, theories, and a new model*. New York: Random House.

Porkorny, B. (1984). A worldwide movement for peace. In A. A. Lee (Ed.), *Circle of unity: Bahá'í approaches to current social issues* (pp. 3–20). Los Angeles, CA: Kalimát Press.

Poe, M. A. (2007). Fairness is not enough: Social justice as restoration of right relationships. *Social Work and Christianity, 34*(4), 449–470.

Powell, K. E., Muir-McClain, L., & Halasyamani, L. (1995). A review of selected school-based conflict resolution and peer mediation projects. *Journal of School Health, 65*(10), 426–432.

Poyyamoli, G. (2003). Promotion of peace and sustainability by community based heritage eco-cultural tourism in India. *International Journal of Humanities and Peace, 19*(1), 40–45.

Pratto, F., Sidanius, J., Stallworth, L. M., & Malle, B. F. (1994). Social dominance orientation: A personality variable predicting social and political attitudes. *Journal of Personality and Social Psychology, 67*, 741–763.

Prejean, H. (1995). Dead man walking. In S. Lynd & A. Lynd (Eds.), *Nonviolence in America: A documentary history* (2nd ed., pp. 344–361). Maryknoll, NY: Orbis Books.

Presbey, G. M. (2006). Evaluating the legacy of nonviolence in South Africa. *Peace & Change, 31*(2), 141–174.

Pruitt, D. G., & Carnevale, P. J. (1993). *Negotiation in social conflict*. Pacific Grove, CA: Brooks/Cole Publishing Company.

Putnam, R. D. (2000). *Bowling alone: The collapse and revival of the American community*. New York: Touchstone Books.

Psychology Today. (2006). The anger profile. Retrieved November 15, 2006, from http://psychologytoday.psychtests.com/tests/anger_access.html

Pyszczynski, T., Greenberg, J., & Solomon, S. (1999). A dual-process model of defense against conscious and unconscious death-related thoughts: An extension of terror management theory. *Psychological Review, 106*, 835–845.

Pyszczynski, T., Solomon, S., & Greenberg, J. (2002). *In the wake of 9–11: The psychology of terror*. Washington, DC: American Psychological Association.

Pyszczynski, T., Vail III, K. E., & Motyl, M. S. (In press). The cycle of righteous killing: Psychological forces in the prevention and promotion of peace. In T. Pick & A. Speckhard (Eds.), *Homegrown terrorism: Understanding and addressing the root causes of radicalization among groups with an international heritage.* Amsterdam: IOS Press.

Queen, C. S. (1998). The peace wheel: Nonviolent activism in the Buddhist tradition. In D. L. Smith-Christopher (Ed.), *Subverting hatred: The challenge of nonviolence in religious traditions* (pp. 25–47). Cambridge, MA: Boston Research Center for the 21st Century.

Radermacher, F. J. (Ed.). (2004). Global Marshall Plan: A planetary contract. Hamburg, Germany: Global Marshall Plan Initiative. Retrieved May 30, 2008, from http://www.globalmarshallplan. org/infocenter/texts/the_initiative/index_eng.html

Raven-Roberts, A. (1999). Participation, citizenship and implications of women's activism in the creation of a culture of peace. In I. Breines, D. Gierycz, & B. A. Reardon (Eds.), *Towards a women's agenda for a culture of peace* (pp. 77–86). Paris: UNESCO.

Raviv, A., Oppenheimer, L., & Bar-Tal, D. (Eds.). (1999). *How children understand war and peace: A call for international peace education.* San Francisco, CA: Jossey-Bass.

Reardon, B. A. (1988a). *Comprehensive peace education: Educating for global responsibility.* New York: Teachers College Press.

Reardon, B. A. (Ed.). (1988b). *Educating for global responsibility: Teacher-designed curricula for peace education, K-12.* New York: Teachers College Press.

Renna, T. (1980). Peace education: An historical overview. *Peace & Change, 6*(1–2), 61–65.

Richins, M. L., & Dawson, S. (1992). A consumer values orientation for materialism and its measurement: Scale development and validation. *Journal of Consumer Research, 19*, 303–316.

Ritter, D. P. (2005, August). *A two-dimensional theory of nonviolence.* Paper presented at the Annual meeting of the American Sociological Association, Philadelphia, PA. Retrieved 2006-10–05 from http://www.allacademic.com/meta/p21970_index.html

Robinson, J. P., Shaver, P. R., & Wrightsman, L. S. (Eds.). (1991). *Measures of personality and social psychological attitudes.* San Diego, CA: Academic.

Robinson, J. P., Shaver, P. R., & Wrightsman, L. S. (Eds.) (1999). *Measures of personality and social psychological attitude* (Vol. 2). San Diego, CA: Academic.

Roe, M. D., McKay, S. A., & Wessells, M. G. (2003). Pioneeers in peace psychology: Milton Schwebel. *Peace & Conflict: Journal of Peace Psychology, 9*(4), 305–326.

Roe, M. D., Wessells, M. G., & McKay, S. A. (2006). Pioneeers in U.S. peace psychology: Morton Deutsch. *Peace & Conflict: Journal of Peace Psychology, 12*(4), 309–324.

Rokeach, M. (1968). *Beliefs, attitudes, and values: A theory of organization and change.* San Francisco: Jossey-Bass.

Rokeach, M. (1973). *The nature of human values.* New York: Free Press.

Rokeach, M. (Ed.). (1979). *Understanding human values.* New York: Free Press.

Rokeach, M., & Ball-Rokeach, S. J. (1989). Stability and change in American value priorities, 1968–1981. *American Psychologist, 44*, 775–784.

Rose, J. (2004). The rule of law in the western world: An overview. *Journal of Social Philosophy, 35*(4), 457–470.

Rosenberg, M. B. (2003). *Nonviolent communication; A language of life.* Encinitas, CA: Puddle Dancer Press

Ross, L. & Nisbett, R. E. (1991). *The person and the situation: Perspectives of social psychology.* Philadelphia, PA: Temple University Press.

Ross, M. R., Powell, S. R., Elias, M. J. (2002). New roles for school psychologists: Addressing the social and emotional learning needs of students. *School Psychology Review, 20*(1), 43–52.

Rotter, J. B. (1971). Generalized expectancies for interpersonal trust. *American Psychologist, 26*, 443–452.

Rouhana, N. N., & Kelman, H. C. (1994). Promoting joint thinking in international conflicts: An Israeli–Palestinian Continuing Workshop. *Journal of Social Issues, 50*(1), 157–178.

Rubin, J. Z., Rubin, J. Z. (1994). Models of conflict management. *Journal of Social Issues, 50*(1), 33–45.

Rubin, J. Z., & Levinger, G. (1995). Levels of analysis: In search of generalizable knowledge. In B. B. Bunker, & J. Z Rubin (Eds.), *Conflict, cooperation, and justice: Essays inspired by the work of Morton Deutsch* (pp. 13–38). San Francisco, CA: Jossey-Bass.

Rubin, J. Z., Pruitt, D. G., & Kim, S. H. (1994). *Social conflict: Escalation, stalemate, and settlement* (2nd ed.). New York: McGraw Hill.

Sabol, W. J., Coulton, C. J., & Korbin, J. E. (2004). Building community capacity for violence prevention. *Journal of Interpersonal Violence, 19*(3), 322–340.

Safilios-Rothschild, C. (1969). 'Honour' crimes in contemporary Greece. *British Journal of Sociology, 20*(2), 205–218.

Salamon, L. M., Haddock, M. A., Sokolowski, S. W., & Tice, H. S. (2007). *Measuring civil society and volunteering: Initial findings from implementation of the UN handbook on nonprofit institutions.* (Working Paper No. 23). Baltimore, MD: Johns Hopkins Center for Civil Society Studies. Retrieved on May 29, 2008 at http://www.jhu.edu/ccss/

Salomon, G. (2002). The nature of peace education: Not all programs are created equal. In G. Salomon & B. Nevo (Eds.), *Peace education: The concept, principles, and practices around the world.* (pp. 3–13). Mahwah, NJ: Lawrence Erlbaum Associates.

Salomon, G. (2004). Does peace education make a difference in the context of an intractable conflict? *Peace and Conflict: Journal of Peace Psychology, 10*(3), 257–274.

Salomon, G. (2006). Does peace education *really* make a difference? *Peace and Conflict: Journal of Peace Psychology, 12*(1), 37–48.

Salomon, G., & Nevo, B. (Eds.). (2002). *Peace education: The concept, principles, and practices around the world.* Mahwah, NJ: Lawrence Erlbaum Associates.

Sanson, A., & Bretherton, D. D. (2001). Conflict resolution: Theoretical and practical issues. In D. J. Christie, R. V. Wagner, & D. D. Winter (Eds.), *Peace, conflict, and violence: Peace psychology for the 21st century* (pp. 193–209). Upper Saddle River, NJ: Prentice-Hall.

Satha-Anand, C. (1993). The nonviolent crescent: Eight theses on Muslim nonviolent actions. In G. D. Paige, C. Satha-Anand, & S. Gilliatt (Eds.), *Islam and nonviolence* (pp. 7–26). Honolulu, HI: Center for Global Nonviolence, Inc. Retrieved June 17, 2008, from http://www.globalnonviolence.org/islam.htm

Scholl, S. (Ed.). (2002). *The peace bible: Words from great traditions.* Los Angeles, CA: Kalimát Press.

Schoonmaker, A. (1984). Revisioning the women's movement. In A. A. Lee (Ed.), *Circle of unity: Bahá'í approaches to current social issues* (pp. 135–153). Los Angeles, CA: Kalimát Press.

Schwartz, S. H. (1990). Individualism-collectivism: Critique and proposed refinements. *Journal of Cross-Cultural Psychology, 21*, 139–157.

Schwartz, S. H. (1992). Universals in the content and structure of values: Theoretical advances and empirical tests in 20 countries. *Advances in Experimental Social Psychology, 20*, 1–65.

Schwartz, S. H. (1994a). Are there universal aspects in the structure and contents of human values? *Journal of Social Issues, 50*(4), 19–45.

Schwartz, S. H. (1994b). Beyond individualism/collectivism: New cultural dimensions of values. In U. Kim, H. C. Triandis, C. Kagitcibasi, S. Choi, & G. Yoon (Eds.). *Individualism and collectivism: Theory, method, and applications* (pp. 85–119). Thousand Oaks, CA: Sage.

Schwartz, S. H. (2003). Robustness and fruitfulness of a theory of universals in individual human values. In A. Tamayo & J. Porto (Eds.), *Valores e trabalho* [Values and work]. Brasilia: Editora Universidade de Brasilia.

Schwartz, S. H. & Bilsky, W. (1987). Toward a universal structure of human values. *Journal of Personality and Social Psychology, 53*, 550–562.

Schwartz, S. H. & Bilsky, W. (1990). Toward a theory of the universal content and structure of values: Extensions and cross-cultural replications. *Journal of Personality and Social Psychology, 58*, 878–891.

Schwartz, S. H., Melech, G., Lehmann, A., Burgess, S., Harris, M., & Owens, V. (2001, September). Extending the cross-cultural validity of the theory of basic human values with a different method of measurement. *Journal of Cross-Cultural Psychology, 32*(5), 519–542.

Schwarzschild, S. S. (1981). Introduction. In A. Solomonow (Ed.), *Roots of Jewish Nonviolence* (pp.1–2). Nyack, NY: Jewish Peace Fellowship.

Schwebel, M. (2006). Realistic empathy and active nonviolence confront political reality. *Journal of Social Issues, 62*(1), 191–208.

Schwebel, M., & Christie, D. J. (2001). Children and structural violence. In D. J. Christie, R. V. Wagner, & D. D. Winter (Eds.), *Peace, conflict, and violence: Peace psychology for the 21st century* (pp. 120–129). Upper Saddle River, NJ: Prentice-Hall.

Scott, W. A. (1965). *Values and organizations.* Chicago: Rand McNally.

Seligman, M. E. P. (1991). *Learned optimism.* New York: Knopf.

Shafer-Landau, R. (2004). *Whatever happened to good and evil?* New York: Oxford University Press.

Shapiro, D. L., & Watson, A. (2000). Using the theory of planned behavior to induce problem solving in schools. *Negotiation Journal, 16*(2), 183–190.

Sharma, I. C. (1965). The ethics of Jainism. In R. L. Holmes (Ed.), (1993). *Nonviolence in theory and practice* (pp. 10–14). Belmont, CA: Wadsworth Publishing Company.

Sharp, G. (1959). The meanings of nonviolence: A typology revised. *Journal of Conflict Resolution, 3,* 41–67.

Sharp, G. (1967). A study of the meanings of nonviolence. In G. Ramachandran, & T. K. Mahadevan (Eds.), *Gandhi: His relevance for our times* (pp. 21–66). Berkeley, CA: World Without War Council.

Sharp, G. (1970). *Exploring nonviolent alternatives.* Boston, MA: Extended Horizon Books.

Sharp, G. (1973). *The politics of nonviolent action.* Boston, MA: Porter Sargent Books.

Sharp, G. (1979). *Gandhi as political strategist.* Boston, MA: Porter Sargent Books.

Sharp, G. (1985). *National security through civilian-based defense.* Omaha, NE: Association for Transarmament Studies.

Sharp, G. (1990). *The role of power in nonviolent struggle. (Monograph Series Number 3)* Cambridge, MA: The Albert Einstein Institute.

Sharp, G. (1992). Nonviolent struggle: An effective alternative. In K. Kraft (Ed.), Inner peace, world peace: Essays on Buddhism and nonviolence (pp. 111–125). Albany, NY: State University of New York Press.

Sharp, G. (1999). Nonviolent action. In L. Kurtz (Ed.), *Encyclopedia of violence, peace, and conflict (Vol. 2,* pp. 567–574). New York: Academic.

Sharp, G. (2003). *There are realistic alternatives.* Boston, MA: The Albert Einstein Institution.

Sharp, G., & Paulson, J. (2005). *Waging nonviolent struggle: 20th century practice and 21st century potential.* Manchester, NH: Extending Horizons Books.

Shastri, S. Y., & Shastri, Y. S. (1998). Ahimsa and the unity of all things: A Hindu view of nonviolence. In D. L. Smith-Christopher (Ed.), *Subverting hatred: The challenge of nonviolence in religious traditions* (pp. 67–84). Cambridge, MA: Boston Research Center for the 21st Century.

Sherman, L. (1999). Sticks and stones: Name-calling, put-downs and bullying. *Northwest Education, 4*(3), 2–11.

Siddiqui, W. (2005). Nonviolence in Islam. In R. L. Holmes & B. L. Gan (Eds.), *Nonviolence in theory and practice* (2nd ed.). (pp. 36–40). Long Grove, IL: Waveland Press.

Sivaraksa, S. (1992). Buddhism and contemporary international trends. In K. Kraft (Ed.), *Inner peace, world peace: Essays on Buddhism and nonviolence* (pp. 127–137). Albany, NY: State University of New York Press.

Smith, E. R., & Mackie, D. M. (2000). *Social psychology* (2nd ed). Philadelphia, PA: Taylor and Francis.

Smith, M. B. (1968). *Social psychology and human values: Selected essays.* Chicago: Aldine.

Smith, P. B., & Bond, M. H. (1993). *Social psychology across cultures: Analysis and perspectives.* Boston, MA: Allyn and Bacon.

Smith-Christopher, D. L. (Ed.) (1998a). *Subverting hatred: The challenge of nonviolence in religious traditions.* Cambridge, MA: Boston Research Center for the 21st Century.

Smith-Christopher, D. L. (1998b). Indigenous traditions of peace: An interview with Lawrence Hart, Cheyenne Peace Chief. In D. L. Smith-Christopher (Ed.), *Subverting hatred: The challenge of nonviolence in religious traditions* (pp. 85–94). Cambridge, MA: Boston Research Center for the 21st Century.

Smith-Christopher, D. L. (1998c). Political atheism and radical faith: The challenge of Christian nonviolence in the third millennium. In D. L. Smith-Christopher (Ed.), *Subverting hatred: The challenge of nonviolence in religious traditions* (pp. 141–165). Cambridge, MA: Boston Research Center for the 21st Century.

Smithey L., & Kurtz, L.R (1999). "We have bare hands" Nonviolent social movements in the Soviet block. In S. Zunes, L. R. Kurtz, & S. B. Asher (Eds.), *Nonviolent social movements: A geographical perspective* (pp. 96–124). Malden, MA: Blackwell Publishers.

Smock, D. R. (1995) *Perspectives on pacifism: Christian, Jewish, and Muslim views on nonviolence and international conflict.* Washington, DC: United States Institute of Peace Press.

Solomon, N., Harries, R., & Winter, T. (Eds.). (2005). *Abraham's children: Jews, Christians, and Muslims in conversation.* New York: T & T Clark.

Solomon, S., Greenberg, J., & Pyszczynski, T. (1991). Terror management theory of social behavior: The psychological functions of self-esteem and cultural world views. In M. Zanna (Ed.), *Advances in experimental social psychology* (*Vol. 24*, pp. 91–159). Orlando, FL: Academic.

Solomonow, A. (Ed.). (1981). *Roots of Jewish nonviolence.* Nyack, NY: Jewish Peace Fellowship.

Southern Poverty Law Center (2008). *Southern Poverty Law Center.* Retrieved May 4, 2008, from http://www.splcenter.org/

Spense, R., & McLeod, J. (2002). Building the road as we walk it: Peacebuilding as principled and revolutionary nonviolent praxis. *Social Alternatives, 21*(2), 61–64.

Sponsel, L. E. (1994). The mutual relevance of anthropology and peace studies. In L. E. Sponsel, & T. Gregor, T. (Eds.), *The anthropology of peace and nonviolence* (pp. 1–36). Boulder, CO: Lynne Rienner Publishers.

Sponsel, L. E. & Gregor, T. (Eds.). (1994). *The anthropology of peace and nonviolence.* Boulder, CO: Lynne Rienner Publishers.

Stacey, S., & Meyer, M. (2005). Civil society and violence: A research agenda. *Journal of Civil Society, 1*(2), 181–190.

Staub, E. (1972). Instigation to goodness: The role of social norms and interpersonal influence. *Journal of Social Issues, 28*(3), 131–150.

Staub, E. (1992). The origins of caring, helping, and nonaggression: Parental socialization, the family system, schools, and cultural influence. In P. M. Pearl, S. P. Oliner, L. Baron, L. A. Blum, D. L. Krebs, & M. Z. Smolenska (Eds.), *Embracing the other: Philosophical, psychological, and historical perspectives on altruism* (pp. 390–412). New York, NY: New York University Press.

Staub, E. (1993). *The roots of evil: The origins of genocide and other group violence.* New York: Cambridge University Press.

Staub, E. (2004). Justice, healing, and reconciliation: How the people's courts in Rwanda can promote them. *Peace and Conflict: Journal of Peace Psychology, 10*(1), 25–32.

Staub, E., & Pearlman, L. A. (2001). Healing, reconciliation, and forgiving after genocide and other collective violence. In R. G. Helmick & R. L. Petersen (Eds.), *Forgiveness and reconciliation: Religion, public policy, and conflict transformation* (pp. 195–217). Philadelphia, PA: Templeton Foundation Press.

Steckel D. S. (1994). *Compassionate communication training and levels of participant empathy and self-compassion.* Unpublished doctoral dissertation, United States International University, San Diego, CA.

Steger, M. B. (2003). *Judging nonviolence: The dispute between realists and idealists.* New York: Routledge.

Steihm, J. (1968). Nonviolence is two. *Sociological Inquiry, 38*(1), 23–29.

Steinberg, M. (1947). *Basic Judaism.* New York: Harcourt, Brace, & World, Inc.

Stolzfus, N. (1996). *Resistance of the heart: Intermarriage and the Rosenstrasse protest in Nazi Germany.* New York: W.W. Norton & Co.

Swearer, D. K. (1992). Exemplars of nonviolence in Theravada Buddhism. In K. Kraft (Ed.), Inner peace, world peace: Essays on Buddhism and nonviolence (pp. 63–76). Albany, NY: State University of New York Press.

Sylvester, C. (1989). Patriarchy, peace, and women warriors. In L. R. Forcey (Ed.), *Peace: Meanings, politics, and strategies* (pp. 97–112). New York: Praeger.

Teichman, J. (1986). *Pacifism and just war: A study of applied philosophy.* New York: Basil Blackwell.

Teixeira, B. (1987). Comments on ahimsa (nonviolence). *The Journal of Transpersonal Psychology, 19*, 1–17.

Teixeira, B. (1999). Nonviolent theory and practice. In L. Kurtz (Ed.), *Encyclopedia of violence, peace, and conflict* (*Vol. 2*, pp. 555–565). New York: Academic.

Thomas, J. M. (1984a). Poverty and wealth in America: A Bahá'í perspective. In A. A. Lee (Ed.), *Circle of unity: Bahá'í approaches to current social issues* (pp. 91–116). Los Angeles, CA: Kalimát Press.

Thomas, R. W. (1984b). A long and thorny path: Race relations in the American Bahá'í community. In A. A. Lee (Ed.), *Circle of unity: Bahá'í approaches to current social issues*, (pp. 37–65). Los Angeles, CA: Kalimát Press.

Thompson, L. Y., & Snyder, C. R. (2003). Measuring forgiveness. In S. J. Lopez & C. R. Snyder (Eds.), *Positive psychological assessment: A handbook of models and measures* (pp. 301–312). Washington, DC: American psychological Association.

TIKKUN Community. (2008). http://www.tikkun.org/community

Tolman, C. E. (1942). *Drives toward war.* New York: Appleteton-Century.

Triandis, H. C. (1995). *Individualism and collectivism.* San Francisco, CA: Westview Press.

Thurman, R. A. F. (1992). Tibet and the monastic army of peace. In K. Kraft (Ed.), *Inner peace, world peace: Essays on Buddhism and nonviolence* (pp. 77–90). Albany, NY: State University of New York Press.

Trumblety, J. (2003). Responses to women's enfranchisement in France, 1944–1945. *Women's Studies International Forum, 26*(5), 483–497.

Tsang, J., & McCullough, M. E. (2003). Measuring religious constructs: A hierarchical approach to construct organization and scale selection. In S. J. Lopez & C. R. Snyder (Eds.), *Positive psychological assessment: A handbook of models and measures* (pp. 345–360). Washington, DC: American psychological Association.

Tuck, S. (2006). Making the Voting Rights Act. In R. M. Valelly (Ed.), *The Voting Rights Act: Securing the ballot* (pp. 77–94). Washington, DC: CQ Press.

Turay, T. M. (2000). Civil society and peacebuilding: The role of the Inter-Religious Council of Sierra Leone. *Conciliation Resources.* Retrieved May 30, 2008 from http://www.c-r.org/our-work/accord/sierra-leone/inter-religious-council.php

Umbreit, M. S. (1995). *Mediating interpersonal conflicts: A pathway to peace.* West Concord, MN: CPI Publishing.

Underwood, L. G., & Teresi, J. (2002). The Daily Spiritual Experience Scale: Development, theoretical description, reliability, exploratory factor analysis, and preliminary construct validity using health related data. *Annals of Behavioral Medicine, 24*(1), 22–33.

Unger, R. K. (1998). *Resisting gender: Twenty-five years of feminist psychology.* Thousand Oaks, CA: Sage Publications.

United Nations (1948). *Universal declaration of human rights.* Retrieved April 30, 2008, from http://www.un.org/Overview/rights.html

United Nations adopts Declaration on Rights of Indigenous Peoples. (2007, September 13). UN News Centre. Retrieved May 20, 2008 at http://www.un.org/apps/news/story.asp?NewsID=23794&Cr=indigenous&Cr1#

United States Department of State (n.d.). *The rule of law.* Retrieved May 4, 2008, from http://usinfo.state.gov/dhr/democracy/rule_of_law.html

United States Institute of Peace (n.d.). *About the rule of law.* Retrieved May 4, 2008, from http://www.usip.org/ruleoflaw/about.html

Universal House of Justice (1985). *The promise of World Peace.* Thornhill, Ontario: Bahá'í Peace Council of Canada.

Universal House of Justice (2008). Official website of the Universal House of Justice. Retrieved June 12, 2008 from http://info.bahai.org/universal-house-of-justice.html

Valelly, R. M. (Ed.) (2006). *The Voting Rights Act: Securing the ballot.* Washington, DC: CQ Press.

Van Inwegen, P. (2006). Velvet Revolution: An actor-based model. *Peace & Change, 31*(2), 175–203.

Van Slyck, M., & Stern, M. (1999). A developmental approach to the use of conflict resolution interventions. In L. R. Forcey & I. M. Harris (Eds.), *Peacebuilding for adolescents: Strategies for educators and community leaders* (pp. 177–193), New York: Peter Lang Publishing, Inc.

Vilela, M. (2007). The Earth Charter endeavor: Building more just and sustainable societies through a new level of consciousness. *Social Alternatives, 26*(3), 34–37.

Vriens, L. (1999). Children, war, and peace: A review of fifty years of research from the perspective of a balanced conception of peace education. In A. Raviv, L. Oppenheimer, & D. Bar-Tal, (Eds.), *How children understand war and peace: A call for international peace education* (pp. 27–58). San Francisco, CA: Jossey-Bass.

Wagner, R. V. (2001). Peacemaking. In D. J. Christie, R. V. Wagner, & D. D. Winter (Eds.). *Peace, conflict, and violence: Peace psychology for the 21st century* (pp. 169–172). Upper Saddle River, NJ: Prentice-Hall.

Wagner, R. V., & Bonzaft, A. L. (1987). Sprinkling psychology courses with peace. *Teaching of Psychology, 14,* 75–81.

Waines, D. (1995). *An introduction to Islam.* London: Cambridge University Press.

Wall, J. A., Stark, J. B., & Standifer, R. L. (2001). Mediation: A current review and theory development. *Journal of Conflict Resolution, 45*(3), 370–391.

Waller, J. (1993). Correlation of need for cognition and modern racism. *Psychological Reports, 73*(2), 542.

Wallis, J. (2006). *God's politics: Why the right gets it wrong and the left doesn't get it.* New York: Harper Collins Publisher.

Warfield, W. (1997). Moving from civil war to civil society. *Peace Review, 97*(9), 249–254.

Warraich, S. A. (2005). 'Honour killings' and the law in Pakistan. In S. Hossain & L. Welchman (Eds.), *'Honour': Crimes, paradigms, and violence against women* (pp. 78–110). London: Zed Books.

Washington, J. M. (Ed.). (1992). *I have a dream: Writings and speeches that changed the World.* Sunnyvale, CA: Scott Foresman.

Watt, J. D., & Blanchard, M. J. (1994). Boredom proneness and the need for cognition. *Journal of Research in Personality, 28*(1), 44–51.

Webb, W. M., & Worchel, P. (1986). Trust and distrust. In S. Worchel & W. G. Austin (Eds.), *Psychology of intergroup relations* (2nd ed., pp. 213–228). Chicago: Nelson Hall.

Webster's third new international dictionary of the English language, unabridged (1971). Springfield, MA: G. & C. Merriam Co.

Wessells, M. G. (1998). The changing nature of armed conflict and its implications for children: The Graça Machel/UN study. *Peace and Conflict: Journal of Peace Psychology, 4*(4), 321–334.

Wessells, M. G., & Monteiro, C. (2001). Psychosocial interventions and post-war reconstruction in Angola: Interweaving western and traditional approaches. In D. J. Christie, R. V. Wagner, & D. D. Winter (Eds.), *Peace, conflict, and violence: Peace psychology for the 21st century* (pp. 262–275). Upper Saddle River, NJ: Prentice-Hall.

Wessells, M. G., Schwebel, M., & Anderson, A. (2001). Psychologists making a difference in the public arena: Building cultures of peace. In D. J. Christie, R. V. Wagner, & D. D. Winter (Eds.), *Peace, conflict, and violence: Peace psychology for the 21st century* (pp. 350–362). Upper Saddle River, NJ: Prentice-Hall.

Wessells, M. G., & Strang, A. (2006). Religion as resource and risk: The double-edged sword for children in situations of armed conflict. In N. Boothby, A. Strang, & M. G. Wessells (Eds.), *A world turned upside down: Social ecological approaches to children in war zones.* (pp. 256–286). Bloomfield, CT: Kumarian Press

White, R. K. (1984). *Fearful warriors: A psychological profile of U.S.-Soviet relations.* New York: Free Press.

White, R. K. (Ed.). (1986). *Psychology and the prevention of nuclear war.* New York: Free Press.

White, R. K. (1991). Empathizing with Saddam Hussein. *Political Psychology, 12*(2), 291–308.

White, W. H. (2007). Protecting and advancing the international rule of law. *Human Rights: Journal of the Section of Individual Rights and Responsibilities, 34*(1), 8–14.

Williams, R. M. (1968). The concept of values. In D. L. Sils (Ed.), International encyclopedia of the social sciences (*Vol. 16,* pp. 283–287). New York: Free Press.

Wink, W. (1992). *Engaging the powers: Discernment and resistance in a world of domination.* Minneapolis, MN: Fortress Press.

Wink, W. (2003). *Jesus and nonviolence: A third way.* Minneapolis, MN: Fortress Press.

Willer, R. (2004). The effects of government issued terror warnings on presidential approval ratings. *Current Research in Social Psychology, 10*(1), 1–12.

Worthington, E. L. (2001). Unforgiveness, forgiveness, and reconciliation and their implications for social interventions. In R. G. Helmick & R. L. Petersen (Eds.), *Forgiveness and reconciliation: Religion, public policy, and conflict transformation* (pp. 161–182). Philadelphia, PA: Templeton Foundation Press.

Worchel, P. (1979). Trust and distrust. In W. G. Austin & S. Worchel (Eds.), *The social psychology of intergroup relations* (pp. 174–187). Belmont, CA: Wadsworth Publishing.

Worchel, S. (1986). The role of cooperation in reducing intergroup conflict. In S. Worchel & W. G. Austin (Eds.), *Psychology of intergroup relations* (2nd ed., pp. 288–304). Chicago: Nelson Hall.

Yoder, J. H. (1992). *Nevertheless: Varieties of religious pacifism*. Scottsdale, PA: Herald Press.

Yum, Y., & Schenck-Hamlin, W. (2005). Reactions to 9/11 as a function of terror management and perspective taking. *Journal of Social Psychology, 145*, 265–286

Zajonc, R. B. (1966). *Social psychology: An experimental approach*. Belmont, CA: Wadsworth Publishing Company.

Zeiger, S. (2000). Teaching peace: Lessons from a peace studies curriculum of the progressive era. *Peace & Change, 25*(1), 52–69.

Zhou, Q., Valiente, C., & Eisenberg, N. (2003). Empathy and its measurement. In S. J. Lopez & C. R. Snyder (Eds.), *Positive psychological assessment: A handbook of models and measures* (pp. 269–284). Washington, DC: American psychological Association.

Ziller, R. C., Moriarty, D. S., & Phillips, S. T. (1999). The peace personality. In A. Raviv, L. Oppenheimer, & D. Bar-Tal (Eds.), *How children understand war and peace: A call for international peace education* (pp. 78–90). San Francisco, CA: Jossey-Bass.

Zinn, H. (Ed.). (2002). *The power of nonviolence: Writings of advocates of peace*. Boston, MA: Beacon Press.

Zins, J. E., Weissberg, R. P., Wang, M. C., & Walberg, H. J. (Eds.). (2004). *Building academic success on social emotional learning: What does the research say?* New York: Teachers College Press.

Zunes, S. (1999a). Unarmed resistance in the Middle East and North Africa. In S. Zunes, L. R. Kurtz, & S. B. Asher (Eds.), *Nonviolent social movements: A geographical perspective* (pp. 41–51). Malden, MA: Blackwell Publishers.

Zunes, S. (1999b). The origins of People Power in the Philippines. In S. Zunes, L. R. Kurtz, & S. B. Asher (Eds.), *Nonviolent social movements: A geographical perspective* (pp. 129–157). Malden, MA: Blackwell Publishers.

Zunes, S. (1999c). The role of nonviolence in the downfall of apartheid. In S. Zunes, L. R. Kurtz, & S. B. Asher, (Eds.), *Nonviolent social movements: A geographical perspective* (pp. 203–230). Malden, MA: Blackwell Publishers.

Zunes, S., Kurtz, L. R., & Asher, S. B. (Eds.). (1999). *Nonviolent social movements: A geographical perspective*. Malden, MA: Blackwell Publishers.

Name Index

Subject Index

Breinigsville, PA USA
21 August 2009
222732BV00007B/49/P